MW01131684

Biology
for CSEC®

2nd Edition

Karen Morrison

Peta-Gay Kirby

Lucy Madhosingh

OXFORD
UNIVERSITY PRESS

Great Clarendon Street, Oxford, OX2 6DP, United Kingdom

Oxford University Press is a department of the University of Oxford.
It furthers the University's objective of excellence in research, scholarship,
and education by publishing worldwide. Oxford is a registered trade mark of
Oxford University Press in the UK and in certain other countries

First published by Nelson Thornes Ltd in 2008
Second edition published by Nelson Thornes Ltd in 2014
This edition published by Oxford University Press in 2014

British Library Cataloguing in Publication Data
Data available

978-1-4085-2508-1

10 9 8

Printed in India

Acknowledgements

Illustrations: Hart McLeod Limited, Cambridge, Tech-Set Ltd, Gateshead and Peters and Zabransky Ltd
Page make-up: Tech-Set Ltd, Gateshead

Contents

Contents

Biology for CSEC® 2nd Edition covers all the syllabus objectives for the CSEC® examination. It has been carefully structured to help you achieve the best possible results in your examinations.

The following features are found in the units.

Objectives

- This box summarises the syllabus requirements for each unit of work.

Diagrams

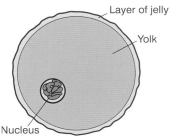

▲ **Figure 23.1.3** An ovum

In Biology the diagram forms an important part of the content. Read the labels and captions carefully to make sure you know what the diagram represents.

Key terms

Important terms are shown in **bold** in the text. These are carefully explained or defined in context.

 Key fact

These boxes highlight important or interesting facts related to the topic.

Exam tip

The authors of this book are experienced teachers who write exam items and mark examinations. These hints come from their experience and highlight some of the common mistakes that students make.

 Practical activity

Practical activities are an important part of the course and you are expected to do a number of them throughout the year. The skills contained in each activity are listed.

Safety

Some experiments can be dangerous. The safety boxes highlight any potential hazards in a practical activity and tell you how to avoid them.

Case study

The case studies are real-life examples of Biology at work and they give you data and other information about the issue under study.

Questions

Each topic is concluded by a set of questions to help you recall what you have learnt and to apply your knowledge to answer questions related to the content.

Revision sections

At the end of each section you will find:
- case studies related to the content in the section to help you relate your learning to the real world
- a summary of the key concepts in each unit
- a list of the key terms you should know, with page references to help you find those you may have forgotten
- practice exam-style questions to help you revise and prepare for examinations. Allocated marks are provided for knowledge and comprehension (KC) and using knowledge (UK).

CD resources

The student CD accompanying this book has interactive activities, multiple-choice practice questions and many other useful features to make learning more interesting and to help you understand concepts fully. You will also find a glossary of key terms, information to help you prepare for your examinations and School-Based Assessment (including a sample investigative project), and answers to the practice exam-style questions.

A1 Grouping living organisms

In biology, we study living things (organisms) and we compare them to find out how they are similar or different. In this unit, you will work inside and outside the classroom to observe living organisms and record what you find out.

A1.1 Observing living organisms

The Earth is home to millions of living plants and animals (organisms). We don't know exactly how many types of organism there are, but about 1.8 million different living things have been found, described and named so far. New organisms are being found all the time.

Characteristics of living organisms

Living organisms look different from each other and they range in size from microscopic, single-celled bacteria to giant trees and whales. However all living organisms share some characteristics. These are:

- **Reproduction** – living organisms are able to produce new organisms like themselves.
- **Nutrition** – plants make food, animals take in food.
- **Respiration** – the cells in living organisms release energy from food, often this involves oxygen.
- **Growth** – living organisms develop and increase in size.
- **Excretion** – living organisms get rid of waste produced in cells.
- **Movement** – plants move by growing, animals move from place to place.
- **Sensitivity** – living organisms interact with their surroundings and respond to them.

Making observations

Scientists use their scientific knowledge and their senses to observe things in the world around them. For example, a scientist might notice that the banana trees growing on one side of the road were much bigger than the banana trees growing on the other side of the road. The scientist has made an observation.

When you observe living organisms, you will focus on their visible characteristics. Visible characteristics are the things you can see. For example, colour, shape, size, number of limbs, whether the body surface is smooth, hairy or scaly, and so on.

Different species

In biology, a species is a group of organisms that share physical characteristics. For example, parrots and frigate birds both belong to the bird family but they are different species of birds. The organisms in a species have similar biological features that allow them to reproduce with each other.

Objectives

By the end of this topic you will be able to:

- recognise the characteristics of living organisms
- observe living organisms in your environment
- record your observations in table format.

▲ **Figure 1.1.1** Coral reefs are home to thousands of living organisms. How many can you find in the photo?

Members of one species cannot interbreed with members of another species and produce fertile offspring.

Naming organisms

Living things are often given different names. For example, the fruit of the *Melicoccus bijugatus* tree is called an 'ackee' in Barbados. In Jamaica, people call these fruits 'guineps' and they call the fruit of the *Blighia sapida* tree an 'ackee'. This can get very confusing, so scientists use a system of two-part Latin names to precisely name and identify different species. The two-part naming system is called the binomial system. In the trees named above, the first part of the Latin name is the genus and the second part is the species of the tree.

It is important to understand how organisms are named in biology. However for your work in this course, you can use the common names of organisms.

 Practical activity

Observing living organisms

Your teacher may use this activity to assess: ORR

1 Find an area outside the classroom where there are living organisms. Observe the area and list:
   a the living organisms in the area
   b the non-living components of the area.

2 Copy the table **below**. Choose two animals in your area that are quite different. Write their names in the correct place at the top of the table. Observe the animals closely and record what you observe in the table.

Observed characteristics	Animal 1	Animal 2
Habitat (where does it live?)		
Conditions it prefers		
Size (estimate its size)		
Shape		
Body covering		
Body parts		
Food (what does it eat?)		
How does it eat?		
Type of movement		
What does it use to move?		
Why does it move?		

3 Use your table to find three similarities and three differences between the two animals you observed.

4 Plants are also living organisms. Draw up your own table that lists the characteristics you could observe in plants.
   a Choose two different local plants to observe and record their characteristics using your own table.
   b List five differences between plants and animals.

 Key fact

Insects make up around half of the named and described organisms (plants and animals) on Earth. In fact about three quarters of the known animals are insects.

Objectives

By the end of this topic you will be able to:

- observe living organisms in your environment
- classify living organisms according to physical similarities.

A1.2 Identifying and grouping organisms

The science of classification is called taxonomy.

Scientists have classified all known living organisms by placing them in five main groups called kingdoms. Table 1.2.1 shows the names of the five kingdoms, the characteristics that organisms in each kingdom share and some examples of the organisms found in each kingdom.

In this course, you will focus on the plant and animal kingdoms, but you will also refer to the others when you study health and disease.

▼ **Table 1.2.1** The five kingdom classification system

Monera	Protoctista	Fungi	Plantae (plants)	Animalia (animals)
Simple, single-celled bacteria; absorb food	Most are single-celled but some are multi-cellular; they can absorb, photosynthesise or ingest food	Mostly multi-cellular, but some are single-celled; absorb food	Multi-cellular with specialised cells; produce food by photosynthesis	Multi-cellular with specialised cells; ingest food
This bacteria causes TB	An amoeba is uni-cellular	Yeast is a single-celled fungus		
This bacteria causes pneumonia	Sea bamboo is multi-cellular	Mushrooms are multi-cellular		

Key fact

There is some disagreement among scientists about the actual number of kingdoms, with some scientists dividing the Monera into two groups to make six kingdoms.

Groups of animals

Each of the five kingdoms contains many different species with distinguishing characteristics. To make it easier to place organisms in groups, the kingdoms are divided into smaller groups. The animal kingdom can be divided into two large groups: invertebrates (animals with no spine) and vertebrates (animals with a spine). Each of these groups can be further divided. Table 1.2.2 shows the main groups of vertebrates and the approximate number of known species in each group.

▼ **Table 1.2.2** The main groups of vertebrate animals

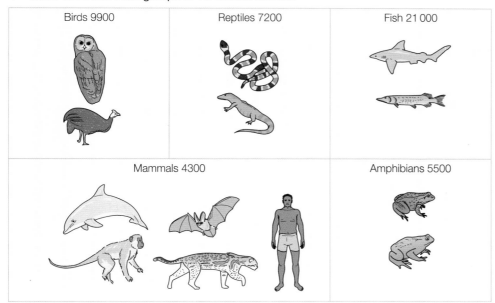

Groups of plants

If you look around outside, you will realise that the plant kingdom also contains many different species of plant. Like animals, plants can be divided into sub-groups. The main sub-groups of plants are shown in Figure 1.2.1. You will deal mainly with flowering plants for your work in this course.

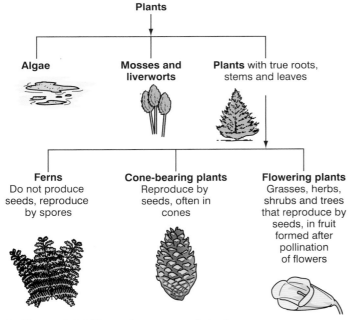

▲ **Figure 1.2.1** The major groups of plants

Putting organisms into groups

One method of grouping organisms is to observe them to find characteristics that they share. Some shared characteristics are colour, number of legs, wings, shape and size. Organisms that share the same characteristics are then placed in the same group. This is the method you will use to group organisms in this topic.

Questions

1 Use information from Table 1.2.2 to draw a bar graph that compares the number of known species in each of the five groups of vertebrates.

2 Look at these three organisms:

a Are these plants or animals? How do you know this?

b Write down three visible characteristics that these organisms share.

c These organisms all belong to the same group. Which group is this?

d How is organism B different to the other two organisms?

3 Choose the odd one out in each of the following groups of organisms and give a reason for your choice:

a bread mould, yeast, algae, mushroom

b leaf of life plant, spider plant, ginger, fern

c frog, toad, newt, lizard

d banana tree, sugar cane, black mangrove tree, pine tree.

4 Choose three groups of vertebrates from Table 1.2.2. Draw up a table of your own and fill in at least three examples of animals from your country in each group.

5 Look at the leaves opposite:

a Find an example of a local plant that has a leaf similar in shape and structure to each of these leaves. Collect or draw a leaf from the plants you have chosen. Give the name of the plant if you can.

b Choose any two of the leaves you have collected and write down three visible differences that you observe.

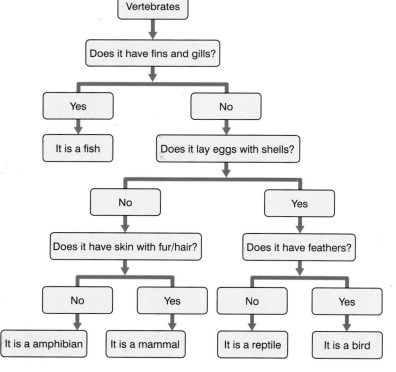

Using a flow diagram to group organisms

To decide whether an organism belongs in a particular group, you can generally ask a question that requires a 'yes' or 'no' answer. For example, is its skin covered with hair? Or, does it reproduce with spores? In order to fully classify organisms you usually have to ask a series of questions to narrow down the groups. These questions may be laid out in the form of a flow diagram (also called a dichotomous key) like the one in Figure 1.2.2. This flow diagram can be used to classify vertebrates into one of the five sub-groups shown on p5.

◀ **Figure 1.2.2** A possible flow diagram (dichotomous key) for classifying vertebrates

Using DNA analysis to group organisms

Grouping organisms using visible characteristics has some disadvantages. This is because organisms that belong to different scientific groups may share the same visible characteristics. For example, bats and birds both have wings, but bats are mammals and birds are not. Scientists therefore group organisms using a combination of what they can see (visible characteristics) and what they know about the organisms from studying them in more detail (internal structures and behaviour).

Some living organisms are difficult to classify because they share the same visible characteristics and internal structure, plus they behave in similar ways to each other. Consider, for example, a group of single-celled algae (*Symbiodinium*) that live inside corals. When scientists study these, they cannot classify them easily by visible characteristics, structure or behaviour because they all look like brown specks, even under a powerful microscope. Other organisms are difficult to classify because they look different to other members of the same group. For example, members of the palm family or members of the fern family may all look very different and this makes it difficult for scientists to decide whether a plant is a fern or not.

With advances in science and technology, scientists are now able to use the DNA sequences of different organisms as an aid to classification. If two organisms share a great many DNA sequences, it is likely that they are closely related. Looking at patterns of nucleotides in the DNA of an organism allows scientists to determine how closely related species may be.

Scientists in New Zealand have used DNA sequencing to study different plant species. This work has actually led to some plants which were considered to be 'fern-like' being reclassified as actual ferns. Dr Leon Perrie, a Te Papa scientist who studies ferns and fern-like plants, says this about DNA and classification:

> With DNA work, we have been able to get a better idea of how things are related. We have learnt more about the evolutionary history of plants and animals. As we've updated our understanding of how plants and animals are related to one another, we've had to change the taxonomic classification in order to reflect that improved updated understanding of their evolutionary history.
>
> A great example within the fern type of plants is that there are several small groups of plants which used to be regarded as fern allies. In particular, there is the *Tmesipteris* fork ferns. They were previously grouped with plants like *Lycopodium* and *Selaginella* in the fern allies, but with DNA analyses, people have worked out that *Tmesipteris* fork ferns are actually more closely related to ferns. So they are now regarded as ferns, rather than as fern allies.

Scientists who study coral reefs have also used DNA sequencing to show that the single-celled algae found inside corals actually belong to different and distinct species. This will allow them to understand coral reefs better and perhaps take steps to prevent coral bleaching. Read the case study that follows to find out more about this work.

Case study

DNA analysis aids in classifying single-celled algae

20 September 2012

For nearly 260 years – since Carl Linnaeus developed his system of naming plants and animals – researchers classified species based on visual attributes like colour, shape and size. In the past few decades, researchers found that sequencing DNA can more accurately identify species. A group of single-celled algae – *Symbiodinium* – that live inside corals and are critical to their survival – are only now being separated into species using DNA analysis, according to biologists.

'Unfortunately with *Symbiodinium*, scientists have been hindered by a traditional morphology-based system of species identification that doesn't work because these organisms all pretty much look the same – small round brown cells,' said Todd LaJeunesse, assistant professor of biology at Penn State. 'This delay in adopting the more accurate convention of identifying species using genetic techniques has greatly impeded progress in the research of symbiotic reef-building corals, especially with regard to their ability to withstand global warming.'

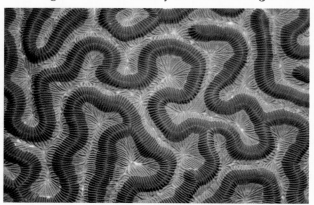

Corals are able to build large reef structures in many of the world's shallow tropical environments because they contain symbiotic micro-algae called *Symbiodinium*. Different species found in different corals look nearly identical.

LaJeunesse and his colleagues looked at *Symbiodinium* that previously had been grouped together as sub-sets of the same species. They report their results in the September issue of the *Journal of Phycology*. They examined specific DNA markers – identifiers – from the organisms' cell nuclei, mitochondria and chloroplasts. Even though the symbionts appeared very much the same, except for their size, genetic evidence confirmed that the two are different species altogether.

These findings indicate that hundreds of other coral symbionts already identified with preliminarily genetic data are also distinct species with unique ecological distributions.

'The recognition of symbiont species' diversity should substantially improve research into reef-building corals and facilitate breakthroughs in our understanding of their complex biology,' said LaJeunesse.

He began his work of classifying *Symbiodinium* using genetic techniques as part of his research into their ecology and evolution and in later studies of coral bleaching events related to global warming.

'Knowing exactly which *Symbiodinium* species you're dealing with is important because certain species of Symbiodinium associate with certain species of coral,' he said. 'Although many corals are dying as a result of global climate change, some may be able to survive because they associate with Symbiodinium species that are better adapted to warm water temperatures.'

Other researchers on this project were John Everett Parkinson, graduate student in biology, Penn State, and James Davis Reimer, associate professor of biology, University of the Ryukyus, Okinawa. The National Science Foundation supported this research.

Extract from: http://www.sciencedaily.com

Questions

1   A student saw these four marine organisms (A to D) on a scuba diving trip.
    Use the flow diagram below to correctly name the organisms.

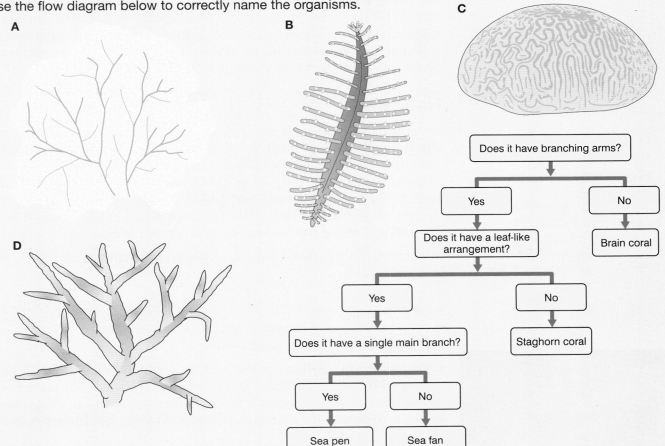

2   Modern technology allows scientists to use DNA to assist in classification of different species.
    a   What is DNA?
    b   How can DNA help scientists decide whether an organism belongs to a taxonomic group or not?
    c   DNA analysis has recently helped scientists to distinguish different species of single-celled algae that live in corals. What are the advantages of knowing that these algae belong to distinct species?

Living organisms do not live in isolation. They interact with each other and they interact with the environments in which they live. In this unit, you are going to look at organisms in their environments to learn more about inter-relationships and the factors that affect both the organisms and their environments. You will then carry out a simple ecological study in your own environment.

A2.1 What makes an environment?

Everything around you is part of your environment. If you are in a classroom environment, then you are probably surrounded by living and non-living things such as desks, books, a teacher, other students, windows, doors, air, bacteria and perhaps plants. We call the living things in an environment the biotic factors. These include the plants, animals and other living organisms found in the environment. The non-living parts of an environment are called the physical factors or abiotic components of the environment. These include factors such as wind, water, light and temperature.

Habitats

Organisms are not found just anywhere in the environment. We do not find fish living in trees or birds living underwater. The type of place where an organism lives is called its habitat. Living organisms need particular things in order to survive. They will only live in habitats where they can find the things they need to survive. For example, tropical fish need warm salty water, so they are found in habitats like the Caribbean Sea where this is available. They are not found in the cold, icy waters near the poles.

Some of the things that organisms need in their habitats are:
- food
- water
- shelter and space to live
- other members of the same species for reproduction
- gases (oxygen and carbon dioxide).

Living organisms are suited to the habitats in which they live. We say that they are adapted to their habitats. An adaptation is a special characteristic that an organism has which helps it to obtain food and water, to move from place to place, to protect itself from predators and to find shelter or to reproduce.

Figure 2.1.1 shows a tree frog in its natural habitat in Belize. The frog's red eyes are an adaptation used to scare off predators. When the frog is asleep during the day, its eyes look green. If something attacks it, it opens its eyes and the red flash scares the predator. The frog's feet are also adapted to living in trees. The feet are shaped like suction cups, which allow the frog to cling to leaves. Its back legs are strong for jumping and its webbed feet allow it to swim well. Because the frog is an amphibian, it needs to conserve body moisture so that its skin does not dry out. The frog has adapted to living in

(!) Key fact

Many organisms can survive outside their natural habitats. For example, the mango tree (*Magnifera indica*), which is native to India and south-east Asia, was imported to the Caribbean. It has adapted to its new habitat and it flourishes here.

▲ **Figure 2.1.1** The red-eyed tree frog in its natural habitat in Belize

trees by sheltering under leaves during the day with its limbs close to its body to prevent loss of moisture.

Plants are also adapted to suit their habitats. Water lilies, for example, have large flat leaves that float on top of the water they live in. Cactuses, like the one in Figure 2.1.2, are well adapted to dry conditions. They have thick, spongy stems that can store lots of water and deep grooves in their stems to allow them to expand and fill up with water whenever it rains. Their stems have a waterproof layer to prevent water loss. Their leaves are reduced to thin spikes that lose very little water. They have roots that spread out near the surface of the soil to absorb any water from rain or dew.

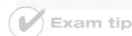

Exam tip

Remember to learn definitions for biotic, abiotic, habitat, adaption, population, community, and niche. In an examination you may be asked to give an example to support your definition.

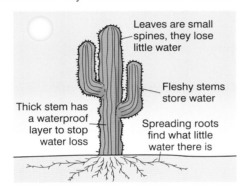

▲ **Figure 2.1.2** Cacti are well adapted to dry conditions

Populations and communities

When a group of organisms that belong to the same species are found living together in a habitat, we call them a population. For example, we could talk about a population of banana trees in a field or a population of ants living in a tree trunk or a population of keskidees living in a hotel garden.

All species of organisms found living together in a particular place are called a community. Figure 2.1.3 shows a fresh water pond community. The different populations that make up this community live in different habitats in and around the water.

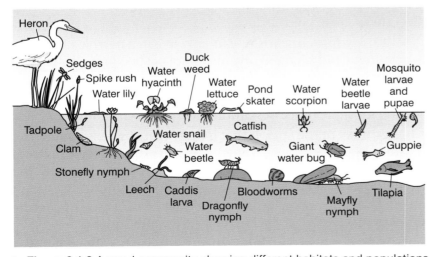

▲ **Figure 2.1.3** A pond community showing different habitats and populations

Each organism in a community has a particular position or role that it is suited to. This role or position is known as the organism's niche. For example, the heron's niche is the water's edge where it eats large fish. There are no other organisms in this niche.

Questions

1 Define the term 'environment' as it applies to living organisms.

2 What do biologists call a group of the same species living in a particular area?

3 How do rainfall and temperature affect the natural environment?

4 Figure 2.1.4 shows you the community living round a tree.
   a Identify the physical factors in this environment.
   b Identify the biotic factors in this environment.
   c List five different habitats in this environment.
   d Give three examples of populations found in this community.
   e How do the different factors that make up this environment depend on each other? List five examples of inter-dependence and say how the different organisms in your examples need each other to survive in their habitats.

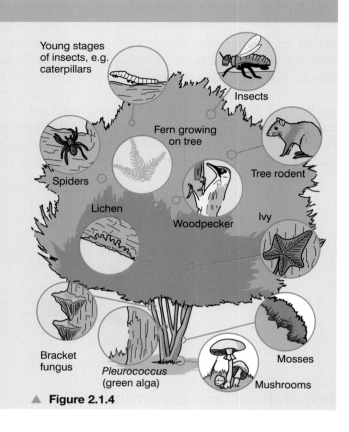

▲ **Figure 2.1.4**

Objectives

By the end of this topic you will be able to:

- explain the importance of the abiotic (physical) factors that make up an environment
- discuss the importance of soil for survival of organisms
- investigate the constituents and properties of different soils
- describe the role of microorganisms in soil.

A2.2 The importance of the abiotic environment

Abiotic factors that affect the environment

To survive in an environment, organisms need to make effective use of the non-living or abiotic factors that surround them. Some of the abiotic factors that affect survival are given below.

- Temperature – most organisms can only live in a narrow range of temperatures. Cold-blooded organisms are particularly affected by changes in temperature.
- Water – most organisms need water to survive. Cell functions rely on water and most life processes cannot take place without water.
- Sunlight – most of the energy that living organisms use comes from the Sun. Green plants rely on this energy in order to photosynthesise and produce food. You will look at energy flows through ecosystems in more detail in topics A2.4 and A3.1.
- Humidity – many organisms need a certain level of moisture in the air in order to survive and conserve their own water supplies.
- Wind – wind is moving air, but it affects survival because it helps disperse plant seeds. Strong winds can also make it difficult for plants and animals to survive in an environment.
- Soil – plants depend on soil for survival and other animals depend on plants in turn. Most plants are very sensitive and they cannot survive in infertile soils that are too acid or too alkaline.

Now you are going to look at aquatic (water) and terrestrial (ground) habitats to see how the physical factors interact and their impact on the organisms that live in the habitat.

Aquatic habitats

In topic A2.1 you studied a community living in water in a pond. A habitat in water is called an aquatic habitat. The pond is an example of an aquatic habitat. So is a rock pool, a river, a coral reef and the water in a mangrove swamp.

Organisms that live in aquatic habitats are affected by the abiotic factors in their environment: temperature, sunlight, wind and condition of the water. However, they are also affected by other unique factors that are not experienced by organisms living on land. These include:

- Water movement and speed of flow – plants and animals that live in rivers have to adapt to the fact that the water is moving. Similarly, plants and animals that live along ocean shores have to adapt to changing water levels as the tides change, as well as wave action.

- Depth – oxygen levels and the amount of sunlight that penetrates the water vary with depth. Some organisms can only survive in shallow water, others need deeper water.

- Water clarity – clear water allows more sunlight to reach the bottom layers than muddy or polluted water. Without light, water plants cannot photosynthesise and they will die.

- Oxygen – organisms need oxygen from the water for respiration and other metabolic functions. If oxygen levels drop, many organisms cannot survive. There is more oxygen in moving water than in stagnant pools.

- Salinity – this is the concentration of salt in the water. Salinity is important in ocean environments, particularly rock pools, where evaporation leads to higher salt levels at certain times. Estuaries and mangrove swamps contain a balanced mixture of salt and fresh water that suits the organisms found in these habitats. Too much fresh water or too much salty water will cause organisms to die off. Figure 2.2.2 shows you how different types of mangrove have adapted to the physical conditions in their habitat.

▲ **Figure 2.2.1** Aquatic organisms live in water

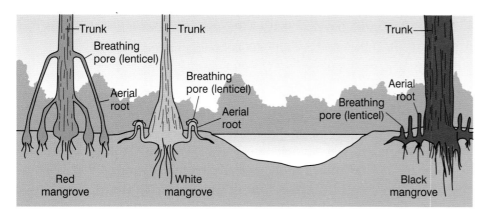

▲ **Figure 2.2.2** Mangroves are well adapted to their habitat

Practical activity

Making inferences

Do this activity in pairs.

◄ **Figure 2.2.3** The physical conditions in a rock pool habitat can change dramatically in a 24-hour period

1 Figure 2.2.3 shows you a small rock pool on the coast of Barbados. The table shows you the water temperatures in the rock pool recorded in one day.

Time	6am	7am	8am	9am	10am	11am	12am	1pm	2pm	3pm	4pm	5pm	6pm
Temperature (°C)	18	19	23	28	28	30	34	23	19	25	25	26	24

a Draw a graph to show the temperature changes during the day.

b What physical factors could cause these changes in temperature?

c Warm water contains less oxygen than cooler water. How do you think this affects the organisms living in this habitat?

d Evaporation leads to increased salinity. How do you think this affects the organisms living in this habitat?

e How do you think the organisms in this rock pool are adapted to cope with changing water levels, strong currents and wave action?

f Draw a labelled diagram of a coastal rock pool showing some of the plants and animals you would be likely to find in it. Draw arrows on your diagram to show some of the ways in which these plants and animals depend on each other and interact with each other.

Questions

1 List five important physical factors that can affect a habitat.

2 Give two local examples of aquatic habitats that are:
   a fresh water habitats
   b marine habitats.

3 Give local examples of habitats that are:
   a very hot   b dry   c damp   d aquatic.

4 As water temperature rises, the amount of oxygen in the water decreases. If a factory pumps thousands of litres of hot water into a river by accident, what effects could this have on the organisms that live in the river?

5 If you could change one thing to improve your own habitat, what would you change? Why?

Terrestrial habitats

Terrestrial means living on land rather than in water. Figure 2.2.4 shows you two of the many different terrestrial habitats in the Caribbean.

Soil

All terrestrial habitats depend on soil. Soil is the thin, top layer of the Earth's crust. Soil is made up of a mixture of rock particles from rocks that are broken down by erosion or weathering, together with organic matter from plants and animals, air, water and living organisms.

Although soil forms only a thin layer of the Earth's surface, it is the most important part of the surface for the survival of all living things. The soil is the part of the crust that contains the nutrients, water and air that plants need to grow. Animals and humans depend on plants for food for their survival. So, plants, animals and humans all depend on soil to survive. Figure 2.2.5 shows how soil is formed.

Because soil is largely made up of small particles of rock (non-living), we can say that soil is a physical factor in a habitat. However living organisms also contribute to the formation of soil by providing the organic products that give different soils their particular characteristics.

There are three main types of soil:

- **Sandy soil** – this has very little organic matter and fairly large rock particles. There are large spaces for air and water so it drains quickly.
- **Clay soil** – this soil is made up of very small rock particles. The small particles do not leave much space for air and water takes a long time to seep through the soil.
- **Loam soil** – this is made up of a mixture of large and small rock particles and organic material. It has enough space for air and water drains through it quickly.

You are going to look at soil in more detail to find out what it is made of and to see why it plays such an important role in habitats.

a

b

▲ **Figure 2.2.4** Terrestrial habitats such as **a** forests and **b** palm plantations are all dependent on soil

▼ **Figure 2.2.5** How soil is formed by mechanical and chemical processes in the environment

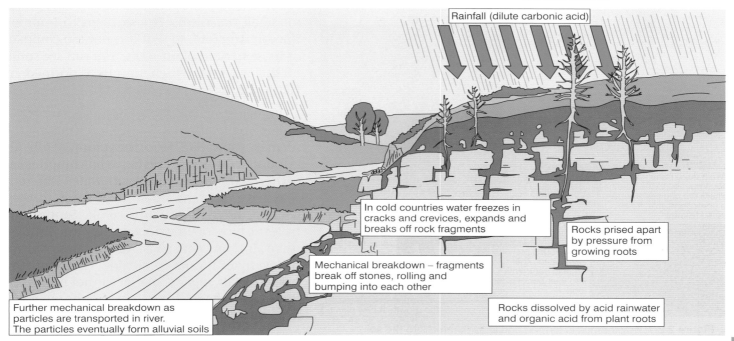

Rainfall (dilute carbonic acid)

In cold countries water freezes in cracks and crevices, expands and breaks off rock fragments

Rocks prised apart by pressure from growing roots

Mechanical breakdown – fragments break off stones, rolling and bumping into each other

Rocks dissolved by acid rainwater and organic acid from plant roots

Further mechanical breakdown as particles are transported in river. The particles eventually form alluvial soils

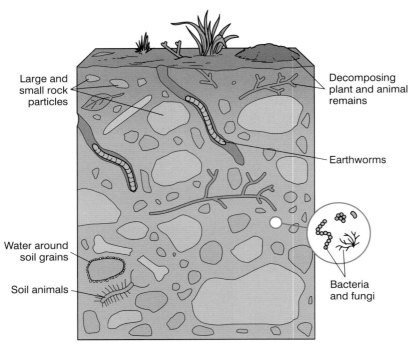

▲ **Figure 2.2.6** The components of soil seen through a magnifying glass

Labels on Figure 2.2.6:
- Large and small rock particles
- Decomposing plant and animal remains
- Earthworms
- Water around soil grains
- Soil animals
- Bacteria and fungi

- Fungi and bacteria feed on dead organic matter causing decay and decomposition
- Woodlice, wood-boring beetles and other wood-eating animals break up plant remains into crumbly pieces called frass. This increases the surface area of the plant remains exposed to attack by fungi and bacteria
- When dead material has decomposed to the point where the original organism is unrecognisable, it is called **humus**
- Earthworms pull dead leaves and other organic fragments into their burrows for food
- Decomposition releases gases, minerals and water from the dead wood into the soil
- Nutrients for the growth of new plants

▲ **Figure 2.2.7** How humus is formed and incorporated into the soil

Components of soil

There are many different soils, but all soils consist of the same basic components: rock particles, organic matter, air, water and living organisms. Soils are different because the amounts of these components vary from soil to soil. For example, a rich fertile soil may have more organic matter and water than an infertile, sandy soil. If you look at soil through a magnifying glass (Figure 2.2.6) you can see examples of the different components.

Rock particles

Rock particles are the largest component of soils and they make up around 45% of the total volume of the soil. The rock particles come from rocks that have been eroded or weathered over thousands of years. Nutrients, in the form of minerals and salts, are slowly released from the rock particles into the soil.

Organic matter

Organic matter forms only about 5% of the total volume of soil, but it is extremely important. Organic matter originates mainly from animal excretions and the remains of dead plants and animals. Small organisms that live in the soil, such as bacteria and fungi, break down the organic matter to release nutrients that plants take up through their roots. This decomposed organic matter in the soil is called humus. Humus is important in soil because it provides the nutrients that plants need as well as food for small organisms. It also helps to improve the soil structure, so that it is not too compact or loose to hold plant roots. You can see some of the ways in which humus is formed in Figure 2.2.7.

Air

Air makes up about 25% of the volume of soil. Air is found in all the spaces between components of the soil that are not filled with water. Different soils have different amounts of space so they contain different amounts of air. Sandy soils have the most open spaces, so they usually have more air than other soils. Air contains oxygen, nitrogen and carbon dioxide. Without the oxygen in air, organic matter cannot be broken down. So, if there is little air in soil, the nutrients from the organic matter are not released quickly and the soil is not very fertile.

Water

Water accounts for about 25% of the volume of soil. Water enters soil as rainfall or when people irrigate the soil. Water is found in the open spaces in the soil and in a thin layer around the soil particles. Different types of soil hold different amounts of water. Clay soils hold more water than sandy soils.

Living organisms

Living organisms make up a very small proportion of the total volume of soil. In most soils they account for only about 0.01% of the volume. Even though they are such a small proportion of the soil, their role is very important for keeping the soil in good condition so that it can provide nutrients for plants and animals.

Macroorganisms are organisms that we can see with the naked eye. Some of the macroorganisms found in soil are earthworms, termites, ants, springtails, beetles, slugs, snails, spiders and woodlice. Macroorganisms keep the soil loose by burrowing and turning the soil over. Their droppings also help to fertilise the soil.

Microorganisms are tiny organisms that we can see only through a microscope. These include bacteria and fungi that break down the organic material in the soil to release useful nutrients for plants.

Without living organisms, the soil would become too compact for plant roots to grow through and nutrients would not be released from organic matter.

The components of soil are important to living organisms:
- rock particles provide an anchor for plant roots and shelter for macroorganisms and microorganisms
- organic matter makes the soil fertile and can prevent erosion
- oxygen in soil is essential for respiration of plant roots and soil organisms
- nitrogen (in air) is essential for the formation of nitrates
- water is essential for plants and animals living in soil.

 Key fact

Not all soil organisms are useful and some can be harmful. The grubs and larvae of some insects eat plant roots and kill the plants. Bacteria, viruses and fungi can attack plants and spread diseases from one plant to another through the soil.

Questions

1. Draw a concept map to show all the different ways in which soil is important. Include what you have learnt in this topic and your own ideas about the importance of soil.

2. Name the three main soil types and give two general characteristics of each type.

3. What is humus and how does it get into soil?

4. Which soil type contains the most humus?

5. Give four reasons why organic material is good for the soil.

6. Sandy soils have large particles and large air spaces. How does this affect:
   a the way the soil holds water
   b how well water drains through the soil
   c how well plants grow in dry and wet seasons
   d how easy it is for plant roots to penetrate the soil
   e the amount of air in the soil
   f the ways in which people cultivate the soil?

Investigating different soils

You are now going to carry out some practical activities to investigate different types of soil.

 Practical activity

Describing soil texture

The three main soil types feel different if you rub them between your fingers. We can say the soils have a different texture (feel). The texture of a soil is related to the size of the particles in the soils.

Soil particles can be grouped into sizes:

- stones or gravel: more than 2 mm in diameter
- coarse sand: 0.2 mm to 2 mm in diameter
- fine sand: 0.02 mm to 0.2 mm in diameter
- silt: 0.002 mm to 0.02 mm in diameter
- clay: less than 0.002 mm in diameter.

1 Collect three different soil samples from your school grounds, from your garden at home and from the roadside.

2 Spread the soil samples out on white paper and examine them. Use a magnifying glass, if you have one, to see the components.
   a Are the particles all the same? Observe any differences in colour and shape.
   b Are there any plant roots, small insects or parts of dead plants or animals in your samples?

3 Compare the texture of each soil sample. Rub the soil lightly between your fingers.
   a Describe how each sample feels. Use the words 'gritty', 'rough', 'smooth' and 'fine'.
   b Are there any clay particles in any of your soil samples? How did you decide this?

 Practical activity

Determining the components of soil

You know that soil is a mixture of different components. You are going to find out what soil is made of and then graph your results.

Materials

- Three soil samples (try to find different types of soil)
- Three identical, clean glass jars with lids
- Water
- Sticky tape

Method

1 Place a sample of soil into each jar. The jars should contain the same amount of soil and they should be about one-third full. Label each jar to show which sample it contains.

2 Fill the jars almost to the top (the same level in each) with water and screw on the lids tightly.

3 Shake each jar well for about a minute to mix the soil sample and the water.

4 Leave the jars to settle for about 15 minutes.

5 The soil in each jar will settle into different layers. The heavier particles will settle at the bottom, with smaller particles in layers above them. Silt particles will settle on the top of the solid particles. Clay particles will not settle; they will float in the water above the silt layer making it look cloudy. The humus from the soil is light and will float on top of the water. Copy the following table. Estimate the percentage of each component in each sample and write it in your table.

6 Work out the degrees each component would take up in a pie chart. Use the formula $\left(\dfrac{x}{100} \times 360°\right)$ to work this out.

7 Draw a pie chart to show the components of each of your samples.

Soil component (%)	Sample 1	Sample 2	Sample 3
Gravel			
Sand			
Silt			
Clay			
Humus			

Practical activity　　　　 **Safety**

Testing for air, water and organic matter in soil samples

Your teacher may use this activity to assess: ORR; M&M

For each test, take a soil sample from a depth of about 30 cm below the surface.

Test 1: Testing for the presence of air in a soil sample

Materials
- A soil sample
- A test tube
- A jug of water

Method
1 Fill one-third of the test tube with soil from your sample.
2 Quickly pour water from the jug into the test tube so that it fills the test tube to the top.
3 Observe the test tube. What do you see? What does this tell you about the soil sample?

Result

This experiment shows that there is air in the soil. As the water filled up the spaces between the particles in the soil, it forced the air out of those spaces. The air rises to the surface of the water as bubbles. If you did not observe any bubbles, repeat the experiment with another sample and observe carefully when you pour the water into the test tube.

Test 2: Determining the volume of air in a soil sample

Materials
- A sample of fairly dry soil
- Two measuring cylinders
- Water
- A stirring rod or spoon

Method
1 Take a handful of soil from your sample. Rub it between your palms to break up any lumps.
2 Put 100 cm³ of soil into one of the measuring cylinders.
3 Put 100 cm³ of water into the other measuring cylinder. Pour this into the cylinder containing the soil.
4 Stir the mixture of soil and water in the measuring cylinder until all the air has escaped (no more bubbles) and the soil is wet.
5 Now read the volume of the soil and water mixture. Why is it not 200 cm³?
6 Work out the **volume of air** in the soil sample by subtracting your reading from 200 cm³.
Write down your results.

Safety

Do not touch hot apparatus or you will burn yourself.

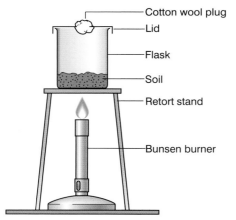

- Cotton wool plug
- Lid
- Flask
- Soil
- Retort stand
- Bunsen burner

▲ **Figure 2.2.8**

Exam tip

Although we are using a Bunsen burner to do these tests, Test 3 is best done using an oven set at 100 °C. The soil is dried out for one day. Test 6 is best done using an oven set at 50 °C. The soil is heated for two days, weighed and then heated for another day.

Safety

Wear eye protection.

Test 3: Testing for the presence of water in a soil sample

Materials

- A sample of fine, dry soil
- A heat-resistant glass flask with a lid (the lid must have a hole in it)
- Cotton wool
- A Bunsen burner
- A retort stand

Method

1 Half-fill the heat-resistant flask with fine, dry soil from the garden or a ploughed field.
2 Close the top of the flask with the lid and plug the hole in the lid with cotton wool. (See Figure 2.2.8.)
3 Heat the flask over a Bunsen burner with a gentle flame. Do not burn the soil, just dry it.
4 Watch what happens in the upper part of the flask. Write down your observations and suggest a reason for what you observed.

Keep this dried soil sample. You will use it again in Test 6.

Test 4: How much water is in soil?

Plan and design another experiment of your own to work out the amount of water in a soil sample.

Test 5: Investigating the water-holding capacity of soils

Imagine you have been given a measuring cylinder, a funnel and cotton wool. How could you use this apparatus to work out how much water a 25g sample of soil can hold?

Test 6: Testing for the presence of organic material in a soil sample

Materials

- Your dry soil sample from Test 3
- Two identical evaporating dishes
- A balance
- A Bunsen burner
- A stirring rod or spoon
- A retort stand

Method

1 Divide the soil sample between the two evaporating dishes. Make sure that you have the same amount in each evaporating dish by putting the dishes on the balance and adding or removing soil from the dishes until the balance stays level.
2 Place one of the evaporating dishes on the retort stand above the Bunsen burner and heat it with a very hot flame. Carefully stir the soil with the stirring rod or spoon as it heats up.
3 Observe whether any smoke rises from the soil. What does it smell like? Can you see parts of the soil glowing red?
4 Keep heating and stirring the dish until no more smoke comes from the soil. Switch off the Bunsen burner and leave the dish to cool for at least 30 minutes.
5 Put the heated evaporating dish and the unheated evaporating dish back on the balance. Which side goes up? Which dish is lighter? Suggest why this happens.

A2.3 Carrying out an ecological study

When you study the organisms in an area you are trying to find information about the species found there, where they are found and how many of each species there are. It is not always practical to try and count all the individuals of every species in the whole area, so scientists study samples (smaller areas) of the habitat and then use the information from the sample to make conclusions about the area as a whole. Sampling is a recognised statistical method that is used in many different areas.

Distribution of species

Think about how the students at your school occupy the school grounds during break times. Are they evenly spread across the grounds? Can you find groups of students in some places? Are there some parts of the grounds that are more popular than others; under a large, shady tree for example? The way the students are spread out is the distribution of the students at break times.

The distribution of a species describes where it is found and how it is spread out in an area. Like students, single species are not evenly distributed in a habitat. Organisms are found in the areas that are most favourable and suitable for their survival.

To study the distribution of species in an area you need to know which species are found in the area and where they are found. You also need to have some method of recording and showing this distribution.

In a small area, you can learn about the distribution of species by observation. For example, if you looked in a small rock pool you could see what species there were and how they were spread out. You could make a list of the species and record on a sketch map (Figure 2.3.1) where each one was found.

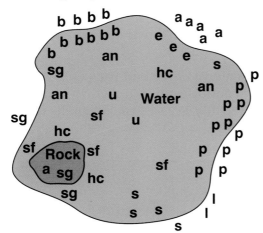

▲ **Figure 2.3.1** The types and distribution of species observed in a rock pool

The transect method

In larger areas we need to use sampling methods to show the distribution of species. One commonly used method is the transect method. The name of the transect method gives you some clues about how it works: *trans* means 'across' and *sect* means 'part'. So, this method means collecting data from across part of the ecosystem.

Objectives

By the end of this topic you will be able to:

- explain why scientists use sampling and how they do this
- explain the terms 'distribution' and 'density'
- use transects and quadrats to find information about species in an area
- choose the best methods of sampling species in a study
- carry out an ecological study in the local environment.

A transect is a line or strip that crosses the entire area of study from one side to the other. You can use a long tape measure or a rope marked with regular intervals to mark the transect. You then walk along the transect and record the species of plants (and/or slow-moving animals) found at each part or at regular intervals.

When you record data you only work along or within the transect, recording what organisms are found. You list the organisms you find and sketch where they are found along the transect. Figure 2.3.2 shows what students found when they did a line transect across a section of waste ground.

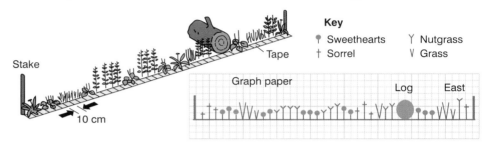

Key
† Sweethearts   Υ Nutgrass
† Sorrel   V Grass

Stake

Tape

10 cm

Graph paper   Log   East

▲ **Figure 2.3.2** The distribution of plants along a line transect

Quadrats and the grid method

A quadrat is a square frame. If you make a quadrat out of 1 m long pieces of wood you will get a square metre. This is a useful size for your purposes. You can divide the quadrat into smaller squares using pieces of string. You can see a quadrat divided into 100 squares (10 cm × 10 cm) in Figure 2.3.3. Each small square represents 1% of the area of the quadrat.

You can use the quadrat to get an idea of the distribution of species in a sample of the area you are studying. When you put it on the ground, you can see what percentage of the area under the quadrat is occupied by different species. Figure 2.3.4 shows you a quadrat that has been placed on a patch of sand near the shore. The shaded areas show you where the grass *Sporobulus virginicus* is found in the square.

You can use your quadrat grid to find the percentage of the area covered by each species by counting the number of squares in which you find the species and converting it to a percentage. In the example above, the *Sporobulus* grass covers 45% of the area.

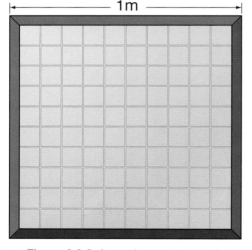

1m

▲ **Figure 2.3.3** A quadrat can be made into a grid using string

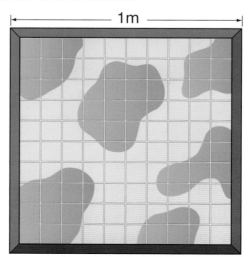

1m

▶ **Figure 2.3.4** The distribution of sand and grass in a square area close to the beach

Random sampling

When you use quadrats in a large area, you will place the quadrats at many different spots and average your results to get a representative figure.

When you do this, you need to place the quadrats randomly in the area being studied. You can select random spots by drawing a rough outline map of the area and throwing dice or coins onto it. Mark the spot that the dice or coin lands on and place your quadrat on that spot. If you want to sample 10 squares, throw the dice or coins 10 times.

 Practical activity

An ecological study

Your teacher may use this activity to assess: ORR; M&M; A&I

Method

Work as a group to do this activity.

1 Select a small open field or an area of waste ground near your school.

2 Carry out a line transect of the field and record the species you find.

3 Build a metre square grid quadrat using poles and string.

4 Choose five random sampling sites on the field. Use your quadrat grid to map the distribution of different plants in the random sample areas.

5 Choose one plant that is found in all the quadrats you use. Calculate the average percentage of the field covered by that plant.

6 Evaluate your data.

Density of species

The abundance of a species is how many members of the species are found in an area. When we work out the abundance of species in different areas, for example, nutgrass plants per square metre, then we are calculating the density of the species.

Density is not a set figure and it changes from time to time. Species may increase in abundance as a result of good conditions for growth or birth. For example, warm, wet conditions might lead to an increase in the density of mosquitoes. Similarly, species may decrease in abundance as a result of poor conditions for growth or deaths. For example, a period of drought might lead to a decrease in the density of some plant species.

Measuring population size

As with distribution, if you are working in a small area, you can observe organisms in the area you are studying and simply count them. For example, you could walk round your school and count the number of breadfruit trees you can find to see how many there are.

When scientists measure numbers of species they use a scale known as the DAFOR scale to describe how abundant a species is. The scale has six categories, each with a descriptive word. The basic categories and what they mean in an ecosystem is given in Table 2.3.1. The DAFOR scale can be adapted for use in different ecosystems. Table 2.3.2 shows you how one group of scientists adapted it to rate the abundance of coral reef fishes.

▼ **Table 2.3.1** The DAFOR scale

Rating	Description	What it means
5	**D**ominant	Found all the time in great numbers. Has the greatest effect on the system
4	**A**bundant	Found all the time
3	**F**requent	Found often
2	**O**ccasional	Sometimes found, but not often
1	**R**are	Hardly ever found
0	Absent	Not found at all

▼ **Table 2.3.2** The DAFOR scale applied to coral reef fishes

Rating	Abundance
5	>200 individuals *and* they form the major part of the overall biomass
4	30 to 200 individuals seen at all times
3	7 to 50 individuals seen
2	2 to 6 individuals seen
1	1 individual seen
0	none found

You can use the quadrat and grid method to measure numbers of plants in an area. Use the same random sampling procedure and record the number of plants of different species per square metre. From this figure you can work out the average population for the whole area you are studying.

Counting populations

Animals can move around and many animals will sense you coming and disappear to avoid you, so it is more difficult to measure the abundance of animals than the abundance of plants.

If the species you are studying moves around a lot, you can measure their population using the capture–recapture method. When you use this method you capture and mark a sample (say 10 members of a species) then release them. When they have had time to mix back with the original population you capture another sample. If 20% (two members) of the new sample is marked, it is mathematically reasonable to expect that the original sample was actually 20% of the whole population. So, the total population is the 10 members of the original population multiplied by five (to get 100%) or 50 individuals. This method is illustrated for beetles in Figure 2.3.5.

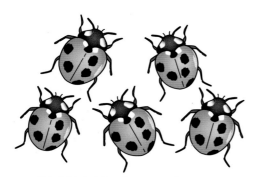

5 ladybirds taken from sample area

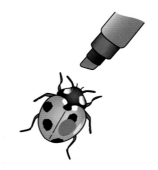

All 5 ladybirds marked and released

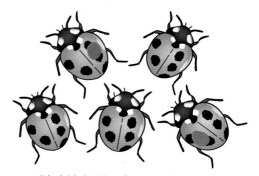

5 ladybirds taken from sample area – percentage marked in blue noted

▲ **Figure 2.3.5** The capture–recapture method of measuring abundance

Capturing and recapturing the animals can be tricky. Figure 2.3.6 shows you some of the methods you can use to capture and recapture the animals in your study. You will need to choose the method that is most suited to the area you are studying.

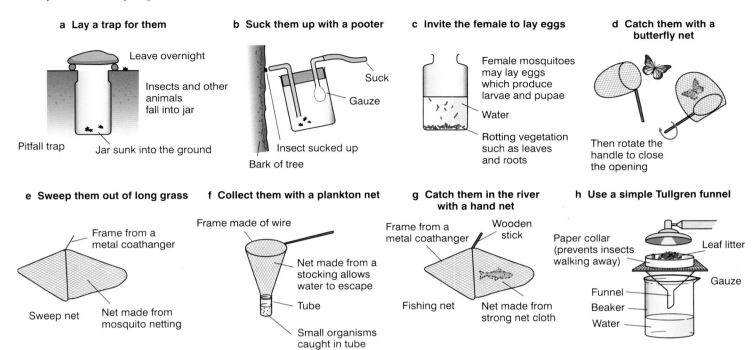

▲ **Figure 2.3.6** Different methods of catching animals without harming them

Questions

1 Use diagrams to show what is meant by:
   a distribution of species
   b population density.

2 Use the DAFOR scale to rate the abundance of the following organisms in your local area:
   a banana trees
   b coconut palms
   c fruit bats
   d mosquitoes
   e lizards.

3 A scientist makes a study of a local river. She uses the capture–recapture method and estimates that the total population of large crabs is eight individuals. On her next field trip she uses the same method and finds the total population to be 50 individuals. Why do you think her results were so much higher on the second visit, even though there was not enough time for birth or immigration to have taken place?

Objectives

By the end of this topic you will be able to:

- define the terms 'ecology' and 'ecosystem'
- explain interdependence of organisms in an ecosystem
- classify organisms according to their mode of feeding
- identify the position of producers and consumers in feeding relationships
- understand the role of decomposers in an ecosystem.

A2.4 Ecosystems

Ecology is the study of plants and animals, their relationships to one another and their relationships with their environments. The word 'ecology' was first used by a German biologist, Ernst Haeckel, in 1866. Ecology comes from two Greek words: 'oikos' which means home and 'logos' which means study. Ecology is thus 'the study of organisms in their homes and habitats'.

An **ecosystem** is the name given to a community of living organisms in a particular habitat together with the physical elements of the habitat.

Ecosystems are varied. Each ecosystem has its own particular characteristics that make it unique. In the Caribbean, we have ecosystems ranging from tropical and equatorial rainforests, mountain forests, grassland savannas, tropical deciduous forests, tropical scrubs, mangrove swamps and coral reefs. Although all these ecosystems are unique and different, they all share a similar structure.

Producers and consumers

The primary source of energy for almost all ecosystems is solar energy from the Sun. The energy from the Sun reaches Earth as radiant energy. The only way that living organisms can use the energy from the Sun is to change it from radiant energy to chemical potential energy.

The only living organisms that can change energy from the Sun into chemical potential energy are the green organisms. Green plants are called **autotrophs** because they can make their own food using energy and materials from the environment. Green plants use sunlight to produce sugars by photosynthesis. Some algae and bacteria are also autotrophs. They get the energy they need to produce food from light or simple chemical reactions. Because autotrophs produce food that is eaten by other organisms, they are called **producers**.

Organisms that cannot produce food from energy and materials in the environment are called **heterotrophs**. These organisms must eat (consume) other living organisms (plants or animals) in order to feed. For this reason they are also called the **consumers** in an ecosystem.

Consumers that eat only plants are called **herbivores**. Examples of herbivores are rabbits, cows, sheep, buffaloes, elephants and giraffes.

Consumers that eat meat (in the form of other consumers) are called **carnivores**. Examples of carnivores are lizards, seagulls, herons, owls, sharks, foxes and lions.

Consumers that eat both plants and meat are called **omnivores**. Spider monkeys and humans are examples of omnivores.

There are three levels of consumers in most ecosystems:
- **primary consumers** eat producers (plants and bacteria)
- **secondary consumers** eat primary consumers
- **tertiary consumers** eat secondary consumers.

When organisms die, their remains are broken down by a group of consumers called decomposers. **Decomposers** are bacteria and fungi that feed on dead and decaying materials. Decomposers are an important part of any ecosystem because they ensure that nutrients are recycled back into the ecosystem.

Organisms in an ecosystem can only survive because they obtain energy in the form of food from various sources. The energy flows through the ecosystem from the source (the Sun) to the producers and consumers and eventually to the decomposers. We will look at energy flow through ecosystems in more detail in Unit A3.

Trophic levels

Each level of feeding in an ecosystem is called a trophic level.

The producers and consumers at different trophic levels in an ecosystem are shown in Figure 2.4.1.

The diagram (Figure 2.4.1) shows that sunlight is converted to chemical energy by the plants (leaves). Plants use some of this energy themselves, but they also store energy in their roots, stems, leaves, flowers, fruits and seeds. Plants are the producers, so they make up the first trophic level in any ecosystem.

Other organisms eat plants to get energy. In this example, the insects eat the leaves of the plants. The chemical energy from the plant is transferred to the insects. They use some of this energy for their own life processes and they lose some in the form of heat. The insects are primary consumers (second trophic level).

The insects are eaten by small birds. The small birds are secondary consumers (third trophic level). The birds receive chemical energy from the insects and more energy is lost as heat. The small birds in turn are eaten by chicken hawks or other tertiary consumers (fourth trophic level).

If any of the producers or consumers dies, their energy will be transferred to the decomposers, again with heat loss.

Because heat energy is lost at each trophic level, only about 10% of the stored chemical energy from each trophic level is passed on to the next level. The amount of energy transferred from level to level is shown as a fraction in Figure 2.4.1. This means that food chains are limited in the number of tertiary consumers they can support.

The feeding relationships between producers and consumers in different ecosystems can be represented as simple food chains and more complex food webs (when a consumer feeds at more than one trophic level). You will learn more about these in topic A2.5.

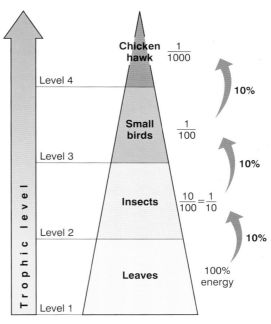

▲ **Figure 2.4.1** Different trophic levels in a terrestrial ecosystem

Questions

1 Copy this table and fill it in to summarise what you have learnt about organisms and how they feed in ecosystems.

Term	Definition	Local examples
Ecosystem		
Autotroph		
Heterotroph		
Producer		
Consumer		
Trophic level		
Decomposer		

2 Identify and list 10 local animals.
   a Classify the animals as herbivores, carnivores or omnivores.
   b Suggest which of the animals are secondary consumers and which are tertiary consumers.

Objectives

By the end of this topic you will be able to:

- define the terms 'food chain' and 'food web'
- draw food chains showing at least four organisms
- read and interpret food webs to identify different feeding relationships
- construct a food web that includes different trophic levels
- understand that organisms in a food chain are interdependent.

The flow of energy from one organism to another can be shown in a simple diagram called a food chain. For example:

leaves ⟶ insect ⟶ bird ⟶ cat

grass ⟶ locust ⟶ lizard

In general, food chains follow the order:

green plant ⟶ herbivore ⟶ carnivore

The arrows in a food chain show the direction in which energy and matter moves through the food chain.

Food webs

If you look around, you will see that in most ecosystems there is more than one primary producer (there are lots of different plants). You will also notice that most animals eat more than one thing. Figure 2.5.1 shows you some feeding relationships in a terrestrial ecosystem and some feeding relationships in an aquatic ecosystem.

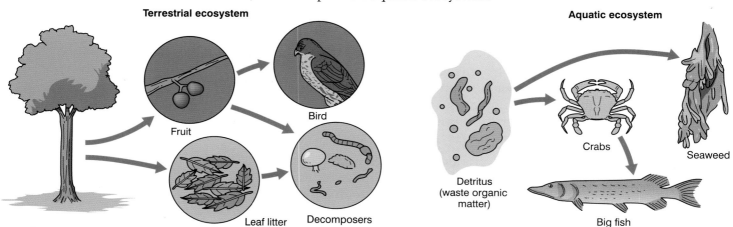

▲ **Figure 2.5.1** Feeding relationships in two different ecosystems

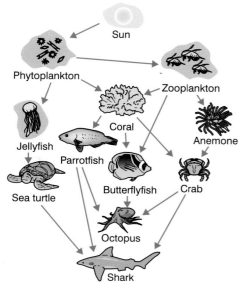

▲ **Figure 2.5.2** A food web for a coral reef

A food chain is too simple to show all these relationships so we use a more detailed diagram called a food web. A food web shows many different food chains and how they are linked together. Food webs give more accurate information about the feeding relationships in a community than food chains can. Figure 2.5.2 shows you a food web for a coral reef community.

How to draw a food web

Food chains all have the same basic features:

- they start with producers (the first trophic level)
- they contain consumers (herbivores, omnivores and carnivores) at different feeding levels
- the arrows show the direction in which energy and matter flows though the ecosystem.

When you have to construct a food web, it helps to identify the trophic levels at which organisms feed. Once you have organised the organisms into levels, you can draw arrows to show feeding relationships. Remember the arrow shows the direction in which energy flows in an ecosystem and energy can flow in one direction only. Figure 2.5.3 shows you the steps in constructing a simple food web for a small part of a tropical forest ecosystem.

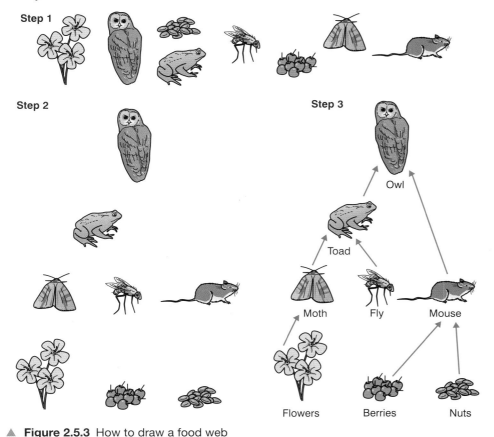

Step 1

Step 2

Step 3

▲ **Figure 2.5.3** How to draw a food web

> ✓ **Exam tip**
>
> In examinations you might be asked to find relationships in a food web that contains unfamiliar examples. It is important to remember that all food webs work in the same way, no matter what organisms they show.

Questions

1 The food web in Figure 2.5.4 is from the Antarctic.

a What are the primary consumers in this food web?

b Identify a herbivore and two carnivores in the food web.

c From the food web, construct two food chains with at least four organisms in each.

d If the killer whales were removed from this food web, what would happen to the size of the population of seals?

e If the krill were over-fished in this system and their numbers dropped, what possible effects would it have on the ecosystem?

f A predator is an animal that catches and kills its own food. Prey is the animals that predators catch and kill. Which animals in this food web are predators and which are prey?

2 Choose one local ecosystem and draw a food web to show the different trophic levels and feeding relationships found in it.

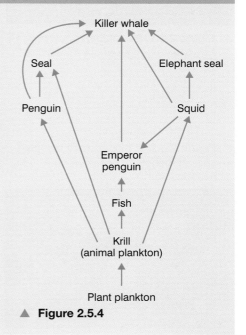

▲ **Figure 2.5.4**

By the end of this topic you will be able to:

- explain what is meant by 'symbiosis'
- define the terms 'commensalism', 'mutualism', 'predation' and 'parasitism'
- identify symbiotic relationships between organisms
- examine symbiotic relationships between organisms
- state the advantages and disadvantages of special feeding relationships for organisms involved.

A2.6 Special relationships among organisms

When organisms live together they interact with each other. These interactions may increase or decrease each other's chances of survival. For example, the presence of cattle increases the chance of survival for ticks because ticks use the cattle's blood as food. This is a beneficial relationship for the ticks. However ticks can spread diseases that decrease the cattle's chances of survival. This is a detrimental relationship for the cattle. The relationship between different organisms that depend on each other in some way is called symbiosis. There are three types of symbiosis: commensalism, mutualism and parasitism.

Beneficial relationships

When organisms interact in ways that benefit and do not harm the organisms involved, the relationship is beneficial. Commensalism and mutualism are beneficial relationships.

Commensalism

When species interact in a way that benefits one species but is neutral or does not harm the other, it is called commensalism. In commensalism, the species are not dependent on each other for survival, that is they can survive without each other.

Epiphytes are orchids or ferns that grow on trees. The relationship between the epiphyte and the tree is an example of commensalism. You can see an epiphyte on a tree in Figure 2.6.1. The epiphytes are supported by the tree but they do not obtain food from the tree. They also do not harm the tree in any way. Both the tree and the epiphyte can survive without the other.

Adult barnacles are sea organisms that cannot move by themselves to find food. They attach themselves to the skin of whales or the shells of large sea molluscs. As the larger animal moves, the barnacles are able to get food from rich sea-currents. The whales and molluscs do not benefit from the relationship but the barnacles do not seem to harm them either. Both species can survive without the other. This is another example of commensalism.

The relationship between cattle egrets and grazing animals is commensal. The birds sit on the backs of the cattle and feed on insects that are disturbed as the cattle move through the grass. The cattle do not benefit from this relationship but they are not harmed by the birds either. Both species can survive without the other.

Mutualism

If two species both benefit from a relationship it is called mutualism. Mutualism is more common than commensalism. Figure 2.6.2 shows you three examples of mutualism in an aquatic environment.

▲ **Figure 2.6.1** An epiphyte growing on a tree is an example of commensalism

▼ **Figure 2.6.2** In these examples, both species benefit from their mutual relationship

Further examples of mutualism are:

- Lichen is an association between an alga and a fungus. The cells of the algae are found among the strands that make up the fungus. In this relationship, the fungus benefits because the green cells in the alga allow it to provide food by photosynthesis. The alga benefits from the moist environment provided by the fungus.

- Nitrogen-fixing bacteria live in nodules (small lumps) on the roots of plants called legumes (beans and peas). The bacteria are able to absorb nitrogen from the air and convert it into a form that plants can use to make proteins. The bacteria benefit by getting sugars from the plant's roots.

- Ants and aphids have a mutualistic relationship. The aphids live among ants. The ants feed on the sugary liquid produced by the aphids. The aphids are protected from other predators by the ants.

- Termites eat wood and other cellulose material but they cannot digest it themselves. The termites have a mutualistic relationship with protozoa in their guts. The protozoa digest the cellulose and have a safe environment to live in whilst the termite gets food.

Detrimental relationships

In detrimental relationships, organisms interact in ways that benefit one species but harm the other. Parasitism is an example of a feeding relationship that is detrimental.

Parasitism

In parasitism one species (the parasite) gets its food from another species (the host). For example, lice are parasites that feed on human blood. Ticks are parasites that feed on the blood of animals (and sometimes people). Tapeworms, bilharzia and malaria parasites get into the bodies of animals or humans and feed off their nutrients. Figure 2.6.3 shows the life cycle of a tapeworm.

Plants can also be parasitic. Dodder is a twisting plant that winds itself round other plants. It sends small suckers into the other plant to feed. Dodder often kills the host plant and spreads to another plant.

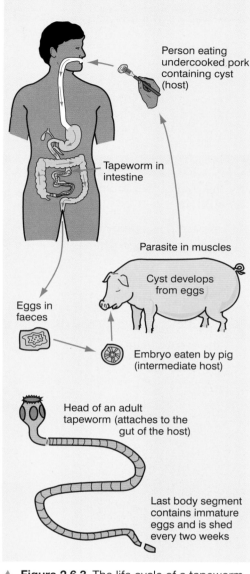

▲ **Figure 2.6.3** The life cycle of a tapeworm

Questions

1 What would you call the following symbiotic relationships? Give a reason for each answer:
   a An oxpecker bird feeds on ticks and other parasites on animals such as cows and buffaloes.
   b Honeybees feed on nectar from flowers.
   c An adult wasp lays its eggs inside the body of a caterpillar. When the larvae hatch, they eat the caterpillar from the inside.
   d Sea anemones sometimes grow on the shells of hermit crabs.
   e Pilot fish swim along in front of sharks and pick up scraps of food left over when the shark feeds.
   f Athlete's foot is a fungus that grows in the damp skin between our toes.

2 Find examples of relationships between bacteria and other organisms. Name the partners in the relationship, say what type of relationship each one is, and identify any advantages or disadvantages for the organisms in the relationship.

You have learnt that all ecosystems depend on energy from the Sun. Now you are going to learn how energy from the Sun enters, then flows through ecosystems, and how it is lost to the environment in the process.

A3.1   Energy flow in ecosystems

The source of all energy for life on Earth is the Sun. Plants use sunlight during photosynthesis to form chemical energy which is stored in the plants as food. This energy is passed onto animals when they eat plants. When animals are eaten by other animals, the energy is passed on again. In this way, the energy from the Sun flows through the ecosystem. Some of the energy is lost (usually in the form of heat) in the transfer of food from one trophic level to the next. We are going to look at how this happens in more detail in this topic.

Energy flow through producers

The energy in ecosystems comes from sunlight. Green plants, algae and some bacteria absorb sunlight and use its energy to convert carbon dioxide and water into sugars in the process called photosynthesis. This is why food chains and food webs all begin with producers (plants, algae or bacteria).

Plants do not absorb much of the sunlight that reaches them. Figure 3.1.1 shows you why they absorb so little sunlight.

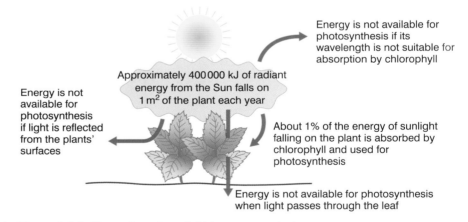

Energy is not available for photosynthesis if its wavelength is not suitable for absorption by chlorophyll

Approximately 400 000 kJ of radiant energy from the Sun falls on 1 m² of the plant each year

Energy is not available for photosynthesis if light is reflected from the plants' surfaces

About 1% of the energy of sunlight falling on the plant is absorbed by chlorophyll and used for photosynthesis

Energy is not available for photosynthesis when light passes through the leaf

▲ **Figure 3.1.1** Absorption of sunlight by a green plant

Plants need energy to stay alive. They get this energy from the sugars they makes during photosynthesis. Some of the energy is used to keep the process of photosynthesis going. However some of the energy is released in the process of respiration (you will learn more about this in Unit B11). Plants use the rest of the energy to grow and live. This is the energy that is available to consumers as food. When a primary consumer eats a plant, energy is transferred to the primary consumer. This energy is transferred indirectly to consumers at higher trophic levels when they feed on the primary consumer. Energy is also transferred from the plant when fruits and seeds are dispersed. When the plant dies or loses its leaves, energy is transferred to decomposers in the ecosystem.

Energy flow through consumers

You read on p27 that only about 10% of available energy is transferred from one trophic level to the level above it. This means that 90% of the energy available at each level is lost to the environment. Why is the transfer of energy from level to level so wasteful? It is because:

● Some plant material is not digested by primary consumers (herbivores). This passes out of their bodies as faeces.

● Some of the plant energy is used by the primary and secondary consumers to stay alive. When the consumers die, their bodies contain stored energy and some of this is transferred to decomposers.

Figure 3.1.2 shows the energy flow through a primary consumer (a cow). You can see from the diagram that more than half of the energy that the cow gets from the grass is transferred to the environment by its urine and faeces. Energy is also transferred to the environment from the cow's body in the form of heat produced by respiration.

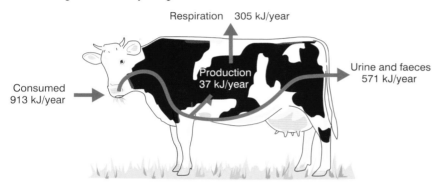

Respiration   305 kJ/year

Production
37 kJ/year

Urine and faeces
571 kJ/year

Consumed
913 kJ/year

▲ **Figure 3.1.2** The energy flow through a primary consumer

The energy flow through a herbivore can be summarised like this:

    energy intake = energy transfer in respiration + energy transfer in
                    production of cow's body mass + energy in urine
                    + energy in faeces

Figure 3.1.3 shows you the energy flow and energy loss for a whole ecosystem.

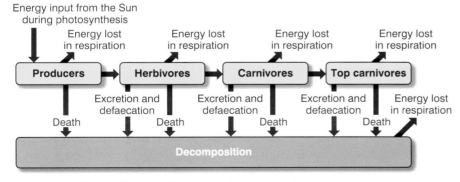

Energy input from the Sun
during photosynthesis

Energy lost
in respiration

Energy lost
in respiration

Energy lost
in respiration

Energy lost
in respiration

Producers ▶ **Herbivores** ▶ **Carnivores** ▶ **Top carnivores**

Excretion and
defaecation

Excretion and
defaecation

Excretion and
defaecation

Energy lost
in respiration

Death

Death

Death

Death

Decomposition

▲ **Figure 3.1.3** Energy flow and loss through an ecosystem

In a long food chain, energy is lost at each trophic level. This means that there is less and less energy available for higher level carnivores at the top of the food chain. A short food chain is far more energy efficient. For example, when humans eat plants directly, less energy is lost than when we feed plants to animals and then eat the animals. A short food chain can thus support more people than a long one with many feeding levels.

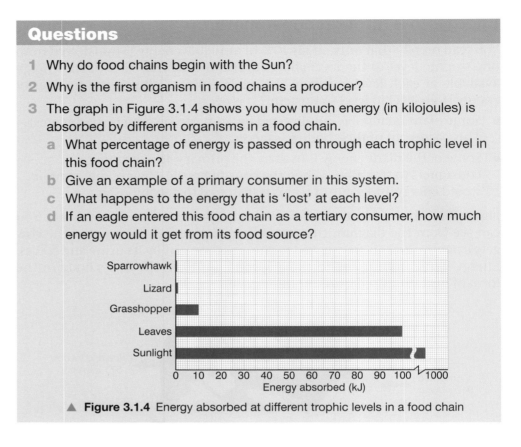

Questions

1 Why do food chains begin with the Sun?

2 Why is the first organism in food chains a producer?

3 The graph in Figure 3.1.4 shows you how much energy (in kilojoules) is absorbed by different organisms in a food chain.

   a What percentage of energy is passed on through each trophic level in this food chain?

   b Give an example of a primary consumer in this system.

   c What happens to the energy that is 'lost' at each level?

   d If an eagle entered this food chain as a tertiary consumer, how much energy would it get from its food source?

▲ **Figure 3.1.4** Energy absorbed at different trophic levels in a food chain

Decomposition and nutrient cycling in an ecosystem

In Unit A2 you learnt that soil is a very important abiotic factor in any ecosystem because plants (producers) absorb nutrients from the soil. Nutrients are the things that organisms need to provide them with energy to function and carry on living. Every ecosystem provides nutrients.

You also learnt that the soil contains microorganisms. In this topic you are going to look at how these microorganisms feed on and break down organic material in the process of decomposition and, in doing so, recycle important nutrients and return them to the soil.

Decomposition

If you have ever walked through a forested area you will have noticed that there is a mass of dead and decaying leaves, flowers and other matter at your feet.

The dead matter in an ecosystem is called detritus. In a terrestrial ecosystem, most detritus is made up of fallen leaves and flowers, broken twigs and dead plants and animals. In an aquatic ecosystem, most detritus is made of dead algae and plants, pieces of plants that get broken off and the remains and waste products of animals.

In all ecosystems, dead matter contains nutrients, so detritus is a source of food. What eats detritus?

Scavengers such as rats and crows are animals that feed on detritus. Small scavengers like earthworms, maggots, snails and insect larvae are known as detritivores.

Objectives

By the end of this topic you will be able to:

- explain the role of decomposers
- investigate the growth of bacteria in soil
- investigate the action of mould on bread
- explain how matter is recycled in nature
- illustrate the carbon cycle and the nitrogen cycle.

Detritivores feed on dead and decaying matter and break it down into small particles. The small particles are then broken down by **decomposers**, such as bacteria and fungi.

Detritivores get some energy from the detritus, but they get most of their energy from the decomposers that live on the detritus.

Decomposers feed by secreting enzymes over their food. The enzymes break down complex substances into simple, soluble substances such as glucose, carbon dioxide, water (hydrogen and oxygen) and nutrients such as sulfates and nitrates. The decomposers release these substances into the soil as they feed. All of these nutrients can be absorbed by plants.

Figure 3.2.1 shows how nutrients are decomposed and recycled in ecosystems.

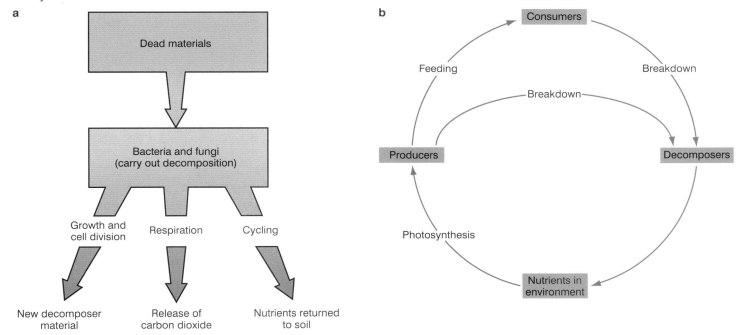

▲ **Figure 3.2.1 a** Decomposition releases nutrients; **b** nutrients are recycled through the ecosystem

Practical activity

Growing microorganisms in soil

Your teacher may use this activity to assess: ORR, M&M; A&I

You are going to grow microorganisms from a soil sample.

Materials

- A sample of topsoil that contains some dead or decaying (organic) matter
- 4 Petri dishes and lids
- 2 beakers
- A Bunsen burner and stand
- Masking tape
- A small glass of milk
- A stirring rod or spoon
- A crucible
- A fibre-tipped pen

Method

1 Place the crucible on the stand and light the Bunsen burner.

2 Place two spoonfuls of soil in the crucible and sterilise it by heating it for 15 minutes. Stir the soil so that it does not overheat. Allow the soil to cool.

3 Pour half the milk into a beaker and sterilise it by heating it gently until it boils. Allow the milk to cool.

4 Place a piece of masking tape on each lid and label them from 1 to 4. Fill the dishes as follows:

Dish 1	A large spoon of sterilised soil plus two teaspoons of sterilised milk
Dish 2	A large spoon of sterilised soil plus two teaspoons of unsterilised milk (the milk you did not heat)
Dish 3	A large spoon of unsterilised soil (the soil you did not heat) plus two teaspoons of sterilised milk
Dish 4	A large spoon of unsterilised soil plus two teaspoons of unsterilised milk

5 Place the labelled lids on the correct dishes and seal them using masking tape.

6 Swirl each dish once or twice to mix the milk and the soil. Then leave the dishes in a warm place (out of the Sun) for four days. Do not open the dishes at all.

Recording your results

Draw and label what you observe in each Petri dish after four days.

Conclusions

1 Which Petri dish showed the greatest growth of microorganisms? Suggest why.

2 Why did you use topsoil with organic matter in it for this experiment?

3 Did any dishes have no growth? Why do you think this was the case?

4 What do you think you have grown: bacteria or fungi? Why?

5 What do you think would have happened if you had put the Petri dishes into a fridge for four days? Why?

 Practical activity

Investigating the action of mould on bread

You can grow mould on bread quite easily. You will need slices of bread, water and clear plastic bags that can be sealed (by tying them or zip-locking them). You simply sprinkle the bread lightly with water and place it in the sealed bag. You then leave the bag in a warm dark place for a few days.

Design a test to find out which types of bread go mouldy the fastest. Try white bread, brown bread, rye bread, shop-bought and home-made bread.

Write a short report on your investigation. Your report should explain:
- what you did (your method)
- what you observed
- suggest likely causes for differences in the results
- what you can conclude from your investigation.

Cycling nutrients

You have just seen that decomposition releases nutrients. Two of the important nutrients that need to be recycled are carbon and nitrogen.

The carbon cycle

Carbon is found in all living organisms. Plants obtain carbon during photosynthesis from the carbon dioxide in the air. Animals get carbon from the food they eat. So plants need carbon dioxide and all other animals, including humans, need plants. This makes carbon dioxide very important in ecosystems.

Plants take in carbon dioxide through their leaves and they take in water through their roots. They use the carbon dioxide and water to synthesise (build) sugars. This reaction is called photosynthesis and you will learn more about it in topic B8.2. Photosynthesis takes place in green leaves in the presence of sunlight. Oxygen is formed during photosynthesis.

Animals eat plants, which contain starches and sugars, which contain carbon. Animals also breathe in air, which contains oxygen. The oxygen that animals breathe in dissolves in the blood supply to the lungs. In the cells, some of the oxygen that is dissolved in the blood oxidises sugars to carbon dioxide and water. This process is called respiration, you will learn more about respiration in Unit B8. Plants and other organisms respire to obtain energy.

Carbon is therefore an essential element in food chains. However the atmosphere does not have an infinite supply of carbon, so carbon needs to be recycled. During respiration, carbon is released and it returns to the atmosphere. Animals also recycle carbon by excreting it into the soil.

When organisms die and they are broken down by decomposers, carbon is released into the air and the soil. Carbon is also released into the atmosphere when we burn fuels such as coal, oil and gas (hydrocarbons).

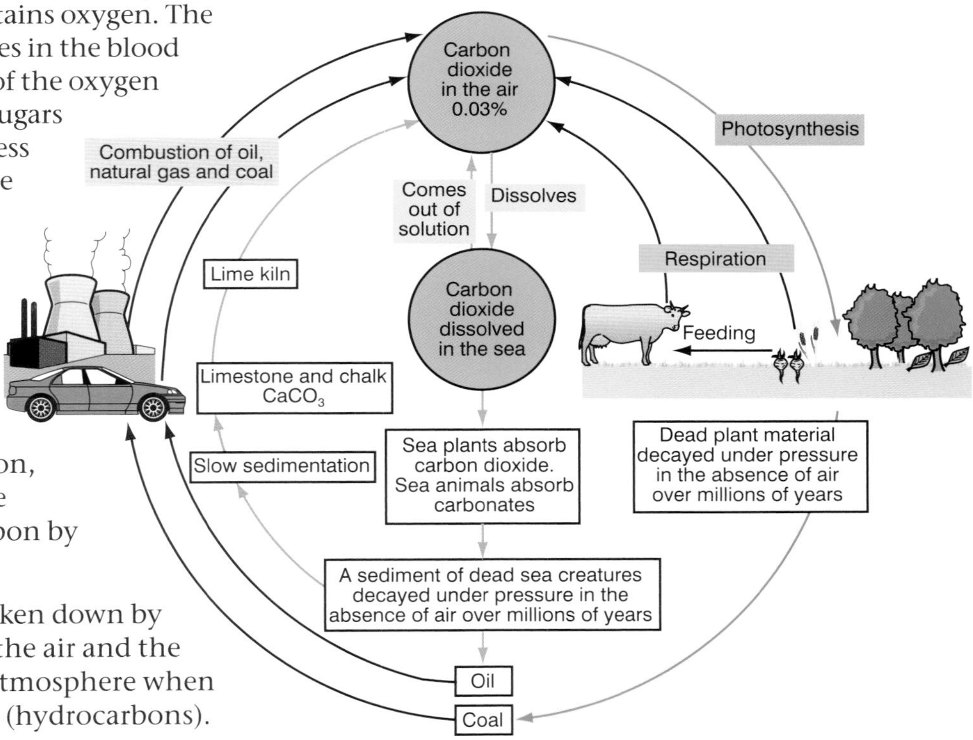

Burning these fuels releases the carbon that has been stored in them for millions of years. The process by which carbon is taken up and released is known as the carbon cycle. You can see how the carbon cycle works in Figure 3.2.2.

▲ **Figure 3.2.2** The carbon cycle

The nitrogen cycle

Nitrogen is an important element in proteins which are manufactured by all living organisms.

Plants cannot absorb nitrogen gas directly from the air. Instead, they absorb nitrogen compounds from the soil. Consumers obtain nitrogen by eating plants.

When organisms die they release nitrogen into the soil in the form of ammonia (NH_3). Certain bacteria in the soil get energy from ammonia and they release nitrates (NO_3^-) that can dissolve in the water in soil. Plants take up nitrates through their root systems.

Nitrogen-fixing bacteria such as those found in the roots of legumes can absorb nitrogen gas from the air. They convert this into nitrogen compounds (such as ammonia) that plants can absorb. Plants make proteins from nitrates in the soil.

Denitrifying bacteria absorb energy from nitrates and release nitrogen back into the atmosphere. This helps to reduce nitrate build-up in the soil.

Nitrogen and oxygen gas can combine to form nitrogen oxides. This happens in the atmosphere during lightning storms and in car engines during combustion. The nitrogen oxides react with water in clouds to from nitric acid. This nitric acid falls to the Earth when it rains and enters the soil. In the soil, the nitric acid reacts with soil minerals to form nitrates. Fertilisers add nitrogen to the soil too. Plants take in these nitrates through their roots and use them to build proteins.

Figure 3.2.3 shows you how nitrogen is recycled in the process known as the nitrogen cycle.

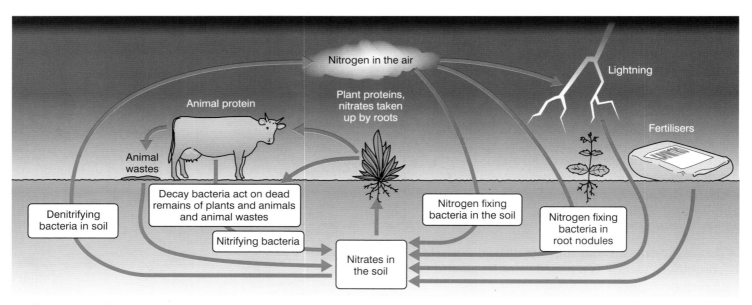

▲ **Figure 3.2.3** The nitrogen cycle

Questions

1 Name two processes by which carbon is released into the air.

2 In what form do plants use carbon? What do they use it for?

3 Why is nitrogen important for plants and animals?

4 Bacteria are very important in the nitrogen cycle. List the roles played by three different types of bacteria.

5 Draw a food web for a local aquatic environment. Include producers, three levels of consumers as well as detritivores and decomposers.

6 Illustrate how the nitrogen cycle and the carbon cycle would operate in the ecosystem you have shown in your food web.

A4 Natural resources

As you will learn in Unit A6, the world's human population is growing at a faster and faster rate. All these people need food, water, shelter and a source of work. Meeting the needs of more and more people is putting tremendous pressure on the Earth's natural resources.

A4.1 Finite resources

You have already seen that the biotic factors are important in ecosystems. Now we are going to think about some of the ways in which we benefit from the natural resources found in our environments. Natural resources are things that we get from our environment. Consider that we get the following from nature:

- provision of food, fuel and fibre
- provision of shelter and building materials
- protection of coastal shores from erosion by waves (including tsunamis)
- renewal of soil fertility
- revenue and employment from tourism
- provision of medicines
- natural purification of air and water
- cycling and movement of nutrients
- enjoyment and aesthetic benefits.

From a purely ecological point of view, it makes sense to use these resources carefully and to make sure that they are available for the future. However, it also makes economic sense. The World Resources Institute estimates that about 40% of the global economy is based on services from nature. In 1997, it was estimated that the services we derive from nature were worth 33 million billion dollars, or 33 trillion dollars, every year. Since then there has been little agreement about the dollar value of these resources, but there is little doubt that they play an important role in the world economy. In island states like ours, we are even more heavily dependent on the natural environment for food, services and to generate income from tourism.

According to the United Nations, in 2013 there were over two billion poor people on Earth. Over 75% of these poor people live in rural areas and they sustain themselves by using the resources in their environment. These people are highly dependent on natural resources and the biodiversity of ecosystems for their survival. Biodiversity is the variety of living things and habitats.

Mineral and energy resources

Many of the natural resources we use are renewable, such as sunlight, soil, plants and water. This means that they can be replaced naturally as they reproduce or cycle through ecosystems. However, some resources,

Objectives

By the end of this topic you will be able to:

- describe various resources and their limits
- describe the impact that human activities may have on natural resources.

Key fact

More than 4.2 billion people (60% of the world's population in 2013) rely on medicines derived from the environment for their health. Examples of medicines derived from natural resources are aspirin, quinine, vinblastine, digitalis, penicillin, codeine, hydrocortisol and taxol. Many other people rely on traditional medicines alone for their health.

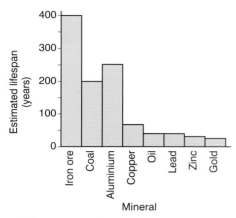

▲ **Figure 4.1.1** Estimated lifespans of different minerals at present rates of use

▲ **Figure 4.1.2** Pitch Lake, Trinidad

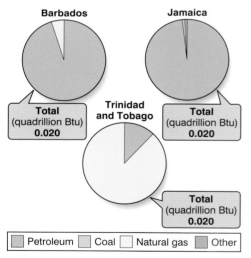

▲ **Figure 4.1.3** Sources of energy used in different countries

particularly those used in mining and industry, are not-renewable in our lifetimes. These resources are called finite resources, because they get used up and they cannot be replaced. Examples are coal, gas and oil. The graph in Figure 4.1.1 shows you how long we can expect some of the most important minerals to last if we continue to use them at present rates.

Our region is not as rich in mineral resources as some other regions, but we do have minerals such as bauxite and nickel and energy resources in the form of oil. Bauxite is found and mined in the Dominican Republic, Haiti, Guyana and Jamaica. Nickel is found in Cuba and the Dominican Republic. Oil is found in Barbados, Cuba and Trinidad but Trinidad is the most important source of oil in the region. Trinidad also has a pitch lake (see Figure 4.1.2) that produces thick asphalt (used to surface roads). A large natural gas plant has been built near the pitch lake to produce electricity for the island.

Levels of resource use

Most of our energy needs are supplied by burning fossil fuels like coal, gas and oil. The pie charts in Figure 4.1.3 show you the main sources of energy used in Trinidad and Tobago, Jamaica and Barbados.

Population growth means that there is a greater demand for resources. In addition, modern lifestyles demand more and more finite resources. More cars mean we use more fossil fuels. More appliances (including cell phones) mean we need more electricity, usually from finite resources. The problem with finite resources is that if we continue to use them at ever increasing rates, they will run out. There is a great need for us to use resources in sustainable ways that conserve them for future generations.

According to the World Wide Fund for Nature (WWF), the Earth has a limited carrying capacity, with only 12 billion hectares of productive land and ocean available to be used by the human population. The carrying capacity is the maximum population size that an environment can support. WWF reports that that was equivalent to 1.8 hectares per person (population in 2008). This amount is called an ecological footprint, and it is an indication of how much of the Earth's resources each person uses as a result of their lifestyle (food, energy, transport and other uses of resources). In 2012, the WWF reported that each person had an ecological footprint of 2.7 hectares per person in 2008, which meant that humans were using 50% more than the Earth could provide and sustain. The graph in Figure 4.1.4 shows that only people in the Asia-Pacific region and Africa were living at or below sustainable levels at the time of the 2012 *Living Planet Report*.

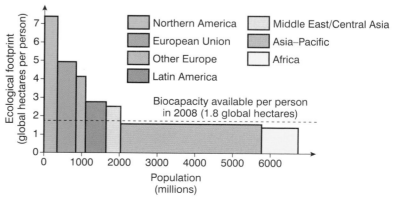

▲ **Figure 4.1.4** Ecological footprint by region

Experts agree that humans cannot continue to use the Earth and its resources at current rates without incurring serious environmental damage. In the long term this will affect our ability to produce food and have access to clean water.

Questions

1 We all use resources. Make two lists, one of renewable resources and one of finite resources, that you use every day.

2 Which of the resources that you listed in Question 1 are most likely to run out in the future? Why?

3 Refer to the graph in Figure 4.1.1. According to these figures:
   a Which of these resources will run out first? Suggest why.
   b Which will last the longest? Suggest why.

4 All indications are that the world is using increasing amounts of energy, mostly in the form of fossil fuels.
   a How will this affect the environment?
   b How could it affect the economies of countries that have to import oil and other fuels?

Human activities and their impact on natural resources

You have seen that biodiversity and a healthy environment are essential for human health and well-being, as well as livelihoods. The interaction of all living organisms in our environment is essential for all life including plants, humans and other animals. We can replace and supplement some of the services and resources that we get from ecosystems using modern technologies. For example, we can synthesise medicines derived from plants in laboratories. However, most ecosystem services and resources cannot be replaced.

All human activities rely on ecosystems to a greater or lesser degree and many of these activities actually threaten or put undue pressure on ecosystems. If you consider the constantly growing human demand for water, food, energy and raw materials, as well as our need for space to build homes, roads, businesses and other infrastructure, you will get some idea of the pressure we put on the Earth and its ecosystems.

Primary activities, such as farming, fishing, forestry and mining, as well as industry and our exploitation of energy resources (particularly non-renewable fossil fuels) and water supplies need to be sustainable and well-managed if we hope to live within the Earth's carrying capacity and ensure that future generations also have access to important natural resources.

WWF have identified the following five greatest threats to ecosystems: pollution, climate change, habitat destruction, extinction of species and invasive species. These threats can all be linked directly to human activities as described below:

- **Pollution** – the main causes of pollution are excessive use of pesticides and other harmful chemicals (including fertilisers) in farming and fishing, solid and liquid waste from urban settlements, industrial pollutants from factories and toxic mining waste, as well as airborne pollutants from burning fossil fuels.

- **Climate change** – burning fossil fuels (including those used in motor vehicles), forest clearing and gases released by industry all contribute to rising levels of greenhouse gases in the atmosphere. These gases, in turn, contribute to global warming. (You will study this in more detail in Unit A5.)

- **Habitat destruction** – human beings change natural environments to use them for farming, fishing, industry or settlement and this destroys natural habitats, decreases space for living organisms or breaks up habitats so that species who live there are put under pressure to survive. Aquatic habitats, such as rivers, are adversely affected by pollutants as well as changed or destroyed by building dams and/or other irrigation systems.

- **Extinction of species** – wild plants and animals are a valuable source of food, raw materials and medicines. However, over-use of these resources, or irresponsible exploitation of limited resources, can deplete them at a faster rate than they can reproduce and this, in turn, leads to species loss (extinctions).

- **Invasive species** – when species of plants or animals are moved deliberately or accidentally from one part of the world to another, they may harm or destroy indigenous species by competing with them for food and space, preying on them for food or parasitising them. Genetically modified organisms (GMO), which are consciously introduced to agriculture, are often infertile and they may impact on indigenous species in ecosystems in negative ways.

Questions

1 In the 1800s a small number of small Indian mongooses (carnivores) were introduced to Jamaica to control rats in sugar plantations. Within a few months, the mongooses had bred and produced young and, as they were considered to be effective in reducing rat numbers, they were exported to other islands in the Caribbean.
   a The small Indian mongoose eats birds, reptiles and small mammals. Many of the native species of these animals have evolved in the absence of predators. How do you think the introduction of a predator would impact on these species? Why?
   b Mongooses also prey on turtle eggs and they have had a negative impact on the number of critically endangered hawksbill turtles in the Caribbean. Conservationists have had some success with trapping programmes around breeding sites. What other measures do you think could be taken to protect endangered turtles from the mongooses?

2 Small Indian mongooses also carry rabies and the *Leptospira* bacteria, which causes leptospirosis in humans.
   a What is rabies and what are the dangers associated with outbreaks of this disease?
   b What is leptospirosis and what are the dangers associated with outbreaks of this disease?
   c Some conservationists suggest the use of poisons to eradicate mongoose populations. What are the advantages and disadvantages of this method of chemical control?

3 The lionfish and crown-of-thorns starfish are invasive species found on Caribbean reefs. Find out more about one of these species and design a poster to warn people about the impact it may have on local ecosystems.

A4.2 Resources for the future?

Humans cannot continue to use resources at the present rate without serious economic and environmental consequences. We need to find ways of protecting the environment and our economic well-being from the effects of using up scarce resources. In other words, we need to find ways of conserving resources. There are three main ways of doing this:

- reduce the amount of resources used
- re-use resources and materials
- recycle waste materials to recover resources.

The diagram in Figure 4.2.1 shows the process.

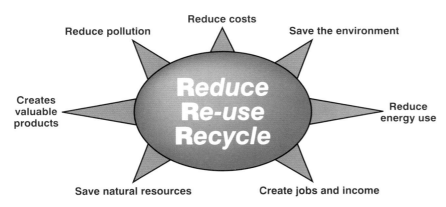

▲ **Figure 4.2.1** Reducing, re-using and recycling can save resources and money

Reducing resource use

At a personal level, reducing resource use means switching off lights and appliances when you are not using them, saving fuel, not buying things you don't need and checking that things you do buy are produced in sustainable ways.

One element of reducing resource use is to buy local products. Think about this: if you buy food that is imported you are actually using up fossil fuels because the food has to be transported by air or sea to the region and this uses fuel. In addition, many imported products are carefully packaged to prevent them from being damaged and the packaging is part of the problem.

At the level of industry and development, this is more problematic. In many industries there is no substitute for the resources that are used. For example, steel (made from iron ore) is used to make vehicles, buildings and bridges. There is no real substitute for steel. In this industry, reducing the use of steel means re-using or recycling scrap metal. Most steel furnaces in the world are partly supplied with scrap metal. The other problem with industry is that reducing consumption often means less income and companies are usually prepared to risk resource damage in the short term in order to make a profit. The government can play a role by passing laws that control the use of resources and force companies to introduce more sustainable practices.

Objectives

By the end of this topic you will be able to:

- discuss the importance of careful use and recycling of resources
- define the terms 'biodegradable' and 'non-biodegradable'
- list some difficulties with recycling manufactured materials.

 Key fact

The packaging of modern products is largely made from plastics. Much of this packaging is thrown away and it ends up in dumps where it pollutes the environment. Plastics are made from oil. So, reducing the amount of packaging could reduce the use of fossil fuel resources, which would conserve resources and protect the environment.

Safety

Always label containers that you re-use so that people know what is inside them. This can prevent people drinking poisonous substances by mistake.

Re-using resources

What do you do with glass bottles? If there is a deposit on these, many people will return them to the store and get their money back. This is an example of re-using resources.

You can also re-use large plastic containers by refilling them with products such as detergents, oil and paraffin. These containers have many uses in domestic and agricultural settings.

Recycling

You have already learnt how bacteria in nature recycle materials and nutrients through the process of decomposition. Materials that can be broken down naturally by bacteria are biodegradable. Biodegradable materials include food waste, paper and human wastes (sewage). Figure 4.2.2 shows you two ways in which we can recycle biodegradable waste.

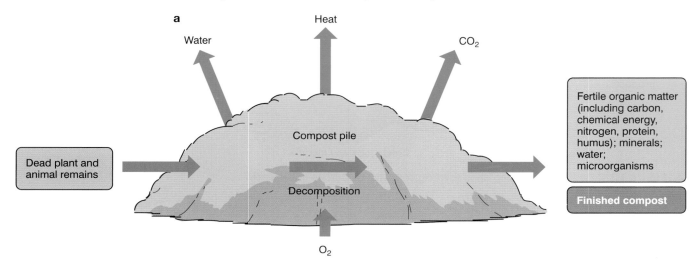

a

Heat

Water

CO_2

Dead plant and animal remains

Compost pile

Decomposition

Fertile organic matter (including carbon, chemical energy, nitrogen, protein, humus); minerals; water; microorganisms

Finished compost

O_2

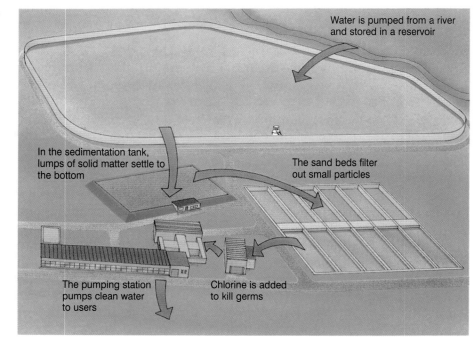

b

Water is pumped from a river and stored in a reservoir

In the sedimentation tank, lumps of solid matter settle to the bottom

The sand beds filter out small particles

The pumping station pumps clean water to users

Chlorine is added to kill germs

▲ **Figure 4.2.2 a** Composting and **b** sewage treatment are both examples of recycling

Most plastics and many other modern materials cannot be broken down by bacteria. They are non-biodegradable.

Recycling means treating used objects so that they can be used again. Recycling has many benefits:

- it conserves raw materials (resources) used to make goods
- it saves energy
- it helps to reduce the amount of non-biodegradable items dumped in the environment.

The pie graphs in Figure 4.2.3 show you how much energy is needed to recycle various materials as a percentage of the energy needed to make them from raw materials.

Exam tip

In an examination you may be asked to give possible solutions to any difficulties associated with recycling.

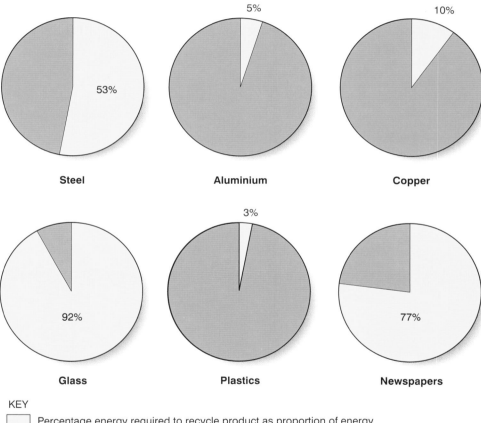

KEY

Percentage energy required to recycle product as proportion of energy needed to manufacture from raw materials

▲ **Figure 4.2.3** Energy needed to make materials from recycled materials as a percentage of energy needed to make the same materials from raw materials

Think about all the things that you throw away and what happens to them when they are dumped. How many of these could be recycled? What prevents them from being recycled?

There are many difficulties involved with recycling. Table 4.2.1 shows you some of these difficulties and how they might be overcome.

▼ **Table 4.2.1** Difficulties encountered with recycling and some solutions

Difficulties encountered with recycling	Possible solutions
People are apathetic and don't bother to recycle.	Introduce incentives, laws which state that certain goods have to be recycled, education campaigns, deposits on containers which are refunded if they are returned for recycling.
Goods need to be sorted by type and stored separately.	Councils can issue separate bins, provide local storage and collection points.
Items for recycling need to be clean and dry, i.e. bottles and cans should be emptied and rinsed, paper should be clean and dry and not contaminated with food waste. This can be inconvenient when people just want to throw things away.	Education campaigns, volunteers to help with cleaning goods for recycling.
Plastics are bulky and heavy when they are compacted, so it is expensive to transport them and not much money is made from recycling.	Develop new methods of recycling to reduce costs and increase profits, add cost of recycling to the containers, reduce plastic use.
It takes time and costs money to sort items at the depot.	Give special subsidies and tax breaks for companies to encourage them to employ people to sort items, working with organisations to provide sheltered employment for the disabled.
Not all paper or glass can be recycled. Paper can only be recycled 4 or 5 times before it becomes useless, brown glass is not very useful in recycling.	Provide separate containers for office and clean paper, bins for different coloured glass.
Recycling depots and large containers are not always central and accessible to everyone in the community, these also take up space.	Consult with community to find best location for recycling facilities. Use local shopping centres and other community centres.
Recycling companies will not pick up small individual loads.	Organise local collection and dumping depots so that loads are consolidated.
Large companies may not recycle unless they see some economic benefit.	Introduce laws and regulations to force companies to recycle, fines and penalties, incentives for recycling. Educate companies about reduced waste removal charges when goods are recycled.

Questions

1 In the past, a great deal of damage to water supplies was caused by detergents containing phosphates. These detergents were non-biodegradable and they provided nutrients for weeds and algae in the water. When the plants died they decomposed. The decomposition process used up the oxygen in the water. Other plants and animals living in the water died from lack of oxygen. Since then, most governments have banned the use of phosphates in detergents and the law requires washing powders and liquids to be biodegradable in many countries.
   a What does 'biodegradable' mean?
   b Examine the labels of detergents and other cleaners that you use at home. Make a list of those that say they are biodegradable.
   c How do detergents and other cleaners get into the water supply?

2 Draw up a table like the one below to show products that are recycled (formally or informally) in your country and the finite resources that are conserved as a result. An example has been filled in for you:

Product that is recycled	Finite resources that are conserved as a result
Tin cans	Tin, iron ore, coal

3 Make a list of renewable resources and finite resources that can be saved by recycling.
   a Explain how you can reduce waste by recycling these resources.
   b Discuss why more of the resources on your list are not recycled locally.
   c What problems would need to be overcome in order to increase recycling of finite resources in your community?

A5 Human activities and their impact on the environment

You read in Unit A4 that humans benefit socially and economically from the environment and the natural resources it provides. Now you are going to look at how we interact with our environment and how we can harm it.

A5.1 Environments under threat

In the past 30 years the Earth's forest species have declined by 15%, marine species have declined by 35% and fresh water species have declined by 54%. Scientists estimate that about 27 000 species are becoming extinct each year. This is equal to 70 species a day (2005 rates). Most of these species are being destroyed by human activity. The graphs in Figure 5.1.1 show you what scientists expect to happen as the human population continues to grow.

Human activity is all the things we do as we go about our daily lives. This includes work activities like farming, mining, manufacturing (industry) and waste disposal. You are now going to look in more detail at how human activity impacts on the environment in different ways.

Objectives

By the end of this topic you will be able to:

- describe the negative effects of human activities on the natural environment.

Habitat loss

The loss of habitats and ecosystems is one of the negative effects of human activity. When people cut down a forest, plough up natural vegetation, trawl or mine seabeds and fill in wetlands, they change the natural habitat of the species that live there. These changes force species to move or die out. They also disrupt the important interactions between organisms and their environments.

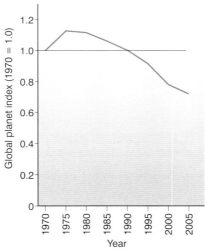

a Average trend in populations of 1686 species of mammal, bird, reptile, amphibian and fish around the world

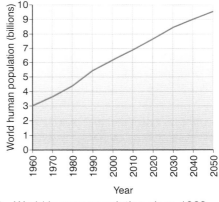

b World human population since 1960 and future predictions

▲ **Figure 5.1.1** Humans are destroying plant and animal species at an alarming rate

Invasive and indigenous species

Alien species are those that do not occur naturally in an environment. When alien species are introduced to an environment on purpose (by farming) or accidentally, they can become invasive. An invasive species is one that takes over the niche of indigenous species and threatens ecosystems. Alien species become invasive when they are introduced to areas that do not have natural predators that can keep their populations in check. The crown-of-thorns starfish is an example of an invader species that destroys coral reefs. The climbing plant dodder (love bush) is an invasive vine that spreads rapidly, choking the indigenous plants.

Population pressure

Look at Figure 5.1.1b again. By 2050, the human population on Earth is likely to be over 9 billion. This means that we will need more space for roads and buildings, more land for farming to produce food, more chemical fertilisers to increase yields, more space to dump waste and more resources to supply our needs. At current rates of use, this is likely to have a very detrimental effect on our planet.

Overconsumption

Modern technology and developments in farming and other industries have led to more intensive use of land and other resources. For example, fishing grounds that have fed communities for many generations are being overfished by sonar-guided boats with large, mechanical nets and other devices aimed at catching more fish. In many places damage to reefs and removal of seaweeds has meant that the predators that used to eat sea urchins have moved away. So the number of sea urchins has increased and these damage reefs further and impact on how you can use water for recreation.

Pollution

The more resources we use, the more pollution we are likely to create. Pollution is anything that damages the environment and affects the living things in it. Pollution can affect the land, the water and the air, all of which we need to survive. You will look at different types of pollution in more detail in the next section.

Practical activity

Investigating your environment

Work in groups to carry out a study in your local environment.

Find out how human activities are negatively affecting the environment.

Write a short report stating what you found out about the 'state of the environment'. Keep this report as you will use it again in topic A5.3 when you deal with conservation and restoration of the environment.

Questions

1 How do the following human activities negatively affect the environment?
   a Building roads
   b Farming
   c Mining
   d Shopping

2 Which human activities in your area have the largest negative effect on the environment? Explain why.

3 Human activities can also impact positively on the environment. Explain how, giving examples to support your explanation.

Key fact

About 45% of the Earth's rainforests have disappeared in the last 100 years. More than 50% of the Earth's wetlands have been drained during the same period and about 30% of coral reefs have been destroyed or degraded.

Key fact

People in different parts of the world consume resources at different rates. According to the 2012 Living Planet Index, the average ecological footprint for people in Europe was 4.7 hectares. In the USA this figure was 7.3 hectares. Jamaica had an ecological footprint of 1.7 hectares, Cuba was lower than average at 1.9 hectares and Haiti was lowest in the region with 0.6 hectare per person. The average for Latin America was 2.6 hectares per person.

You can find the latest figures for different regions in the most up-to-date Living Planet Report published annually by WWF. You can access this online at www.panda.org.

Air pollution

We can't live without the oxygen in air. The average person breathes about 15000–20000 litres of air each day. Unfortunately, for many of us, the air that we breathe is not clean because it has been polluted by dust, gases and other toxins.

Lung diseases, like bronchitis, cancer and emphysema, are more common in areas where the air is highly polluted.

Table 5.1.1 shows you some of the most common pollutants in our air, where they come from and what they do to our bodies.

▼ **Table 5.1.1** Sources and effects of pollutants found in air

Pollutants	Source	Effects
Carbon dioxide (CO_2)	Burning fossil fuels, vehicle emissions	Greenhouse effect (see p50)
Carbon monoxide (CO)	Vehicle emissions and industrial processes	Combines with haemoglobin to reduce oxygen uptake. Continued inhalation will lead to death.
Sulfur dioxide (SO_2)	Burning fossil fuels in power stations and factories	Irritates mucous membranes, causes asthma and bronchitis. Lethal at levels as low as 0.5%. Combines with water vapour to create acid rain.
Hydrocarbons	Unburned chemicals in exhaust fumes, some emissions from factories	Combine with nitrous gases to form smog. Have been linked to cancers.
Nitrogen oxides (NO and NO_2)	Formed at high temperatures in factories, mining industries and metal works, vehicle emissions.	Cause breathing problems and respiratory diseases. Combine with water vapour to form acid rain.
Lead compounds	Exhaust gases from cars, burning coal and industries making metal ores	Toxic to humans, build up in ecosystems and cause nervous system and digestive diseases. Can cause retarded development in children and foetuses.
Dust and other particulates	Grit, dust, fumes and smoke that get into the air from power stations, railways, steel and chemical works, factories and exhaust emissions	Dirty the environment. Breathed in, they carry toxins into the body via the lungs.

Exam tip

In an examination you may be asked to describe how pollution affects plants, animals or the environment.

Effects of air pollution

Acid rain

Acid rain is caused by air pollution. Normal rain has a pH of about 5.5 making it slightly acidic. When sulfur dioxide and nitrogen oxide gases react with water vapour and oxygen in the atmosphere they form sulfuric acid (H_2SO_4) and nitric acid (HNO_3). These acids are carried in water vapour in the air and they form clouds. When it rains, the acidic water falls to Earth in the form of acid rain. Acid rain has a pH of 4.0 or lower.

Acid rain is a problem for many reasons. Rain water is absorbed by the soil. In time, the acid rain reacts with minerals in the soils and converts them to soluble salts. These salts (calcium, potassium and aluminium) are carried in solution in the rain water as it drains down to the water table. In this way, nutrients are leached (washed away) from the topsoil, leaving it less fertile. Some salts, especially aluminium sulfate, damage the roots of plants and make them weak and susceptible to diseases.

Figure 5.1.2 shows you how acid rain is formed and how easily it spreads from place to place.

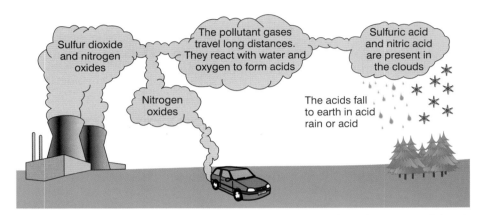

▲ **Figure 5.1.2** The effects of acid rain are often felt far away from the source of the air pollution

Run-off from acid rain enters rivers and lakes where it makes the water acidic. The concentrations of metal salts increase in the rivers and lakes and they build up in the gills of fish. The fish create mucous to get rid of the salts, but this often clogs their gills and they die of suffocation. Plants, insects and other living things cannot survive in acid water and they die.

The greenhouse effect and global warming

Carbon dioxide (CO_2), water vapour and other gases in the Earth's atmosphere absorb sunlight and prevent it from being reflected back into space. This effect is called the greenhouse effect. Figure 5.1.3 shows you how the greenhouse effect happens.

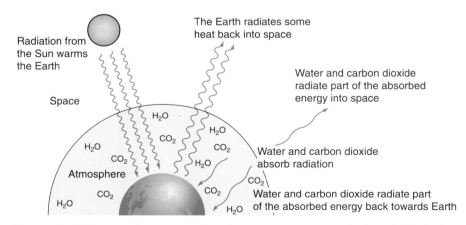

▲ **Figure 5.1.3** The greenhouse effect leads to increased concentration of CO_2 in the atmosphere and contributes to global warming

Over the past decades, average temperatures on Earth have increased steadily. This overall increase in temperature is called global warming. Unless something is done about global warming, the polar ice caps may melt and cause ocean levels to rise and flood densely populated low-lying areas of land, including islands in the Caribbean. Global warming is also likely to change normal weather patterns, making some areas drier than normal and leading to flooding in others.

Air pollution is a major cause of global warming. Burning coal and other fossil fuels releases carbon dioxide and this leads to increased concentrations in the atmosphere. In addition, deforestation removes plants and trees that could absorb excess carbon dioxide from the air during photosynthesis.

Questions

1 An oil refinery has several large chimneys that release emissions into the air.
   a Name two pollutants that could be released from the refinery.
   b Say how each of the pollutants you have named could affect human health.
   c Why do industries have tall chimneys to release emissions?
     Do you think this solves the problem of air pollution?
     Give reasons for your answer.

2 What are the main sources of air pollution in your environment?

3 How would you rate the quality of the air you breathe on a daily basis? Do you think air pollution has increased or decreased in your community over the past 10 years? Suggest why this is.

◄ **Figure 5.1.4** An oil refinery in Trinidad

A5.2 The impact of pollution in the Caribbean

When you live on an island, water is an important element of life. In the Caribbean we use the oceans for food, recreation, tourism and many other activities.

Coral reefs and mangrove swamps along our coasts protect the coastline from erosion. The swamps act as filters to keep the water clean. The importance of these areas was strongly felt in December 2003 in south-east Asia when a tsunami struck. Many communities were totally destroyed by the waves and massive environmental damage was caused by wave action. Scientists found afterwards that areas where mangrove swamps had been cleared to make space for shrimp farming (to feed tourists and make money) were the worst affected by the tsunami. Areas where the mangrove swamps were intact were less damaged by the tsunami. Similarly, in areas where coral reefs had been destroyed the damage was far worse than in areas where the reefs were intact.

Objectives

By the end of this topic you will be able to:

- explain how water resources get polluted
- discuss how pollution affects oceans and wetlands in the Caribbean.

It is clear that our water resources are important. However, they are also damaged by human activity.

Water pollution

You can think of water as nature's transport system. A lot of land and air pollution is eventually carried by water to the oceans. Pollutants in air fall as acid rain into the rivers and oceans. Solid rubbish we throw away as litter gets washed into rivers and storm drains and eventually ends up in the oceans. Sewage water gets cleaned and then pumped out to the oceans. Fertilisers and chemicals from farm land wash away with the rain and end up in our rivers where the water transports them to the oceans. Water filters through waste dumps and enters the groundwater and this water can also end up in the oceans. Table 5.2.1 shows you the sources and effects of pollutants found in water.

▼ **Table 5.2.1** Sources and effects of pollutants found in rivers and oceans

Pollutant	Source	Effects
Oil	Spilled from tankers or off-shore oil rigs, illegally dumped when tanks are cleaned at sea, poured into sewers by motorists	At sea, forms a thick layer or slick which can travel vast distances and ends up on the shore, where it ruins beaches and kills sea life
Detergents	Drains, used to clean and break-up oil spills	Kill organisms living in the water
Sewage	Spills, drainage systems	Decomposed by bacteria which uses up the oxygen in the water; fish and other organisms die from a lack of oxygen
Fertiliser	Runoff from farm lands	Nitrates lead to algal growth. When algae die, bacteria numbers increase and oxygen is depleted.
Warm water	Local power stations, nuclear power stations	Raises temperature of water, allows bacteria to multiply quickly, can kill other organisms which are used to cooler temperatures
Insecticides	Drift from crop sprays, washed from crops and other plants, used to kill mosquitoes in the water	Toxic, builds up in the bodies of organisms and carried along through the food chain
Chemical and industrial wastes	Discharged from factories into water supplies	Can kill organisms quickly if concentrated, at lower levels build up in tissues and passed along the food chain
Solid waste (paper, plastic, bottles, cans and other litter)	Washed into water from storm drains when it rains, left on beaches, dumped from ships and boats, blown into water by wind	Unsightly, takes a long time to degrade, can harm sea animals especially if they get caught in plastic or swallow solid waste thinking it is food

Figure 5.2.1 shows you how fertilisers and sewage can affect water supplies.

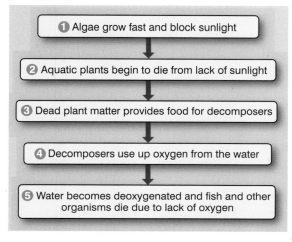

▲ **Figure 5.2.1** Farming contributes to the pollution of water resources

Coral reefs

Coral reefs are important natural resources. They provide a home to many species of plants and animals. They also have an enormous economic value in our region because they provide food and are a tourist attraction.

Figure 5.2.2 shows some of the ways in which human activites damage and destroy coral reefs.

Mangrove swamps (wetlands)

You have seen that mangrove swamps are important ecosystems. You also know they have an important role to play in protecting our coastlines and river estuaries.

Figure 5.2.3 shows a rich mangrove swamp ecosystem and the ways in which it can be damaged or destroyed by human activity.

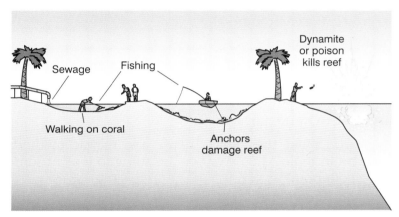

▲ **Figure 5.2.2** Human activities can badly damage coral reefs

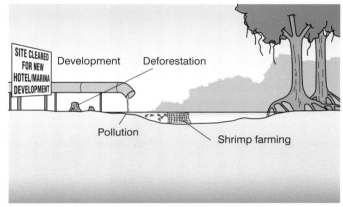

▲ **Figure 5.2.3** Mangrove swamps are important ecosystems that are damaged easily

Questions

1 Figure 5.2.4 shows you part of a river with a factory on its banks. An industrial accident meant that thousands of litres of water contaminated with nitrates were pumped into the river by mistake.
   a What effects of the industrial accident are likely to be observed in the river near the factory?
   b What is likely to happen to oxygen levels in the river at point X? Why?
   c What problems could this accident cause further down the river?
   d How could this accident have an impact on:
      i   the mangrove swamp at the mouth of the river
      ii a coral reef close to the river mouth?

2 What pollutants are the biggest problems in the water resources in your area? How do these pollutants get into the water?

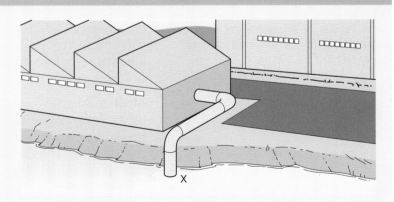

▲ **Figure 5.2.4**

Objectives

By the end of this topic you will be able to:

- identify methods of conserving the environment
- explain how a damaged environment can be restored.

▲ **Figure 5.3.1** Nature reserves, such as this one near Bridgetown in Barbados, are important havens for protected species

A5.3 Conservation and restoration of the environment

In recent years people have become much more aware of the threats that human activities and pollution pose to the environment. Many governments have passed laws and entered into international agreements to limit pollution and conserve natural environments. Environmental groups such as Greenpeace, The World Wide Fund for Nature (WWF) and Caricom Global Environmental Facility Project work with local communities and governments to raise awareness of conservation issues and to educate people to use resources more sustainably.

Conservation

Conservation means saving for the future. Some of the methods used to conserve natural environments (and the species in them) include:

- passing laws to protect the environment
- signing international agreements
- declaring reserves and limiting human access to certain areas (nature reserves)
- controlling pollution from farming and industry
- restoring damage caused by human activity.

You have already learnt about the reduce, re-use and recycle methods of conserving resources in topic A4.2. Now you are going to look at some methods of reducing pollution.

Preventing and controlling pollution

The burning of fossil fuels in industries and in cars is the biggest source of air pollutants. If we want clean air, we have to find ways of preventing and controlling air pollution. One way of doing this is for the government to pass laws that control things like the type of fuel you can use in your car.

Governments can also help to reduce pollution through education. You will know from school that most curriculums (which are drawn-up by government departments) aim to teach you about air pollution and methods of stopping it.

Most industries operate within the law. This means that they have put measures in place to prevent and control emissions and pollutants. These measures include using cleaner fuels, cleaning (scrubbing) smoke before it is released into the air and purifying wastes or disposing of them safely rather than dumping them.

Motor car manufacturers can also help to prevent pollution. Most modern cars now have catalytic converters in their exhaust systems. The catalyst oxidises poisonous carbon monoxide into less harmful carbon dioxide.

Lead-free petrol helps to reduce lead levels in the atmosphere and modern diesel fuels for cars are designed to contain much lower concentrations of sulfur.

Research to find less polluting methods of generating energy is ongoing. However many of these methods are more expensive than using fossil fuels, so they do not always get much support.

 Practical activity

Finding out about local conservation efforts

You will need to do your own research to complete this activity. You can find information at the local library, in the media and on the internet. You can refer back to your report from the practical activity on p48.

Method

1　Identify one human activity that damages or pollutes the environment or a particular species in your country.

2　Briefly describe how this activity damages or pollutes the environment or species.

3　Discuss any conservation methods that are being implemented to reduce the effects of the activity or to restore the damage once it has been caused.

4　Evaluate these conservation efforts and state whether or not they have been effective. Give reasons for your decision.

5　If no conservation efforts are in place, suggest what could be done to reduce or repair the impact of this activity.

Restoration

Restoration is the process of repairing and returning the environment to a healthy state. Restoration is an important issue in mining. Bauxite is a mineral used to produce aluminium. Bauxite is mined in Jamaica and Guyana. However, the mining process from exploration to extraction, to transport of the minerals to processing works disturbs the environment and generally produces some form of pollution.

In the past, mining companies were able to develop mines with little regard for the local environment and little concern for the future. Once the mines were worked out, the companies left, leaving behind mined-out pits, waste dumps, deforested areas and contaminated water. Pressure from environmental groups, such as the Jamaica Environmental Advocacy Network (JEAN), has forced governments to produce laws that have to be obeyed by all mining companies (even international ones). Environmental impact studies have to be done before mining can take place and rehabilitation and restoration of the environment is now a necessity for all mining companies.

Case study 1 is just one example to show how a mining company has been involved in a process to restore the environment. You should try to find out what restoration projects have been undertaken in your own territory.

Case study 1

Jamaican Bauxite Environmental Organization Wins Restoration of Alcan Tailings Pond

Friday, February 02, 2007, 12.22 p.m.

The Jamaican Bauxite Environmental Organization (JBEO) has won a major victory for the environment.

The Jamaican government has approved an Alcan plan for the rehabilitation of a red mud tailings pond at Mount Rosser in the St Catherine's area of Jamaica. The tailings pond was used from the early 1950s until 1991 to store waste from the Alcan alumina refinery at Ewarton.

The tailings pond – which the company calls a 'landfill' – is one of several sites that Alcan retained responsibility for after its operations were sold to Glencore in 2001, although it consistently denied liability for the clean-up. After rehabilitation, it is to be returned to the Jamaican government.

The Jamaican National Environment and Planning Agency (NEPA) web site has a description of the rehabilitation project.

The Jamaican government has been under substantial pressure from JBEO to restore mined-out lands and red mud repositories for a number of years. In 2004, it amended mining laws to fine bauxite companies in breach of the land restoration regulations to be fined $25,000 per acre, plus a fee of $2,500 per year of the breach.

Bauxite companies are also looking to expand in Jamaica, and are facing substantial opposition, particularly for a planned expansion in 'Cockpit Country'. The opposition to this mine has been pointing to the toxic legacy of bauxite mining in Jamaica. A 17 December column in the *Jamaican Observer*, by John Maxwell, quotes from a 2001 report of the US Army Corps of Engineers: 'The Moneague Blue Hole, located in the Dry Harbour Mountains Basin, was once a good fresh water source. However, this has recently become contaminated. The contamination is believed to be from a bauxite lake, Mount Rosser Pond, which has a high sodium effluent.'

Programme of Works

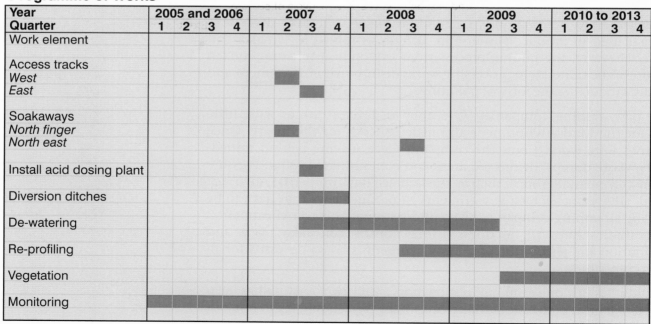

▲ **Figure 5.3.2** Timeline for different aspects of the project

Extract from: http://www.miningwatch.ca

Proposed project

When Alcan sold its factories in 2001 they made a commitment to remediate the bauxite residue landfills they retained, including the largest at Mount Rosser.

The rehabilitation of Mount Rosser requires the de-watering of the pond water on the Mount Rosser landfill site as the first step in the work programme. The work entails building access tracks and ditches to control the rain water entering the Mount Rosser landfill site, building a small water treatment plant, treating and then pumping away the pond water into an adjacent soakaway. The Moneague Blue Hole, which has remained clean since the closure of the landfill in the 1990's is one of a number that will be monitored to ensure that water quality is not affected.

Following extensive consultations and public presentations which are part of the necessary procedure, Alcan have now received from NEPA, permits in order to undertake the construction work and commence the treatment.

When the water has been pumped away, the exposed bauxite residue will be re-graded, so that rain water no longer collects, and the area then re-vegetated. This project will very significantly reduce the current hazards associated with the landfill very significantly and transform it into a safe, aesthetically attractive area that can be returned to the Government.

a

b
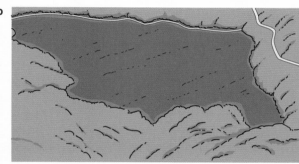

▲ **Figure 5.3.3 a** Mount Rosser before restoration and **b** an illustration of what it will look like after restoration. Remember that the water in the pond is alkaline with elevated levels of sodium.

Extract from: http://www.nrca.org

Questions

1 What is meant by the term 'conservation'? Why is conservation important?

2 How can power stations reduce the amount of air pollution they produce?

3 What can private citizens do to reduce pollution in their own environments?

4 Why is the proposed environmental restoration of Mount Rosser in Jamaica seen as a victory for environmentalists?

5 Mining companies normally have to employ ecologists and botanists to produce an environmental impact report and a rehabilitation plan. What would these scientists need to observe and study in order to produce an environmental impact report and a rehabilitation plan?

6 What steps are necessary to restore Mount Rosser? Why are these steps necessary?

Case study 2

Coral reef conservation and restoration

Coral reef conservation and restoration is an important environmental issue in the Caribbean (and other areas fringed by reefs). There are many organisations and projects which work in this field. Read the information and study the diagrams carefully to learn more about this issue. (You can find additional resources on this topic online. Two useful websites which deal with Caribbean reefs are: www.conservationgateway.org and www.habitat.noaa.gov.)

Coral reefs are among the most diverse ecosystems, but they are also among the most threatened.

'Healthy coral reefs are among the most economically valuable and biologically diverse ecosystems on earth,' said John Christensen, program manager for NOAA's Coral Reef Conservation Program. 'Seafloor habitat maps are vital to understanding the current state of coral reef ecosystems and successfully managing the threats to their survival. Habitat mapping is one of the first steps to conserving coral reef ecosystems,' continued Christensen.

Reefs around the world are threatened by human activities, such as pollution, overfishing and coastal development, as well as natural events, such as tropical storms. As a result, these fragile ecosystems are declining at an alarming rate. In November 2012, after a comprehensive status review of 82 coral species, NOAA proposed Endangered Species Act listings for 66 reef-building coral species, including 59 in the Pacific and seven in the Caribbean.

Adapted from: NOAA Habitat Conservation materials

Coral reefs are home to more than one million species. Reefs protect shorelines from waves and storms that cause flooding and erosion, support commercial and subsistence fisheries at a value of more than $100 million annually and are home to a thriving recreation and tourism industry.

These important ecosystems are in danger. Coral reefs are damaged by pollution, sedimentation, overfishing, invasive species, vessel groundings, increasing tourism and recreation, and marine debris. Reefs are also susceptible to the effects of climate change, such as rising temperatures (which can cause premature spawning and coral bleaching) and ocean acidification.

Can reefs be successfully conserved?

Restoration of reefs can help coral adapt to changing conditions and aid in the recovery of damaged reefs. However, it is important to actively conserve reefs to reduce the need for restoration and to promote healthy, functioning reef ecosystems. This involves:

- responding to and restoring coral reefs after physical impacts such as ship groundings
- implementing projects that address coral conservation priorities, with a focus on land-based sources of pollution
- implementing projects to restore corals listed as endangered
- controlling overgrowth of invasive species and preventing loss of habitat.

In 2009, NOAA received $167 million in funding from the American Recovery and Reinvestment Act for coastal and marine restoration projects. With this funding, NOAA implemented four coral restoration projects – two in the Caribbean and two in the Pacific.

Lessons learned from pilot restoration projects in the Caribbean

Scientists working to restore coral reefs by replanting them with staghorn and elkhorn corals have learned several valuable lessons from their work in a range of pilot projects. These lessons have implications for the success of future projects.

- Choose sites carefully – deeper, protected areas of reef are more suitable for nursery plantings and they have a higher survival rate. Avoid sandy areas and areas with loose broken rock. Similarly, planting new corals closer to the reef edges reduces their exposure to predators. In general, it is important to choose sites where predator populations are lower. Inspect sites to see whether there are juvenile snails or other snail colonies which might eat the corals, and avoid areas where there are dead corals as these may be home to fireworms.

- Start with healthy corals – the fragments with the highest survival rate are those harvested from healthy coral communities.

- Split colonies regularly – new colonies should be split at least twice a year to help them grow better and to prevent the growing platforms from being overloaded and collapsing. Overgrown colonies are attractive to damselfish, which in turn promote the growth of algae.

- Consider the best type of structure for the nurseries – using a range of nursery structures can reduce the risk to colonies in the event of storms. Generally though, A-frames are most cost-effective as the materials are easy to obtain and the structures can be made on land. When placing the structures, make sure they are well secured with nails, underwater epoxy (glue) or cement as this gives them a greater chance of survival than simply wedging them into cracks or placing coral fragments in holes in the reef.

- Monitor sites regularly – it is important to visit the nurseries to check on their stability and health as often as possible, monitoring allows for early detection of problems or predator risk.

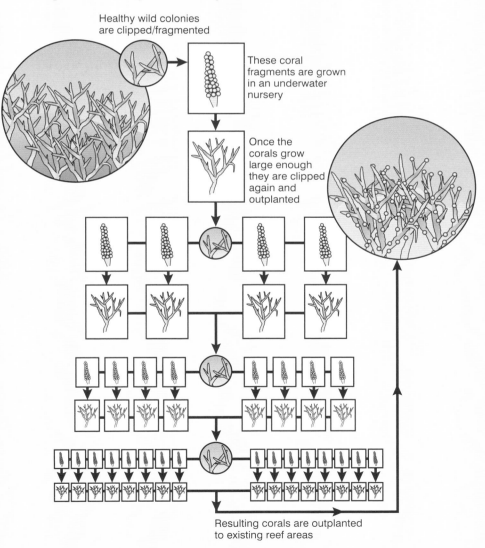

Healthy wild colonies are clipped/fragmented

These coral fragments are grown in an underwater nursery

Once the corals grow large enough they are clipped again and outplanted

Resulting corals are outplanted to existing reef areas

▲ **Figure 5.3.4** The process used to propagate staghorn and elkhorn corals

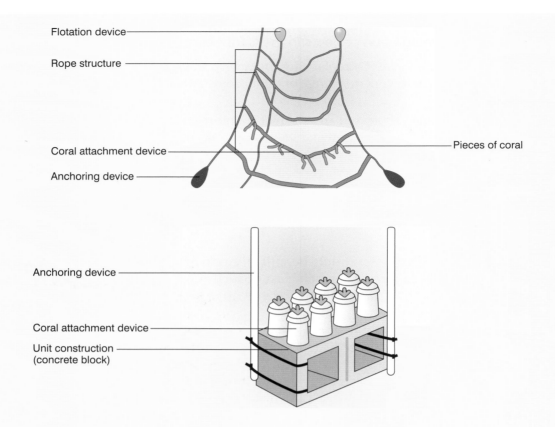

Flotation device

Rope structure

Coral attachment device

Anchoring device

Pieces of coral

Anchoring device

Coral attachment device

Unit construction
(concrete block)

Coral attachment device

Unit construction
(metal frame)

Anchoring device

▲ **Figure 5.3.5** Coral nursery designs. The design that is most suitable will depend on the environmental conditions of the area under restoration. The most effective designs generally use locally available materials as far as possible for convenience and to reduce costs.

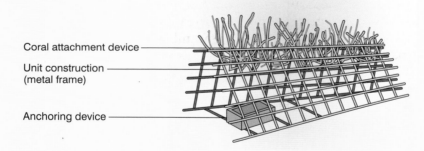

Questions

1 Explain why coral reefs are so important in Caribbean ecosystems.

2 How does tourism impact on coral reefs? What could be done to alleviate the negative effects on reefs?

3 List three strategies used to conserve and/or restore coral reefs.
   a Evaluate the effectiveness of each strategy.
   b What do you think should be done to conserve and restore coral reefs in your country? Give reasons for your choices.

The size and growth of a population depends on many different factors, including how many offspring are produced, how many organisms die naturally or as a result of disease, how many organisms move into an area and how many move away or are dispersed. The amount of space and food that is available can also have an effect on population size and growth.

A6.1   Factors affecting natural population growth

You should remember that a population is a group of one species of organism living in the same environment. The rate at which populations grow depends on the rate of birth, the rate of death, movement into the population (immigration) and movement out of the population (emigration) (see Figure 6.1.1). These four factors are in turn affected by available space, food and water supply, predator–prey relationships, competition between organisms, the presence of invasive species, outbreaks of diseases, pests and natural disasters that destroy the environment.

How these factors affect population growth

Look at the two photographs in Figure 6.1.2. These show two populations of elephants in two national parks in Africa. Population A is growing so rapidly the authorities are considering culling elephants to control the numbers. Population B has declined over the past five years.

Population A

Population B

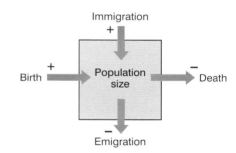

▲ **Figure 6.1.1** Population growth rates are affected by the interaction of four factors

▲ **Figure 6.1.2** Why is population A growing while population B is declining?

Population A is growing because the birth rate among the elephants is higher than the death rate. The elephants breed successfully and produce more offspring because they have an ample supply of food and water. They are free to roam over a large area as the park is not fenced so they are able to co-exist with other animal populations as they are not in competition for space, for food and for water.

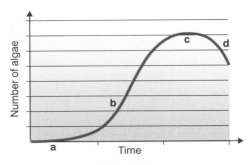

a The new population of algae grows slowly at first. Although they reproduce, the total number of plants does not increase very quickly at first.

b At first, there are no limiting factors, so the population begins to grow at a rapid rate, steadily doubling over time.

c After a while, there is not enough oxygen in the water to sustain all the algae. This causes reproduction rates to slow to a point where there is no increase in numbers.

d As oxygen runs out, more algae die off and the number in the population drops. This is the death phase.

▲ **Figure 6.1.3** Growth of an algae population in a small pond

The death rate is low because the elephants are healthy and able to resist disease. Also they are not the preferred prey of the lions and other large carnivores in the park. There is a plentiful supply of buck antelope and zebra, so the carnivores tend to prey on those instead of the elephants. The elephants are also protected by law from poachers, which means they cannot be hunted and killed.

Population B is declining because the death rate among the elephants is higher than the birth rate. The birth rate is low because the elephants live in a dry area where food and water is scarce. This is one of the main reasons why they do not breed successfully and produce few offspring. Their space is limited by park fencing, they cannot move to other areas in search of food and therefore they have to compete with other animal populations for food.

Population B has a high death rate. The elephants succumb to disease as they are in a weakened state. The lions in the park hunt and kill baby elephants when other prey is scarce in the dry season. The government has little control and poaching is common.

Factors that limit population growth

The same factors which encourage populations to grow can limit the size and growth of populations. Where there is a shortage of space, food or water, successful breeding does not usually take place which reduces the birth rate and leads to a slower increase in the population. Similarly, where there is a large number of predators, an outbreak of a disease that spreads through the population, or a natural disaster, the death rate increases. When the death rate exceeds the birth rate, the population will decrease in size (negative growth).

When a limiting factor causes population growth to decline, we get a typical S-curve graph. Figure 6.1.3 shows you a typical growth curve for a population of algae in a pond of water.

Questions

1 The table shows you some of the factors that contribute to the growth of natural populations. Copy and complete the table by filling in the matching factors that limit population growth.

Factors contributing to population growth	Factors limiting population growth
Adequate space	
Adequate food supply	
Adequate water supply	
Disease resistance	
Ideal abiotic factors (climate, soil, etc.)	
Lack of predators	

2 The graph in Figure 6.1.4 shows the numbers of insects that eat peppers. The insects only have two natural enemies: birds and a parasite that kills the insect larvae. The number of insects is normally not problematic for the pepper farmer, as it remains at a level where they do not seriously damage the crop. At point X on the graph, there was a flood and the parasites that kill the insect larvae were almost entirely wiped out.

   a Explain how the numbers of insect larvae which survive to maturity changes at point X.

   b What effect would this have on the number of peppers eaten by the insects?

   c Why do you think there was a sudden drop in insect numbers after the rapid increase shown on the graph?

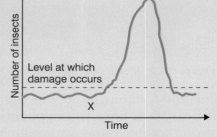

▲ **Figure 6.1.4** Growth of a population of insects that feed on peppers

A6.2 Human population growth and its effects

Humans that live in different areas form separate populations. However, we generally talk about the population of humans on Earth as a whole. The number of people on Earth have increased steadily over time.

The growth curve of the human population

Figure 6.2.1 is a graph that shows how the human population on Earth has increased from AD 1 to the year 2000, when the population reached 6 billion.

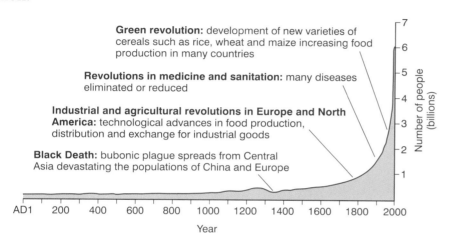

Green revolution: development of new varieties of cereals such as rice, wheat and maize increasing food production in many countries

Revolutions in medicine and sanitation: many diseases eliminated or reduced

Industrial and agricultural revolutions in Europe and North America: technological advances in food production, distribution and exchange for industrial goods

Black Death: bubonic plague spreads from Central Asia devastating the populations of China and Europe

▲ **Figure 6.2.1** Human population growth from AD 1 to 2000

You can see that the graph follows a similar pattern to the start of the other population curves you have studied. In other words, the population grows slowly at first, then it begins to increase rapidly from about 1850 onwards.

What is missing from this graph is a stabilisation phase. (The graph is J-shaped rather than S-shaped.) Population experts predict that the population of Earth will stabilise at about 12 billion people around 2200. However, this depends on many factors, so no one is really sure that this will happen. At current growth rates, the population is expected to reach 7 billion by 2013 and 8 billion by 2028.

Factors affecting human growth rates

The human population on Earth as a whole depends on the relationship between birth and death rates. (Humans can immigrate or emigrate from local populations, but they cannot immigrate or emigrate from the Earth.) As with other species, when the birth rate is higher than the death rate, as it is presently, the size of the population increases.

As mammals, humans have the same needs as other animals. Humans need space, food and water, they are susceptible to diseases that can kill them and although they have few natural predators, humans often kill each other in times of war. The examples in Figures 6.2.2–6.2.4 show how some of these factors can impact on human growth rates.

▲ **Figure 6.2.2** Natural events such as droughts, floods or hurricanes can cause an increase in the death rate as a result of famine or the spread of disease

▲ **Figure 6.2.3** Overcrowding as a result of lack of space can lead to unhealthy conditions and make it easier for disease to spread

▲ **Figure 6.2.4** War and conflict lead to increases in the death rate. They can also lead to a decline in births as family life is disrupted and food and water supplies are damaged.

Effects of human population growth

The human population on Earth is likely to continue growing quickly in the immediate future. This has serious implications for the Earth and its resources. In this topic you will focus on understanding how human population growth impacts the Earth.

As the population increases, people need more and more space to live and more space to farm to produce food for the increasing numbers of people. As a result, more and more natural areas, including the rainforests, are being cleared to make room for farming and housing and to produce resources for building and other industries. The world's rainforests are being cleared at a rate of 160 000 square kilometres per year. Removal of forests and other natural vegetation and using the land for farming leads to increased pollution of soil and water resources (see Figure 6.2.5).

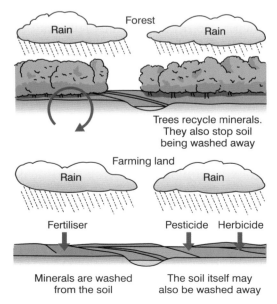

▲ **Figure 6.2.5** Increased food production can damage soil and water

Clearing natural areas also puts pressure on other species and it can lead to extinctions and biodiversity-loss as a result of habitat change and lack of food supplies. A recent report by the United Nations said the following about the loss of biodiversity as a result of human actions:

'The loss of biodiversity is a major barrier to development already and poses increasing risks for future generations,' said Walter Reid, the director of the Millennium Assessment, 'however, the report shows the management tools, policies, and technologies do exist to dramatically slow this loss.'

According to the report, changes in biodiversity due to human activities were more rapid in the past 50 years than at any time in human history and over the last 100 years species extinction caused by humans has multiplied as much as 1000 times.

A proactive approach is needed to solve the problem

About 12% of birds, 23% of mammals, 25% of conifers and 32% of amphibians are threatened with extinction and the world's fish stocks have been reduced by an astonishing 90% since the start of industrial fishing.

'We will need to make sure we don't disrupt the biological web to the point where collapse of the whole system becomes irreversible,' warns Anantha Kumar Duraiappah of Canada's International Institute for Sustainable Development, one of the co-chairs of the report.

The report notes, while efforts have helped reduce the loss of biodiversity, more action is needed as little progress is foreseen in the short-term. The report blames biodiversity change on a number of factors including habitat conversion, climate change, pollution and over-exploitation of resources.

You already know that organisms, including humans, depend on each other and on the abiotic environment. Together, the abiotic environment and the living organisms form essential systems such as the water cycle, the carbon cycle and several other nutrient cycles. The removal or destruction of abiotic or biotic components of the system can disrupt these systems and threaten our survival as a species.

Questions

1 Redraw the world population graph in Figure 6.2.1 (omit the notes). Extend the graph to the year 2200, using the prediction of 12 billion people.

2 Use your graph from Question 1 to answer the following questions.
   a What is the world's population likely to be in 2020?
   b Predict when the world's population is likely to reach 15 billion at this rate.

3 Suggest three things that could happen to slow the growth in world population numbers.

4 Explain how an increase in the human population can lead to increased pollution of soil and water.

5 List two other effects of an ever-increasing human population.

 Exam tip

Learn how to read and interpret graphs properly. In an examination you may be asked to describe the shape of the graph. You may also be asked to explain the shape of the shape.

Biology in the real world

Case study A

Environmental resources and ecosystems

It has long been recognised that in Jamaica farming activities on the slopes are the most notable cause of degradation. Over 170 000 farmers cultivating just fewer than 245 000 hectares, using unsuitable farming practices, have contributed to massive soil loss through soil erosion, siltation of dams and rivers and destructive flooding downstream.

The Millennium Development Goal 7 of the National Environmental and Planning Agency (NEPA) is to ensure environmental sustainability

Forests and watersheds

Jamaica's topography makes soil protection and restoration services of great importance to the country. More than two thirds of Jamaica's land mass is above 300 meters high therefore forest cover plays an important role in preventing soil erosion and landslide from rainfall. These forests also help to conserve surface and groundwater resources particularly in watershed areas.

Source: Statistical Institute of Jamaica (2009)
Environmental Statistics Jamaica 2007–12, p43

The sustainable use of forest resources through appropriate forest management strategies is essential for the protection of watersheds, the conservation of biodiversity, and the maintenance and increase of the economic benefits that forests provide.

Source: Forestry Department (n.d.)
Strategic Forest Management Plan 2009–13, p3

Pressure on Jamaica's forests and watersheds have resulted in concerns such as deforestation, soil erosion, pollution pressures, mining for limestone and bauxite, large- and small-scale cultivation on mountain slopes and lack of public awareness concerning conservation.

Jamaica's response to manage its forests and watersheds

Jamaica has various policies, plans and programmes in place to maintain and protect the country's forests and watersheds and Jamaica is signatory to the major international environmental agreements that address forest and watershed issues. The Forestry Department has also been implementing a range of actions geared towards sustainable forestry. These include:

- Ongoing forest inventory to generate information/data.
- Four draft Local Forest Management Plans developed, using inventory information.
- Improved forest governance structures, through the establishment of 7 Local Forest Management Committees established in several watersheds, using participatory involvement of stakeholders.

- Increased vigilance to reduce forest loss and infringements.
- Research into restoration of forest cover on mined-out bauxite lands.
- Awareness building to protect forest values and benefits.

Approaches to protect Jamaica's forests and watersheds:

- Data collection and research into the restoration of forest cover on mined-out bauxite lands.
- Tax incentives provided for landowners for maintaining existing forest and for establishing or restoring tree cover and inclusion of private lands in conservation efforts.

- Development of private forestry sector production of wood from plantations on private lands in an environmentally-friendly manner. The strategy is based on the assumption that this approach will reduce the pressure on natural forests and sensitive areas.

- Community-based resource management adopted by NEPA who will corroborate with other public sector partners and community organisations, the institutionalisation of this approach and its application to other watersheds will be a priority of the Agency.

- Implementation of watershed management projects and programmes – The Hope River Watershed Slope Stabilisation Project 24, which began in the 2007–8 financial year was successfully finalised over the 2008–9 financial year. Under this project, visible demonstrations of proper land management practices on degraded lands were undertaken in the watershed to enable residents to be able to replicate these practices. This project has

resulted in reduced soil erosion, protection of water resources and enhancement of biodiversity habitat values. The project was implemented via a Memorandum of Understanding (MOU) between NEPA and the Rural Agricultural Development Authority (RADA). Two farming communities in Woodford, namely Windsor Castle and Freetown, St. Andrew, were selected.

- Sustainable farming practices

- Reforestation

- Prevention of soil erosion – pursuing soil stabilisation – engineering solutions are being used at a number of sites to reduce soil erosion. These solutions include:
  - bamboo log barriers to contain sediment,
  - check dams to reduce the velocity of runoff
  - retaining walls and culvert improvement to transport excess storm water into existing gullies.

Extract from: http://www.nepa.gov.jm

Reforestation activities include growing seedlings, slope preparation and replanting. The hard work of planting out the seedlings is often carried out by volunteers.

Case study B

Making a difference – dealing with plastic pollution

The young people in these examples are all using their studies to develop methods of dealing with plastic waste and producing a more environmentally-friendly plastic.

The Ocean Cleanup

Every year we produce about 300 million tons of plastic, and a fraction of that enters rivers, waterways, and eventually the oceans. The plastic primarily concentrates in five rotating currents – called the gyres – where it not only directly kills sea life, but due to the absorption of persistent organic pollutants, also poisons the food chain. Due to the vast size, and the fact that the plastic moves around, the most feasible cleanup concept is predicted to take approximately 79 000 years to remediate just a single gyre.

In 2011, together with friend Tan Nguyen, Boyan Slat embarked on writing his final paper in the last year of secondary education, researching the possibility of remediating the world's *oceanic garbage patches*. Spending over 500 hours on the paper (instead of the required 80 hours), it has won several final paper prizes, including *Best Technical Design 2012* at the Delft University of Technology. In January of 2013, The Ocean Cleanup Foundation was founded, a non-profit organisation which is responsible for the development of our technologies.

Moving through the oceans to collect plastic would be costly, clumsy and polluting, so why not let the rotating currents transport the debris to you? With The Ocean Cleanup Array, an anchored network of floating booms and processing platforms will span the radius of a gyre. These booms act as giant 'funnels', where the angle of the booms creates a component of the surface current force in the direction of the platforms. The debris then enters the platforms, where it will be filtered out of the water, and eventually stored in containers until collected for recycling on land.

By deploying this array in all five gyres, The Ocean Cleanup calculated it is possible to extract approximately 7 million tons, using the natural currents to our advantage. The Ocean Cleanup also wants to develop spinoffs of this technology to be used for intercepting plastic in river deltas before it reaches the oceans. However, Boyan Slat also emphasises the importance of 'closing the tap first', to prevent any more plastic from entering the oceans in the first place.

Adapted from: Boyan Slat, The Ocean Cleanup and http://www.boyanslat.com/

The Truc stops here for old carrier bags

Student Eléa Nouraud has developed a method for recycling old plastic bags and turning them into everyday objects including pots, egg boxes, wallets and long-lasting plastic shopping bags.

The University of Brighton 3D Design Materials and Practice student has come up with 'Truc', or Technique to Recycle Used Carrier bags. Nouraud, 22, hopes to turn her technique into a commercial enterprise in her native France after she graduates next month (July).

"I sort the carrier bags and heat-press them in order to create a sheet [so that they can] then be thermo-formed on top of a shape, either made by myself or in the case of the egg box it's formed on top of the real egg box."

To make long-lasting plastic bags, granules from the polyethylene bags are mixed with a resin to produce tubes of materials which are flattened by rollers. The resulting polyethylene film is cut, rolled rolled up, and ready to be turned into robust bags. Alcohol based ink is applied and the bags are cut and heat sealed.

Nouraud: "The products are really tough and durable."

"The products are really tough and durable – I dropped one recently and accidentally trod on it, and it survived intact," Nouraud said. "I have really enjoyed my course at the University of Brighton and I hope to pursue Truc once I have graduated."

Extract from: http://www.prw.com

Science in Action Winner for 2013: Elif Bilgin

"Genius," Thomas Edison famously said, "is 1 percent inspiration and 99 percent perspiration." He would have found a kindred spirit in Elif Bilgin, 16, of Istanbul, Turkey, winner of the 2013 $50,000 Science in Action award, part of the third annual Google Science Fair. The award honors a project that can make a practical difference by addressing an environmental, health or resources challenge; it should be innovative, easy to put into action and reproducible in other communities.

Bilgin spent two years toiling away on her project to develop a bioplastic from discarded banana peels, enduring 10 failed trials of plastics that weren't strong enough or that decayed rapidly. She was undaunted. As she put it in her project description: "Even Thomas Edison said, 'I have not failed. I have just found 10,000 ways that won't work.'" Finally, in her last two trials, she made plastics with the features she sought, and it did not decay. We admire her persistence, which will be help her to take advantage of another aspect of her Science in Action prize — a year's worth of mentoring to help further her work. I like to think, too, that Edison, who used to stop by the *Scientific American* offices in New York City to demonstrate his latest inventions, would have approved.

The ingredients to make Bilgin's plastic are relatively benign. As she wrote in her entry materials, "it is possible to say that one could do it at home." In her research, she learned that starch and cellulose are used elsewhere in the bioplastic industry (such as from the skin of mangoes) and made the leap that banana peels might be suitable feedstock sources as well. She hopes that the use of the bioplastic could replace some of the petroleum-based plastics in use today for such applications as insulation for electric cables and for cosmetic prostheses. The health application is perhaps no surprise to those who know Bilgin; she hopes to attend medical school one day ("science is my calling," she wrote in her entry).

Bilgin is also a finalist in the overall Google Science Fair for the 15-16-year-old category, and will fly, with the other 14 contenders, to the company's Mountain View, Calif., campus for the awards event in September.

Extract from: http://blogs.scientificamerican.com

Key concepts

A1 Grouping living organisms

- Living organisms have certain characteristics that distinguish them from non-living organisms. These include: reproduction, nutrition, respiration, growth, excretion, movement and sensitivity.

- All organisms can be grouped into one of five kingdoms according to observable similarities and differences.

- The organisms in each kingdom can be further sub-divided into smaller groups based on their similarities.

A2 Living organisms and their environment

- The environment is everything around you. It is made up of biotic (living) components and abiotic (non-living) components.

- The particular place in which an organism lives is called its habitat. Living organisms are adapted to suit the habitats in which they live. Habitats on land are called terrestrial habitats. Habitats in water are called aquatic habitats.

- Organisms from the same species that live in a habitat are called a population. The various populations living in a habitat are called a community.

- The environment is affected and shaped by various factors including temperature, water, sunlight, humidity, wind and soil. Aquatic environments are affected by particular factors such as water movement and speed of flow, depth, water clarity, oxygen levels and salinity.

- Soil is one of the most important factors in a terrestrial habitat. Soil is made up of rock particles, organic matter, air, water and living organisms.

- When scientists study the distribution and density of a population they usually restrict their study to a sample from the whole population. They use the data they collect from the sample to make deductions about the population as a whole.

- Two methods used to sample populations are the transect method and the quadrat method. To get a representative sample when you are using a quadrat you should apply random sampling techniques. When you study animals, you usually use a capture–release method.

- An ecosystem is the name given to a community living together in a particular habitat. Ecosystems vary, but they all have similar feeding relationships involving producers and consumers. Each level of feeding is called a trophic level.

- Simple feeding relationships can be shown as food chains. More complicated feeding relationships can be shown as food webs.

- When organisms depend on each other in some way they have a symbiotic relationship. There are different kinds of symbiotic relationships including commensalism and mutualism. Some relationships, such as parasitism, are detrimental.

A3 Energy flows and cycles

- All ecosystems depend on energy from the Sun. This energy flows through the ecosystem from the producers through the various levels of consumers.

- As the energy is transferred from level to level, almost 90% of the energy is lost to the environment, mostly in the form of heat.

- Decomposers play an important role in all ecosystems because they break down dead and decaying matter and release nutrients in the process. These nutrients can then be recycled.

- Two important nutrients that are recycled in ecosystems are carbon and nitrogen. The carbon cycle shows the passage of carbon through ecosystems. The nitrogen cycle shows the passage of nitrogen through ecosystems.

- Nitrogen-fixing bacteria and denitrifying bacteria play an important role in the nitrogen cycle.

- Human activity puts immense pressure on ecosystems and contributes to habitat destruction and loss, pollution, climate change, depletion of species and introduction of invasive species.

A4 Natural resources

- The Earth provides a range of natural resources, including food, fuel, fibre, medicines and various mineral and energy resources. Some of these resources are replaced as they get used up by natural cycles and processes. However, some resources cannot be replaced easily; when they are used, they are no longer available, so the supply is limited.

- If we wish to conserve resources and make sure that the Earth can provide for future generations, we need to use resources carefully and recycle where possible to prevent over-use and destruction of these resources.

- In order to prevent harm to the Earth, humans need to reduce resource use, recycle resources and materials and recycle waste materials to recover resources.

- Materials that can be broken down naturally by bacteria are biodegradable.

- Recycling means treating used objects so that they can be used again. Recycling has many benefits, including conservation of raw materials, energy saving and reduction of waste materials.

- There are also problems associated with recycling. Not all materials can be recycled. Industries and private citizens are not always keen to recycle and many governments do not make recycling a priority, so it does not happen.

A5 Human activities and their impact on the environment

- Human activity includes work activities like farming, mining, manufacturing and waste disposal. These activities impact on the environment in different ways.

- The loss of natural habitats is one of the negative effects of human activity. This in turn allows invasive species to occupy environments where they wipe out or damage the indigenous populations.

- Pollution is a negative effect of human activity. Anything that dirties or harms the environment can be classified as pollution.

- Air pollution damages the environment but it also impacts on human health. The most common pollutants are carbon monoxide, sulfur dioxide, hydrocarbons, nitrogen oxides, lead compounds, dust and smoke.

- Acid rain is caused by air pollution. Acid rain damages soil, infiltrates and pollutes groundwater and it can damage plants, harm animals and erode structures.

- Increased levels of carbon dioxide in the Earth's atmosphere have contributed to the greenhouse effect and global warming. Global warming is likely to have serious environmental and economic effects in the future. Air pollution is one of the major contributors to global warming.

- Pollution from the land and air usually ends up in water supplies (oceans, rivers and other supplies). The main pollutants of water are oil, detergents, sewage, fertilisers, warm water, insecticides, chemical and industrial wastes and solid waste from the land.

- Coral reefs are important natural resources. The destruction or pollution of coral reefs has ecological and economic impacts, particularly in the Caribbean where the reefs are important sources of food and a major tourist attraction.

- Mangrove swamps are important ecosystems. They protect coastlines, prevent erosion and filter water. They are damaged easily by human activity and pollution.

- In recent years, people have tried to undo or repair the damage caused by human activity. Conservation projects aim to save the Earth for future generations. Preventing and controlling pollution is an important aspect of conservation, so is restoration of damaged environments.

A6 Population growth

- The rate at which populations grow depends on the birth rate, the death rate, emigration and immigration. These four factors are affected in turn by the environmental conditions and relationships between species.

- The same factors which encourage population growth can limit the size and growth of populations. When the death rate exceeds the birth rate, the population will decrease in size (negative growth).

- The human population is affected by the same factors as natural populations. Currently, the population of Earth is growing rapidly because the birth rate remains higher than the death rate.

- As the human population grows, it puts pressure on the Earth's resources. People need space to live and grow food; they use natural species for food, building equipment and economic wealth. The result is habitat loss, decreasing biodiversity and increased exploitation and pollution of natural resources.

Do you know these key terms?

- biotic factors (p10)
- habitat (p10)
- abiotic factors (p12)
- macroorganisms (p17)
- microorganisms (p17)
- distribution (p21)
- transect (p22)
- quadrat (p22)
- abundance (p23)
- density (p23)
- ecology (p26)
- ecosystem (p26)
- autotrophs (p26)
- producers (p26)
- heterotrophs (p26)
- consumers (p26)
- herbivores (p26)
- carnivores (p26)
- omnivores (p26)
- decomposers (p26)
- trophic level (p27)
- food chain (p28)
- food web (p28)
- symbiosis (p30)
- commensalism (p30)
- mutualism (p30)
- parasitism (p31)
- detritus (p34)
- scavengers (p34)
- detritivores (p34)
- carbon cycle (p37)
- nitrogen-fixing bacteria (p38)
- denitrifying bacteria (p38)
- nitrogen cycle (p38)
- renewable (p39)
- finite resources (p40)
- population growth (p40)
- ecological footprint (p40)
- biodegradable (p44)
- recycling (p45)
- human activity (p47)
- alien species (p47)
- invasive species (p47)
- pollution (p48)
- acid rain (p49)
- greenhouse effect (p50)
- global warming (p50)
- conservation (p54)
- population (p61)
- immigration (p61)
- emigration (p61)

Practice exam-style questions

Working through these questions will help you to revise the content of this section and prepare you for your examination.

The number of marks available for each question gives you an idea about how much detail to put in your answer.

1 A sample of a food chain is shown below:

hibiscus leaf ⟶ caterpillar ⟶ lizard ⟶ garden snake

  a) From the food chain, which of the following is:
    i) the producer
    ii) the secondary consumer
    iii) the herbivore?   [3KC]

  b) The carbon dioxide from the air around the leaves of the hibiscus tree becomes part of the flesh of the garden snake.
    i) Name and describe the process by which the carbon dioxide is incorporated into the leaf.   [1KC, 2UK]
    ii) This carbon dioxide is eventually returned to the atmosphere from the body of the snake. Name this process.   [1KC]
    iii) Draw a simple diagram to depict how the processes named in **b i)** and **b ii)** are related.   [3UK]

  c) With reference to the diagram below:

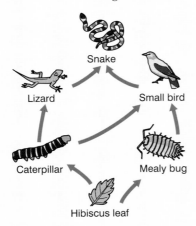

    i) State ONE process that results in the loss of energy between the secondary and tertiary consumer.   [1KC]
    ii) State TWO possible effects on the rest of the ecosystem if the lizard was removed from the ecosystem.   [2UK]
    iii) Do you think that removing the snake from the ecosystem would have a similar effect as removing the lizard? Give a reason for your answer.   [1KC, 1UK]

                 [Total 15 marks]

2 **a)** Copy and complete the following cycle to show how the falling leaves of the almond tree contribute to the mineral nutrients supplied to the plant.   [3KC]

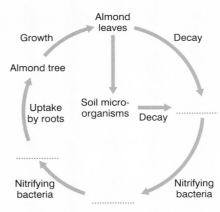

  b) **i)** Give TWO reasons why recycling of minerals is important.   [2UK]
    ii) Explain why some types of material, for example plastics, are difficult to return to natural cycles.   [2UK]

  c) Using an example, explain the negative impact of human activity on the environment.   [1KC, 4UK]

  d) Give one example for each of the following symbiotic relationships:
    i) parasitism   **iii)** commensalism.
    ii) mutualism   [3KC]

                 [Total 15 marks]

3 Caribbean coral reefs are habitats for several different species of fishes and algae. World-wide, reefs are being destroyed as a consequence of human activities.

  a) **i)** Using appropriate examples, distinguish between the terms 'community' and 'population'.   [4KC]
    ii) With reference to the above ecosystem, discuss THREE factors that affect the growth of the natural population of the fishes.   [6UK]

  b) **i)** Give TWO examples of human activities that are contributing to the destruction of the coral reefs.   [2KC]
    ii) Based on the problems identified in part **b i)**, what advice would you give the Caribbean governments to help preserve the reefs.   [3UK]

                 [Total 15 marks]

4 **a)** A smelter plant has been built recently on a Caribbean island. The island also contains an oil refinery and several quarries.
    i) Give ONE major environmental problem that you would expect to be encountered on the island.   [1KC]
    ii) Discuss THREE activities you would recommend to prevent complete destruction of the island's forests.   [6UK]

  b) It is important for manufactured materials to be recycled since most of the raw materials are finite.
    i) Using appropriate examples, distinguish between the terms 'biodegradable' and 'non-biodegradable'.   [2KC]
    ii) Discuss TWO advantages and ONE disadvantage of recycling manufactured materials.   [6UK]

                 [Total 15 marks]

Cell biology

Organisms are made up of simple units called 'cells'. The invention of powerful electron microscopes in the 1930s allowed scientists to learn much more about cells than they knew before. In this unit you will look at cells to learn more about how they function, how substances move in to and out of cells and how cells group together and perform specialised functions to form living organisms.

Objectives

By the end of this topic you will be able to:

- draw and label diagrams of cells to show their structure
- name the structures found in cells
- state the functions and importance of different cells' structures
- tabulate the differences between plant and animal cells
- examine plant and animal cells under a microscope
- construct a model of a cell using found materials.

B7.1 The structure of cells

The cell is the basic unit of life. Some organisms, such as bacteria and protozoa, consist of one cell. We call these uni-cellular organisms. (You can see diagrams of these organisms in Figure 7.2.1.) Most plant and animal species are multi-cellular. This means consist of have many cells that work as a system to keep them alive.

Figure 7.1.1 shows the structure of an animal cell and the structure of a plant cell. Plant and animal cells are different, but all cells have the following properties:

- The cell is covered by a cell membrane.
- The cytoplasm is the living part of the cell.
- The organelles are small structures found in the cytoplasm. They are mostly too small to be seen with the naked eye but they can be seen with an electron microscope.
- The nucleus controls the working and function of the cell, it also contains the chromosomes.
- The vacuole is an organelle with a membrane that holds liquid.
- The mitochondria are organelles which are responsible for cellular energy.

Animal cell

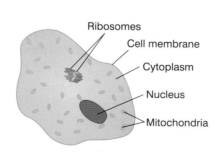

Plant cell

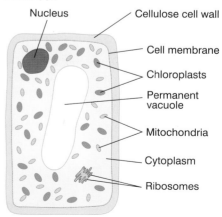

▲ **Figure 7.1.1** The basic structures found in animal cells and in plant cells

Animal cells

Animal cells do not have rigid cell walls so they may not have a fixed shape. If vacuoles are present in the cell they are normally small.

Plant cells

Plant cells are normally larger than animal cells. They have a strong cell wall that encloses the cell and gives it a fixed shape. Plant cells usually have a large vacuole which is filled with cell sap (a solution of water and sugars).

Plant cells that are involved in photosynthesis also have organelles called chloroplasts. Chloroplasts are organelles that contain the chemical chlorophyll.

Table 7.1.1 lists the differences between animal and plant cells.

▼ **Table 7.1.1** The differences in structure of animal and plant cells

Animal cells	Plant cells
No cell wall	Have a cell wall
No chloroplasts	Many contain chloroplasts
Not rigid, can change shape	Rigid, have a fixed shape
Often don't have vacuoles	Have a central vacuole with cell sap
When present, vacuoles are very small	Vacuole is normally single and large

The different cell structures

The structures found in cells all have specific functions that are important for keeping each cell alive and helping it to function properly. Table 7.1.2 summarises the function and importance of the different structures found in cells.

▼ **Table 7.1.2** The function and importance of cell structures

Type of cell	Structure	Function and importance
Animal and plant cells	Cell membrane	Forms the boundary between the cell and its surroundings. Controls the movement of substances in to and out of the cell
	Nucleus (contains the chromosomes)	The **chromosomes** contain the **genetic code** or **DNA**. Information in the chromosomes is used to control the development and function of the cell. Without a nucleus, most cells will die.
	Cytoplasm	Contains many cell organelles. Is where cell activities take place.
	Mitochondria (singular is 'mitochondrion')	Small organelles responsible for cellular energy
Plant cells	Cell wall	Gives protection and shape to the cell. Helps plants stay upright
	Vacuole	Stores water and dissolved substances. Important for the exchange of various substances.
	Chloroplasts	Contain the green pigment chlorophyll. Are important because they are the sites of food production in plants (photosynthesis takes place here).

Exam tip

In an examination you may be asked to annotate the labels on a drawing of a plant/animal cells, use the function to do this.

Safety

Take care when using sharp instruments in practical activities.

 Practical activity

Looking at and modelling cells

1 a Cut an onion into pieces and soak the pieces in a beaker of water.

 b Extract a small piece of a thin layer from the onion (it will slide off easily from the thick piece of onion).

 c Place specimen on a slide and cover with a drop of water.

 d Place cover slip over specimen, dry and observe using a microscope.

2 Build a model of a plant cell using materials that you can find in your environment. For example, you could use wire to form the cell wall and a plastic bag to represent the cell membrane.

 Exam tip

In an examination you may be asked to give differences between plant and animal cells. Be sure to write complete sentences, for example: A plant cell has a cell wall while an animal cell does not.

Questions

1 Why are microscopes needed to study cells?

2 What is an 'organelle'?

3 What substance gives plants their green colour? Where in cells is this substance stored and what does it do?

4 What do you think would happen to an animal cell if its cell membrane burst? Would the same thing happen to a plant cell? Explain why or why not.

5 Would you expect to find chloroplasts in the root cells of a plant? Why?

6 Draw and label a typical plant cell. Remember to use a double line to show the cell wall.

7 Make a list of three differences between the plant cell you have drawn and a typical animal cell.

Objectives

By the end of this topic you will be able to:

- explain cell specialisation
- give some examples of cell specialisation in plants and animals
- define 'cells', 'tissues', 'organs' and 'organisms' and show how they are connected
- give examples of tissues from both plants and animals.

B7.2 From cells to organisms: specialisation

You have learnt in topic B7.1 that all plant and animal cells have certain things in common. By studying the insides of cells and how they work, scientists have discovered that cells are highly organised. They have also learnt that different cells are specialised to carry out various tasks in living things and that cells can group together to work as a unit. In this topic you are going to learn more about cell specialisation and groups of cells.

Single cells can live as organisms

Unicellular organisms consist of only one cell that carries out all the functions the organism needs to survive. Different types of unicellular organism look different to each other, but they all have the same basic structure: a cell membrane, a nucleus and other organelles in their cytoplasm. You can see a generalised bacterium cell and an amoeba (a protozoan) in Figure 7.2.1.

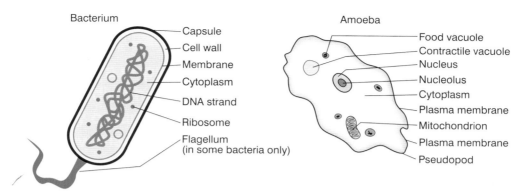

▲ **Figure 7.2.1** Bacteria and protists, such as amoeba, are single-celled organisms

Multicellular organisms

Most cells cannot survive on their own, so they join together to function as multicellular organisms. Humans are multi-cellular organisms made up of billions of cells. In multicellular organisms, cells can become specialised to perform different functions in the body. These cells have different structures and functions, but they work together so that the organism can function as a whole.

A group of similar cells form a tissue. For example, muscle cells form the tissue of your stomach wall and your heart. Different tissues together form an organ. The stomach is an organ and the heart is an organ. The organs work together in an organised system. For example, the stomach, together with other organs, forms the digestive system. You can see the different levels of organisation in cells in Figure 7.2.2.

In plants, the groups of cells form tissue, but we do not often talk about the organs of plants, we usually talk about the 'structures' or 'parts' of plants.

A closer look at specialised cells

The human body has more than 200 different types of cell. Figure 7.2.3 shows some of the cells that you will learn more about in this course.

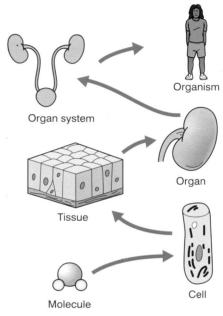

▲ **Figure 7.2.2** Different levels of organisation of cells

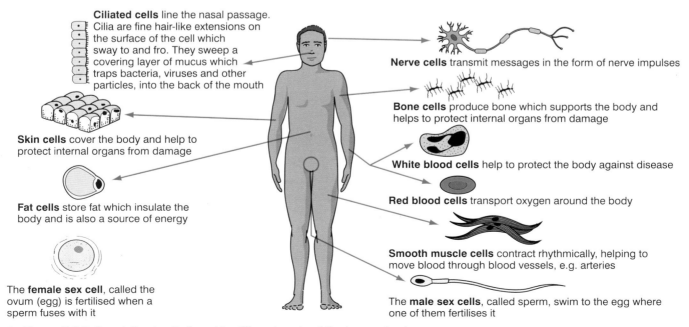

Ciliated cells line the nasal passage. Cilia are fine hair-like extensions on the surface of the cell which sway to and fro. They sweep a covering layer of mucus which traps bacteria, viruses and other particles, into the back of the mouth

Skin cells cover the body and help to protect internal organs from damage

Fat cells store fat which insulate the body and is also a source of energy

The **female sex cell**, called the ovum (egg) is fertilised when a sperm fuses with it

Nerve cells transmit messages in the form of nerve impulses

Bone cells produce bone which supports the body and helps to protect internal organs from damage

White blood cells help to protect the body against disease

Red blood cells transport oxygen around the body

Smooth muscle cells contract rhythmically, helping to move blood through blood vessels, e.g. arteries

The **male sex cells**, called sperm, swim to the egg where one of them fertilises it

▲ **Figure 7.2.3** Specialised cells found in different parts of the human body

Figure 7.2.4 shows some of the specialised cells that you find in flowering plants. You will learn more about the functions of these cells later.

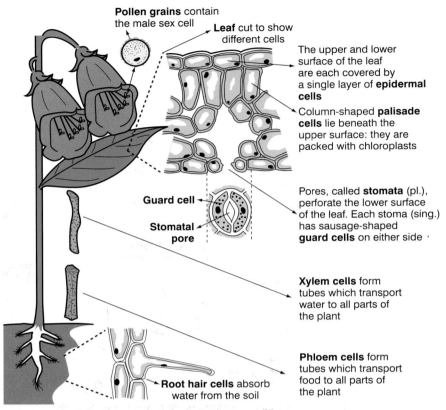

Pollen grains contain the male sex cell

Leaf cut to show different cells

The upper and lower surface of the leaf are each covered by a single layer of **epidermal cells**

Column-shaped **palisade cells** lie beneath the upper surface: they are packed with chloroplasts

Guard cell

Stomatal pore

Pores, called **stomata** (pl.), perforate the lower surface of the leaf. Each stoma (sing.) has sausage-shaped **guard cells** on either side ·

Xylem cells form tubes which transport water to all parts of the plant

Phloem cells form tubes which transport food to all parts of the plant

Root hair cells absorb water from the soil

▲ **Figure 7.2.4** Specialised cells found in different plant structures

Questions

1 Why are cells not all the same? Give examples to support your answer.

2 Which types of cell are needed to perform the following functions in a multi-cellular animal?
   a Protective covering
   b Carry messages between cells
   c Move oxygen round the body
   d Prevent dirt and bacteria from getting into the lungs

3 What is the function and importance of the following specialised plant cells?
   a Root cells   c Guard cells
   b Chloroplasts   d Phloem cells

4 What do you think happens to the fat cells in your body when you eat more food than you need for your body functions?

A closer look at tissue

You have learnt that cells differentiate and specialise so that they can perform specific tasks. When cells that are alike group together to perform the same function they form tissue. Plants and animals contain many different types of tissue.

Plant tissue

Plant tissue is made up of cells that have the same function and structure. Table 7.2.1 gives some examples of plant tissue, where each type is found and what it does. The different types of tissue can be seen in Figure 7.2.5.

▼ **Table 7.2.1** Plant tissue and its functions

Type of tissue	Where it is found	What it does
Epidermal tissue	Found in the outer covering layers of plants	Protects the plant and prevents it from drying out by means of a waxy layer called the **cuticle**
Photosynthetic tissue	Mainly inside green leaves	Contains chloroplasts that allow photosynthesis to take place
Packing tissue (**parenchyma cells**)	All over the plant between more specialised parts, **cortex** of roots	Provide support and useful for food storage
Transport or vascular tissue (**xylem** and **phloem**)	In the stems and leaves – forms the veins of the plant	Forms tubes that allow food, mineral salts and water to move through the plant
Supportive or strengthening tissue (**collenchyma** and **sclerenchyma**)	Below the surface of stems and leaves	Thick walls allow them to support the plant and also allow it to be flexible

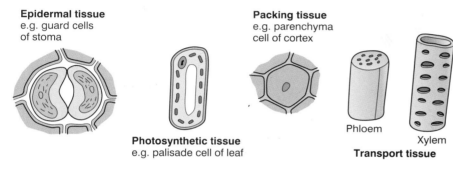

Epidermal tissue e.g. guard cells of stoma

Packing tissue e.g. parenchyma cell of cortex

Photosynthetic tissue e.g. palisade cell of leaf

Phloem

Xylem

Transport tissue

▲ **Figure 7.2.5** Different types of tissue are made up of groups of cells such as these

Animal tissue

Animal tissue can be grouped into epithelial tissue, muscle tissue, connective tissue and nerve tissue. Each of these larger groups contains several sub-groups of tissue types. Table 7.2.2 shows the main groups of tissue and gives examples of tissue found in each group. The different types of tissue can be seen in Figure 7.2.6.

▼ **Table 7.2.2** Main groups of animal tissue

Type of tissue	Examples of this type of tissue
Epithelial tissue	Epidermal tissue, found on the surface of the skin.
	Mucous membrane, found lining the nose, throat and other body parts.
	Glandular epithelium, found in glands, such as milk glands and sweat glands.
	Endothelium, smooth tissue found in the blood vessels and the heart.
	Mesothelium, found in the lining of body spaces and on the surfaces of organs.
Muscle tissue	Skeletal or striated tissue, connected to the skeleton to help with movement.
	Smooth muscle tissue, found in the internal organs.
	Cardiac muscle tissue, forms the heart.
Connective tissue	**Areolar** connective tissue, found covering the organs, skeletal muscle and blood vessels, also in the skin.
	Fibrous connective tissue, found in **ligaments** and **tendons**.
	Bone, forms the skeleton.
	Cartilage, not as hard as bone, covers surfaces of bone and forms the nose and ears.
	Adipose tissue, fatty tissue found beneath the skin and around organs.
	Blood, a liquid tissue found throughout the body.
Nerve tissue	The brain and spinal cord, which contains special cells called **neurons**.

| Epithelium cells | Muscle cell | Connective tissue e.g. bone cells | Connective tissue e.g. blood cells | Nerve cell |

▲ **Figure 7.2.6** Different types of animal tissue are made from specialised cells such as these

Questions

1 Copy and complete the following sentences:
  a Bone is a type of … .
  b Tendons and ligaments are examples of … .
  c The heart is made of … .
  d … is the only tissue that is in a liquid form.
  e … tissue forms a protective layer round your liver and other organs.

2 Name the main group to which each of these animal tissue types belongs:

a 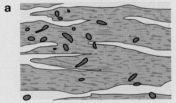 b 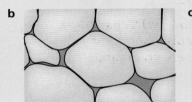 c 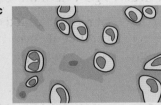 d

▲ **Figure 7.2.7**

B7.3 Movement of substances through cells

Cells need a supply of water and other substances that dissolve in water so that they can stay alive. Cells also need to get rid of waste products. Dissolved substances move in to and out of cells across the cell membrane through the processes of diffusion and osmosis.

Diffusion

If you walk past the kitchen when someone is cooking you can usually smell the food from some distance away. This shows that smells spread through the air. Smells can also spread in water. Sharks, for example, can smell blood in the water from some distance away. We can smell food cooking and sharks can smell blood because of diffusion.

The molecules or particles of gas and liquid move around at random. The natural tendency of these particles is to move from where they are highly concentrated (close together) to where they are less concentrated (more spread out). The result is a movement of molecules of a substance along a concentration gradient from where the substance is highly concentrated to where it is in low concentration. This movement of particles through a gas (like air) or through a solution (when they are dissolved in liquid) is called **diffusion**.

Table 7.3.1 gives some examples of diffusion in living organisms.

▼ **Table 7.3.1** Diffusion takes place in the cells of all living organisms

Where diffusion takes place	Substance that is diffused	How substances move
Small intestine	Glucose and amino acids from dissolved food	From small intestine, through capillary walls into blood
Lungs	Oxygen (from the air)	From the lungs through alveoli walls into the blood
Lungs	Carbon dioxide	From the blood through the alveoli walls into the lungs for exhalation
Pores of leaves	Oxygen	From the air spaces in the leaf, through the pores into the air (during photosynthesis)
Pores of leaves	Carbon dioxide	From the air, through pores into the air spaces in the leaf
Cell membrane of amoeba	Amino acids, sugars and vitamins (products of digestion)	From a food vacuole, through the membrane around it into the cytoplasm of the cell

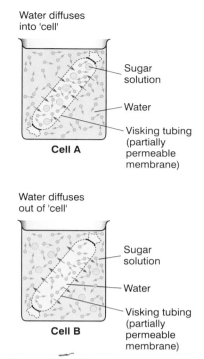

▲ **Figure 7.3.1** Substances move into and out of our cells by diffusion

Figure 7.3.1 is a simplified version of diffusion. It shows how diffusion allows substances like oxygen and food to get in to our cells and waste products like carbon dioxide and other chemicals to get out of our cells.

Diffusion is a passive process. It does not require added energy. Diffusion will continue until the molecules of the substance are evenly distributed through the gas or liquid. You are now going to do an experiment to demonstrate diffusion.

 Practical activity

Demonstrating diffusion

Materials

- A beaker of clean water
- A crystal of potassium permanganate (Condi's crystals)

Method

1 Drop a crystal of potassium permanganate into the water by letting it slide down the side of the glass.

2 Observe what happens.

3 Try to explain your observations based on what you have learnt about diffusion.

Questions

1 Charles was walking through shallow water when he cut his foot on a shell.
   a Explain, with reference to diffusion, why the cut looked much more serious in the water than it would have looked if he had cut his foot on a shell while walking across the sand.
   b Explain, with reference to diffusion, how sharks are able to smell blood in water.

2 Explain, giving an example, why diffusion is important in living cells.

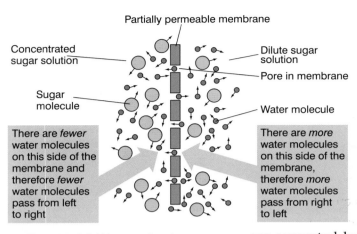

Concentrated sugar solution

Partially permeable membrane

Sugar molecule

Dilute sugar solution

Pore in membrane

Water molecule

There are *fewer* water molecules on this side of the membrane and therefore *fewer* water molecules pass from left to right

There are *more* water molecules on this side of the membrane, therefore *more* water molecules pass from right to left

▲ **Figure 7.3.2** Water molecules can pass through the membrane, but the sugar molecules cannot

Osmosis

The most important function of the cell membrane is that it allows water and nutrients to pass in and out of cells. The cell membrane is partially permeable. This means that some substances can pass through it, but others can't. The membrane has small pores (openings) in it that allow the movement of substances. In general, substances pass through a membrane if their particles are smaller than the pores in the membrane. You can see how this happens in Figure 7.3.2.

Water is one of the important substances that can move through cell membranes. When two solutions are separated by a partially permeable membrane, water passes through the membrane in both directions. The net flow of water is from the more diluted solution, which has a high concentration of water molecules, to the more concentrated solution, which has a lower concentration of water molecules. Water will continue to move through the membrane until the two concentrations are equal. The movement of water molecules from a more dilute solution to a more concentrated solution through a partially permeable membrane is called osmosis. You can think of osmosis as a special type of diffusion, in which only water molecules move from one area to another. You are now going to do some experiments on osmosis.

 Practical activity

Demonstrating osmosis

Your teacher may use this activity to assess: ORR; M&M; A&I.

Materials

- Half a potato, peeled (share with another student)
- A scalpel or knife
- A dish to hold the potato
- Sugar
- Water
- A pin

Method

1 Use the scalpel or knife to carve out a hollow cup-shape in the top of your potato.

2 Stand your potato in a dish of water as illustrated in Figure 7.3.3.

3 Make a strong solution of sugar and water.

4 Half-fill the hollow in the top of the potato with the sugar solution.

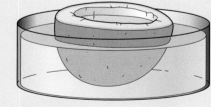

▲ **Figure 7.3.3**

5 Stick a pin into the potato to mark the level of the sugar solution.

6 Leave the potato as it is for half an hour.

Observations

1 What happened to the level of the sugar solution?

2 Try to explain how and why this happened.

Practical activity

Investigating and measuring osmosis

Your teacher may use this activity to assess: ORR; M&M; A&I.

Materials

- Three potato sticks of dimensions 1 cm × 1 cm × 5 cm
- Three test tubes
- 0.1 M saline solution
- 1 M saline solution
- Pure water
- Ruler

Method

1 Place a potato stick in each test tube and label them A, B and C.

2 To test tube A, add 0.1 M saline solution until the potato stick is covered.

3 To test tube B, add 1 M saline solution until the potato stick is covered.

4 To test tube C, add pure water until the potato stick is covered.

5 Leave for 30 minutes.

6 Record all observations and take measurements of each potato stick's new dimensions. Explain what happened in each test tube.

7 Observe whether the potato stick is floating or sinking and suggest a reason for this.

Osmosis in plant cells

Osmosis is the way that plants take up the water they need to stay alive. The cell membrane of the plant is a partially permeable membrane and allows the movement of water molecules into the cell.

Turgidity

Osmosis takes place across the cell membrane that separates solutions inside the cell from solutions outside the cell. The changes that happen inside plant cells as a result of osmosis cause visible changes in the plant.

When plant cells are placed in a solution that is less concentrated than the solution inside them, water passes through the cell wall and cell membrane, through the cytoplasm and into the vacuole. The cell fills with water and become **turgid**. You can see this illustrated in Figure 7.3.4.

The diagram shows that water flows from the less concentrated solution outside the cell, through the cell wall and cell membrane into the cytoplasm and into the vacuole. The increased pressure in the vacuole is called **turgor pressure** and it causes the cytoplasm to press up against the cell wall. When the cell contains as much water as it can hold, it is said to be fully turgid. Turgid cells do not burst because the cell wall is strong enough to withstand the turgor pressure.

Turgidity is important in plants because the turgid cells allow the plant to stay upright and gives it support. When cells lose water they become flaccid and the plant droops or wilts.

> **!** **Key fact**
>
> You can use cucumber in place of potato in this experiment. You will get similar results.

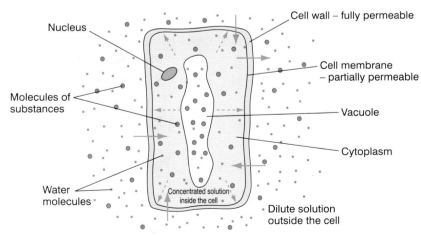

More water molecules pass from the solution outside the cell into the cell than from the solution inside the cell to the outside

The pressure of the solution in the vacuole increases, pressing the cytoplasm against the cell wall

▲ **Figure 7.3.4** A turgid cell

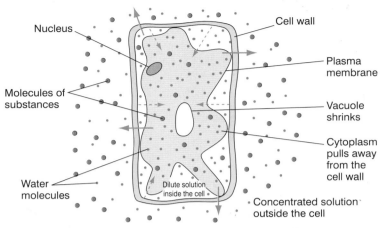

Nucleus

Molecules of substances

Water molecules

Dilute solution inside the cell

Cell wall

Plasma membrane

Vacuole shrinks

Cytoplasm pulls away from the cell wall

Concentrated solution outside the cell

→ More water molecules pass from the solution inside the cell to the outside than from the solution outside the cell to the inside

- - -→ The pressure of the solution in the vacuole decreases, reducing the pressure pressing the cytoplasm against the cell wall. Eventually the cytoplasm pulls away from the cell wall

▲ **Figure 7.3.5** A plasmolysed cell

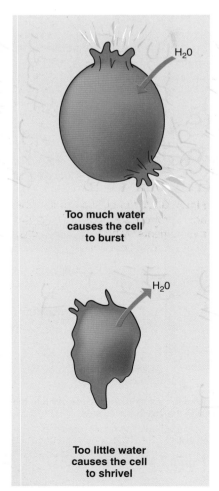

Too much water causes the cell to burst

H_2O

H_2O

Too little water causes the cell to shrivel

▲ **Figure 7.3.6** Osmosis in an animal cell

Plasmolysis

If plant cells are placed in a solution that is more concentrated than the solution inside them, then water passes out of the cells by osmosis. Water passes out of the vacuole, out of the cytoplasm, out through the cell membrane and cell wall and into the solution outside the cell. The pressure of the vacuole on the cytoplasm decreases until the cytoplasm pulls away from the cell wall, causing the cell to become flaccid. Cells in this condition are said to be plasmolysed. You can see the process of plasmolysis in Figure 7.3.5.

Osmosis in animal cells

If animal cells are placed in a solution that is less concentrated than the solution inside them, water moves into the cells by osmosis and they swell up. If too much water flows into the cells they may burst because they have no cell walls.

When animal cells are placed in a solution that is more concentrated than the solution inside them, water flows out of the cells as a result of osmosis. This causes the cells to shrivel up (see Figure 7.3.6).

For animals is it very important to maintain an osmotic balance between cells and body fluids. Maintaining this balance is called osmoregulation. You will learn more about this process in topic B14.5.

Active transport

Sometimes substances move across the cell membrane and other cell membranes from a region where they are present in low concentration to a region where they are present in high concentration. That is, they move against a concentration gradient in the reverse direction to normal diffusion. Such movement is called active transport. It allows cells to build up stores of substances which otherwise would be spread out by diffusion. Active transport is an active process, which means that it requires energy, unlike diffusion which is a passive process and does not require energy.

Questions

1 Define 'osmosis'.

2 Explain, with reference to osmosis, why the following advice is sound:
   a To make limp salad leaves crisp, you can soak them in cold water for an hour.
   b To preserve fruit, you can cover it with a concentrated sugar solution.
   c When you add fertiliser to pot plants, read the instructions carefully. Too much fertiliser is as bad as too little fertiliser.

3 Explain why dehydration is dangerous and potentially fatal in humans.

4 Explain, with reference to their structure, why animal cells are more likely than plant cells to burst if too much water flows into them.

You learnt in Unit A2 that plants are autotrophs which make their own food. Now you are going to learn more about different types of nutrition and then you are going to learn how plants gain nutrients through the process of photosynthesis.

B8.1 Types of nutrition

In Unit A1 you learned that nutrition is one of the characteristics of all living organisms. Nutrition, or feeding, provides organisms with the substances they need to grow and repair cells, and it also provides the energy the organism needs for survival.

Autotrophic and heterotrophic nutrition

Organisms can generally be placed into two main groups depending on how they obtain their nutrients:

- **Autotrophs** are organisms that essentially make their own food. In autotrophic nutrition, organisms use simple inorganic substances from the air and soil (such as carbon dioxide and water) to build the organic molecules (such as glucose) they need. All green plants are autotrophs. Plants use energy from sunlight for this process (photosynthesis). Some bacteria are autotrophic. They use carbon dioxide and energy from the oxidation of substances such as iron, ammonia and nitrites to synthesise carbohydrates. Autotrophic bacteria are important in processes such as nitrogen fixation.

- **Heterotrophs** are organisms that cannot make their own food. In heterotrophic nutrition, the organism takes in complex organic substances which are generally made by plants (this is why plants are called the producers in any ecosystem). Heterotrophs break down, or digest, the complex organic substances to produce the food substances they need. Animals are heterotrophs which feed on plants and/or other animals. Fungi, some bacteria and some protoctists also rely on heterotrophic nutrition to meet their energy and nutrient needs.

Saphrotrophs and saphrophytic nutrition

Fungi and other decomposers are heterotrophic but they do not obtain nutrients by eating other organisms. Instead, they obtain nutrients by breaking down complex organic material from the dead and decaying remains of other organisms in the process of saprophytic nutrition. ('Sapros' means rotten and 'phyton' means plant.) As saprotrophs feed, they release vital chemical elements into the soil. These elements, in turn, are absorbed by autotrophs.

You will learn about plant nutrition and photosynthesis in more detail in this unit. You will then learn about the substances that organisms need to survive before studying the human digestive system in more detail.

Objectives

By the end of this topic you will be able to:

- distinguish between autotrophic, heterotrophic and saprophytic nutrition
- compare the substances used by plants to make food with the substances used by animals to make food.

▲ **Figure 8.1.1** Fungi, such as this one, are saprotrophs which obtain energy and nutrients by breaking down organic matter in dead or decaying organisms

▲ **Figure 8.1.2** This sundew plant is an autotroph, but it also obtains organic matter and nitrogen from the insects it traps. The plants need to supplement their nitrogen intake as they generally live in nitrogen-poor soils.

1   For each of the following organisms, state the type of nutrition it relies on and identify two possible sources of its nutrients.

   a A mushroom   e An aphid

   b A palm tree   f A mosquito

   c A horse   g Yeast (a single-celled fungus)

   d A human being

2   Think back to what you learned about symbiotic feeding relationships in Unit A2. In which ways are saprotrophs different from parasites?

Objectives

By the end of this topic you will be able to:

● describe photosynthesis and give a generalised equation for the process

● outline the main stages in photosynthesis and where they occur

● state what happens to the products of photosynthesis.

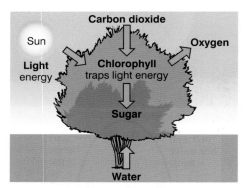

▲ **Figure 8.2.1** Plants use sunlight and simple inorganic substances to produce sugars and oxygen

B8.2 Photosynthesis

Feeding, or nutrition, in plants involves taking in the substances that the plants need to survive. Green plants can take in simple inorganic substances and use them to make more complex carbohydrates. Animals get their food and energy indirectly by eating plants or by eating other animals that have eaten plants.

The process of photosynthesis

Photosynthesis is the process by which plants use energy from sunlight to change the simple inorganic substances of water and carbon dioxide into food. Plants take in water through their roots. The water is transported up the plant to the leaves. Plants take in carbon dioxide gas (CO_2) from the air. The carbon dioxide enters the leaves through microscopic pores called stomata. Chlorophyll (in the chloroplasts of cells) in the leaves absorbs radiant energy from the Sun. The leaf cells use this energy to change carbon dioxide and water into glucose (a simple sugar). Oxygen is released as a waste product during the process and returned to the air through the stomata in the leaves. Figure 8.2.1 is a simplified diagram that shows what happens during the process of photosynthesis.

Photosynthesis is a complicated process, but is can be summarised using the following equation:

$$\text{carbon dioxide} + \text{water} \xrightarrow[\text{chlorophyll}]{\text{light energy}} \text{glucose} + \text{oxygen}$$

The arrow in the equation means 'changes to'. Light energy and chlorophyll are written above the arrow because they are necessary for the process to take place.

If we use the chemical formulae for the substances the equation looks like this:

$$6CO_2 + 6H_2O \longrightarrow C_6H_{12}O_6 + 6O_2$$

This is a chemical equation. You may remember from chemistry that chemical equations have to be balanced. This means that the number of atoms you start with has to be same as the number of atoms you end up with. To balance the equation you have to write numbers in front of the substances to show how many molecules are involved in the reaction.

The main stages in photosynthesis

Photosynthesis takes place continuously in plants, but we can think of it as a process that happens in two stages. The products of the first stage become the raw materials for the second stage. Sunlight is necessary for the first stage, so this is called the light stage. The second stage uses carbon dioxide and it can take place in the dark, so it is called the dark stage.

The light stage

In this stage, the chlorophyll in the leaves converts sunlight (light energy) into chemical energy. Some of the light energy is used to split water molecules (H_2O) into hydrogen (H) and oxygen (O_2). This process is called the evolution of oxygen. You will carry out an experiment to show that plants produce oxygen during photosynthesis in topic B8.4.

The dark stage

The hydrogen released (from water molecules) in the light stage combines with carbon dioxide to form glucose (a sugar). This process is called the reduction of carbon dioxide. The process requires some of the energy that was absorbed during the light stage but it does not require sunlight.

What happens to the products of photosynthesis?

Most photosynthesis takes place in the leaves of plants. However all parts of the plant need food, so the glucose needs to be transported to other parts. This is done through the phloem tubes. (You will learn more about this in Unit B14.) Glucose can also be converted to starch and stored in different parts of the plant.

Figure 8.2.2 shows how plants use the glucose made during photosynthesis.

Oxygen is also produced during photosynthesis. This is released into the atmosphere through the stomata of the leaves.

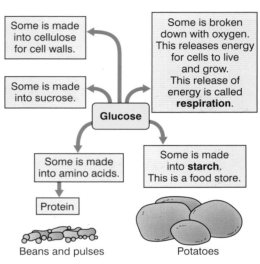

▲ **Figure 8.2.2** Plants use the glucose made during photosynthesis in different ways

Questions

1 Figure 8.2.3 shows a leaf from a green plant where photosynthesis takes place.

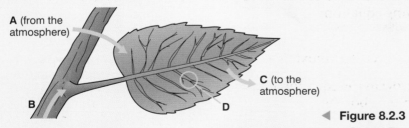

◄ **Figure 8.2.3**

a Identify the products of photosynthesis represented by C and D.
b Name the inorganic substances needed for photosynthesis.
c Where does the plant get substance B?
d What happens to substance A during photosynthesis? Show this using an equation.

2 State two ways in which plants use the glucose produced during photosynthesis.

3 Explain why photosynthesis is important for animals as well as plants.

Key fact

The rainforests are sometimes called the 'lungs' of the world because the trees absorb carbon dioxide and release oxygen. Scientists estimate that 50% of the oxygen in the atmosphere comes from small ocean plants called **phytoplankton**. If the environmental balance is disturbed by water pollution or deforestation the atmosphere will change and less oxygen will be available for living things.

By the end of this topic you will be able to:

- relate the structure of a leaf to its functions during photosynthesis
- draw and label diagrams to show the external and internal structure of a leaf.

B8.3 How leaves are adapted for photosynthesis

Most photosynthesis takes place in the leaves of plants. The leaves are adapted to allow for maximum photosynthesis. In this topic you are going to look at leaves in more detail, to identify leaf structures and to relate structures to their functions.

The external features of leaves

Look at the pictures in Figure 8.3.1 carefully. Figure 8.3.1a shows the top and underside of a leaf. Figure 8.3.1b shows what the underside of a leaf looks like when viewed with a light microscope.

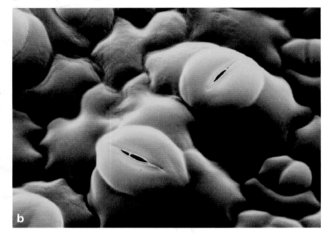

▲ **Figure 8.3.1 a** The top and bottom surfaces of a leaf; **b** the bottom surface of a leaf as viewed with a microscope

Table 8.3.1 is a summary of how the external features and structures of leaves are adapted for photosynthesis.

▼ **Table 8.3.1** How the external structures of a leaf are adapted to maximise photosynthesis

Visible feature/structure	How feature/structure relates to photosynthesis
Colour (most leaves are green)	Leaves are usually green because they contain chlorophyll, a chemical that absorbs sunlight.
Shape and size (surface area)	Leaves are generally flat with a large surface area to absorb maximum amounts of sunlight and carbon dioxide.
Thickness	Leaves are quite thin (usually less than 1 mm thick) if you look at them from the side, this is to allow carbon dioxide and oxygen to diffuse in to and out of the leaf easily.
Veins	Because leaves are thin, the veins help to support the leaf. They also carry substances to and from the cells in the leaves.
Pores (stomata)	The top and bottom surfaces of leaves contain tiny pores called stomata. There are more stomata on the underside of leaves. These allow gases to pass in to and out of the leaf.

The internal structure of leaves

You cannot see the structures inside a leaf just by looking at it. To find out more about the internal structures you have to cut a very thin slice of leaf (a transverse section). Figure 8.3.2 shows what a transverse section of a leaf looks like when viewed through a light microscope.

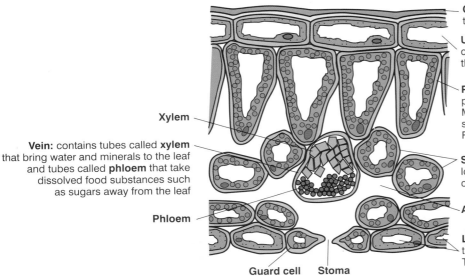

Cuticle: waterproof layer that reduces the water lost by evaporation

Upper epidermis: single layer of cells with no chloroplasts. Light passes straight through these cells

Palisade layer: layer of palisade cells. The palisade cells contain lots of chloroplasts. Most photosynthesis occurs here. You can see the structure of a palisade cell in Figure 7.3.4 on p83

Spongy layer: a layer of rounded cells with lots of air spaces between them. Diffusion of carbon dioxide and oxygen occurs here

Airspace

Lower epidermis: no thick cuticle. Has lots of tiny holes called stomata (singular stoma). These allow gases to diffuse in and out

Xylem

Vein: contains tubes called **xylem** that bring water and minerals to the leaf and tubes called **phloem** that take dissolved food substances such as sugars away from the leaf

Phloem

Guard cell   Stoma

▲ **Figure 8.3.2** Transverse section of a leaf

If you look at Figure 8.3.2 closely, you can see that the cells in the leaves are arranged so that photosynthesis can take place. Table 8.3.2 summarises the internal structures of a leaf and explains how these help to maximise photosynthesis.

◄ **Table 8.3.2** How the internal structures of a leaf are adapted to maximise photosynthesis

Internal structure	Description and functional role
Waxy cuticle	A waxy waterproof layer that protects the leaf and allows light through for photosynthesis, also prevents water loss from the surface of the leaf
Upper epidermis	Thin, transparent cells that do not contain chlorophyll but allow light to pass through, act like a skin to protect the leaf
Palisade layer	Tightly packed layer of long, thin palisade cells packed with chloroplasts to absorb light, these cells are most active in photosynthesis
Spongy layer	A layer of more rounded cells, loosely arranged with many air spaces between them to allow diffusion of carbon dioxide and oxygen through the leaf. These cells contain some chloroplasts, but not as many as palisade cells.
Leaf vein (vascular bundle)	Made from xylem and phloem cells. Xylem transports water and minerals into the leaf. Phloem transports food substances from the leaf to other parts of the plant.
Lower epidermis	Protects the leaf and contains stomata, controls water movement in to and out of leaf and is where most carbon dioxide and oxygen move in to and out of the leaf
Stomata	Pores that allow carbon dioxide and oxygen to move in to and out of the leaf. Guard cells can open or close stomata to prevent water loss from the leaf.

Questions

1   Choose one local plant. Sketch a leaf from this plant and label the external features. Write a short statement about each feature explaining how it helps photosynthesis to take place.

2   Copy and label Figure 8.3.2 to show the internal structures of a leaf.

3   Explain why the underside of leaves is often a paler green than the upper side.

4   Which cells contain most chloroplasts? Where are they situated?

5   What role do stomata play in helping photosynthesis take place?

Objectives

By the end of this topic you will be able to:

Objectives

By the end of this topic you will be able to:

- test for reducing sugars and starch
- carry out controlled investigations to show that light and chlorophyll are necessary for photosynthesis
- show that carbon dioxide is needed for photosynthesis.

B8.4 Investigating the conditions necessary for photosynthesis

You have learnt that plants need sunlight and chlorophyll in order for photosynthesis to take place. During photosynthesis plants produce glucose (known as a reducing sugar) and give off oxygen. Plants rapidly convert some of the glucose into starch. In this topic you are going to do some practical investigations to prove that light and chlorophyll are necessary for photosynthesis. You will carry out tests to show that plants make sugar and starch and do an experiment to show that plants give off oxygen during photosynthesis.

Investigating photosynthesis

Photosynthesis is the process by which plants make food. So, to find out whether photosynthesis has taken place, we have to be able to check whether a plant has made sugars or stored sugars in the form of starch.

- To test for reducing sugars (such as glucose) we can use Fehling's solution or Benedict's solution. Both solutions contain copper sulfate. If a reducing sugar is present, it reacts with the copper sulfate and forms a **precipitate** (solid particles that sink to the bottom of the container), which is usually green or brown.

- To test for starch we use iodine. If starch is present, the iodine turns **blue-black**.

However both sugar and starch are found in the cells of the plant, so if you want to test leaves, they need to be carefully prepared before you test them.

Now you are going to learn how to test for reducing sugar and starch so that you can apply these tests in other investigations to find out whether photosynthesis has taken place or not.

Safety

Wear goggles. Reagents are toxic and heating a water bath is potentially dangerous.

Practical activity

Testing for reducing sugars

Your teacher may use this activity to assess: M&M.

- You are going to test the leaves of a plant to see whether they contain any reducing sugars.

Materials

- Some green leaves from an onion plant
- Two test tubes
- A Bunsen burner and stand
- Benedict's or Fehling's solution
- A funnel and filter paper
- A pestle and mortar
- A beaker of water

Method

1 Tear a few pieces of onion leaf into the mortar.
2 Cover them with water and grind them into a paste.
3 Pour the mixture through the funnel and filter paper into the test tube.
4 Put some plain water into another test tube to act as a control.
5 Add the same amount of Benedict's or Fehling's solution to both test tubes.
6 Stand the test tubes in the beaker and heat them over a Bunsen burner until the mixture boils.

What happens to the solutions in the test tubes?

A green-brown or red colour means that there are reducing sugars present.

Plants do not absorb sugars from the soil because there are no sugars in soil (you can test soil to check), so how do the sugars get into the plant?

Practical activity

 Safety

Testing for starch

Your teacher may use this activity to assess: M&M.

- You are now going to learn how to test leaves for starch. Remember that starch is stored in the plant cells so you have to break down the cell walls before you can test the leaf. To do this, you boil the leaf in alcohol.

Materials

- A beaker
- A large test tube half full of alcohol (ethanol or methylated spirits)
- A leaf
- A Bunsen burner and stand
- Boiling water
- Iodine solution

Method

1 Place the leaf in a beaker of boiling water for about one minute to soften it.

2 Transfer the softened leaf to the test tube containing alcohol.

3 Place the test tube in the beaker of hot water. Allow the heat of the water to boil the alcohol. The leaf will turn white and become brittle.

4 Remove the leaf from the alcohol and dip it in hot water to soften it again.

5 Spread the leaf out on a white tile.

6 Add a few drops of iodine solution to the leaf.

Why do you think that the various steps in the method are necessary?

What do you notice?

If starch is present, the leaf will turn blue-black. If no starch is present, the iodine will remain brown.

We will use the starch test to check whether photosynthesis takes place in plants under certain conditions.

 Practical activity

Do plants need chlorophyll for photosynthesis?

Your teacher may use this activity to assess: ORR; M&M; A&I.

Materials

- A variegated leaf from a plant, such as a coleus (if you use a pot plant, make sure it has been in the Sun for several days)
- Materials to test for starch (see practical activity above)

Method

1 Remove a leaf from the plant.

2 Trace around it and colour your drawing to show which parts of the leaf are green.

3 Carry out a starch test on the whole leaf.

What do you notice?

Which parts of the leaf turned blue-black in iodine?

What can you conclude from this?

Practical activity

Do plants need light for photosynthesis?

Your teacher may use this activity to assess: ORR; M&M; A&I.

To do this experiment you will need two plants. One plant will serve as your control.

Both plants need to be de-starched before you start. To de-starch a plant you put it into a dark place, such as a cupboard for 24–48 hours. In this time, the plant will use up the starch in its leaves. Because we are going to test for starch as an end-product of photosynthesis, we have to make sure that there is no starch present to start with.

Method

1 Place one of the de-starched plants back in the cupboard.

2 Place the other one in the light. This is your control plant.

3 After two or three days, take a leaf from each plant and test it for starch.

Which plant has formed starch?

What can you conclude about light and photosynthesis from this?

(There are other methods of testing whether light is necessary for photosynthesis. Try to find out how you can do this test using one plant only.)

Safety

Sodium hydrogen carbonate is toxic, take care when using.

Practical activity

Showing that carbon dioxide is necessary for photosynthesis

Two students set up the experiment shown in Figure 8.4.1 to prove that carbon dioxide is necessary for photosynthesis. Study their experiment carefully and answer the questions that follow.

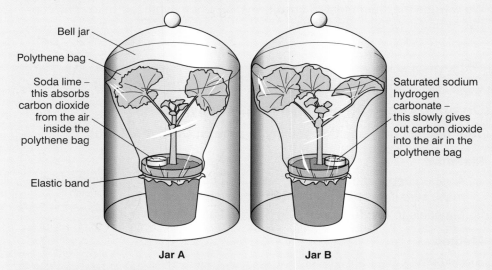

Bell jar

Polythene bag

Soda lime – this absorbs carbon dioxide from the air inside the polythene bag

Elastic band

Saturated sodium hydrogen carbonate – this slowly gives out carbon dioxide into the air in the polythene bag

Jar A   Jar B

▲ **Figure 8.4.1** An experiment to show that plants need carbon dioxide for photosynthesis

Our results

When we tested the leaves for starch, we found that the control plant had formed starch, but the experimental plant had not. As the conditions in both jars were the same, except that Jar A contained no carbon dioxide, we concluded that plants need carbon dioxide to form starch.

Questions

The students kept both plants in a cupboard for two days before the experiment.

1 Why was this necessary?

2 Why was it important to seal jar A properly?

3 Why did the students have to place soda lime in jar A?

4 Where did the plant in jar B get carbon dioxide from?

After carrying out these experiments, we know that plants need chlorophyll, light and carbon dioxide in order for photosynthesis to take place. Now you are going to do an experiment to show that oxygen is given off by plants during photosynthesis.

You cannot really show that terrestrial plants produce oxygen in a school laboratory. However, you can show this if you use aquatic plants such as *Elodea* or *Hydrilla*.

 Practical activity

To show that oxygen is given off during photosynthesis

Materials

For the experiment and the control:

- A beaker
- A funnel
- Modelling clay to support the funnel
- Sodium hydrogencarbonate powder
- A test tube
- Water and water plants

Method

1 Set up the apparatus as shown in Figure 8.4.2.

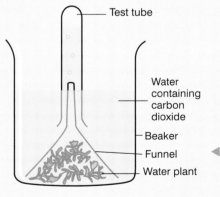

Test tube

Water containing carbon dioxide

Beaker

Funnel

Water plant

◀ **Figure 8.4.2** Experiment to show that oxygen is given off during photosynthesis

2 Place your experiment in the light and place your control in a dark place.

3 Leave them for two days.

What happens to the test tubes? Why?

How can you check whether the gas that has been produced in your experiment is oxygen?

Questions

1 Why do you test for starch as proof of photosynthesis?

2 Why do you need a control when you do experiments or investigations?

3 How can you prove that plants do not get starch and sugar from soil?

Environmental factors and rates of photosynthesis

You have seen that plants need chlorophyll, light and carbon dioxide for photosynthesis. However, the amount of light and carbon dioxide varies, so does temperature and the amount of water available to plants. These factors affect the rate at which plants make food by photosynthesis. They are called the **limiting factors** because if any of them falls to a low level, photosynthesis slows down or stops.

Light

Look at the graph in Figure 8.4.3. The graph shows how two plants photosynthesise in different light conditions. The rate of photosynthesis increases as the light intensity increases. Notice that once a particular light intensity is reached, the rate of photosynthesis stays constant even if the light intensity increases.

This graph also shows that the maximum rate of photosynthesis in plant A occurs at a lower level of light intensity than for plant B. However the maximum rate of photosynthesis for plant B is greater than the maximum rate for plant A. This suggests that plant A is more adapted to shady conditions because it can reach its maximum rate with lower levels of light. It also suggests that plant B needs a sunny place for maximum photosynthesis.

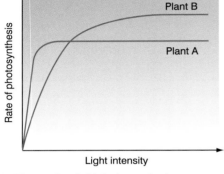

▲ **Figure 8.4.3** Light intensity is a limiting factor

Carbon dioxide

Figure 8.4.4 shows how the rate of photosynthesis increases with increased carbon dioxide concentrations. Again, the rate of photosynthesis reaches a maximum level at a particular concentration of carbon dioxide. The optimal rate for growing plants seems to be around 0.1% carbon dioxide. Some plant growers pump carbon dioxide into glass houses or tunnels to improve their crop yields.

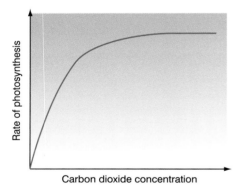

▲ **Figure 8.4.4** Carbon dioxide is a limiting factor

Warmth

Most plants grow best in warm conditions. Tropical plants (like those found in the Caribbean) thrive in temperatures of 20–30 °C. Above 40 °C enzymes are not able to work and photosynthesis cannot take place.

Water

Water is one of the raw materials of photosynthesis, but it is also essential for plant growth, for the transportation of foods and so many other cell processes that it is difficult to single it out as a specific condition for photosynthesis.

Plants need to make sure that they have enough nutrients for their life processes when there is no actual sunlight. Scientists now think that plants do fairly sophisticated arithmetic to distribute nutrients and to make sure their food supply lasts through the night (or through other periods with no sunlight). Read the article on p95, which appeared in the media in 2013, to find out more about this.

Plants are good at maths

PLANTS do maths every night to prevent themselves starving before dawn, scientists have discovered.

To keep themselves going in the absence of sunlight, they need to make their food-producing photosynthesis system work. Plants use division equations throughout the night to eke out their stores of starch until the sun reappears.

This is the first known example in nature of relatively sophisticated arithmetic being carried out by a relatively primitive life form, as opposed to the brain of an animal, scientists said.

If plants were to be without starch at night, they would quickly begin to starve, would stop growing and it would take several hours for them to recover, even after light returned.

'The capacity to perform arithmetic calculation is vital for plant growth and productivity,' Professor Alison Smith, a metabolic biologist who helped make the discovery, explained.

'The calculations are precise so that plants prevent starvation.'

© The Daily Telegraph (published in *The Times*, 3 July 2013)

Source: http://www.timeslive.co.za

Questions

1 The table shows the number of bubbles of gas given off in one minute by water weed grown under light of different colours.

Colour of light	Number of bubbles given off per minute
Blue	85
Green	10
Red	68

a What gas is given off by the plants? How could you check this?

b What does this suggest about the colour of light and the rate at which photosynthesis takes place?

c Suggest how this information could help gardeners to grow bigger plants in a shorter time.

2 Suggest why plants such as crotons (*Codiaeum*), which are found in many parts of the world are often bigger and healthier in tropical regions like the Caribbean.

B8.5 Mineral nutrition in plants

In order to grow well, plants need mineral nutrients which they absorb through their roots as solutions of salts from the soil. Plants need some minerals (macro-nutrients) in large amounts (kilograms per hectare). Trace minerals, or micro-nutrients, are the nutrients that plants need in very small amounts (a few parts per million by weight in the soil).

The importance of minerals for plants

Plants need the following mineral nutrients in large amounts:

- Nitrogen (N): is taken up in the form of nitrates and is used by the plants to make protein.

Objectives

By the end of this topic you will be able to:

- discuss the importance of minerals for plant nutrition
- explain the importance of nitrogen and magnesium in plant nutrition
- investigate the effects of nitrogen deficiency on plants.

- Phosphorus (P): is taken up in the form of phosphates and is used by plants to make cell membranes, for the development of roots and for the synthesis of nucleic acids.
- Potassium (K): is taken up as potassium salts and is used in the process of photosynthesis.

Plants also need calcium, magnesium and sulfur, but in much smaller amounts.

Table 8.5.1 shows three important plant nutrients. The table describes the effects each element has on plant growth, explains what happens to plants when this mineral is deficient in plants and lists the main sources of these nutrients.

▼ **Table 8.5.1** Plant nutrients and their effects on plants

Elements	Effect on plant growth	Signs of deficiency	Source of nutrient
Nitrogen (N)	Plants use it to: – form chlorophyll – photosynthesise – increase their biomass – build up proteins – produce larger 'crops' – control and regulate the uptake of P and K	Plants are: – small and stunted as they cannot make proteins – slow-growing – yellow, with weak leaves – over-mature, producing flowers and seeds before they have reached a good size	Nitrogen fixation, nitrates and ammonium compounds, artificial fertilisers
Phosphorus (P)	Plants use it to: – develop strong, healthy root systems – absorb food and water from soil – develop flowers and fruit – increase resistance to disease	Plants: – grow slowly and do not develop fully – have poorly developed roots – wilt quickly in dry conditions due to poor roots – have few flowers, most will drop off – develop red or purple patches on the leaves and stems	Can be supplied by fertilisers made from crushed rock, phosphate, superphosphate and bone meal
Potassium (K)	Plants use it to: – photosynthesise – develop strong stems – form seeds and grow well-developed fruits – resist disease	Plants are: – unable to photosynthesise well, so yellow spots form and leaves die off at the edges – small and stunted – weak-stemmed – discoloured, with yellow or orange margins on leaves – unable to form seeds and fruit properly	Most sandy soils are deficient. Can be supplied in the form of potassium chloride and potassium sulfate

Mineral deficiencies

Plants absorb mineral nutrients from the soil as they grow. If the plants die and decompose, the nutrients can be returned to the soil. However, if plants are harvested (crops and fruits), then the nutrients are removed from the soil. This can lead to deficiencies, particularly of the macro-nutrients.

Plant nutrients dissolve in water and they may be washed away (leached) when water drains down through the soil. Leached nutrients may end up in water sources, like streams or rivers, or they may remain trapped in the groundwater far below the surface of the soil.

Farming can make natural soil deficiencies much worse. For example, recent research in Latin America and the Caribbean region showed that crops are removing significantly more nutrients from the soils than are being replenished either naturally or with fertilisers. Without nutrients, plants cannot grow well and this has serious implications for food production in the future.

You are now going to do an experiment to see what happens when plants do not have enough nitrogen.

Practical activity

Investigating the effect of nitrogen deficiency

Your teacher may use this activity to assess: ORR; M&M; A&I.

You are going to see what happens when you plant seedlings in clean sand (nitrogen-poor soil).

Materials
- Bean or other seedlings
- Two trays of clean sand
- Plant fertiliser containing nitrogen

Method

1 Plant seedlings in both trays.

2 Add fertiliser (according to instructions) to the sand in one tray. This is your control.

3 Water the trays and place them in a sunny spot where they will not be disturbed. Leave them there for at least two weeks. Water both trays regularly during this time so that they do not dry out.

Observe what happens to the plants in each tray.

Write a short report outlining what you can conclude from this investigation.

⚠ **Safety**

Wash your hands after using fertiliser.

Questions

1 Look at the leaf in Figure 8.5.1 from a field with very well-drained sandy soil.

   a What can the leaf tell you about the soil?

   b What mineral do you think is deficient in this soil?

   c How could it be replaced?

2 A local gardener finds that the plants in one bed have very small roots and purple patches on some younger leaves. What advice could you give this gardener to help him deal with the problem?

3 The graph in Figure 8.5.2 shows you how fertiliser use increased in the Caribbean over a 36-year period.

   a Why is it necessary to use fertilisers on agricultural soils?

   b The most common fertilisers are called NPK fertilisers. Why?

   c What are the effects on plants likely to be if the soil becomes deficient in nitrogen?

   d What are the long-term effects of poor soil likely to be for plants, humans and other animals?

   e Find out two ways in which fertilisers can harm the environment.

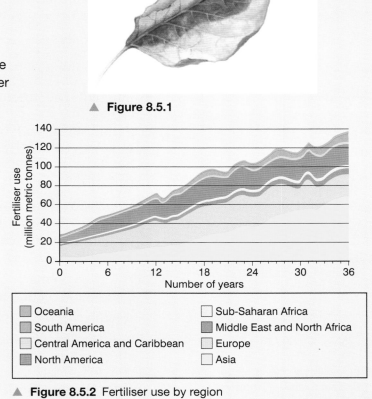

▲ **Figure 8.5.1**

▲ **Figure 8.5.2** Fertiliser use by region

B9 Life chemicals and nutrition

Chemical substances such as carbohydrates (sugars and starches), lipids and proteins are the basic building blocks of all living organisms. In this unit you are going to learn more about these substances and their role in providing nutrition for humans and other animals.

B9.1 Food substances

Objectives

By the end of this topic you will be able to:

- identify and describe carbohydrates, lipids and proteins as food substances
- state the chemical and physical properties of different food substances.

All life processes require energy. Energy for life processes comes from the carbohydrates, proteins and lipids contained in the food we eat. The energy is stored in the chemical bonds of their molecules and it is released during cellular respiration. (You will learn about cellular respiration in topic B11.1.) Carbohydrates, proteins and lipids are also called food substances or energy nutrients.

Carbohydrates

Carbohydrates are compounds containing carbon, hydrogen and oxygen only. Carbohydrates are very important for all living organisms because they provide energy. When carbohydrates react with oxygen, water and carbon dioxide are formed and energy is released. This reaction takes place slowly inside cells and energy is released in a controlled way to be used by cells for all their life processes. Carbohydrates include sugars, starches and cellulose.

The formula for glucose in full

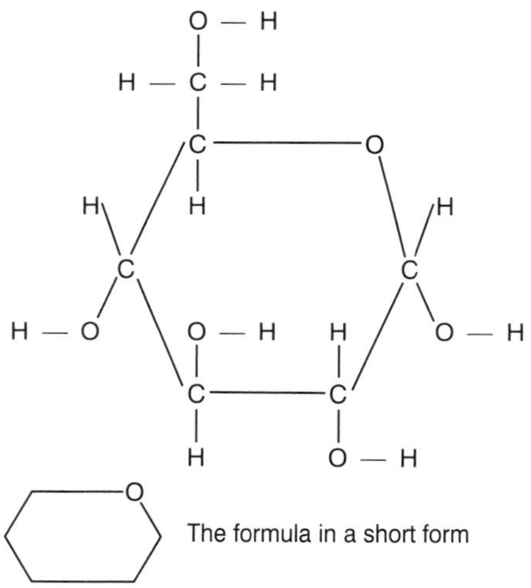
The formula in a short form

▲ **Figure 9.1.1** The arrangement of atoms in a molecule of glucose

Sugars

Glucose and fructose are simple sugars. They both have the same chemical formula of $C_6H_{12}O_6$, but the way atoms are arranged in their molecules is different. The structure of a molecule of glucose is shown in Figure 9.1.1. You can see that six of the atoms (five carbon and one oxygen) are joined to form a ring. Sugars with one ring of atoms are called monosaccharides. Simple sugars are soluble (they dissolve) in water and they taste sweet.

Two molecules of glucose can join together to form one molecule of maltose, another sugar. Maltose ($C_{12}H_{22}O_{11}$) is a disaccharide because each molecule contains two sugar rings. You can see a simplified representation of this in Figure 9.1.2. Table sugar (sucrose) is also a disaccharide. Glucose combines with fructose to form sucrose. Maltose and sucrose are complex sugars. Complex sugars, like simple sugars, are soluble in water and they taste sweet.

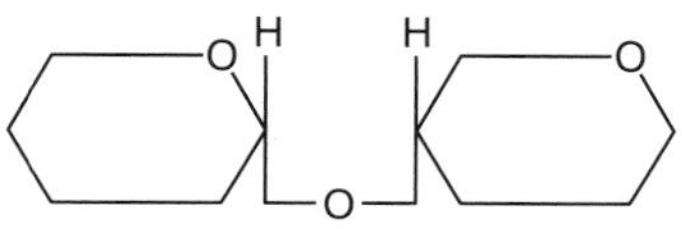

▲ **Figure 9.1.2** The structure of sugar rings in maltose (simplified)

Condensation and hydrolysis

When two organic molecules such as glucose and fructose join together to form disaccharides, a condensation reaction occurs. Condensation is a reaction in which two molecules join together and a water molecule is released. Disaccharides can be broken down into simple monosaccharides again by hydrolysis. Hydrolysis is a reaction in which the chemical bonds of a molecule are split by the addition of water (H_2O).

Starch, glycogen and cellulose

Starch, glycogen and cellulose are all carbohydrates. Starch is a stored food substance in plants cells. Glycogen is a stored food substance in animal cells. Cellulose is the name given to fibres in the walls of plant cells. These compounds are called polysaccharides because their molecules contain many (hundreds) of sugar rings, as you can see in Figure 9.1.3.

Polysaccharides do not taste sweet. Starch and glycogen are slightly soluble in water and cellulose is insoluble. As starch and glycogen are only slightly soluble, they can stay in the cells of an organism without being dissolved. This makes them good food stores. Cells convert starch and glycogen into glucose which is soluble. Glucose is oxidised in cells to release energy.

Some polysaccharides are used as building materials in organisms. Cellulose fibres are used to form the walls of plant cells. The tough framework of fibres is what makes the plant cell wall rigid.

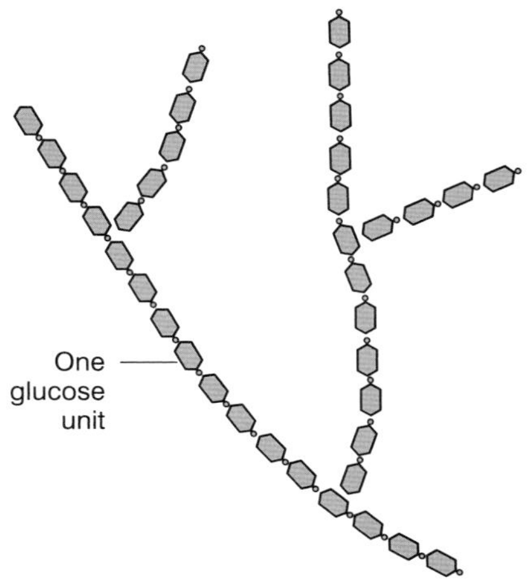

▲ **Figure 9.1.3** Model of part of a starch molecule

Lipids

Lipids are fats and oils. Lipids are made of carbon, hydrogen and oxygen. Most fats are solid at room temperature while most oils are liquid at room temperature. Fats and oils feel greasy and they are not soluble in water.

Lipids are a mixture of compounds of glycerol with fatty acids. Saturated fats have only single bonds between the carbon atoms in their fatty acids. Monounsaturated fats have one double bond between carbon atoms in their fatty acids. Polyunsaturated fats have more than one double bond per molecule. Scientists believe that a diet high in saturated fats is unhealthy and they have linked saturated fats to an increased risk of heart disease.

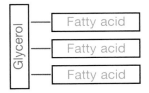

▲ **Figure 9.1.4** The general structure of a lipid

Proteins

Proteins are compounds that contain carbon, hydrogen, oxygen, nitrogen and sometimes sulfur or phosphorus. Proteins are very important for the following reasons:

- Proteins are needed to make new tissues. In order to grow and repair damaged tissue, organisms need proteins.

- Enzymes are proteins. The reactions that take place in living organisms could not happen quickly enough without enzymes.

- Hormones are proteins which control the activities of organisms.

- Proteins can be oxidised during respiration to provide energy.

Every protein molecule is made up of a long chain of amino acids. There are 20 amino acids and they all have the general formula shown in Figure 9.1.5. Because each amino acid is different, they can form quite complex patterns and large molecules when they are joined together to form proteins.

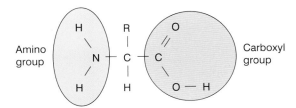

▲ **Figure 9.1.5** The general structure of an amino acid

Key fact

Cellulose is not soluble so humans cannot digest it. It does however form an important part of our diet because it provides roughage and fibre.

Questions

1 Which three elements are found in carbohydrates, lipids and proteins?

2 Define the terms: 'monosaccharide', 'hydrolysis', 'condensation' and 'polysaccharide'.

3 In which kind of food would you find the following substances: fructose, cellulose, sucrose, oil, fat, amino acids.

4 What is the main function of proteins?

Objectives

By the end of this topic you will be able to:

- carry out tests to identify different food substances
- explain the role of hydrolysis and neutralisation in testing for non-reducing sugars.

B9.2 Testing for food substances

You can carry out various simple tests in the classroom or laboratory to find out whether foods contain certain chemical nutrients. In this topic you will learn more about the types of tests that you can use on different foods to find out whether they contain sugars, starch, lipids or proteins.

Simple food tests

Table 9.2.1 describes the tests that you can use to investigate whether foods contain different substances. Pay particular attention to the last column which tells you about the colour changes you can expect when each substance is present.

▼ **Table 9.2.1** Tests for different food substances

Food substance	Test	Method	Additional information	Results
Simple sugar (reducing sugar) e.g. glucose	Benedict's test	Mash food and mix it with water. Put each suspension into a test tube and add equal amounts of Benedict's solution. Boil the mixture.	Benedict's solution will not react with non-reducing sugars. These will only react if they are first broken down to simple sugars (see below).	If an orange-red precipitate forms, reducing sugars are present
Complex sugar (non-reducing sugar) e.g. sucrose	Hydrolysis and neutralisation, then Benedict's test	Boil the food with a few drops of diluted hydrochloric acid to break down the sugar. Add sodium bicarbonate to neutralise the mixture. When it stops fizzing, do the Benedict's test.	Test for simple sugars first. If the solution reacts there is no point in testing for complex sugars as your results will be biased.	If an orange-red precipitate forms, reducing sugars have been produced by breaking down the complex sugar in the food
Starch	Starch test with iodine	Add a few drops of iodine solution to the food	There is no need to 'de-starch' food like you do with leaves	A blue-black colour indicates starch is present
Lipids	Grease spot test	Rub a small piece of the food onto filter paper. Hold the paper up to the light to check if food has left a translucent mark.	To make sure the mark is not water, dry the paper carefully. If the mark remains, it was made by lipids, not water.	A translucent greasy mark indicates food contains lipids
Lipids	Emulsion test	Dissolve the food in ethanol. Pour the solution into a clean test tube of water.	Fat is not water soluble, but it will dissolve in pure alcohol (ethanol)	A white cloudy emulsion shows lipids are present in the food
Proteins	Biuret test	Mash the food and mix it with water. Add a few drops of potassium hydroxide until the solution clears. Then add a few drops of dilute copper sulfate and shake the mixture.	You can use sodium hydroxide in place of potassium hydroxide in this test, but you should be careful as it is harmful to the skin	A violet or purple colour shows that protein is present in the food

Practical activity

Testing food substances

Your teacher may use this activity to assess: ORR; M&M; A&I.

You are going to test a range of foods to see what chemical nutrients each contains.

Materials

- Samples of orange juice, banana, bread, milk, egg white, butter, breakfast cereal and sweet biscuits or cake
- Two other samples of foods that you eat regularly
- Equipment for testing

Method

1 Divide the foods into groups and decide which test(s) you will perform on each.
2 Carry out the tests.
3 Record your results using a table like this one:

Food sample	Test carried out	What we noticed (observations)	What this tells us (deductions)

 Safety

When you perform tests to find out about food substances, it is important to keep the different foods you are testing separate from each other to avoid contamination. This means you should keep them in separate dishes, use separate knives or spatulas to cut them up and clean test tubes after each test. For most tests, you will need to mash the food up or cut it into small pieces before you can test it. If you use a pestle and mortar for this, remember to clean it properly after each test to remove all traces of the previous food.

Questions

1 Copy and complete the following table to show which reagents you would use to test for each compound and what changes you would observe for a positive result.

Chemical compound	Reagent(s)	Change for a positive result
Starch		
Proteins		
Fats		
Glucose solution (concentrated)		

2 Explain the role of hydrochloric acid and bicarbonate of soda in the test for non-reducing sugars.

B9.3 Enzymes

The molecules in cells are constantly broken down and rebuilt in an ongoing series of chemical reactions. The rate at which chemical reactions take place is controlled by a special group of large proteins called enzymes. This makes enzymes very important in all cell functions.

The importance of enzymes

The chemical reactions that take place in living organisms constitute the organism's metabolism. Enzymes are essential for breaking down and building up reactions in metabolism.

Enzymes can be used over and over again, so only small amounts are needed in cells. Cells make enzymes as they are needed (this is controlled by the cell nucleus). Different types of cell make different types and amounts of enzymes depending on the metabolic functions that the cell carries out.

Objectives

By the end of this topic you will be able to:

- explain the importance of enzymes for cells
- list the characteristics of enzymes
- investigate the effect of temperature and pH on enzyme action
- interpret graphs and tables to deduce the effects of temperature and pH on enzyme action.

Key fact

Aspirin slows down the enzyme amylase therefore enzyme activity is lessened.

How enzymes work

Enzymes are catalysts. Catalysts help chemical reactions take place but they are not used up in the reaction itself. Catalysts control the rate of a reaction (speeding it up or slowing it down) and they remain chemically unchanged at the end of the reaction.

Enzymes are specific in their action. This means that they catalyse only one type of reaction. They work by providing an active site (surface) where the reaction can take place. The substance that the enzyme helps to react is called the substrate. The substances formed in the reaction are called the products of the reaction. Figure 9.3.1 shows you how an enzyme called amylase (found in our saliva) acts as a catalyst to break down starch to form sugar molecules.

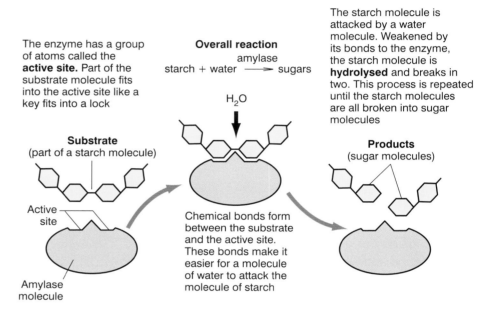

▲ **Figure 9.3.1** How the enzyme amylase catalyses the breakdown of starch

Optimal conditions for enzyme action

Enzymes need certain conditions to work well. Most enzymes work best at a certain temperature. If the temperature varies from this level, the rate of the reaction that the enzyme is catalysing will decrease.

Acidity and alkalinity (pH) are also important for enzyme functioning. Enzymes work best at a particular pH. If the pH varies from this level, the rate of the reaction will decrease.

Enzymes are sensitive to temperature and pH because of their protein structure. High temperatures and extreme acidity or alkalinity cause enzymes to stop working. We say that they are denatured. When an enzyme is denatured, the active site breaks down and the substrate no longer fits. The graphs in Figure 9.3.2 show how enzyme action is affected by temperature and pH.

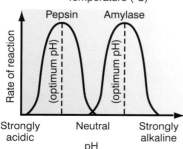

▲ **Figure 9.3.2** The effects of temperature and pH on enzyme action

You are now going to investigate the effect of temperature on the activity of the digestive enzyme amylase and the effect of changing pH on the enzyme catalase.

 Practical activity

Investigating the effect of temperature on enzyme activity

The enzyme amylase breaks down starch into simple sugars. You can find out how temperature affects this process by mixing a starch solution with amylase and then keeping the mixtures at different temperatures in a water bath.

Use iodine solution to test a drop of each mixture for starch at regular intervals and record your results. When the iodine no longer turns black, the reaction has finished and the starch has been broken down.

Your results will show you how temperature affects the rate of enzyme reaction.

What to do

1 Plan and carry out an investigation based on the information given above.

2 Write a short report of your investigation.

 **Exam tip**

In an examination you might be asked how different factors affect enzyme activity, for example how amylase is affected when it reaches the stomach.

 Safety

Iodine is an irritant. Wear goggles and wash off skin.

 Practical activity

Does pH affect enzyme activity?

You have seen that amylase reacts with starch to break it down into sugar and you know you can test for starch using an iodine solution. In this experiment you are going to see how changing the pH of the reaction affects the enzyme activity.

1 Set up four test tubes as indicated in Figure 9.3.3.

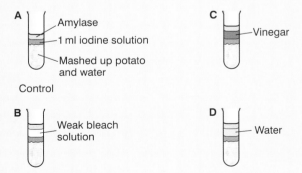

A — Amylase
— 1 ml iodine solution
— Mashed up potato and water
Control

B — Weak bleach solution

C — Vinegar

D — Water

▲ **Figure 9.3.3**

2 Add 1 ml of iodine solution to each test tube. It should turn blue-black because there is starch in each test tube.

3 The colour will disappear as the starch breaks down. Time how long it takes for the colour to disappear in each test tube.

What does this experiment suggest about pH and the action of amylase?

Safety

Take precautions when using bleach and iodine.

Exam tip

In an examination you might be asked how to perform a food test or the results when the test is positive for unfamiliar samples. Remember the tests work the same way as long as the food is present.

Questions

1   Many metabolic processes are controlled by enzymes, for example respiration. When you are ill and have a fever, your body temperature may rise to 40 °C. How do you think this would affect your metabolic processes? Why?

2   Table 9.3.1 gives you the optimum pH values for different enzymes.

▼ **Table 9.3.1** Optimum activity pH for different enzymes

Enzyme	Optimum pH
Lipase (pancreatic)	8.0
Lipase (stomach)	4.0–5.0
Pepsin	1.5–1.6
Trypsin	7.8–8.7
Urease	7.0
Invertase	4.5
Maltase	6.1–6.8
Amylase (pancreatic)	8.0
Catalase	7.0

The graph in Figure 9.3.4 shows how pH affects the rate of three enzyme-controlled actions.

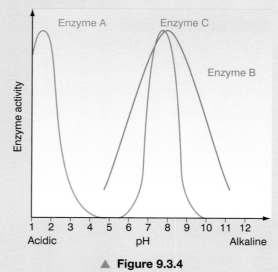

▲ **Figure 9.3.4**

a   Which enzyme works best in strongly acid conditions?

b   Which enzyme works best in a neutral pH?

c   Which enzyme works best in alkaline conditions?

d   Which enzyme works in the biggest range of pH?

e   Based on the information in the table, which enzymes could these be?

Food contains nutrients that our bodies need to survive. However, these nutrients need to be converted into substances that our bodies can absorb and use. In this unit you will learn how this happens in the digestive system.

B10.1 The digestive system

Cells are microscopic. So, how do the large pieces of food we eat get into our cells? Obviously the pieces of food we eat are too big to enter our cells. These pieces of food must be broken down into smaller, simpler, soluble substances so that they can enter our cells and be used in our bodies. This means that carbohydrates have to be broken down into simple sugars, proteins into amino acids and lipids into fatty acids and glycerol.

The process of breaking down food is called digestion and it takes place in the organs of our digestive system. (The digestive system is shown in detail in Figure 10.1.3 on p107.)

The process of digestion

Food enters our digestive system through the mouth (ingestion). Before the food can be distributed and used in our bodies it has to be broken down or digested. There are two kinds of digestion: mechanical digestion and chemical digestion. Once food is digested, it is absorbed from the digestive system into the bloodstream. The blood transports the digested food throughout the body where it is assimilated to be used in metabolic processes. Any food which cannot be digested or absorbed is passed out of the body (egestion).

Mechanical digestion

Mechanical digestion is the process by which large food particles are physically broken down into smaller food particles (see Figure 10.1.1a). Your teeth start the process of mechanical digestion by tearing and grinding up food. You will study teeth in more detail in topic B10.2.

Muscles in the organs of the digestive system also play a role in mechanical digestion as they squeeze and push food through the system, mixing it with digestive juices as they do so.

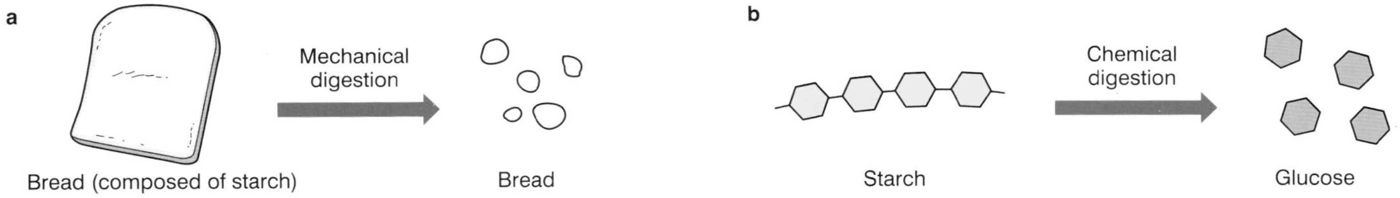

Objectives

By the end of this topic you will be able to:

- define the terms 'ingestion', 'digestion' and 'egestion'
- identify the enzymes involved in digestion and name their products
- describe the structure of the human digestive system
- relate the parts of the digestive system to their functions.

a Bread (composed of starch) → Mechanical digestion → Bread

b Starch → Chemical digestion → Glucose

▲ **Figure 10.1.1 a** Mechanical digestion and **b** chemical digestion

Chemical digestion and digestive enzymes

Chemical digestion is the process by which food molecules are chemically changed into smaller, water-soluble molecules (see Figure 10.1.1b). Chemical digestion takes place as a result of digestive juices that are produced by different organs in our digestive system. The digestive juices contain digestive enzymes which are vital in chemical digestion.

Digestion uses nearly one hundred different enzymes to speed up the chemical reactions that break down food. Without these enzymes the food we eat would break down so slowly that we would starve to death.

Digestive enzymes catalyse the breakdown of food by hydrolysis. In hydrolysis, water splits molecules of carbohydrates, proteins and lipids into smaller molecules, as shown in Figure 10.1.2.

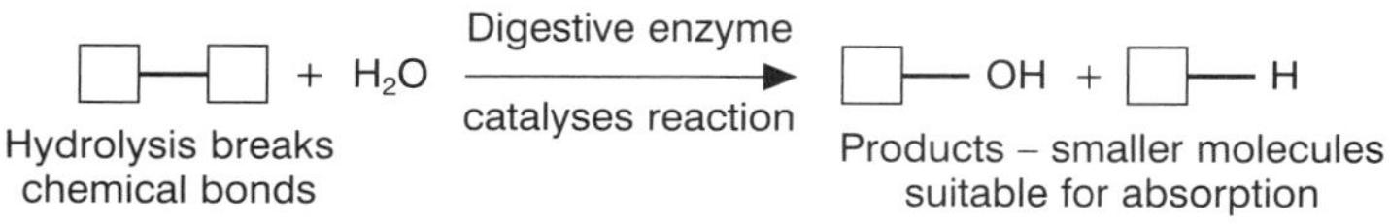

▲ **Figure 10.1.2** Enzymes break down food components by hydrolysis

The main digestive enzymes are listed in Table 10.1.1. These enzymes are grouped according to the reactions they catalyse. For example, carbohydrate digesting enzymes are grouped as 'carbohydrases'. The table also lists where these enzymes are found in the digestive system.

▼ **Table 10.1.1** Enzymes that digest carbohydrates, proteins and lipids

Enzyme group	Examples	Where found	Food component digested	Products of digestion
Carbohydrases (catalyse digestion of carbohydrates)	Amylase Maltase	Mouth Small intestine	Starch Maltose	Maltose Glucose
Proteases (catalyse digestion of proteins)	Pepsin Chrymotrypsin Dipeptidase	Stomach Small intestine	Proteins Polypeptides Dipeptides	Polypeptides Dipeptides Amino acids
Lipases (catalyse digestion of lipids)	Lipase	Small intestine	Fats	Fatty acids Glycerol

When digestion is complete, the food has been broken down into glucose, amino acids, fatty acids and glycerol. These particles are small enough to pass into the bloodstream by diffusion. Once in the blood, they are carried to the cells of our bodies where they are used for energy, growth and repair.

Key fact

The absence of even one digestive enzyme can make you ill. People who do not produce the enzyme lactase are lactose intolerant. They cannot digest the sugars found in milk (lactose) and they get cramps and diarrhoea if they drink milk or eat milk products because the sugar builds up in their digestive system.

Questions

1 Why do living things need food?

2 What are the main components of our food?

3 When we eat food, it needs to be digested. Explain what is meant by digestion and why it is important.

4 Explain the difference between mechanical digestion and chemical digestion and give an example of each type.

5 Why are enzymes important in the process of digestion?

The human digestive system

Figure 10.1.3 shows the human digestive system. The tube which extends from the mouth to the anus in the digestive system can also be called the gut or the alimentary canal. The functions of the main organs and the time that food spends in that region are described next to the diagram.

The digestive system is 7–9 m long. Food moves through the digestive system in one to three days.

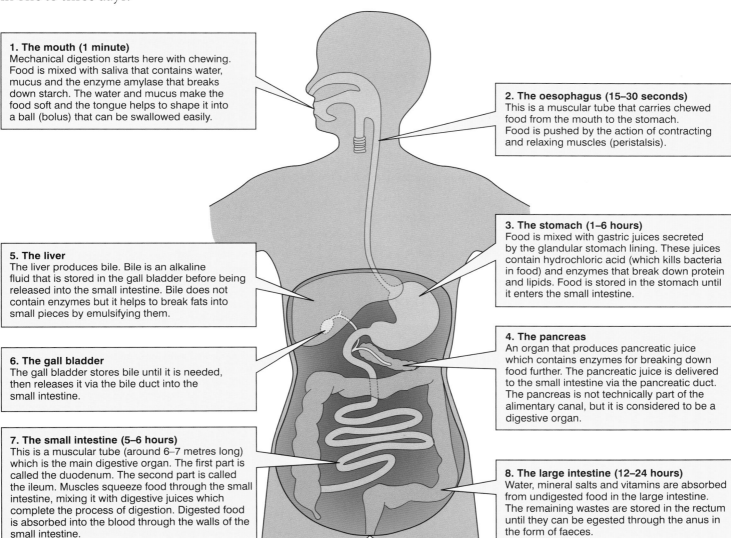

1. The mouth (1 minute)
Mechanical digestion starts here with chewing. Food is mixed with saliva that contains water, mucus and the enzyme amylase that breaks down starch. The water and mucus make the food soft and the tongue helps to shape it into a ball (bolus) that can be swallowed easily.

2. The oesophagus (15–30 seconds)
This is a muscular tube that carries chewed food from the mouth to the stomach. Food is pushed by the action of contracting and relaxing muscles (peristalsis).

3. The stomach (1–6 hours)
Food is mixed with gastric juices secreted by the glandular stomach lining. These juices contain hydrochloric acid (which kills bacteria in food) and enzymes that break down protein and lipids. Food is stored in the stomach until it enters the small intestine.

5. The liver
The liver produces bile. Bile is an alkaline fluid that is stored in the gall bladder before being released into the small intestine. Bile does not contain enzymes but it helps to break fats into small pieces by emulsifying them.

6. The gall bladder
The gall bladder stores bile until it is needed, then releases it via the bile duct into the small intestine.

4. The pancreas
An organ that produces pancreatic juice which contains enzymes for breaking down food further. The pancreatic juice is delivered to the small intestine via the pancreatic duct. The pancreas is not technically part of the alimentary canal, but it is considered to be a digestive organ.

7. The small intestine (5–6 hours)
This is a muscular tube (around 6–7 metres long) which is the main digestive organ. The first part is called the duodenum. The second part is called the ileum. Muscles squeeze food through the small intestine, mixing it with digestive juices which complete the process of digestion. Digested food is absorbed into the blood through the walls of the small intestine.

8. The large intestine (12–24 hours)
Water, mineral salts and vitamins are absorbed from undigested food in the large intestine. The remaining wastes are stored in the rectum until they can be egested through the anus in the form of faeces.

▲ **Figure 10.1.3** The structure of the human digestive system and how it functions

Some food does not need to be digested

Not all food is digested. Vitamins do not need to be digested because they are already small, soluble molecules that can pass into the bloodstream by diffusion.

Humans cannot digest cellulose (fibre). However, fibre is important in the digestive system as it provides bulk that helps the movement of food through the digestive system and has been shown to stimulate peristalsis (muscular action of the intestines). Fibre is one of the main components of the solid waste (faeces) that passes out of the digestive system during egestion. The formation of faeces is easier if your diet contains lots of plant materials. One of the best sources of dietary fibre is unprocessed bran.

Moving food through the digestive system

Food is moved through the intestines by the repeated contraction and relaxation of muscles. This muscular action is called peristalsis. Figure 10.1.4 shows you how this happens.

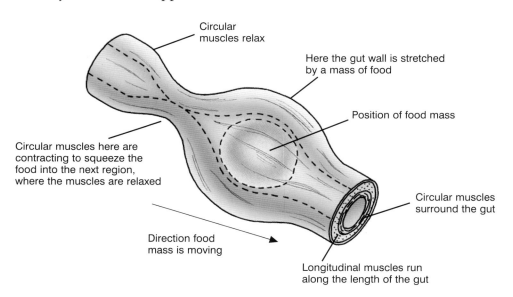

Circular muscles relax

Here the gut wall is stretched by a mass of food

Position of food mass

Circular muscles here are contracting to squeeze the food into the next region, where the muscles are relaxed

Circular muscles surround the gut

Direction food mass is moving

Longitudinal muscles run along the length of the gut

▲ **Figure 10.1.4** Peristalsis moves food through the digestive system

Questions

1 Copy and complete the flow diagram to the right to summarise the parts of the human digestive system.

2 What sort of food is digested by saliva?

3 How does chewing food aid digestion?

4 How does food get down your oesophagus?

5 What two important things are produced by the stomach lining?

6 What is the optimum pH for the digestive enzymes in the stomach likely to be? How do you know this?

7 Why is the small intestine the main digestive organ?

8 The large intestine absorbs water from food. Where does this water come from?

9 Why is fibre the main component of faeces?

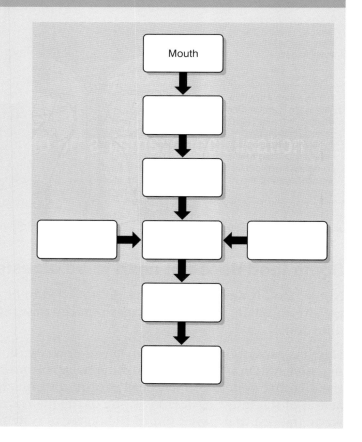

Mouth

B10.2 Teeth and their role in digestion

Humans need teeth. Without teeth we would not be able to talk properly and we would not be able to eat solid foods.

Chewing food

Think about how you bite and chew a piece of fruit. Your front teeth cut a piece out of the fruit. Your back teeth grind up the piece of fruit that you have eaten. The process of chewing food by moving your jaws and teeth is called mastication. Teeth are our feeding structures and they allow us to break food down into smaller pieces so that we can swallow it. Breaking down the food also increases the surface area of the food so that enzymes can act on it more easily.

What are teeth made of, and why do we have different types?

Human teeth

Humans have four basic types of teeth. The shape of each type of tooth is related to the function it plays in biting and chewing food. We can say that teeth are adapted for different kinds of feeding. Table 10.2.1 shows the four main types of human teeth and their functions.

▼ **Table 10.2.1** Human teeth and their functions

Type of tooth		Function
Incisor Chisel-shaped tooth		Biting off pieces of food Cutting food
Canine (also called eye tooth) Pointed cone-shaped tooth		Biting food Cutting food and tearing off pieces of food
Premolar Broad, uneven surfaced tooth with 'bumps' called cusps		Crushing and grinding food
Molar Broad, flattened but uneven-surfaced tooth with 'bumps' called cusps		Crushing and grinding food

The different types of tooth are positioned in the mouth according to their function. Figure 10.2.1 shows you the position of teeth in an adult human jaw. Note that there are 32 teeth in a full set of adult teeth: eight incisors, four canines, eight premolars and 12 molars.

Humans have two sets of teeth. The first set of teeth is called milk teeth. These form in the jaw before birth and they begin to appear through the gums at the age of three to six months in most children. There are 20 milk teeth in a full set. The milk teeth are pushed out and replaced by permanent teeth between the ages of 6 and 12. A third set of molars, called wisdom teeth, only appear after the age of 18. In some people, these do not appear at all.

By the end of this topic you will be able to:

- describe the role that teeth play in mechanical digestion
- identify different types of teeth and their functions
- draw and label a simple diagram of a tooth.

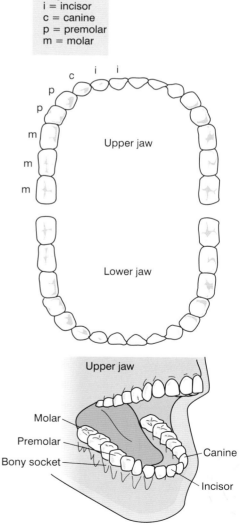

Key
i = incisor
c = canine
p = premolar
m = molar

▲ **Figure 10.2.1** How human teeth are arranged in the mouth

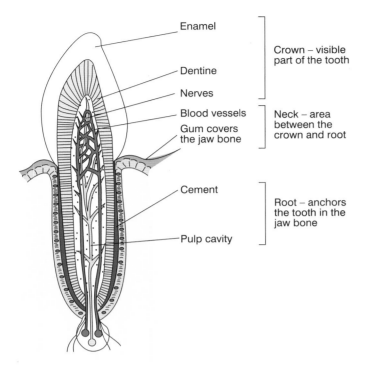

▲ **Figure 10.2.2** The internal structure of a human tooth

Enamel
Dentine
Nerves
Blood vessels
Gum covers the jaw bone
Cement
Pulp cavity

Crown – visible part of the tooth
Neck – area between the crown and root
Root – anchors the tooth in the jaw bone

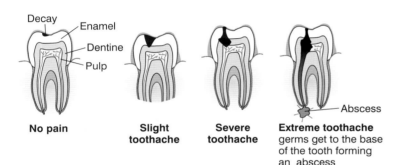

Decay
Enamel
Dentine
Pulp

No pain

Slight toothache

Severe toothache

Extreme toothache
germs get to the base of the tooth forming an abscess

Abscess

The structure of a tooth

Figure 10.2.2 shows you the structure of a canine tooth.

If you look at the diagram you can see that blood vessels and nerves enter the pulp cavity through a hole at the base of the tooth's root. In carnivores, such as dogs and cats, and omnivores, such as humans, this hole closes up when the tooth is fully grown. We say that the tooth has a closed root. The tooth no longer produces dentine and it stops growing. In herbivores, this doesn't happen – their teeth get worn away by the abrasive food they eat, so the teeth need to keep growing. For this reason, their roots stay open and the tooth continues to make dentine and grow throughout the animal's life.

Tooth decay

Tooth enamel is very hard. However, it can be dissolved by acids. When you eat food, especially foods rich in sugar, the remains of the food can settle on your teeth and in the spaces between them. Bacteria in your mouth mix with saliva and collect on these food remains where they multiply to form plaque. The bacteria use the sugars on your teeth for their own metabolic processes and excrete acids that wear away the enamel on your teeth.

Figure 10.2.3 shows the process of tooth decay. You can reduce the risk of tooth decay by brushing your teeth properly and regularly. Reducing the amount of sugar in your diet also helps to prevent tooth decay.

◀ **Figure 10.2.3** Tooth decay can lead to serious pain, gum disease and the eventual loss of teeth

Questions

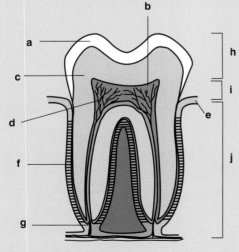

▲ **Figure 10.2.4** The internal structure of a molar

1 Copy Figure 10.2.4 showing the internal structure of a molar into your book. Replace the letters **a** to **j** with the correct labels.

2 Figure 10.2.5 shows you the teeth of a sheep and the teeth of a dog.

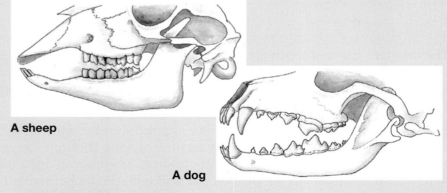

A sheep

A dog

▲ **Figure 10.2.5** The teeth of a sheep and a dog

a Describe two ways in which the teeth of a sheep are different to those of a human. Give a reason for each difference.

b Describe two ways in which the teeth of a dog are different to those of a human. Give a reason for each difference.

B10.3 Absorbing and assimilating food

Figure 10.3.1 summarises what happens to food as it moves through the digestive system to reach the small intestine.

Food at start	In mouth	In stomach	In small intestine	After digestion
Protein				Amino acids
Carbohydrate				Simple sugars
Fats				Fatty acids and glycerol
Minerals				Minerals
Vitamins				Vitamins

Objectives

By the end of this topic you will be able to:

● describe how the products of digestion are absorbed

● explain the role of the liver in relation to the products of digestion

● define 'assimilation'.

◄ **Figure 10.3.1** The progress of digestion. Solid blocks of colour represent the nutrients in food before digestion.

Absorption is the movement of substances into the cells of an organism. In humans, most absorption takes place in the ileum (small intestine) although small amounts of minerals, vitamins and water are absorbed by the lining of the stomach. Water is absorbed by the large intestine.

If you refer back to Figure 10.1.3 on p107, you can see that our intestines are folded and coiled to fit as much of the alimentary canal as possible into the restricted space in the abdominal cavity. The extra length gained by folding and coiling means that food travels a greater distance through the digestive system so that enzymes have more time to digest the food.

The extra length also provides a greater surface area for absorption. Inside the small intestine, the surface area is further increased by closely packed finger-like structures called **villi**. Figure 10.3.2 will help you to understand how the villi increase the surface area.

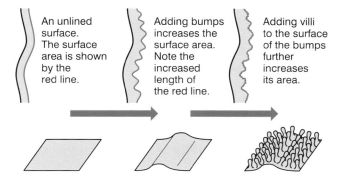

An unlined surface. The surface area is shown by the red line.

Adding bumps increases the surface area. Note the increased length of the red line.

Adding villi to the surface of the bumps further increases its area.

◄ **Figure 10.3.2** Villi cover the inside surface of the small intestine and increase its surface area

Figure 10.3.3 shows you the inside structure of a villus (singular of villi). Absorption takes place when nutrients pass through its cells and into the blood and lymph vessels. Most fatty acids and fat-soluble vitamins pass into the lymph vessels. Water, glucose, glycerol, amino acids and other substances pass into the network of capillary blood vessels. From there they are transported to the liver. Microvilli project from the surface of each cell lining the villus. These increase the surface area for absorption about 20 times more than the villi alone and enable nutrients to be absorbed quickly from digested food before peristalsis moves it on.

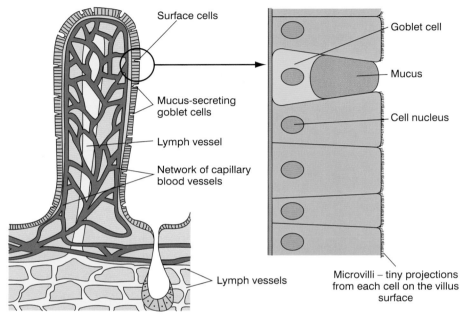

▲ **Figure 10.3.3** The structure of a villus

The role of the liver in distributing and using products of digestion

Once food has been absorbed it is transported to the liver. The fate of the products depends largely on what cells need.

The liver is very important because it controls the levels of many substances as they are transported through the body. The liver also breaks down unwanted or toxic substances.

Glucose is one substance whose level is controlled by the liver. As the cells of the body demand glucose for respiration, the liver releases more glucose into the bloodstream. If glucose levels are sufficient, the liver is able to store excess glucose in the form of glycogen. The liver also controls the levels of amino acids by converting excess amino acids to urea in the process of deamination. The urea is excreted in urine.

You have already learnt that the liver produces bile which is stored in the gall bladder. The liver releases bile into the small intestine as it is needed to digest lipids.

The liver regulates cholesterol levels in the blood and it can store excess lipids. Vitamins A, B and D and iron can also be stored in the liver.

An important role of the liver is to break down substances we do not need or that are toxic to the cells. These substances include some drugs and alcohol.

Assimilation of products of digestion

Once food has been ingested, digested, absorbed and transported to our cells it can become part of our body and play a role in our metabolic processes. We say the food has been assimilated. Once food has been assimilated, you cannot tell where it came from originally. Assimilated food forms part of your cells or it can be used to supply energy or provide raw material for metabolic processes or take part in chemical reactions in the cells. Indeed, cells are made mainly of water, carbohydrates, proteins and lipids (fats), all of which we get from our diet.

Questions

1 Which has the greater surface area: the outside wall or the inside wall of your small intestine? Why?

2 What happens to the products of digestion after they have been absorbed:
   a if they are needed by your cells
   b if they are in excess of cell requirements
   c if they are toxic?

3 Why is the liver important in relation to the products of digestion?

B10.4 What is a balanced diet?

You learnt in topic B10.1 that carbohydrates, lipids and proteins are important nutrients. However in order to be healthy, our diet (what we eat) has to include other components. The other components of a healthy diet are vitamins, mineral salts, fibre and water. A balanced diet contains all these components in the right amounts and proportions.

Vitamins and minerals

Vitamins are organic substances that play an important part in the control of metabolism. We need small amount of vitamins for good health. A few vitamins are produced in our bodies, the rest come from the food we eat. Some vitamins, such as vitamin K, are produced by bacteria in our intestines. Table 10.4.1 lists the sources and functions of some vitamins needed by humans.

Objectives

By the end of this topic you will be able to:

- explain what is meant by a 'balanced diet'
- identify the sources of the components of a balanced diet
- discuss the results of a deficiency or surplus of various nutrients
- describe how age, gender and occupation affect dietary needs
- discuss the advantages and disadvantages of vegetarianism.

▼ **Table 10.4.1** Some of the vitamins needed by humans

Vitamin	Sources	Importance	Results of deficiency/surplus
A (fat soluble)	Liver, fish-liver oil, milk, dairy products, green vegetables, carrots	Gives resistance to disease, protects eyes, helps us to see in the dark	Deficiency leads to infections, poor vision in dim light (night-blindness). Excess can cause liver damage.
B6 (water soluble)	Eggs, meat, potatoes, cabbage	Helps to digest protein	Deficiency leads to anaemia. Excess can cause irreversible nerve damage and kidney stones.
B12 (water soluble)	Meat, milk, yeast, comfrey (a herb)	Helps in formation of red blood cells	Deficiency leads to pernicious anaemia. Large excesses can lead to skin problems.
C (water soluble)	Oranges, limes and other citrus fruits, guavas, mangoes, green vegetables, potatoes, tomatoes	Helps to bond cells together. Helps in the use of calcium by bones and teeth.	Deficiency leads to scurvy (bleeding gums and internal organs). Excess can cause nausea and diarrhoea.
D (fat soluble)	Fish-liver oil, milk, butter, eggs. Made by the body in sunlight.	Helps body absorb calcium from food	Deficiency leads to rickets in children, brittle bones in adults. Excess causes vomiting, cramps, dehydration.

Some minerals are important for the growth and repair of our bodies, others control metabolism. We need small amounts of minerals from our food for good health.

Calcium is an important mineral. We need calcium for strong bones and teeth and in order for our blood to clot. An adult needs about 1.1 g of calcium a day. Iron is used by our bodies to make the blood protein, haemoglobin. An iron deficiency results in anaemia. An adult needs about 16 mg of iron a day.

Table 10.4.2 lists the sources and functions of some minerals needed by humans.

▼ **Table 10.4.2** Some of the minerals needed by humans

Mineral	Sources	Importance	Results of deficiency
Calcium	Milk, cheese and other dairy products, bread	Forms bones and teeth. Blood clotting.	Rickets (soft bones). Osteoporosis (brittle bones in adults).
Sodium and chlorine	Table salt (NaCl), cheese, green vegetables	Keeping levels of body fluids correct. Transmission of nerve impulses.	Cramps
Iron	Liver, eggs, meat, cocoa	Making haemoglobin	Anaemia
Iodine	Drinking water, seafoods	Needed to make the hormone thyroxine	Thyroid problems, goitre
Phosphorus	Present in most foods	Main calcium salt in teeth and bones	Deficiency is rare but alcoholics may be deficient and suffer bone loss

Water

Our body is about two-thirds (almost 70%) water. We take water in directly by drinking or indirectly in the food we eat.

Water is important in the body. It is the solvent in which chemical reactions take place. It is also the solvent in which waste matter is transported and passed out of the body in solution. Water in blood and lymph fluids is used to transport materials around our bodies. Water also allows us to keep cool.

Adults need about 2.5 litres of water every day. The body loses and gains water through its different activities. We gain water by drinking, from eating and as a product of cellular processes. We lose water in urine and faeces, through evaporation from our lungs and by sweating.

When you do not have enough water, you become dehydrated and your cellular processes cannot take place. Humans cannot survive longer than a few days without water.

Fibre

The fibre in our diets comes from plant foods. Soluble fibre dissolves in water to produce a gel. Insoluble fibre does not dissolve, but it holds water and swells up when mixed with water.

● Soluble fibre comes from fruit pulp, vegetables, oat bran and dried beans.
● Insoluble fibre comes from the cellulose of plant cell walls and the husks that cover wheat, rice and other grains.

Insoluble fibre adds to the bulk of undigested food passing through the intestines and maintains peristalsis by giving the muscles something to push against. Fibre can also reduce the amount of fat absorbed from food and this in turn reduces the risk of bowel cancer.

A lack of fibre leads to constipation. In the longer term, this can lead to bowel cancer.

Questions

1 Why do we need vitamins and minerals in our diet?

2 What is the difference between a fat-soluble and a water-soluble vitamin? Which are most likely to be stored in the body? Why?

3 What foods are good sources of vitamins A and C?

4 What could you eat to build up your iron levels if you had a deficiency?

5 Water and fibre have no nutritional value, so why are they important in our diet?

6 Why is whole wheat bread a better source of fibre than white bread?

7 Write down the five foods that you eat most of. What do these foods contribute to your diet?

How much food do we need in a balanced diet?

Food supplies us with energy. The amount of energy in food is measured in kilojoules (kJ). The amount of food (kilojoules) you need each day depends on your age, whether you are male or female, how active you are and where you live. Men generally need more energy than women. Children and young adults who are still growing need more energy than people who have stopped growing. People who are very active or who do very physical work will have greater energy needs than people who do not do much activity. People who live in cold places burn more energy to keep themselves warm, so they may need to eat more than people who live in warm places.

Figure 10.4.1 shows the daily energy requirements of different people (male and female) based on their age and activity level.

Food groups and portions

There are many different opinions about what constitutes a balanced diet. One method involves the concept of groups of foods that should be eaten every day. Table 10.4.3 lists five food groups and shows you how much you should eat from each group. Figure 10.4.2 is a food pyramid that shows the proportions of each food group that you should eat each day.

▼ **Table 10.4.3** Five food groups and the recommended daily intakes of each

Food group	What this supplies	Recommended daily intake
Bread and cereals (includes rice and pasta)	Carbohydrates, vitamins and fibre	4 servings
Fruit and vegetables	Vitamins, minerals, fibre	5 servings
Dairy products (milk and milk products like cheese and yoghurt)	Calcium, protein, vitamins	Adults: 300 ml milk, children: 600 ml milk
Meat and other proteins (chicken, fish, eggs, beans, nuts and lentils)	Protein, minerals, vitamins	2–3 servings Women: 50–60 g, men: 60–80 g
Fats and oils (including butter and margarine)	Lipids, vitamins	15–30 g

 Key fact

Anaemia causes a shortage of oxygen as a result of reduced haemoglobin levels. People who are anaemic are usually very tired all the time and they have heart palpitations. Other symptoms include paleness, shortness of breath and dizziness, fainting or angina.

 Key fact

Fat-soluble vitamins (A and D) can reach toxic levels if a person exceeds their normal daily amounts. This is because these vitamins are stored in the liver for months. Water-soluble vitamins (B and C) seldom reach toxic levels since they are not stored in the organs and are thus excreted easily.

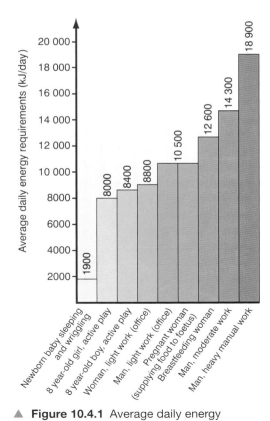

▲ **Figure 10.4.1** Average daily energy requirements for different groups of people

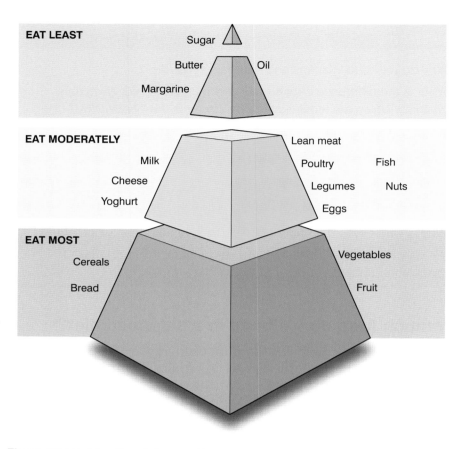

▲ **Figure 10.4.2** A healthy diet pyramid

In general, the rule for a healthy diet is to eat a variety of foods that are low in sugar and fats and high in fibre. For most people this means eating more wholegrain cereals, vegetables and fruit.

The effects of an unbalanced diet

Malnutrition means bad nourishment. Malnutrition results from an unbalanced and unhealthy diet. People who are malnourished may not be getting enough to eat or they may not be getting enough variety of foods. However, malnutrition can also result from eating too much food. Table 10.4.3 summarises some of the effects of an unbalanced diet.

▼ **Table 10.4.3** Some effects of malnutrition

Problems related to excess	Problems related to shortages
Too much food (taking in more kilojoules than your body uses) can result in obesity. This in turn can lead to diabetes and heart disease.	Too little food (getting less kilojoules than your body needs) can lead to starvation. People who are starving have restricted growth and development; they will become weak and eventually die. A general lack of food and nutrients, particularly in children, can lead to a deficiency disease known as marasmus, which causes severe weight loss and diarrhoea.
Too much animal fat in the diet can result in high cholesterol. This causes arteries to become blocked and it can lead to angina and heart attacks.	Vitamin and mineral deficiencies that lead to deficiency diseases (see Tables 10.4.1 and 10.4.2) can result from a diet that is lacking in fresh fruits and vegetables
Too much carbohydrate and too little protein can lead to deficiency diseases such as kwashiorkor	A lack of fibre in the diet can lead to constipation and bowel cancer in the long term

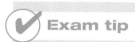

Exam tip

In an examination you may be asked to describe problems associated with an unbalanced diet. This would include eating in excess, not eating enough and vegetarian diets. You should also be able to give recommendations to fix problems.

Vegetarian diets

Vegetarians do not eat meat. People choose to follow a vegetarian diet for different reasons: some people believe it is cruel to kill animals for food, some people are vegetarian for cultural or religious reasons and some people are vegetarian because they think it is a healthier diet choice.

If foods are chosen carefully you can get a complete range of nutrients from a vegetarian diet, especially if you eat eggs, milk and cheese. A balanced vegetarian diet offers some health advantages because it usually offers more fibre, less saturated fat and cholesterol and less high-energy foods.

Research has shown that vegetarians are less likely to be overweight than people who regularly eat meat. Vegetarians also have a lower risk of heart disease, diabetes and some types of cancers than non-vegetarians.

Questions

1 Are the following statements true or false?
   a Milk contains many of the nutrients our bodies need.
   b Diets are only for people who want to lose weight.
   c Everyone needs to eat meat, fish or chicken.
   d You should never eat fried chips.
   e Whole wheat bread is better for you than white bread.
   f Yoghurt is good for you.
   g Liver and eggs are rich in iron.
   h Old vegetables are just as good as fresh ones.
   i Humans can get the water they need just by eating food.
   j A growing child needs fewer kilojoules of food than an adult.

2 Correct the false statements in Question 1 to make them true.

3 Vegans do not eat any animal products at all (not even milk, cheese or eggs). Explain why vegans may struggle to get the vitamins and minerals they need from their diet alone.

Respiration

We take in oxygen and produce carbon dioxide in our bodies. In this unit you are going to look in more detail at cells to understand how and why this happens during the process of respiration.

Objectives

By the end of this topic you will be able to:

- distinguish between breathing and respiration
- show that respiration takes place at a cellular level
- understand the function and role of ATP in transferring energy
- describe the process of aerobic respiration
- tabulate the differences between aerobic and anaerobic respiration
- carry out investigations to find out about the products of respiration.

B11.1 Releasing energy by respiration

All living organisms need energy, in the form of chemical energy, in order to move, to send nerve messages, to build large molecules and to release heat. We get the chemical energy we need from the food we eat. The food is converted into usable energy by a series of chemical reactions called cellular respiration.

It is important to understand that cellular respiration does not mean the same thing as breathing. When we breathe we inhale air that contains about 20% oxygen and around 0.04% carbon dioxide. When we breathe out, the air we exhale contains only about 16% oxygen but around 4% carbon dioxide. The 'missing' oxygen is used up inside our cells to release energy and carbon dioxide in the process of respiration.

All living cells respire continuously in order to produce the energy they need to carry out metabolic processes. When they use oxygen in the process, it is called aerobic respiration.

Aerobic respiration

Aerobic respiration is the release of fairly large amounts of energy using oxygen to break down digested food. It involves many different chemical reactions which are all catalysed and controlled by enzymes. Aerobic respiration can be summed up in words like this:

$$\text{glucose} + \text{oxygen} \longrightarrow \text{energy} + \text{carbon dioxide} + \text{water}$$

We can also represent this reaction as a balanced chemical equation:

$$C_6H_{12}O_6 + 6O_2 \longrightarrow \text{energy} + 6CO_2 + 6H_2O$$

Glucose and oxygen are the raw materials for aerobic respiration. Energy (approximately 16 kJ/g of glucose), carbon dioxide and water are the products of aerobic respiration. The energy released in the process is used by cells. The carbon dioxide and water are expelled as wastes. Aerobic respiration releases the maximum amount of energy from the glucose because the molecule is completely broken down in the process.

The reactions that take place in aerobic respiration occur in the mitochondria of cells. Cells that need large amounts of energy, such as muscle cells and nerve cells, have many mitochondria. Cells that do not need a lot of energy, such as fat cells, have few mitochondria.

ATP and energy release

During respiration, energy is released slowly in small amounts. If energy was released quickly in cells, the sharp rise in temperature would kill the cells. As glucose breaks down, the energy that is released is used to convert a substance known as ADP (adenosine diphosphate) into energy-carrying molecules of ATP (adenosine triphosphate). Each molecule of glucose that is broken down produces about 38 molecules of ATP. ATP is the chemical that carries energy to the parts of the body that need it.

ATP is sometimes called the energy currency of cells. This makes sense if you think of your cells as a 'bank' that stores energy in the form of ATP (the currency). The cells 'earn' ATP by 'working' to convert glucose to energy. They bank or store the products of these reactions, building up a positive balance of ATP. When you need a small amount of energy, you withdraw a small amount of ATP from the bank in the cells. When you need a larger amount of energy, you withdraw more ATP from the bank in the cells. Using ATP as you need energy is more efficient than producing large amounts of energy that gets wasted.

The energy that is released by ATP is used by your cells in different ways:

- to synthesise (build) complex molecules, such as proteins, carbohydrates and lipids
- for cell growth
- to repair and maintain cells
- in the process of active transport to move materials across cell membranes
- to provide energy to specialised cells, such as nerve, muscle, sperm, liver and kidney cells.

Only about 40% of the energy stored in glucose is converted to ATP and stored. The rest is released as heat. The energy from respiration that is released in the form of heat is useful because it helps to keep our body temperature constant at around 37 °C. This is the temperature at which our cells and enzymes function well.

Questions

1 Define the terms 'respiration' and 'aerobic respiration'.

2 Write a generalised equation for respiration.

3 Why is respiration important to cells?

4 Why is there less oxygen in exhaled air than in inhaled air?

5 Suggest an experiment you could do to show that oxygen is taken up and carbon dioxide is released during respiration.

6 A petrol engine converts fuel to energy with about 25% efficiency. Cellular respiration is about 40% efficient. Explain why.

Anaerobic respiration

Think about what happens when you run: you breathe heavily and your heart beats faster. Both of these things help to get more oxygen to your cells. Sometimes this is not enough and oxygen cannot reach your cells fast enough to supply their needs.

Key fact

Lactic acid is a mild poison. When it builds up in muscles it makes them stiff and sore.

When cells do not get enough oxygen to meet their needs, they can switch from aerobic respiration to anaerobic respiration to release energy without using oxygen. We can represent this process using the general formula:

$$glucose \longrightarrow lactic\ acid + energy$$

Anaerobic respiration takes place in the cytoplasm of cells and it does not involve the production of ATP.

The reactions in anaerobic respiration release only a fraction (about 0.8 kJ/g of glucose) of the energy that is released during aerobic respiration. This is because the glucose molecules are not broken down completely in the process.

During this process, lactic acid is produced as a waste product. This builds up in muscles and causes them to ache. At this point you feel fatigued (tired). Muscles become fatigued as a result of lactic acid build-up.

As we continue to breathe, more oxygen reaches the cells and aerobic respiration can take place again. The oxygen breaks down the lactic acid in our muscles and converts it to carbon dioxide and water, producing ATP in the process.

Anaerobic respiration in muscle cells can take place only for a few minutes since lactic acid is toxic. After muscles have respired anaerobically for a few minutes, the lactic acid they have built up stops them from working. During the recovery period, the rush of oxygen to the muscles promotes aerobic respiration. Some lactic acid is oxidised and the rest is converted to glucose. In this way, the oxygen debt is repaid.

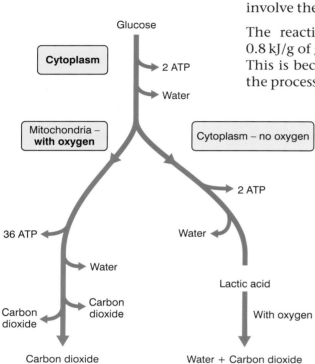

▲ **Figure 11.1.1** Respiration in animals

Figure 11.1.1 shows you how both aerobic respiration and anaerobic respiration takes place in animals.

Bacteria, yeasts and the root cells of plants can also change from aerobic respiration to anaerobic respiration if oxygen is in short supply.

Yeast cells use anaerobic respiration to convert glucose into ethanol and carbon dioxide, with the release of energy (some ATP is produced). Again, less energy is released in this process (about 1.2 kJ/g of glucose) than in aerobic respiration.

$$glucose \longrightarrow ethanol + carbon\ dioxide + energy$$

This series of reactions is called fermentation and it is used to make alcoholic drinks and breads.

You have seen in this topic that glucose can be used by organisms in three different ways to produce different amounts of energy and different products (see Figure 11.1.2).

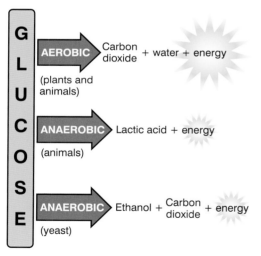

▲ **Figure 11.1.2** Glucose is one of the raw materials for energy production in both aerobic and anaerobic respiration

Table 11.1.1 compares aerobic respiration and anaerobic respiration.

▼ **Table 11.1.1** A comparison of aerobic and anaerobic respiration

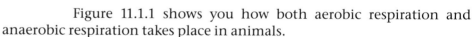

Process	Oxygen used or not used	Products	Energy released (kJ/g of glucose)
Aerobic respiration	Used	Carbon dioxide and water	16.1
Anaerobic respiration in yeast	Not used	Ethanol and carbon dioxide	1.17
Anaerobic respiration in muscles	Not used	Lactic acid	0.83

Cellular respiration and photosynthesis

As you can see in Figure 11.1.3, cellular respiration and photosynthesis in plants form a cycle. The products of one are the raw materials for the other.

During the day, photosynthesis produces more oxygen than the plant needs for aerobic respiration. The surplus oxygen diffuses out of the leaves of the plant through the stomata. At night, photosynthesis stops but plant cells still need oxygen for aerobic respiration. Oxygen from the air diffuses back into the leaves through the stomata. The carbon dioxide produced by aerobic respiration in the plant's cells diffuses out of the leaves through the stomata.

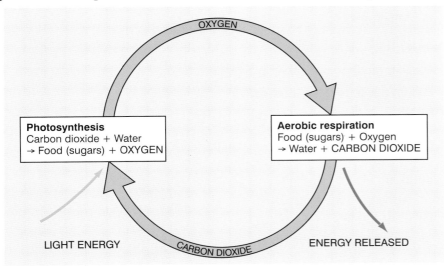

▲ **Figure 11.1.3** Respiration and photosynthesis form a cycle in plants

Questions

1 The graph in Figure 11.1.4 shows the amount of lactic acid in the blood of an athlete who exercised vigorously for 10 minutes.
   a How much lactic acid was in the athlete's blood before exercise?
   b Describe the change in lactic acid concentration as shown on the graph.
   c Explain why there was a sharp increase in lactic acid concentration during exercise.
   d What causes the concentration of lactic acid to drop after exercise?
   e How long did it take for the lactic acid level to return to the pre-exercise level?

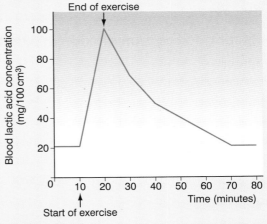

▲ **Figure 11.1.4**

2 Copy this table and complete it to show the differences between aerobic and anaerobic respiration.

Aerobic respiration	Anaerobic respiration
Uses oxygen	
	Produces lactic acid or ethanol
Releases large amounts of energy	
Always produces carbon dioxide as a waste product	

3 Why is bread dough containing yeast usually left in a warm place? In your answer refer to the action of enzymes and the products of respiration.

B11.2 Investigating the products of respiration

Objectives

By the end of this topic you will be able to:

- carry out investigations to find out about the products of respiration.

Safety

Wear goggles. Once heating is stopped, the lime water is drawn back into the boiling tube and may cause it to shatter. Also lime water is toxic – take care in this practical activity and the one below.

Practical activity

Does burning food give off carbon dioxide?

Materials

- A teaspoon of sugar
- Two test tubes, a delivery tube, a stopper/bung and clamp
- Lime water
- A Bunsen burner

Method

1 Place a teaspoon of sugar in a test tube.

2 Set up the apparatus as shown in Figure 11.2.1.

3 Heat the sugar over a moderate flame.

Questions

What happens to the lime water as you heat the sugar?

What can you deduce from this?

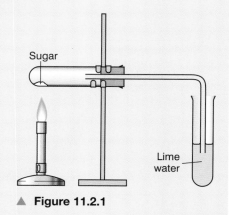

Sugar

Lime water

▲ **Figure 11.2.1**

Practical activity

Testing for carbon dioxide in exhaled air

Materials

- A test tube half-full of lime water
- A straw

Method

1 Put the straw into the lime water.

2 Breathe out gently through the straw.

Questions

What happens to the lime water as you breathe out?

What can you deduce from this?

A student sets up the equipment in Figure 11.2.2 to perform the same investigation.

Explain why this is a more precise method of proving that you breathe out carbon dioxide.

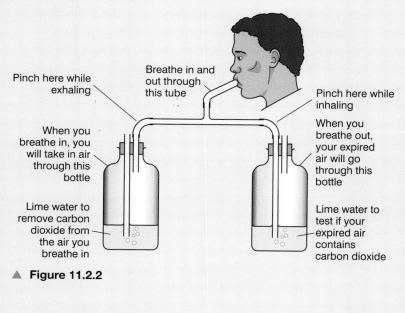

Pinch here while exhaling

Breathe in and out through this tube

Pinch here while inhaling

When you breathe in, you will take in air through this bottle

When you breathe out, your expired air will go through this bottle

Lime water to remove carbon dioxide from the air you breathe in

Lime water to test if your expired air contains carbon dioxide

▲ **Figure 11.2.2**

 **Practical activity**

Measuring heat energy from germinating seeds

Your teacher may use this activity to assess: ORR; A&I.

You have learnt already that respiration releases energy in the form of heat. This investigation will allow you to measure the amount of heat produced by germinating peas.

Materials

- Germinating peas (or beans) – rinse them in a dilute disinfectant solution before you begin, to kill all microbes and fungi
- Two thermos flasks
- Two thermometers
- Cotton wool

Method

1 Boil half the germinating peas to kill them and stop germination.

2 Set up the two flasks as shown in Figure 11.2.3.
Record the starting temperature in each flask.

3 Leave the two flasks for 24 hours. Then note the temperature in each flask.

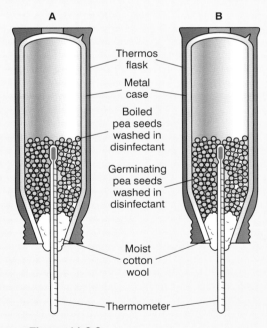

▲ **Figure 11.2.3**

Questions

What is the role of the following?

- The thermos flasks.
- The moist cotton wool.
- The dead peas.

What conclusions can you draw from this experiment?

Practical activity

Does yeast give off CO$_2$ during anaerobic respiration?

Your teacher may use this activity to assess: ORR; A&I.

Materials

- Glucose
- Pipette
- Liquid paraffin
- Bicarbonate indicator
- Two test tubes, a stopper and a delivery tube
- Yeast

Method

1 Make a 10% glucose solution using boiled water. Let it cool.

2 Add live yeast to the cooled glucose solution. Cover it with a layer of liquid paraffin (trickle this on gently using a pipette).

3 Set up the apparatus as shown in Figure 11.2.4.

4 Set up a control for your experiment using dead yeast (boil it to kill it).

Questions

What happens to the indicator in the second test tube?

How long does this take?

How could you speed up the fermentation reaction?

Investigate to find out whether or not your ideas work.

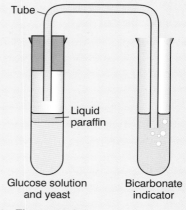

▲ Figure 11.2.4

Practical activity

Investigating the effect of temperature on the action of yeast

Materials

- Three measuring cylinders
- Bread dough

Method

1 Make a mixture of bread dough using live yeast.

2 Place an equal amount of dough in three measuring cylinders.
- Place one measuring cylinder in the fridge.
- Leave one measuring cylinder in a shady spot at room temperature.
- Put one measuring cylinder in a warm spot in the sun.

3 Use a table to record the volume of dough in each cylinder at 10-minute intervals for one hour.

4 Write a short report in which you explain:
- what causes the dough to rise
- why the dough in this experiment rose at different rates.

B12 Gaseous exchange

You have seen that respiration uses oxygen and releases carbon dioxide. In this unit you are going to look at how these two gases move through surfaces to get in to and out of the cells of living organisms.

B12.1 Gaseous exchange in humans

The ability to exchange gases across a surface is a vital life process in both plants and animals.

Human cells need oxygen for cellular respiration. However, the cells cannot inhale oxygen directly from the air. They get the oxygen they need from the blood. This means that the oxygen has to be able to move across surfaces in our bodies to get from our lungs (where we inhale it), into our blood and into our cells. The carbon dioxide that is produced as a waste product in cellular respiration has to move across surfaces in the opposite direction: from the cells, into the blood and back into our lungs so we can exhale it.

The importance of gaseous exchange

The function of our respiratory system is to provide oxygen for cellular respiration and to remove the carbon dioxide that cells produce during the process. If cells do not get oxygen, they cannot respire and they will die fairly quickly. If the carbon dioxide is not removed, it combines with water in the blood to form carbonic acid. This acid lowers the pH of the blood and disturbs the delicate balance inside cells.

Breathing and gaseous exchange

Breathing is a mechanical process that involves inhaling air, which contains oxygen, into the lungs and exhaling air that contains carbon dioxide. Breathing allows gaseous exchange to take place across the respiratory surfaces in the lungs.

Gaseous exchange is the exchange of gases across a respiratory surface. This takes place in the lungs where oxygen and carbon dioxide are exchanged between the alveoli of the lungs and the blood. Gaseous exchange also takes place between the blood and the cells. These processes are illustrated in Figure 12.1.1.

The human respiratory system

The respiratory system in humans (and other mammals) consists of:

- air passages, which allow air to move in to and out of the lungs
- a pair of lungs, which provides a gaseous exchange surface
- breathing muscles, which move the chest and allow air to enter and exit the lungs.

Breathing is involuntary and controlled by our brain. The brain controls the rate at which we breathe and also the depth of breathing. Figure 12.1.2 shows the human respiratory system.

Objectives

By the end of this topic you will be able to:

- explain what is meant by 'gaseous exchange'
- understand the need for a continuous supply of oxygen and the removal of carbon dioxide and other waste products
- describe and explain the importance of breathing in humans
- draw and label simple diagrams of the human respiratory system
- make a model to demonstrate how the thorax works.

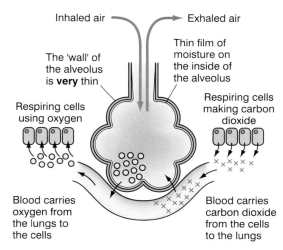

▲ **Figure 12.1.1** Gaseous exchange across different surfaces

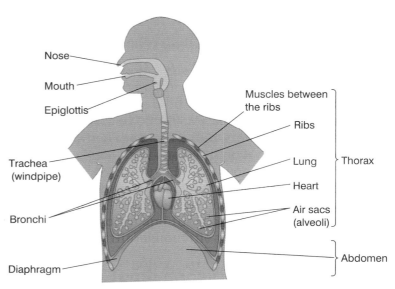

▲ **Figure 12.1.2** The human respiratory system

The respiratory system at work

Our upper respiratory tract, or air passage, consists of a tube from the nostrils and mouth to the lungs. The air passage is lined with a mucous membrane made up of ciliated columnar epithelial cells. The mucus that covers the membrane is produced by goblet cells in the membrane. Rows of fine hair-like structures called cilia, move backwards and forwards to sweep the mucus. The mucus is very important because it traps bacteria, viruses and dust and prevents them from getting into our lungs. The mucus membrane also helps to keep air moist and warm so that dry air does not enter and harm our lungs.

Figure 12.1.3 is a representation of the mucus membrane showing the different types of cell found there.

Air enters our respiratory tract through our nose and then passes through the throat and larynx (voice box) to our trachea (windpipe). The trachea divides into two branches called bronchi which lead into our lungs. The trachea and bronchi are kept open by C-shaped rings of cartilage.

In the lungs, each bronchus branches many times into small tubes called bronchioles. These form a network called the bronchial tree. The bronchioles divide and sub-divide into even smaller tubes which end in clusters of small sacs called alveoli.

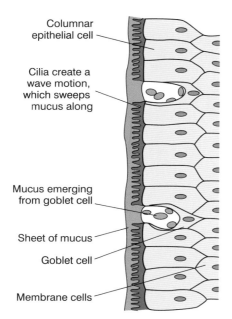

▲ **Figure 12.1.3** The cells and functions of the mucus membrane

The walls of the alveoli are very thin and they are surrounded by capillary blood vessels. The alveoli enlarge the surface area for gaseous exchange (in almost the same way as the villi enlarge the surface area of the small intestine). There are millions of alveoli in our lungs with a combined surface area of approximately 90 square metres – almost the area of a tennis court!

Gases are exchanged between the air and the blood inside the alveoli. Oxygen passes through the walls of the alveoli into the blood in the capillaries. Some of the oxygen dissolves in the blood, but most of it combines with haemoglobin to be transported to the cells of the body. At the same time as oxygen passes into the blood, carbon dioxide leaves the blood so that it can be exhaled from the lungs.

Figure 12.1.4 shows you how gases are exchanged in the alveoli.

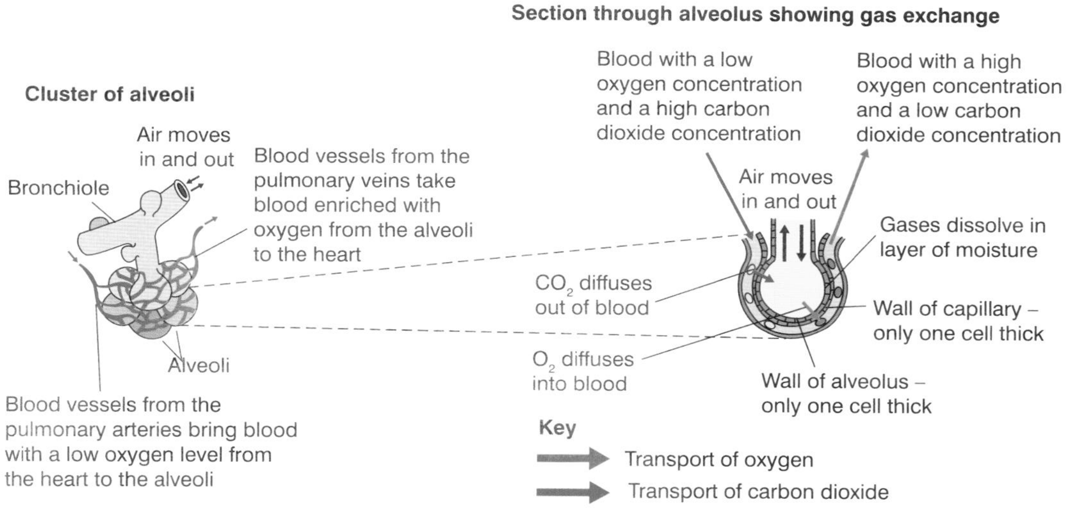

Section through alveolus showing gas exchange

Cluster of alveoli

Bronchiole

Air moves in and out

Blood vessels from the pulmonary veins take blood enriched with oxygen from the alveoli to the heart

Alveoli

Blood vessels from the pulmonary arteries bring blood with a low oxygen level from the heart to the alveoli

Blood with a low oxygen concentration and a high carbon dioxide concentration

Blood with a high oxygen concentration and a low carbon dioxide concentration

Air moves in and out

Gases dissolve in layer of moisture

CO_2 diffuses out of blood

Wall of capillary – only one cell thick

O_2 diffuses into blood

Wall of alveolus – only one cell thick

Key

Transport of oxygen

Transport of carbon dioxide

▲ **Figure 12.1.4** The alveoli are adapted so that gas exchange can happen efficiently

Questions

1 Why do we need to breathe?

2 Where does gaseous exchange take place in humans?

3 Why is mucus important in the respiratory system?

4 What function do the following have in the respiratory system?
  a C-shaped rings of cartilage   c Bronchi
  b Cilia   d Alveoli

5 Draw a flow diagram to show the passage taken by oxygen from your nose to the cells of your body.

The mechanisms of breathing

Breathing relies on movements in the chest cavity. The process of breathing has three phases:

● inhalation (breathing in or inspiration) where air flows into the lungs

● a short resting period

● exhalation (breathing out or expiration) where air is moved out of the lungs.

Inhalation

Figure 12.1.5 shows you what happens inside your chest when you inhale.

The thorax or chest cavity is a cage formed by your ribs and your diaphragm. It is elastic. The diaphragm is a dome-shaped plate of muscle that stretches across the chest cavity. When you inhale, the diaphragm contracts and flattens. The intercostal muscles between the ribs also contract, lifting the ribs upwards and outwards.

These movements increase the volume of the thorax. This causes the air pressure inside the lungs to decrease so that it is lower than the pressure of the air in the atmosphere. Air therefore is drawn down the trachea into the lungs. The lungs enlarge like balloons to contain the inhaled air.

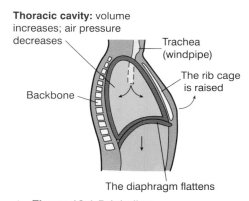

Thoracic cavity: volume increases; air pressure decreases

Trachea (windpipe)

The rib cage is raised

Backbone

The diaphragm flattens

▲ **Figure 12.1.5** Inhaling

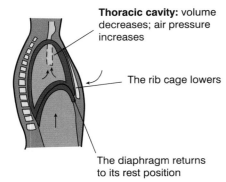

Thoracic cavity: volume decreases; air pressure increases

The rib cage lowers

The diaphragm returns to its rest position

▲ Figure 12.1.6 Exhaling

Exhalation

Figure 12.1.6 shows what happens in your chest when you exhale.

When you exhale, the diaphragm relaxes and returns to its resting position. The intercostal muscles also relax and the ribs return to their original positions. The volume in the chest cavity is reduced. As a result, the air pressure in the lungs increases and the air is forced out of the lungs through the trachea.

You can demonstrate the action of inhaling and exhaling by building a model of the thorax.

Practical activity

Making a model thorax

Aim

To build a model to show how humans breathe.

Method

1 Make a model using the apparatus shown in Figure 12.1.7.

2 Use the model to investigate how moving the rubber sheet affects the movement of the balloons.

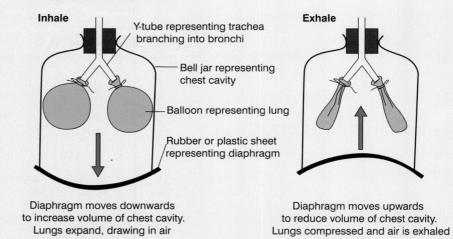

Inhale

Y-tube representing trachea branching into bronchi

Bell jar representing chest cavity

Balloon representing lung

Rubber or plastic sheet representing diaphragm

Diaphragm moves downwards to increase volume of chest cavity. Lungs expand, drawing in air

Exhale

Diaphragm moves upwards to reduce volume of chest cavity. Lungs compressed and air is exhaled

▲ Figure 12.1.7

Questions

Copy and complete this paragraph, which analyses the results of this investigation, by filling in the missing words.

In this model, the airtight … represents the chest cavity or … . The chest cavity is connected to the air in the atmosphere by the … and the …, which are represented by the glass tube. The balloons are elastic and they represent the … . They change shape when air is … and … . The rubber sheet represents the …, a sheet of muscle that moves … when it contracts and … back to its original position when it relaxes.

Explain the shortcomings in this model that prevent it from correctly representing what happens when you breathe in and out.

Questions

1 Below are some statements about breathing. Write them in the correct columns in a table, like the one below, to summarise the differences in the processes of inhalation and exhalation.
   - Intercostal muscles relax/intercostal muscles contract.
   - Rib cage moves upwards and outwards/rib cage moves down and inwards.
   - Diaphragm relaxes/diaphragm contracts.
   - Diaphragm becomes rounded/diaphragm flattens.
   - Volume of chest cavity decreases/volume of chest cavity increases.
   - Volume of lungs increases/volume of lungs decreases.
   - Pressure in thorax and lungs decreases/pressure in thorax and lungs increases.
   - Air is drawn into the lungs/air is expelled from the lungs.

Inhalation	Exhalation

2 Describe what happens in the thorax during the process of inhalation.

B12.2 Other gaseous exchange surfaces

In topic B12.1 you learnt that gases are exchanged in solution across the gaseous exchange surfaces of the alveoli in humans. These surfaces are well adapted for diffusion because they are:

- thin, so that it is easy for gases to be exchanged
- moist, so that gases can dissolve
- large in surface area to allow for maximum diffusion
- well supplied with blood vessels to provide transport throughout the body
- in contact with the atmosphere through the tubes of the bronchioles, bronchi and trachea.

These characteristics of gaseous exchange surfaces are important because they ensure that a sufficient supply of gases can move across the surfaces quickly and continuously. You will find that these characteristics are common to all gaseous exchange surfaces. This includes the leaves of plants, although blood is not the transport medium in plants, and insects.

Gills and other surfaces

Fish and other organisms that live in water use oxygen that is dissolved in the water.

In small animals, like *amoeba*, *hydra* and *Planaria* (flat worms), gas exchange occurs across the body wall. The surface area of the organism is large enough to let in enough oxygen and get rid of enough carbon dioxide. The flat body of *Planaria* increases its surface area and allows gases to diffuse through it easily (see Figure 12.2.1).

▲ **Figure 12.2.1** *Planaria* lives in water where gases are in solution. The gases are exchanged across the body wall of the animal.

Gills

Fish breathe through specialised organs called gills. If you look at the fish in Figure 12.2.2 and the shark in Figure 12.2.3 you can see the location of the gill covering and the gill slits.

▲ **Figure 12.2.2** Bony fish have gill slits that are covered by a flap of bony skin called the operculum

▲ **Figure 12.2.3** Cartilaginous fish, such as sharks, do not have opercula covering their gills

A single gill

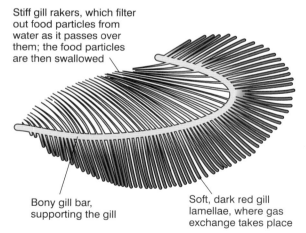

Stiff gill rakers, which filter out food particles from water as it passes over them; the food particles are then swallowed

Bony gill bar, supporting the gill

Soft, dark red gill lamellae, where gas exchange takes place

▲ **Figure 12.2.4** A single gill showing how the lamellae increase the surface area for diffusion

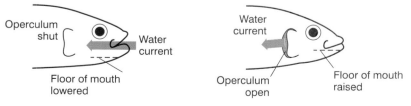

Operculum shut

Floor of mouth lowered

Water current

Water current

Operculum open

Floor of mouth raised

▲ **Figure 12.2.5** Inspiration and expiration in fish are continuous processes

Figure 12.2.4 shows the structure of a single gill.

The outside of each gill bar is covered by rows of leaf-like tissue called lamellae (singular lamella). Each lamella is folded into gill plates, which greatly increases the surface area of the gills. Blood vessels at the base of each gill branch into dense networks of capillaries in the lamellae.

As water passes over the lamellae, the dissolved oxygen in the water diffuses into the blood flowing through the dense network of capillaries. At the same time, carbon dioxide diffuses out of the blood into the gills, where it is carried away in the water.

The exchange of gases in gills is efficient because the flow of blood through the lamellae and the flow of water over the lamellae are in opposite directions.

The flow of water through the mouth and over the gill lamellae is called the respiratory current. Figure 12.2.5 shows what happens as fish breathe. The coordinated opening and closing of the mouth and opercula results in a continuous flow of water over the surfaces of the lamellae. The water does not enter the gut because muscles at its upper end contract, closing off the opening.

Fish die when they are taken out of water because the gill surfaces all stick together if there is no water flowing through them. When this happens, the surface area is reduced and the fish cannot get enough oxygen from the air, so they die.

Questions

1 Write a few sentences explaining how it is possible for fish to absorb oxygen even though they live in water.

2 To be efficient, gaseous exchange surfaces must:
- be thin
- be moist
- have a large surface area
- have constant movement or transport to maintain a concentration gradient for diffusion.

a List the sites of gaseous exchange surfaces in plants, mammals and fish.

b Explain, using examples, how each of these surfaces fulfils the requirements for efficient gaseous exchange.

B12.3 Smoking and the respiratory system

Objectives

By the end of this topic you will be able to:

- discuss how smoking affects our lungs and other body systems.

Cigarette smoking poses some serious health risks. It is the single largest preventable cause of disease and premature death. It is a factor in heart disease, strokes and chronic lung disease. It can cause cancer of the lungs, larynx, oesophagus, mouth and bladder, and contributes to cancer of the cervix, pancreas and kidneys.

Why is smoking a health risk?

Cigarette smoke contains around 4000 poisonous chemicals. The main poisons are tar, carbon monoxide and nicotine. Table 12.3.1 shows how these chemicals affect your respiratory system.

▼ **Table 12.3.1** The harmful effects of chemicals in cigarette smoke

Harmful chemical	How it affects your body
Tar	Contains chemicals that cause cancer (carcinogenic). Lines the air passages and leads to increased mucus production. Paralyses and damages cilia. When smoke cools, tar settles in the lungs.
Carbon monoxide	A poisonous gas that combines irreversibly with haemoglobin and prevents haemoglobin from transporting oxygen to your cells.
Nicotine	One of the most powerful known poisons It raises your heart rate and increases your blood pressure. Addictive and leads to more smoking.

In addition, smoking among teenagers is considered to be an early warning sign of additional substance abuse problems. The Campaign for Tobacco-Free Kids (www.tobaccofreekids.org) reports that teenagers between the age of 12 and 17 who smoke are 11 times more likely to use illegal drugs, including marijuana, and 16 times more likely to drink alcohol than those who do not smoke. The earlier a person starts to smoke, the higher the likelihood that they will use an illicit drug, and teenagers who smoke more than 15 cigarettes a day are much more likely to use marijuana and/or other drugs. Even young people who use smokeless tobacco (chewing or spit tobacco) are four times more likely to abuse illegal drugs than non-users.

The pie chart in Figure 12.3.1 shows you the main components of cigarette smoke. The advert shows you some of the common household poisons found in cigarette smoke.

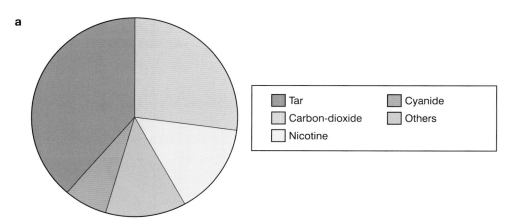

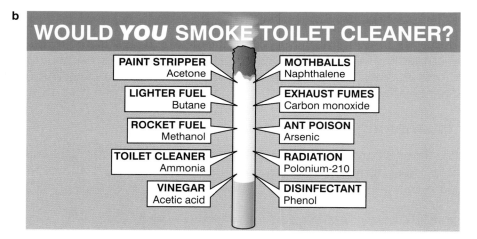

▲ **Figure 12.3.1 a** The main components of cigarette smoke and **b** an advert showing harmful chemicals of cigarette smoking; there is no scientific doubt that cigarette smoking is bad for your health

The chemicals in cigarette smoke are generally considered to be harmful. Some irritate the lining of your upper respiratory tract. Others destroy cilia and stop them from moving. When this happens, extra mucus (phlegm) forms in the trachea and bronchi. This is the cause of smoker's cough. Smokers have to cough to get rid of the phlegm that builds up in their air passages.

Smoking also weakens the walls of the alveoli and a serious smoker's cough can destroy some of them. When the alveoli break down, the smoker gets a serious lung disease called emphysema. People with emphysema are short of breath because the gaseous exchange surface in their lungs is reduced. They cannot get enough oxygen into their blood so they are also often exhausted and unable to move around well.

Smoking can cause cancer of the lungs and other organs of the body. Figure 12.3.2 shows the development of lung cancer.

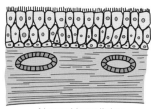 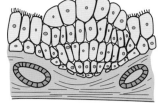

Normal lung lining   Lung lining with cancerous growth

▲ **Figure 12.3.2** Smoking can cause lung cancer

Pregnant women are always advised not to smoke. The chemicals in cigarette smoke pass across gaseous exchange surfaces into the mother's blood. This blood reaches the baby across the placenta.

Babies born to mothers who smoke are generally smaller and lighter than babies born to mothers who do not smoke. Smoking also increases the mother's chances of giving birth prematurely. Research suggests that the chemicals in the cigarette smoke stop the unborn baby from getting the nutrients it needs from its mother.

Passive smoking

Passive smoking means breathing in the smoke from other people's cigarettes. Nicotine can be found in the bloodstream of non-smokers for up to 40 hours after they have been exposed to smoke from other's people's cigarettes. If you spend an hour in a smoky room, you probably inhale the same amount of toxic chemicals as a person who smokes a few cigarettes. The World Health Organisation (WHO) estimates that there is no safe level of exposure to second-hand cigarette smoke.

The Pan American Health Organisation (PAHO) together with the World Health Organisation (WHO) have carried out a decade-long (2000–2010) research survey into tobacco use and exposure among 13–15-year-olds in the region. Tables 12.3.2 and 12.3.3 show some of the results of this study.

▼ **Table 12.3.2** Percentage of 13–15-year-olds who were using tobacco products at the time of the survey

Country and year of survey	Percentage of all respondents who use tobacco	Percentage of boys who use tobacco	Percentage of girls who use tobacco
Antigua and Barbuda (2009)	20.1	24.3	15.9
Barbados (2007)	28.6	34.5	23.2
Dominica (2009)	25.3	30.4	19.8
Grenada (2009)	20.5	24.5	16.7
Jamaica (2010)	28.7	31.3	24.6
St Kitts and Nevis (2010)	9.2	10.4	13.6
St Lucia (2007)	17.9	22.4	14.5
St Vincent and the Grenadines (2007)	19.1	22.0	16.6
Trinidad and Tobago (2007)	19.9	20.8	17.8
Regional average (mean)	23.2	25.7	19.7

Key fact

According to the WHO, diseases linked to smoking kill one in 10 adults globally, or cause four million deaths. By 2030, if current trends continue, smoking will kill one in six people. Half of long-term smokers will die from tobacco. Every cigarette smoked cuts at least five minutes off life expectancy on average – about the time taken to smoke it!

▼ **Table 12.3.3** Percentage of 13–15-year-old smokers who had their first smoke before the age of 10

Country and year of survey	Percentage of boys	Percentage of girls
Antigua and Barbuda (2009)	24.6	35.5
Barbados (2007)	33.1	29.3
Dominica (2009)	20.5	17.1
Grenada (2009)	40.1	33.9
Jamaica (2010)	23.5	27.9
St Kitts and Nevis (2010)	37.6	25.0
St Lucia (2007)	22.9	26.7
St Vincent and the Grenadines (2007)	31.9	25.4
Trinidad and Tobago (2007)	26.0	24.9

Questions

1 Name three toxic substances in cigarette smoke.

2 What is a smoker's cough? How is it caused by smoking?

3 Draw a simple labelled diagram of the parts of the human respiratory system. State how smoking affects each part.

4 How does smoking affect the levels of oxygen available for cell processes?

5 Explain the health risks associated with passive smoking.

6 Study the data in Tables 12.3.2 and 12.3.3.
   a Draw suitable graphs to display both sets of data visually.
   b Describe the trends shown in the graphs.
   c How does your country compare with others in the region and with the region as a whole? (You may need to do some online research to find data for your own country if it is not shown here.)
   d How might the fact that the survey data Is for different years affect how you interpret the data?

All animal cells have to get oxygen and nutrients and give off carbon dioxide and other wastes. Small aquatic animals can exchange these substances directly with their environment. In larger animals, these substances need to be transported and circulated throughout the body. In this unit you are going to learn about the structure and functions of the human circulatory system and the role it plays in defending the body and fighting disease.

B13.1 Why animals need a transport system

Figure 13.1.1a shows an amoeba. The amoeba is a unicellular organism found in water, wet soil or inside other organisms. The amoeba is a good example of an animal cell, and like all animal cells, it has to exchange oxygen and carbon dioxide, absorb nutrients and get rid of wastes. Figure 13.1.1b–c shows how this happens in an amoeba.

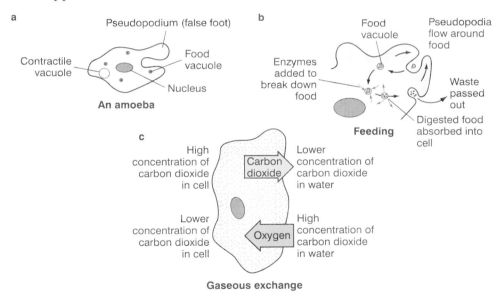

▲ **Figure 13.1.1** The amoeba can meet all its cellular needs by diffusion

Objectives

By the end of this topic you will be able to:

- explain why multicellular organisms need a transport system
- understand the limitations of diffusion in multi-cellular organisms
- identify the relationship between surface area and volume in cells
- list examples of types of material that need to be transported in animals.

You can see from the diagrams that an amoeba does not have a complicated system of moving substances through its body (the cell). Oxygen diffuses into the cell from the environment and carbon dioxide diffuses out into the environment. Digested food is absorbed into the cell by diffusion from the food vacuole and waste products are expelled from the cell when the amoeba moves around.

Diffusion is sufficient for the amoeba cell to get all its life requirements because the organism has a very large surface-area-to-volume ratio. The surface area is large enough that diffusion of gases across the surfaces provides all the cell's needs. Once inside the cell, gases and nutrients do not have to travel large distances, so they can move through the cell by diffusion.

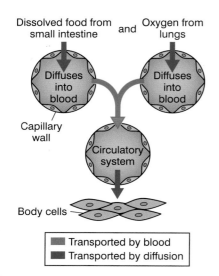

Transported by blood
Transported by diffusion

▲ **Figure 13.1.2** Larger organisms need both diffusion and transport to get substances to all the cells in their bodies

Simple organisms like amoeba and paramecium, as well as some multi-cellular organisms like flat worms and sea anemones (cnidarians), do not need an internal transport system because they have a large surface-area-to-volume ratio and cells can get everything they need by diffusion. Larger organisms, however, have a small surface-area-to-volume ratio and they cannot survive without a transport system to move things in to and out of cells. Figure 13.1.2 shows you how multi-cellular organisms get food and oxygen into their cells.

Diffusion is not sufficient in multi-cellular organisms

Bigger organisms with tissues and organ systems cannot rely only on diffusion to meet all their cellular needs. Compared to the volume of cells in their bodies, their surface area is small. Plus, many organisms are protected by skin, hair, scales and shells that do not act as semi-permeable membranes to allow diffusion to take place.

Think about your own body. You inhale oxygen through your nose and mouth into your lungs. From the lungs, this oxygen has to be transported to every cell in your body. You eat and digest food to break it down into nutrients which have to be transported from your intestines to all the cells in your body (see Figure 13.1.2).

Diffusion is not efficient enough or fast enough to allow substances to move through your body and reach all your cells quickly enough for them to survive. It is therefore necessary for you to have another way of transporting substances throughout your body. In humans this system is called the circulatory system and blood is the medium of transport.

Materials transported in blood

Table 13.1.1 shows you some of the materials (including heat) that are transported in the blood in our circulatory system and why these substances need to be transported throughout our bodies.

▼ **Table 13.1.1** Substances transported in the blood

Substance	Transported from	Transported to	Why it needs to be transported
Oxygen	Lungs	Body cells	Respiration
Carbon dioxide	Body cells and tissues	Lungs	Excretion
Digested foods (fats, glucose and amino acids)	Digestive organs (intestinal villi) and liver	Body cells	Growth and cell metabolism
Urea and other nitrogenous wastes	Liver and body cells	Kidneys	Excretion
Hormones	Ductless endocrine glands	Various organs as needed	Regulation of body functions
Heat	Muscles, liver	All tissues	Regulation of body temperature

Questions

1 What is the advantage of a large surface-area-to-volume ratio in small uni-cellular and simple multi-cellular organisms?

2 In a sea anemone, each cell in the organism is exposed to the water in which the animal lives. Explain why this organism does not need an internal transport system.

3 Why can humans not rely on diffusion alone to transport substances that cells need from place to place?

4 Use cardboard or modelling clay to build a set of four cubes with different dimensions. (Remember a cube is a regular solid with six square faces.)

  a Use the formula: volume = length × breadth × height, to find the volume of each cube in millimetres cubed (mm^3).

  b Use the formula: total surface area = 6 × (area of one face), to find the surface area of each cube in millimetres squared (mm^2).

  c Calculate the ratio of the surface area to the volume of each cube. What happens to this ratio as the volume of the cube increases?

  d Relate your findings in this activity to the need for transport systems in multi-cellular organisms.

B13.2 The circulatory system

The circulatory system in humans and other mammals is made up of the heart and blood vessels. The heart acts as a pump to keep blood circulating throughout the body in the blood vessels. Blood passes through the heart twice as it is circulated round your body.

Blood vessels

Blood flows through the body in a network of tubes called blood vessels. There are three main types of blood vessels: arteries, veins and capillaries. Blood that flows from the heart travels through the arteries. The arteries branch into arterioles and become smaller and smaller until they form a network of thin vessels called capillaries around the cells of body tissue. Small veins, called venules branch out from the capillary network into veins to return the blood to the heart.

The major blood vessels are the arteries and veins. Table 13.2.1 compares arteries and veins.

Objectives

By the end of this topic you will be able to:

- name the parts of the human circulatory system
- describe the structure and function of the human heart
- discuss how the human heart works
- examine a mammalian heart to learn more about its internal and external features.

▼ **Table 13.2.1** A comparison of arteries and veins

Arteries	Veins
Carry oxygenated blood away from the heart to organs and tissues (except for the pulmonary artery which carries deoxygenated blood from the heart to the lungs)	Return deoxygenated blood to the heart from organs and tissues (except for the pulmonary vein which carries oxygen-rich blood from the lungs to the heart)
Blood is at high pressure	Blood is at low pressure. Body muscles squeeze the veins to help push the blood to the heart
Have a pulse, because the vessel walls expand and relax as blood is pumped from the heart	Do not have a pulse, since blood flows smoothly at low pressure
Have thick elastic and muscular walls to withstand pressure of blood	Have thin walls and a large diameter which reduces the resistance to the flow of blood returning to the heart, also contain valves to keep blood flowing in one direction only

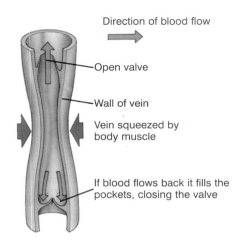

Figure 13.2.1 Valves inside veins make sure blood flows in one direction only

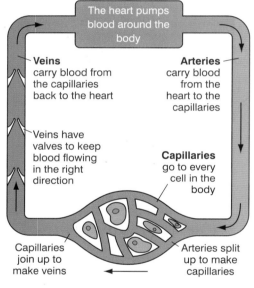

Figure 13.2.2 A simplified representation of the circulatory system

Blood in the veins is at a much lower pressure than in the arteries. One-way valves inside the veins prevent blood from flowing backwards. You can see this in Figure 13.2.1.

Arteries do not have valves like this because the force of the heart beating is strong enough to keep blood flowing away from the heart.

Capillaries

Capillaries are tiny vessels, with walls one cell thick, that link arteries to veins. They form dense networks, called beds, in the tissues of the body and carry blood through the organs and tissues so that materials can be exchanged. The networks of capillaries are very dense, so all the cells in your body are close to capillaries. This makes it easy for oxygen and nutrients to diffuse from capillaries into cells and for carbon dioxide and other wastes to diffuse from cells into capillaries to be carried away.

Figure 13.2.2 shows how arteries, capillaries and veins are linked in the circulatory system of humans.

Tissue fluid

The capillaries are the sites of exchange between blood and the cells of the body. Blood is contained in a closed system, but capillaries leak fluid from the blood into the tiny spaces between cells. This fluid is known as tissue fluid. Tissue fluid is the medium that allows exchanges of materials between cells and blood. Some tissue fluid diffuses back into the capillaries but the majority of tissue fluid passes back into the circulatory system through the lymphatic system. Figure 13.2.3 shows you the relationship between arteries, capillaries, veins and lymph vessels.

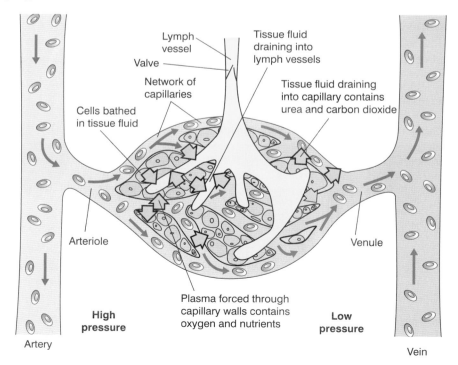

Figure 13.2.3 The relationship between arteries, capillaries, veins and lymph vessels

The lymphatic system

The lymph vessels return excess tissue fluids to the blood system. Capillary lymph vessels are blind-ended tubes which form a network in the body's tissues. Tissue fluid diffuses through their walls and slowly passes into the larger lymph vessels. The fluid is now called lymph and it is moved by the contraction of muscles during normal activities.

Lymph drains back into the circulatory system by joining the veins in the neck before they enter the vena cava and the heart.

A double circulation

During one complete circulation (in mammals) the blood flows through the heart twice. The heart is divided into two halves. The blood in these two halves does not mix. Figure 13.2.4 shows how blood arrives at the heart from the organs and tissues of the body and then travels to the lungs. From the lungs, the blood travels back to the heart and then to the organs and tissues of the body. The route followed by the blood is:

body ⟶ heart ⟶ lungs ⟶ heart ⟶ body.

Blood vessels and major organs

Figure 13.2.5 shows the routes that blood takes as it circulates round the major organs of your body. Pay attention to the names of the blood vessels that supply your major organs with the substances they need.

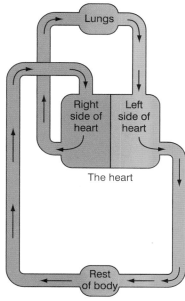

▲ **Figure 13.2.4** All mammals have a double circulation system

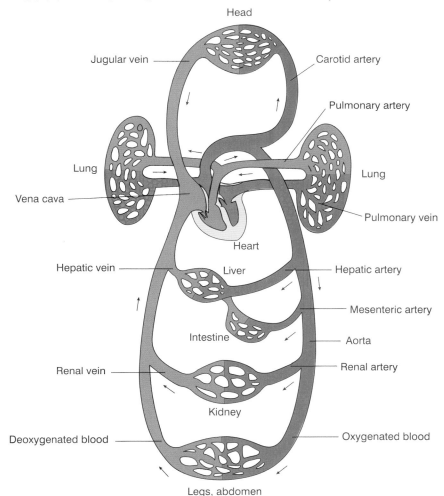

◀ **Figure 13.2.5** Major blood vessels and the routes followed by oxygenated and deoxygenated blood

The structure and functions of the heart

The heart is a pump that moves blood through the arteries and veins. The heart is made of cardiac muscle which contracts and relaxes rhythmically throughout your life without getting tired. The more efficient the heart is, the more efficiently you can exchange food, oxygen, carbon dioxide and other dissolved substances between the blood and tissues of the body.

The structure of the heart

The heart lies in the chest cavity surrounded by a membrane called the pericardium. The heart is protected by the rib cage. Figure 13.2.6 shows the heart and the blood vessels leading in to and out of it. Figure 13.2.6a shows a longitudinal-section through the heart and Figure 13.2.6b shows the whole heart. Note that heart diagrams are always shown from the front as if you were looking at someone else's heart, so the right chambers are always on the left of the diagram.

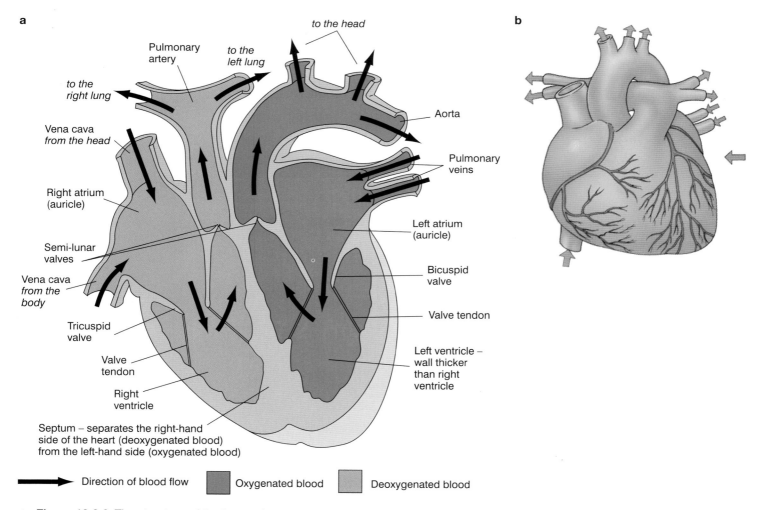

▲ **Figure 13.2.6** The structure of the human heart

You can see that the heart is divided into two parts: the right side receives deoxygenated blood from the body and pumps it to the lungs where it is oxygenated and the left side receives the oxygenated blood from the lungs and pumps it throughout the body.

The heart is made up of four chambers. The top two are thin-walled chambers called atria (singular atrium). The lower two chambers are called ventricles. The ventricles are larger than the atria and they have thicker walls. The two halves of the heart are separated by the septum and blood in the left and right halves does not mix.

Even though the heart is full of blood, it is muscle tissue, so it needs a supply of blood, just like any other muscle tissue does. The walls of the heart muscle are so thick that oxygen and nutrients from the blood cannot diffuse from the blood inside the heart fast enough to supply its cellular needs. So, some of the heart muscle is supplied with blood by the coronary arteries.

How the heart works

Put simply, the heart is a pump. When the muscles relax, the heart fills up with blood. When the muscles contract, the heart pumps the blood through the body. The muscles then relax again and the heart fills up with more blood so that it can continue pumping. This process continues in an ongoing cycle called the cardiac cycle. You can see the two main phases in the cardiac cycle in Figure 13.2.7.

In the diastole phase, the atria and ventricles are relaxed. Blood from the body and lungs flows into the atria. The valves between the atria and ventricles are open at this stage, allowing blood from the atria to flow into the ventricles. As the ventricles fill, the semi-lunar valves close and prevent the blood from flowing backwards into the atria.

During the systole phase, both atria contract together, forcing more blood into the ventricles. Both ventricles then contract at the same time forcing blood out of the heart. The right ventricle pumps blood into the pulmonary artery to be carried to the lungs. The left ventricle pumps blood into the aorta to be carried to the rest of the body.

The right ventricle pumps blood into the pulmonary artery to be carried to the lungs. The left ventricle pumps blood into the aorta to be carried to the rest of the body. The semi-lunar valves close when the ventricles relax.

Each ventricle pumps blood along a different path through the body. Look at Figure 13.2.5 on p139 again. Notice that the blood which travels through the head and body path has to travel a greater distance than the blood that travels through the lung circuit. This means that the left ventricle has to pump harder to move the blood over the longer distance. This is why the left ventricle walls are thicker than the right ventricle walls.

Heartbeats

The opening and closing of heart valves produces a two-tone sound that can be heard easily through a stethoscope. This sound is called a heartbeat. In a healthy adult, the heart beats an average of 70 times per minute (but it can range from 60 to 80).

The beating of the heart is controlled by a group of special cells in the right atrium known as the pacemaker. Occasionally the natural pacemaker malfunctions and the heart starts to beat more slowly causing drowsiness and shortage of breath. When the heart's natural pacemaker does not function properly, an electronic pacemaker can be placed in the chest next to the heart to keep it beating at a normal rate.

The heart is relaxed and the atria and then ventricles fill with blood

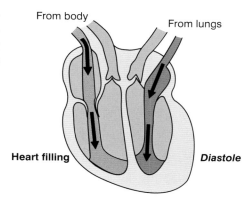

From body   From lungs

Heart filling   Diastole

The heart contracts (first the atria then the ventricles) and blood is pumped out into the body

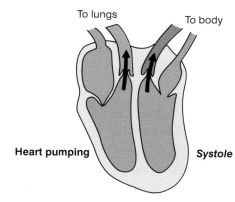

To lungs   To body

Heart pumping   Systole

▲ **Figure 13.2.7** The action of the heart

Safety

Wash your hands afterwards.

 Practical activity

Examining a mammalian heart

Your teacher may use this activity to assess: Drawing.

Your teacher will supply you with the heart of an ox or sheep that has been cut open so that you can look inside.

1 Identify the atria and ventricles. Feel them and explain why they feel different.

2 Which is the left ventricle? How can you tell?

3 If the blood vessels are still intact, try to identify them.

4 Find the valves between the atria and ventricles and the valves at the base of the pulmonary artery and aorta. State the function of each.

5 Draw a labelled diagram showing the longitudinal-section of the heart. Do not forget to show your magnification.

Questions

1 List the differences between arteries and veins and state why these differences are necessary.

2 Arteries and veins are connected by small blood vessels just one cell thick. What are these small blood vessels called?

3 Blood spurts from a cut artery but it seeps more slowly from a cut vein. Explain why.

4 Copy Figure 13.2.8 and label parts **a** to **h** of the heart. Add arrows to the diagram to show the path taken by blood through the heart.

5 How does the blood entering the left atrium differ from blood leaving the right ventricle?

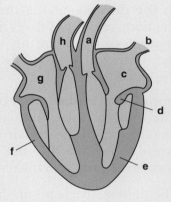

▲ **Figure 13.2.8**

Objectives

By the end of this topic you will be able to:

- identify the components of mammalian blood
- describe the functions of different blood components
- draw and label red and white blood cells
- state the functions of plasma, red and white blood cells and platelets.

B13.3 The functions and composition of blood

Blood has many different functions in mammals. You have already learnt that blood transports substances to and from the capillaries where exchanges take place between the blood and the cells of the body (see p138). Blood helps the body to fight invasions by bacteria and viruses. Blood also helps to regulate body temperature and it clots if the skin is broken to prevent excessive blood loss.

If you take a sample of blood from a mammal and spin it in a special machine called a centrifuge, the blood separates out into two parts, as shown in Figure 13.3.1. The blood separates into a clear liquid fraction called plasma and a dark reddish-brown solid fraction consisting of blood cells.

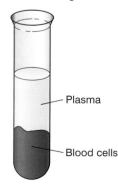

Plasma

Blood cells

▶ **Figure 13.3.1** A centrifuge separates blood into plasma and blood cells

Plasma

Plasma is a sticky, yellowish liquid. It is 90% water and 10% substances carried in solution. These substances include digested food, such as sugars, amino acids, vitamins and minerals, excretory products, such as carbon dioxide and urea, hormones and large protein molecules, such as antibodies.

Blood cells

Blood cells are made in bone marrow. There are three main groups of blood cells:

- Red blood cells – these are cells that contain the red pigment haemoglobin that gives blood its colour. Red blood cells do not have nuclei.
- White blood cells – there are two types of white blood cell: lymphocytes and phagocytes. The nucleus of each type has a characteristic shape.
- Platelets – these are fragments of cells made in the bone marrow. They are very small (about 3 μm) but they are important for blood clotting.

Figure 13.3.2 shows the main groups of blood cells.

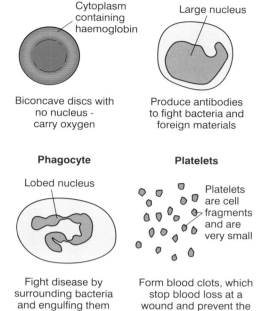

▲ **Figure 13.3.2** Different types of blood cells

Red blood cells

Red blood cells do not have a nucleus so they cannot survive for more than three months. Old red blood cells are destroyed in the liver or the spleen.

Red blood cells contain the protein haemoglobin. Haemoglobin readily combines with oxygen in the tissues to form a bright red, unstable compound called oxyhaemoglobin. Where the oxygen concentration is low, oxyhaemoglobin breaks down to release free oxygen.

$$\text{haemoglobin} + \text{oxygen} \rightleftharpoons \text{oxyhaemoglobin}$$

This allows red blood cells to pick up oxygen molecules in the lungs and transport the oxygen to the cells and tissues of the body.

Cellular respiration releases carbon dioxide which diffuses into the blood. Some of this forms hydrogencarbonate ions in the plasma. Haemoglobin carries the rest of the carbon dioxide in the red blood cells. When blood reaches the lungs, carbon dioxide diffuses from the plasma and the red blood cells into the alveoli where it is exhaled.

Figure 13.3.3 shows what happens to the red blood cells in the lungs and in other parts of the body.

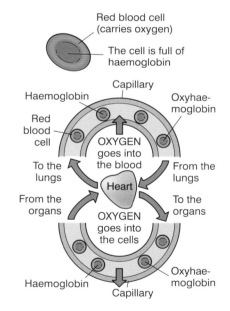

▲ **Figure 13.3.3** The main job of red blood cells is to carry oxygen throughout the body

White blood cells

White blood cells are larger than red blood cells. They do not contain haemoglobin so they appear translucent under a microscope unless they are stained. They have a nucleus.

Some microorganisms (bacteria and viruses) can get into the blood and tissues where they cause infection or disease. The two types of white blood cells, lymphocytes and phagocytes, protect the body by working quickly to destroy harmful microorganisms and any other foreign substances that the body does not recognise in the blood. Foreign substances are called antigens. When antigens come into contact with lymphocytes they stimulate the lymphocytes to produce antibodies which begin the process of destruction. The phagocytes complete the job by engulfing the foreign substances, such as bacteria, digesting and killing them. Figure 13.3.4 shows you how this process happens in our blood.

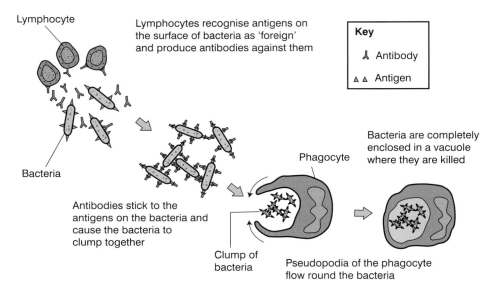

▲ **Figure 13.3.4** White blood cells protect the body from infection and illness

Table 13.3.1 summarises the components of blood and the main functions of each component.

▼ **Table 13.3.1** Components and functions of blood

Component of blood	Functions
Plasma 90% water with substances in solution	Blood cells float in the plasma and are transported by it. Transport dissolved food, wastes, hormones and heat throughout the body.
Red blood cells Cells with no nucleus that contain haemoglobin	Main function is to transport oxygen. Some carbon dioxide is also transported.
White blood cells Larger than red blood cells, with a nucleus. Two types: lymphocytes and phagocytes	Fight and destroy microbes. (Note: 'Microbe' and 'microorganism' mean the same.) Produce antibodies.
Platelets Small particles of cells	Help blood to clot at a cut.

Questions

1 Copy Figure 13.3.5 and label the components of the blood.

2 What is the biggest fraction of blood? What does this contain?

3 Where are red blood cells made? Why are they red? How are they adapted for carrying oxygen?

4 List three ways in which white blood cells are different from red blood cells.

5 What is the main function of white blood cells?

6 What are platelets and what do they do?

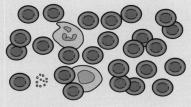

▲ **Figure 13.3.5**

B13.4 Human body defence systems

The human body has several defences against pathogens. External defences aim to prevent pathogens from entering the body. Internal defences operate inside the body to disable and kill pathogens which have managed to enter the body. The body's defences against disease are known collectively as the immune system. The immune system consists of the skin, parts of the respiratory system, parts of the digestive system and the blood. Figure 13.4.1 shows you the main components of the immune system and their role in defending the body against pathogens.

Objectives

By the end of this topic you will be able to:

● state how the body defends itself against pathogens
● describe the role of blood in defending the body and in developing natural immunity.

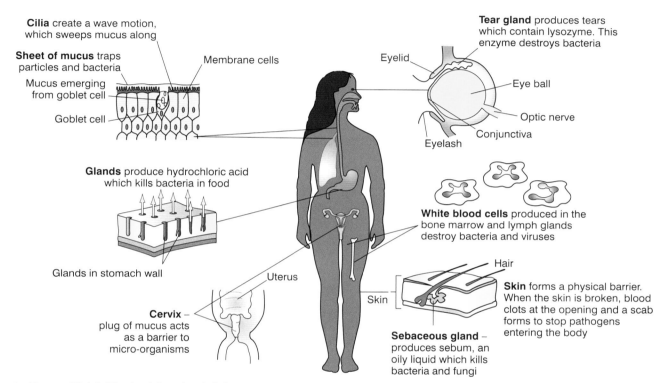

▲ **Figure 13.4.1** The body's natural defences

Internal defence systems

In topic B13.3 you learnt that platelets cause blood to clot at wounds and that white blood cells (lymphocytes and phagocytes) in the blood system protect the body by working quickly to destroy viruses and bacteria. The blood plays an important role in protecting the body and is responsible for immunity and the immune response.

Immunity and the immune response

Immunity is the body's resistance to a specific condition or disease. When a specific pathogen, such as measles, enters the body and is destroyed by the internal defences, we describe the person as being 'immune' to that disease. The immunity may last for a short time or for life.

The body's immune response is its reaction to being invaded by specific foreign materials, such as viruses, bacteria, toxins or other unrecognised proteins. The body recognises that these substances are foreign and it responds by trying to destroy them. Substances which cause an immune response are called antigens. The immune response involves the

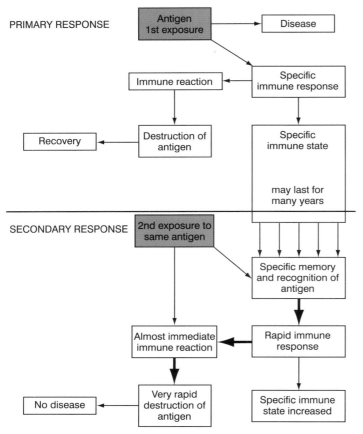

PRIMARY RESPONSE

SECONDARY RESPONSE

▲ **Figure 13.4.2** The body's immune response

lymphocytes and the production of antibodies. These are proteins which the body produces in response to specific antigens. The antibodies bind onto the targeted antigens and destroy them.

Antibodies produced against a particular antigen will attack only that antigen. The antibody is said to be specific to that antigen. This means that the antibodies produced against the typhoid bacteria will not attack the pneumonia bacteria. The body is able to produce tens of millions of specific antibodies in a lifetime.

Natural immunity

The antibodies that are produced against a microorganism may stay in the body for some time ready to attack the same microorganisms when they attack the body again. Even if the antibodies do not remain in the body, the antigens of the microorganism are recognised by the lymphocytes on further attacks. The lymphocytes then rapidly produce large quantities of the antibody. This means that the re-infection is dealt with by an immune reaction which is even more effective than the first reaction. We say the body has become 'resistant' to the disease. This is why you rarely contract diseases like chicken pox and measles more than once. Figure 13.4.2 shows you the body's immune response.

The action of lymphocytes and phagocytes

You should remember that lymphocytes are a type of white blood cell produced in the bone marrow. Lymphocytes work together with phagocytes to keep the body healthy. They quickly destroy pathogens that infect the blood or tissues and which the body does not recognise as its own. Lymphocytes produce antibodies in response to antigens. Phagocytes engulf and destroy antigens.

 Key fact

The body sometimes produces antibodies against harmless substances. When this happens, the person suffers from allergies. Common allergens are pollen and animal hair. Common symptoms of an allergy are itchy and swollen skin, red eyes and a runny nose.

Questions

1 What role do the skin, cilia and mucous membranes play in preventing disease?

2 What is an 'antigen'?

3 Describe the body's response to antigens with reference to the role of the white blood cells and the production of antibodies

Objectives

By the end of this topic you will be able to:

● explain how the principles of immunisation are used in disease control

● discuss how vaccines are used to provide artificial immunity.

B13.5 Immunisation and disease control

Immunisation is the process of protecting a person from a disease (or making them immune to a disease) by giving them a substance (by mouth or by injection) that provides artificial immunity. Immunisation can promote active or passive immunity to disease-carrying microorganisms.

The substance that is injected or swallowed is called a vaccine and the process of being immunised is called immunisation or vaccination.

Vaccines are made from one of the following:

- Dead microorganisms, for example, whooping-cough vaccine is made from dead bacteria.
- A weakened form of the microorganism that is harmless. Vaccines made like this are called attenuated vaccines. The vaccine against tuberculosis is an attenuated vaccine.
- A substance from the disease-causing microorganism, which does not itself cause the disease, for example, the diphtheria vaccine.

The processes of genetic engineering are also used to produce new vaccines.

How do vaccines work?

There are two types of vaccination. One provides active immunity, the other provides passive immunity.

Active immunity is acquired when the person is given a vaccine consisting of antigens. This stimulates the lymphocytes to produce antibodies specific to that antigen. These antibodies remain in the blood for a long time to provide a defence that can eliminate the microorganism should it infect the body in the future. Active immunity is acquired when you are vaccinated against diseases such as measles, tuberculosis, polio, diphtheria and whooping cough. In some cases, the levels of immunity may drop off over time and booster injections may be needed to maintain the levels of immunity. For example, the polio vaccine is given to babies and then a booster injection is given at ages five and 15.

Passive immunity is acquired when the person is given a vaccine consisting of antibodies produced by another organism in response to infection by a specific pathogen. This method is used when the person has been exposed to an antigen but has no immunity. For example, pregnant women who are exposed to German measles may be given a vaccine made from human serum or with antibodies from human serum. Similarly, if you cut yourself deeply on something dirty, you are given a tetanus injection made from antibodies. Passive immunity is important for babies. Babies are not able to make their own antibodies until they are one to three months old, so they are dependent on antibodies from their mothers. Some antibodies cross the placenta to provide immunity before the baby is born. However, most babies receive antibodies from their mother's milk when they are breastfed. The passive immunity they acquire is short-lived, but by the time it wears off, they are able to produce their own antibodies.

You have probably been immunised against some communicable diseases. Children are routinely vaccinated against six diseases that used to cause many deaths. These are:

- diphtheria, which affects the throat and releases toxins that can damage the heart;
- tetanus, which causes the muscles in the body to permanently contract and which can lock the jaw so that the person cannot swallow;
- whooping cough, which is a serious cough that can lead to pneumonia and an increased risk of brain damage;
- poliomyelitis, which damages the nervous system and can cause paralysis;
- tuberculosis, which affects the lungs and is very infectious;

- and German measles, which is not serious in children but can damage unborn babies if the mother is exposed to the virus.

The result of immunisation campaigns is that these diseases are now rare in most countries. However, if the number of people who are vaccinated were to drop, the number of cases would rise among unprotected people.

Problems in the immune system

The immune system does not always work properly.

In some cases, the immune system may over-function and lead to hypersensitivity reactions and auto-immune diseases. In a hypersensitivity reaction, the immune system attacks body tissues instead of the microorganism. An example of this is an allergic reaction that leads to asthma. In an auto-immune disease, the T-lymphocytes treat the body's own proteins as antigens. Rheumatoid arthritis is an auto-immune disease in which cells in the joints of the hands and feet are attacked and inflammation sets in.

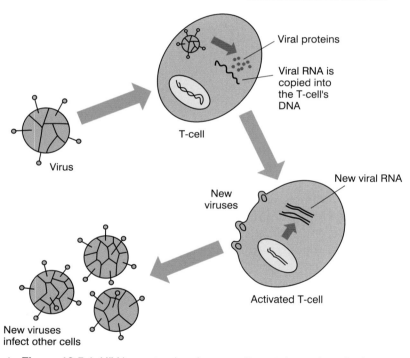

▲ **Figure 13.5.1** HIV is a retrovirus because it contains only a single strand of RNA in a protein coating

The immune system may also under-function and lead to immune deficiency diseases. In an immune deficiency disease, the body's defences become suppressed and they are not able to defend against invading microorganisms. AIDS is probably the best-known immune deficiency disease. In AIDS, the HIV attacks the T-lymphocytes causing the body to be vulnerable to opportunistic infections it would otherwise be able to fight off. The most common infections in AIDS patients are Kaposi's sarcoma (a type of skin cancer), a type of pneumonia and leucoplakia which causes thick white patches to develop on the tongue.

HIV spreads by invading T-lymphocytes. At first the virus does not multiply. When the T-lymphocyte is activated to fight another pathogen, the virus is activated and it spreads in the T-lymphocytes as they clone themselves and differentiate. By invading T-lymphocytes, the HIV effectively breaks down the body's own defences. Figure 13.5.1 shows you how HIV infects cells.

Questions

1 What is the difference between 'active immunity' and 'passive' immunity?

2 What is a vaccine?

3 Explain how vaccines work in the body.

4 Illnesses which are normally not serious, such as flu, can lead to death in people who have developed AIDS. Explain why.

Like humans and other multi-cellular organisms, plants need to move substances from place to place. Plants have a specialised transport system that allows water and food to be moved around the plant to supply its cellular needs.

B14.1 Transport structures

Plant leaves are able to get the carbon dioxide they need for photosynthesis directly from the air by diffusion. They get the oxygen they need for respiration in the same way. However, for the plant to survive, cells in different parts of the plant need to be supplied with the water and nutrients. Plants therefore have a transport system to allow for the movement of water from the roots to the leaves and other parts of the plant and for the movement of food made in the leaves to other parts of the plant.

The transport system of plants

The transport system in plants consists of a network of very fine tubes made of specialised tissue known as xylem and phloem. Xylem vessels transport water and phloem tubes transport food. You can see a simplified version of how this transport system works in Figure 14.1.1.

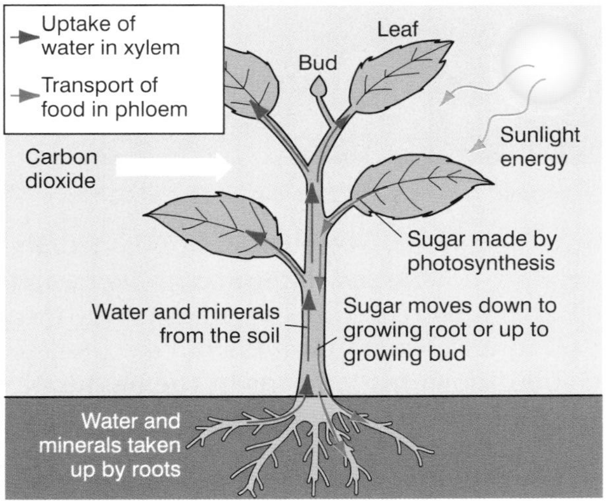

Objectives

By the end of this topic you will be able to:

- explain the importance of a transport system in plants
- identify the two main transport structures: xylem and phloem
- describe the structure of xylem vessels
- draw and label xylem vessels
- explain how the structure of xylem vessels suits their function
- observe water movement through the xylem.

▲ **Figure 14.1.1** The transport system in plants

A network of vessels for circulation is called a **vascular system**. The vessels or vascular tubes formed from xylem and phloem are grouped closely together in plants to make up a vascular bundle. This is a long, continuous strand of tissue that extends from the roots, up the stem to the leaves of plants. The arrangement of vascular bundles in the stems and leaves of flowering plants is shown in Figure 14.1.2.

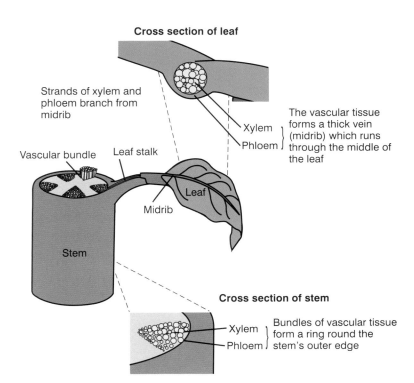

▲ **Figure 14.1.2** The arrangement of vascular bundles in a flowering plant

You will learn more about the structure and functions of phloem tubes in topic B14.4 which deals with the movement of food through plants. Now you will focus only on xylem vessels because they play an important role in water relations in plants.

Xylem

Xylem transports water and mineral ions upwards from the roots to the leaves of plants. Xylem tubes or vessels are made from dead cells thickened with woody material called lignin. Lignin strengthens the cells walls and helps to make xylem vessels waterproof. The xylem cells join end to end and their cross walls break down to form long continuous hollow vessels through which water can pass freely. The strong walls of these non-living tubes also help to give support, rigidity and strength to the stems of plants. You can see a scanning electron micrograph of xylem vessels in Figure 14.1.3. Figure 14.1.4 shows how xylem vessels are formed.

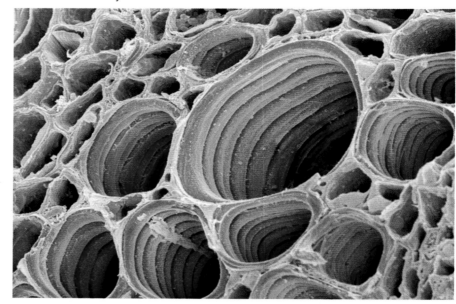

▲ **Figure 14.1.3** Xylem vessels are supported by thick bands of cellulose and lignin

You can see from the diagrams that xylem vessels are well suited for transporting water. They are long, thin, hollow and waterproof so that water can move freely upwards through them. You can think of them as very thin drinking straws that the plant uses to suck water upwards from the roots to the leaves. You will learn more about how this happens in the next topic (B14.2) when you deal with the transpiration stream.

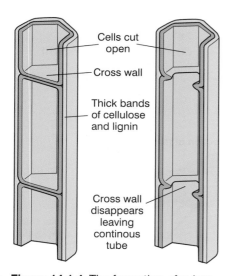

Cells cut open

Cross wall

Thick bands of cellulose and lignin

Cross wall disappears leaving continous tube

▲ **Figure 14.1.4** The formation of xylem vessels

 **Key fact**

You should remember that osmosis is the movement of water from an area of higher water potential to an area of lower water potential.

 Practical activity

Observing water movement through a plant

You will need two small plants with their root systems intact.

Method

1 Wash the roots of the plants to remove the soil.

2 Stand one plant in a jar of clear water and the other in a jar of water containing a coloured dye (use eosin or red or blue ink) for about 4 hours.

3 Remove the plants. Cut through both stems and compare them.

What do you notice?

Explain your observations.

How could you check that the dye solution was transported in xylem vessels?

Place a balsam plant, which has a transparent stem, in the dye solution. The transparent stem allows you to see the movement of dye upwards through the plant.

Use this to try and work out the rate at which water moves upwards through the plant. Record your results.

Questions

1 List two differences between the transport system in humans and the transport system in plants.

2 Explain what is meant by the term 'vascular bundle'.

3 Draw and label a section through a xylem vessel to show its structure.

B14.2 Transpiration

The movement of water through the xylem of plants depends on transpiration. Transpiration is the evaporation of water from the leaves of plants to the air. As water is lost from the leaves of the plant more water is pulled upwards through the xylem vessels. In this topic you are going to learn more about this process.

Water movements in plants

Water enters the plant through the root hairs by osmosis. The water moves across the root cortex by osmosis and passes into the xylem vessels. Figure 14.2.1 shows the path taken by water from the soil through the roots to the xylem.

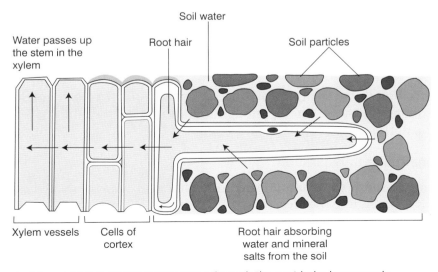

Water passes up the stem in the xylem

Root hair

Soil water

Soil particles

Xylem vessels

Cells of cortex

Root hair absorbing water and mineral salts from the soil

▲ **Figure 14.2.1** Water enters roots through the root hairs by osmosis

Once in the xylem vessels, water forms unbroken columns from the roots, through the stem and into the leaves. Water evaporates from the leaves, mainly through the stomata (tiny pores) on the underside of the leaf by transpiration (see Figure 14.2.2).

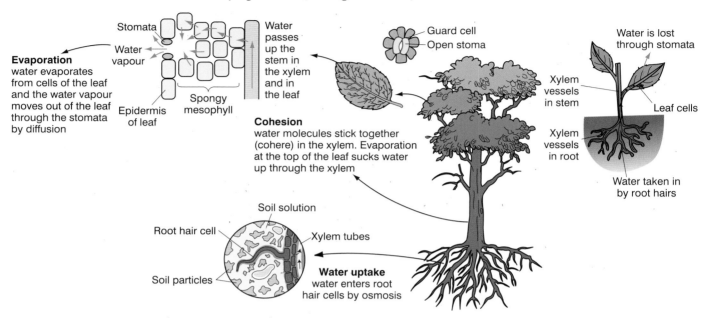

▲ **Figure 14.2.2** The transpiration stream

The water that is lost through transpiration from the plant has to be replaced by water taken in through the roots, otherwise the plant will wilt and die. The constant upward flow of water through a plant is known as the transpiration stream.

The water that evaporates from the leaves during transpiration gets the transpiration stream going. This is called the transpiration pull. Water is drawn up the xylem vessels to replace the water that is lost. Xylem vessels are well suited to the process because they are very narrow and they act as capillaries for the water. The forces of attraction between water molecules and the adhesive force between the water and the cell walls also help to move water upwards. This action is known as capillarity.

As water is sucked up through the xylem in the stem, more water is supplied to the bottom of the xylem vessels by the roots. This water increases the pressure in the root xylem. The higher root pressure pushes the water up the xylem to the areas of lower pressure created as water is lost. In this way, there is a continuous flow of water from the roots to the leaves.

The force that drives the transpiration stream is equivalent to as much as 30 atmospheres pressure – strong enough to move water from the roots to the very top of the tallest tree.

Demonstrating transpiration

Figure 14.2.3 shows you a simple experiment that you can carry out to show that plants lose water from their leaves, in other words, to show that plants transpire.

This experiment demonstrates that transpiration takes place. You can test that the liquid inside the bell jar is water using cobalt(II) chloride paper (which turns pink in water) or anhydrous copper(II) sulfate crystals (which turn blue in water).

The pot is placed in a plastic bag to contain any water that evaporates from the soil

The leaves are removed from the control because we are trying to show that the leaves lose water

▲ **Figure 14.2.3** After 24 hours, water droplets will condense on the inside of the jar with the leafy plant

Transpiration takes place at different rates. In the next topic you will investigate the factors that affect transpiration and carry out an investigation with a potometer to measure how these factors affect the rate of transpiration.

Questions

1 Define the terms:
   a transpiration
   b transpiration stream
   c transpiration pull
   d root pressure
   e capillarity.

2 Describe how water moves from the soil, through the roots and up to the leaves of plants. Use the correct biological vocabulary in your description.

3 Explain why it is a bad idea to plant out young seedlings on a bright, windy day.

4 How is it possible for water to reach the topmost branches of very tall trees?

B14.3 Factors affecting transpiration

Plants need to maintain their water balance. If the water that is lost through transpiration is not balanced by the uptake of water from the soil then the stomata on the leaves close to reduce the rate of transpiration. If the plant still does not get enough water from the soil, then the cells begin to lose turgor and the plant wilts (see pp83 and 158).

Normally stomata are open during the day, so that gases can be exchanged during photosynthesis, and almost closed at night. So more transpiration takes place during the day. However, various environmental factors also affect the rate of transpiration.

External factors that affect transpiration

Evapo-transpiration is a geographical term which describes how water is returned to the atmosphere to form part of the water cycle, by evaporation from land and water surfaces and from plants by transpiration. The rate at which water evaporates from plants is affected by the conditions in the environment (see Figure 14.3.1). Transpiration is affected by:

- temperature
- humidity
- wind velocity
- light intensity
- water content of the soil.

Temperature

The graph in Figure 14.3.1a shows how temperature affects the rate of transpiration. When the temperature rises, the relative humidity of the air around the plant is lowered. Relative humidity is a measure of how much water vapour the air contains expressed as a percentage of how much it

Objectives

By the end of this topic you will be able to:

- identify the environmental conditions that affect the rate of transpiration
- explain the terms evapo-transpiration and relative humidity
- carry out an investigation to demonstrate how light, humidity and air movement affect transpiration rates.

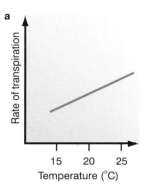

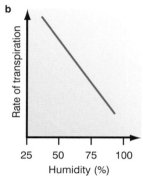

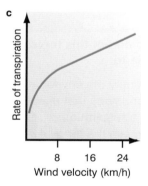

▲ **Figure 14.3.1** The conditions in the environment affect transpiration

could hold. So, for example if the relative humidity is 80%, then the air contains 80% of the total water vapour it could hold. Warm air is less dense that cold air, so it can hold more water vapour. This is what causes the drop in relative humidity when the temperature increases. At the same time, higher temperatures increase the rate of evaporation from the plant's leaves and water vapour diffuses more quickly from the leaves to the air.

Humidity

You know that diffusion takes places from areas of high concentration to a lower concentration. So, when the humidity in the air is low, water vapour from moist leaves diffuses more quickly into the air. Similarly, when the humidity is high, less transpiration takes place because there is less of a diffusion gradient between the water content of the air and the water content of the leaves. You can see how humidity affects transpiration rates in Figure 14.3.1b.

Wind velocity

When the air is still, the water vapour that diffuses out of a plant's leaves builds up around the leaves, creating a humid environment that does not favour transpiration. When the wind blows, the moist air is blown away from the plant and the rate of transpiration increases. When it is very windy, plants may close their stomata to prevent too much transpiration taking place. The graph in Figure 14.3.1c shows how wind velocity affects the rate of transpiration.

Light intensity

Light does not affect the rate of transpiration directly, but it does affect the opening and closing of the stomata, which in turn affect how much transpiration can take place. Transpiration is more rapid in bright sunlight because the stomata are fully open.

Water content of the soil

The amount of water in the soil affects the rate at which water can be taken up by the plant. If the soil dries out so that roots cannot take in water, the rate of transpiration in the plant slows down. The plant closes its stomata to stop transpiration. In conditions where the ground remains dry, the plant will eventually wilt and die.

You are now going to do an investigation to show how temperature, humidity, wind and light affect transpiration from a plant. You are going to use a piece of apparatus called a potometer. The potometer does not actually measure transpiration, it measures the rate at which water is taken up by the plant. Because these two processes are related, we can use the potometer to draw conclusions about transpiration rates.

 Key fact

Some plants have special adaptations to reduce the transpiration rate. These adaptations include a thick waxy cuticle on leaves, a reduced leaf surface (small leaves or spines instead of leaves), hairy leaves or stems to trap water vapour, thick stems and sunken stomata. You will learn more about this in topic B14.5.

Practical activity

Investigating and measuring transpiration rates with a potometer

Your teacher may use this activity to assess: ORR; M&M; A&I.

You will need to set up a potometer as shown in Figure 14.3.2. Your teacher will assist with this (your equipment may be slightly different to that shown).

Method

- Cut a shoot from a leafy plant and place it in water immediately. Keeping the end of the plant under water, make a slanting cut a few centimetres above the first cut you made. The stem must fit tightly into the hole of your potometer.
- Transfer the cut shoot to the apparatus under water to avoid air bubbles getting in the system.
- Remove the system and seal the plug around the shoot with Vaseline.
- Release the valve and let the air bubble settle close to zero.
- Measure how long it takes for the water column to move a given distance along the capillary tube. This will be your control rate for comparison. Each time the air bubble reaches the end of the measuring section of the tube, re-set it to zero by releasing the valve again.

Use your equipment to investigate the following:

1 The effect of temperature on transpiration – you could do this by placing the apparatus in a warm place and in a cool place and comparing rates.

2 The effect of humidity on transpiration – you can enclose the plant in a transparent plastic bag to increase the humidity.

3 The effect of wind on transpiration – use a small electric fan, but do not allow it to move the leaves too much or the stomata will close.

4 The effect of light and darkness on transpiration – place the apparatus in a dark place and measure the rate of water uptake.

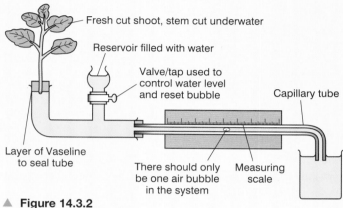

▲ **Figure 14.3.2**

Copy and complete this table based on your investigations and changing conditions:

	Conditions	Average time taken for air bubble to move 100 mm
Control set up	Normal classroom air	
Normal air around plant	Hot, still air	
	Hot, windy air	
	Cool, still air	
	Cool, windy air	
	Light conditions	
	Dark conditions	
High humidity (plant enclosed in plastic bag)	Hot, still air	
	Cool, still air	
	Light conditions	
	Dark conditions	

B14.4 Transport of minerals and food

You have learnt how water is transported through plants by the xylem. In this topic you will learn how plants take in mineral ions through their roots and how these are transported by the xylem. You will also learn more about phloem tissue and its role in transporting food made in the leaves to other parts of the plant.

Mineral ions

Mineral ions enter the plant through the root hairs by active transport. The concentration of mineral ions is normally higher in root tissue than in the soil. Normally, therefore, mineral ions would diffuse down their concentration gradient from the roots to the soil. However, roots take up mineral ions against their concentration gradient in the reverse direction to normal diffusion. This process is called active transport and it allows cells to build up stores of substances that would otherwise be spread out by diffusion. Active transport uses a lot of energy, which is supplied by mitochondria in the cells of the root hair.

The mineral ions which are now in the root cells are dissolved in water for transportation to the rest of the plant through the xylem.

Phloem and the movement of food

Phloem transports food materials, mostly in the form of sugars, up and down the stem to all parts of the plant.

Xylem vessels consist of dead cells. Phloem tissue consists of living cells. The most important of these cells are the sieve cells and companion cells. Sieve cells are cylindrical and joined at their end walls to form strands of tissue called sieve tubes. Figure 14.4.1 shows the structure of phloem tissue.

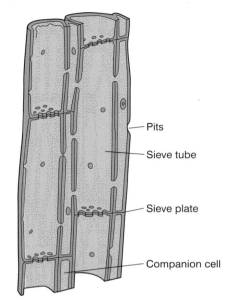

▲ **Figure 14.4.1** Sieve tubes of phloem with companion cells

Mature sieve cells are alive. They contain cytoplasm but they do not have a nucleus. The end wall of each cell is called a sieve plate because it is pierced with small holes. There is a companion cell next to each sieve plate. The companion cells and sieve cells work together to transport sugars to where they are needed in the plant. The movement of sugars and other substances from one region to another through the sieve cells is called translocation.

Figure 14.4.2 shows how translocation takes place. Sugar passes from the leaf cells to the sieve cells by active transport. Once it enters the sieve tubes, the sugar and other substances are carried to the parts of the plant where they are needed. The translocation of sugar depends on the differences in sugar concentration in different parts of the plant. Diffusion transports sugar from areas of high concentration, such as the leaves, to areas of lower concentration, such as the roots which cannot produce their own sugar by photosynthesis. Sugar that passes to the roots can move out of the sieve tubes and into the cells of the cortex. The sugar is converted to starch in the roots and stored.

How do we know that phloem transports food?

Earlier you carried out simple experiments to show that water is transported in the xylem. Scientists have done experiments to show that xylem transports water for over 300 years. Experiments to show that food is transported by the phloem are more recent. Two of the best known experiments involve ringing trees by removing bark and using aphids to track radioactive tracers.

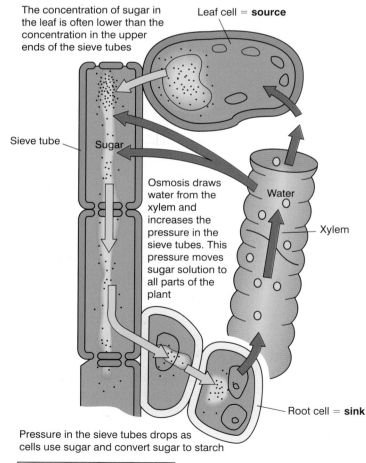

◄ **Figure 14.4.2** Translocation of sugars and other substances through the sieve tubes

Aphids and radioactive tracers

Small insects, called aphids, can be used to study the transport of sugar in the sieve tubes of the phloem. To feed, the aphid pushes its tube-like mouthpart, called a stylet, through the stem into a sieve tube. The pressure of the liquid in the sieve tube is so great that it force-feeds the aphids to the point where drops ooze from its anus. When aphids are anaesthetised with carbon dioxide and cut from their stylets, the liquid from the sieve tube continues to ooze for several days. Radioactively labelled glucose is injected into a leaf and samples are collected from the stylet. The presence of the radioactive tracers in the liquid shows that the sugar is transported in the sieve tubes. This method can also be used to work out the rate of flow through the sieve tubes.

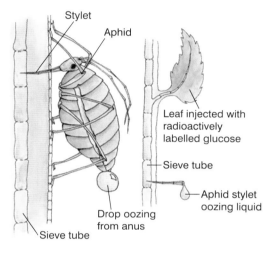

▲ **Figure 14.4.3** Aphids feed on plant sugars by pushing their mouthparts into the phloem

Tree ringing experiments

In these experiments a strip of bark is cut from the stem of a woody plant. The strip is just thick enough to contain phloem from the vascular bundles. The xylem is not removed. After a few days, there is a bulge of growth above the ringed section and no further growth below the ringed section. This is because the movement of sugars downwards is stopped by the ring. The tree does not die immediately because water can still move upwards, but it will die eventually as the roots will not be able to receive nutrients.

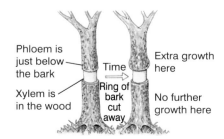

▲ **Figure 14.4.4** Tree ringing involves removing a strip of bark and phloem

 Key fact

Experiments with ringing cotton plants done by T. G. Mason and E. J. Maskell at the Cotton Research Station in Trinidad in the 1920s are often quoted in biology books because they showed that food moves downwards in phloem not in xylem.

Questions

1 What is the difference between active and passive transport systems in cells? Give an example of each from a plant.

2 Draw labelled diagrams to show the structure of phloem vessels.

3 How are sugars transported by the phloem?

4 What evidence do scientists have that phloem transports sugars?

5 Chemicals to control pests and diseases are often sprayed onto the leaves of plants. How can these control or kill insect pests such as aphids?

Osmoregulation in plants   **Transport and water relations in plants**

Objectives

By the end of this topic you will be able to:

- discuss ways in which plants are adapted to conserve water
- observe xerophytic plants to see how they are adapted to conserve water
- model plant leaves to see how leaf shape affects water loss.

B14.5 Osmoregulation in plants

Plants also need to maintain a water balance so that they can keep their cells turgid and as a means of transporting food and other substances throughout the plant. Because plants have strong cell walls, they do not have the same problems with osmosis that animal cells have. For this reasons, osmoregulation in plants normally focuses on conserving water and preventing water loss through transpiration.

Plant habitats and osmoregulation

Plants are found in many different environmental conditions. The environment that plants live in affects the structures they develop for absorbing, storing and preventing the loss of water. We can place plants into four main groups based on their environmental conditions:

- Hydrophytes are plants, such as water lilies and *Elodea*, which live in fresh water. They have a constant supply of water and they do not develop special structures for osmoregulation.

- Halophytes are plants that live in areas of high salinity (salt), such as mangroves and various seaweeds. These plants have to withstand salty conditions and some are able to regulate levels of salt in tissues by excreting salt from special glands in their leaves.

- Mesophytes are land plants that normally have enough water to meet their needs. The majority of flowering plants are mesophytes. Their biggest problem is water loss through transpiration. They may develop structures or behaviours to prevent water loss, for example, a waxy cuticle on leaves, protected stomata and curled or small leaves.

- Xerophytes are plants that are adapted to survive in dry regions. Xerophytes, such as cacti, marram grass and oleanders, have developed many different structures for conserving water. These are summarised in Table 14.5.1. Examples of xerophytic plants and their adaptations are shown in Figure 14.5.1.

▼ **Table 14.5.1** Xerophytes are well-adapted to conserve water

Method of saving water	Structures adapted for this purpose
Slowing or reducing rate of transpiration	Waxy covering (cuticle) on leaves.
	Fewer stomata.
	Sunken stomata which provide a moist micro-environment.
	Stomata that close in daytime and open at night.
	Fine hairs on the surface of plant to trap moisture.
	Curled leaves to provide a moist micro-environment.
	Small leaves or spines that reduce surface area for water loss.
	Leaf loss during times of dryness.
Storing water for times of shortage	Fleshy, succulent leaves with flexible surface.
	Fleshy, thick stems that can store water.
	Fleshy underground tubers.
Increased water uptake	Shallow, widespread roots to absorb maximum surface water.
	Very long deep roots to reach underground water.
	Some plants have a dual root system, which combines a deep tap root with shallow radial roots for maximum water uptake.

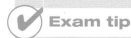

Exam tip

In an examination you may be asked to suggest adaptations a plant may have to survive in a hostile environment, for example a desert or a mountain top.

158

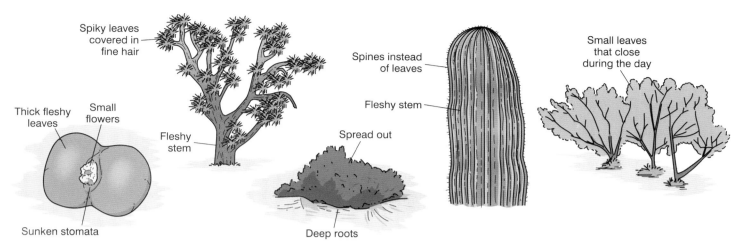

▲ **Figure 14.5.1** Some xerophytic plants and their adaptations for conserving water

 Practical activity

Modelling how leaf shape affects water loss

In this investigation you are going to model different leaf shapes to see how the shape of leaves affects the rate of transpiration. Modelling allows you to make conclusions about what will happen in the real world without using complicated procedures and expensive equipment.

Hypothesis
Plants with narrow leaves will lose less water through transpiration than plants with broad leaves.

Materials
- Thick white paper
- Scissors
- Measuring cylinder
- Plastic wrap
- Beakers or test tubes
- Water

Narrow leaf with stem   Broad leaf with stem

▲ **Figure 14.5.2**

Method

1 Cut out paper leaves in two different shapes, one narrow and one broad as shown in Figure 14.5.2.
2 Make the stems the same length and width and try to keep the total leaf area (length × breadth) more or less the same.
3 Make five copies of each leaf shape.
4 Cover the containers with plastic wrap to reduce surface evaporation. (Make a small hole to fit the stem through and do not cover the actual leaves.)
5 Place each leaf stem in a separate container with the same amount of water.
6 Place the containers in the same location.
7 After one hour check to see which leaf shape has used the most water. Measure the volume of water left in each container and subtract this from the original amount.

Questions

These questions relate to the practical activity above.

1 Which shape of leaf lost most water? Suggest why.
2 Calculate the rate of transpiration from each leaf area using the formula: water lost (ml) ÷ leaf area (mm²).
3 Calculate the average water lost from each leaf shape.
4 Did your results support the hypothesis?
5 What do your results suggest about the shape of leaves likely to be found in xerophytic plants?

Animals and plants use food for energy. Food that is not needed immediately is stored in various places in animals and plants. These stores of food are converted to energy to be used when food is in short supply or unavailable.

B15.1 Food storage in animals

Humans and other animals use energy all the time: breathing, thinking, moving and even sleeping use energy. We get the energy we need from the food we eat. However, we don't need to eat all the time in order to have enough energy. In fact, if we don't eat for a day or two we will still have enough energy to function because our bodies are able to store energy in the form of glycogen and fat.

Glucose and fats

You know that animals digest their food to form glucose and other products. Excess glucose in the blood is transported to the liver where it is changed into a substance called glycogen and stored in the liver or in muscles. Glycogen is a carbohydrate that is also known as animal starch. It is made when glucose molecules join together to form tiny solid, granules that are stored in cells. Because glycogen is insoluble, it does not interfere with osmosis or other cellular processes. When the body needs extra energy, the glycogen is broken down by enzyme action to form glucose that cells can use.

Excess amino acids cannot be stored. These are converted to urea and an organic acid that can be converted to carbohydrate and used for energy in the liver. This process is called deamination.

Humans and other animals store lipids in the form of fat. Fat supplies twice as much energy per gram as carbohydrates. Fat is also insoluble in water, so it does not interfere with osmosis.

If there is not enough glucose or glycogen available, fat reserves in the body are broken down to produce energy. Once the fat reserves have been used up, the body starts to break down proteins (the main component of muscles) to produce energy.

Sites of food storage

The main storage organ for glycogen is the liver. However, glycogen is also stored in muscles where it is rapidly converted into glucose by metabolic processes.

The liver also stores fat-soluble vitamins A and D and water-soluble vitamin B15. There is normally at least a year's supply of these vitamins stored in your liver.

Fat is an important storage compound for energy. It is lighter than carbohydrates and proteins and it contains more energy per gram. Fat is stored in adipose tissue under the skin of humans and other animals.

Key fact

Animals that hibernate during winter slow down their metabolic processes and live off their food stores for up to three months at a time.

▲ **Figure 15.1.1** Seals, and other animals that live in cold water, have a thick layer of blubber to store energy and protect them from the cold

Animals that live in cold conditions such as seals (Figure 15.1.1) and whales have a thick layer of fat, called blubber, under their skins. This serves as an energy store and provides insulation against the cold.

Penguins do not eat when they are moulting or when they are breeding (Figures 15.1.2 and 15.1.3). Before these times they take in enormous amounts of food. Their body mass increases by about 45% and they store between 75% and 85% of their energy in the form of fat (under their skin). This allows them to survive without eating for months at a time.

Hibernating animals store special brown fat that contains energy but which is also able to generate heat. When they end their hibernation period, this fat produces heat which allows them to warm up again and survive. New-born human babies have about 5% brown fat in their bodies, but as they grow to adulthood this disappears.

The eggs of birds and other animals, such as turtles, are also an important site of food storage. The yolk of the egg is rich in fat and protein that is used to feed the growing animal until it hatches.

Too much food

Wild animals do not become overweight. Humans and domestic pets do become overweight. This is because humans and their pets often eat more food than their bodies need. If your energy intake (the amount of food you eat) is greater than your energy output (how much energy you use) then you put on weight. The graph in Figure 15.1.4 shows you healthy and unhealthy weights for adults of different heights.

▲ **Figure 15.1.2** These arctic penguins do not eat for months while they are caring for their eggs. They lose more than half their body mass during this time as they use up fat reserves.

▲ **Figure 15.1.3** These African penguins cannot go to sea to catch food while they are moulting so they have to rely on their fat stores for energy

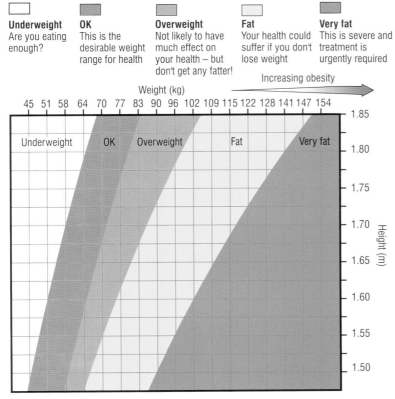

Underweight	OK	Overweight	Fat	Very fat
Are you eating enough?	This is the desirable weight range for health	Not likely to have much effect on your health – but don't get any fatter!	Your health could suffer if you don't lose weight	This is severe and treatment is urgently required

Increasing obesity

Weight (kg)

45 51 58 64 70 77 83 90 96 102 109 115 122 128 141 147 154

Underweight   OK   Overweight   Fat   Very fat

1.85
1.80
1.75
1.70
1.65
1.60
1.55
1.50

Height (m)

▲ **Figure 15.1.4** People who are overweight are more likely to have health problems. Eating less and exercising more is the best way to lose excess weight.

Questions

1 Why do humans and other animals need to store food?

2 In what form do animals and humans store food?

3 What role does the liver play in food storage?

4 Where do animals store fat?

B15.2 Food storage in plants

Humans and animals store food so that they do not have to eat all the time to provide energy for cellular processes. Plants store food so that they have a supply of glucose for cellular respiration during periods when they are not producing food by photosynthesis, for example, during the night. They also store food for times when food may be scarce as a result of unsuitable conditions in the environments, for example, water shortages, heavy winds or very cold temperatures, which prevent food production.

In addition, plants store food so that they can provide the energy needed to produce new plants. For example, when a new plant sprouts from a potato, stored food moves into the new plant to give it the energy it needs to grow until it can photosynthesise by itself. Plants also store food in their seeds and fruits. This stored food is used as a supply of nourishment for newly germinated plants, such as beans or corn, until they can provide their own food.

Figure 15.2.1 shows you how newly developing plants make use of food stored by the parent plant.

Starch and oils

Plants make their own food, in the form of glucose, by photosynthesis. Some of this glucose is used immediately for cellular processes. The rest is normally stored in various parts of the plant in the form of starch. The starch is converted back to glucose as the plant needs it.

Some plants do not store much starch, instead they store surplus glucose in the form of sugar or oil. Sugar cane and sugar beets are good sources of stored sugar, and fruits such as mangoes and peaches have a high sugar content. Sunflower seeds, peanuts, brazil nuts and castor oil seeds have a very high oil content, so do some fruits, such as avocados and olives.

Storage organs in plants

Plants can store food in their roots, stems, leaves, fruits and seeds. Table 15.2.1 shows some plants you probably know and the organs they use to store food.

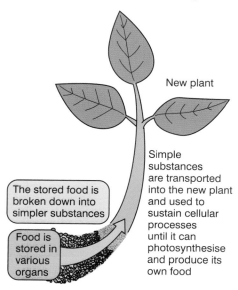

New plant

Simple substances are transported into the new plant and used to sustain cellular processes until it can photosynthesise and produce its own food

The stored food is broken down into simpler substances

Food is stored in various organs

▲ **Figure 15.2.1** Food storage is important for reproduction in plants

You have seen that the food stored in plants is used by plants themselves. However these stores of food are also very useful as sources of nutrients for animals and humans. Remember that plants are the producers in all ecosystems so consumers at every level rely on the energy stored in plants for survival.

▼ **Table 15.2.1** Some of the food storage sites used by different plants

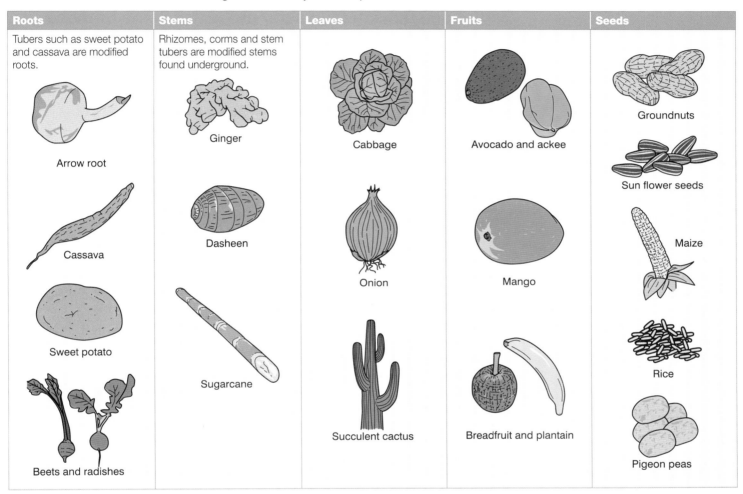

Roots	Stems	Leaves	Fruits	Seeds
Tubers such as sweet potato and cassava are modified roots.	Rhizomes, corms and stem tubers are modified stems found underground.			
Arrow root	Ginger	Cabbage	Avocado and ackee	Groundnuts
Cassava	Dasheen	Onion	Mango	Sun flower seeds
Sweet potato	Sugarcane	Succulent cactus	Breadfruit and plantain	Maize
Beets and radishes				Rice
				Pigeon peas

Questions

1 Why is it important for plants to store food?

2 Why is it important to humans and animals that plants store food?

3 Where, and in what form, do each of the following plants store food?
   a Carrots   c Sugar cane   e Sunflowers
   b Rice plants   d Onions

4 What plant products could you eat if you wanted to get a good supply of the following?
   a Sugar   b Starch   c Oil

B16 Excretion and osmoregulation

Excretion and osmoregulation are important because they help organisms maintain a constant internal environment. Metabolic processes in plants and animals produce unwanted (waste) products. Some of these are harmful or poisonous so the organism needs to get rid of them by excretion. Osmoregulation is the maintenance of constant conditions (fluid and solute levels) that allow osmosis to take place.

 **Key fact**

'Excretion' should not be confused with 'defecation'. Faeces are non-digested materials which are **egested** from the digestive system. Faeces are not involved in metabolic processes, so they are not excretory. The only excretory products in faeces are bile pigments.

B16.1 Excretion

The word metabolism is used to describe the thousands of chemical reactions that take place inside cells. Cell metabolism breaks down compounds and makes new compounds. The waste products formed during metabolism could be harmful to the body if they were allowed to build up in the body, so they need to be removed by excretion.

Excretion is the removal of the waste products that are formed by metabolic activity. These products include water, carbon dioxide, oxygen, nitrogenous compounds (ammonia, urea and uric acid) and bile pigments.

Diffusion of waste products from the body is the simplest means of excretion. This occurs in plants and uni-cellular organisms like amoeba. Animals have many specialised organs and organ systems for excretion. Examples of excretory organs are the lungs (for carbon dioxide and water) and the kidneys (for nitrogenous waste and water). Mammals also excrete small amounts of urea, salts and water from the skin when they sweat. Table 16.1.1 summarises the main waste products produced by metabolism.

▼ **Table 16.1.1** Waste substances produced by metabolism

Waste substance	How it is produced	Where it is produced	Where it is excreted
Carbon dioxide	Cellular respiration	All cells	From lungs or other gas exchange surfaces (including stomata of leaves)
Urea and other nitrogenous compounds	Deamination of amino acids	Liver cells	From the kidney
Bile pigments	Breakdown of haemoglobin from red blood cells	Liver cells	In bile, which passes into the duodenum
Oxygen	Photosynthesis	Inside chloroplasts of plant cells	From leaf cells through the stomata

Excretion in plants

The main waste product in plants is oxygen, which is produced by photosynthesis. This is excreted through the stomata of the leaves (during the day) by diffusion into the air in terrestrial plants and into the water in aquatic plants.

Plants also produce some organic wastes. These are stored in non-living plant tissues so that they do not have a harmful effect on living cells. For example, wastes are stored in bark or leaves. When the plant loses its leaves and bark the waste products are lost at the same time. Substances stored in the plant are also lost when petals fall off, fruit drops or seeds are dispersed.

Some waste products, such as acids which may be harmful to the plant, are stored in the plant in an insoluble form so that they do not interfere with the osmotic process in cells. Calcium ions, for example, combine with oxalic and pectic acids to produce crystals of calcium oxalate or calcium pectate. Some plants, such as dumbcane or mother-in-law's tongue (*Dieffenbachia seguine*) have such high concentrations of calcium oxalate in their leaves that they are poisonous to humans and animals. Figure 16.1.1 shows the main excretory products of plants.

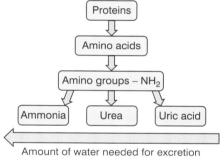

O_2 during day

CO_2 during night

Waste stored in leaves

Waste stored in bark

Leaf fall

Waste stored in woody trunk

Bark fall

▲ **Figure 16.1.1** Plants excrete wastes by diffusion and when they lose parts

Excretion in animals

Table 16.1.1 showed that the three main excretory products in animals are:

- carbon dioxide from cellular respiration
- nitrogenous compounds (urea, uric acid and ammonia) from the breakdown of proteins
- bile pigments from the breakdown of haemoglobin in the liver.

Nitrogenous compounds all contain amino groups ($-NH_2$) from amino acids because these are not needed when amino acids are oxidised to generate energy or converted to fats or carbohydrate to store energy (see Figure 16.1.2).

The amino groups need to be excreted from the body. Table 16.1.2 shows you the form in which different species produce and excrete these compounds.

Proteins

Amino acids

Amino groups – NH_2

Ammonia | Urea | Uric acid

Amount of water needed for excretion

▲ **Figure 16.1.2** Nitrogenous waste production

▼ **Table 16.1.2** Excretion of nitrogenous waste

Product	Habitat	Animals
Ammonia (toxic – requires large amounts of water to remove it from the body)	Water	Uni-cellular organisms such as amoeba, aquatic invertebrates, bony fish (fresh water), amphibian larvae
Uric acid	Land	Insects, birds, reptiles
Urea	Land	Amphibians (mature), mammals

Excretory structures

Different animals use different organs and structures for excretion:

- Uni-cellular organisms excrete wastes directly from their cell membranes into the environment.
- Insects, crustaceans, arachnids and other arthropods excrete through Malphigian tubules and tracheae.
- In fish and amphibians, the excretory structures are the gills, skin, liver and kidneys.
- In humans and other mammals, the excretory structures are the skin, lungs, liver and kidneys.

In humans, water, urea and salts are excreted through the skin in sweat. Carbon dioxide and water vapour diffuse from the lungs. Bile pigments are produced in the liver and pass into the duodenum in bile to be removed with faeces. The liver also produces urea from amino acids, which is transported to the kidneys, the main excretory organs in humans. You will learn more about the kidneys and their role in excretion and osmoregulation in topics B16.2. and B16.3

Questions

1 What are the main excretory products of:
   a plants
   b animals?

2 How do plants excrete waste products?

3 What are the main excretory structures in humans?

4 Which of these statements is false?
   a Insects excrete uric acid.
   b Humans excrete urea.
   c Fishes excrete ammonia.
   d Birds excrete ammonia.

Objectives

By the end of this topic you will be able to:

- identify the parts of the excretory system
- relate the structure of the kidney to its functions
- label diagrams of parts of the kidney
- state the functions of different parts of the kidney.

B16.2 The human excretory system

You have read that metabolism produces waste substances that have to be removed from the body by excretion. Water and salts, in excess of the body's needs, also have to be excreted. In humans and other mammals, the kidney is the main excretory organ. The kidney also plays a role in osmoregulation because it regulates the amount of water and the concentration of salts and other useful substances in the blood.

The structure of the kidneys

Figure 16.2.1 shows you where the kidneys are in the human body. Each kidney receives blood from a renal artery. Blood is returned to the circulatory system through a renal vein.

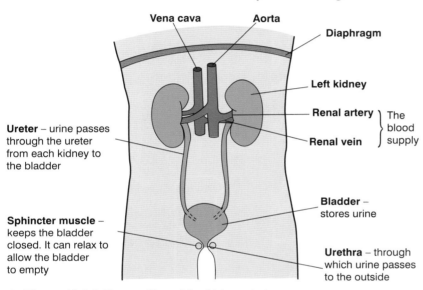

Vena cava | Aorta
Diaphragm
Left kidney
Renal artery } The blood supply
Renal vein
Ureter – urine passes through the ureter from each kidney to the bladder
Bladder – stores urine
Sphincter muscle – keeps the bladder closed. It can relax to allow the bladder to empty
Urethra – through which urine passes to the outside

▲ **Figure 16.2.1** The position of the kidneys in humans

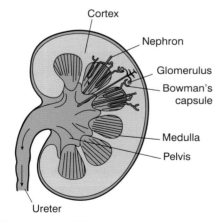

Cortex
Nephron
Glomerulus
Bowman's capsule
Medulla
Pelvis
Ureter

▲ **Figure 16.2.2** The internal structure of a kidney

 Key fact

The ureter is not the same as the urethra. Make sure that you know the difference between these and that you can label the parts and spell the names correctly on a diagram.

The ureter is a narrow tube that carries urine from the kidney to the bladder. Figure 16.2.2 shows the internal structure of a kidney. You can see that the kidney has three main areas: the cortex, the medulla and the pelvis. If you look at a kidney through a microscope, you can see that it consists of about one million tiny tubules called nephrons. Each nephron consists of two main structures (see Figure 16.2.3):

- a renal tubule attached to a cup-shaped capsule known as a Bowman's capsule
- a bunch of capillaries, called a glomerulus, which is contained inside the Bowman's capsule.

Figure 16.2.3 shows the position of nephrons in the kidney and the detailed structure of one nephron.

The nephron is the working unit of the kidney. Blood is carried to the glomerulus via the afferent arteriole. This blood contains wastes (mostly urea) which the nephrons filter from the blood together with glucose, salts and other substances in solution. Some of these substances are useful, so they are reabsorbed into the blood as the filtrate moves through the nephron. The cleaned blood returns to the circulatory system via the renal vein. The nephrons thus have an important role to play in keeping the composition of the blood constant. Figure 16.2.4 shows how a nephron functions. Remember there are about a million nephrons in each kidney.

The fluid which is left in the kidney after filtration and reabsorption is called urine. This passes down the ureter to the bladder where it is stored until it can be excreted through the urethra during urination. A sphincter muscle controls the release of urine through the urethra.

Table 16.2.1 shows the composition of 'dirty' blood in the glomerulus before it is filtered and reabsorbed by the nephrons. It also shows the composition of the urine which is left over at the end of the process.

▼ **Table 16.2.1** Percentage by mass of different substances in blood and urine before and after treatment by the nephron

	Blood in the glomerulus (%)	Urine (%)
Water	91.7	96.5
Proteins	7.5	0
Urea	0.03	2
Ammonia	Trace amounts	0.05
Sodium ions	0.3	0.6
Potassium ions	0.02	0.15
Chloride ions	0.36	0.6
Glucose	0.1	0

Functions of the kidneys

The kidneys have four main functions:

- they are the main excretory organs for waste products such as urea
- they play a role in regulating the water content of the body (osmoregulation)
- they help to maintain the osmotic pressure of body fluids by excreting excess salts and by retaining water as needed
- they regulate the pH of the blood by controlling the acid–base balance in the blood.

You will look at the role of the kidneys in osmoregulation in more detail in topic B16.3 and at the role the kidneys play in internal control in Unit B20.

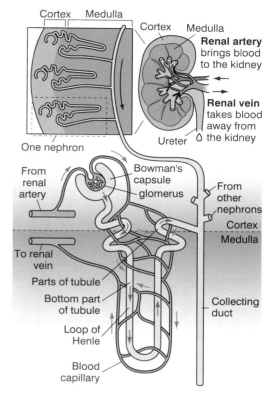

▲ **Figure 16.2.3** The position and structure of a nephron

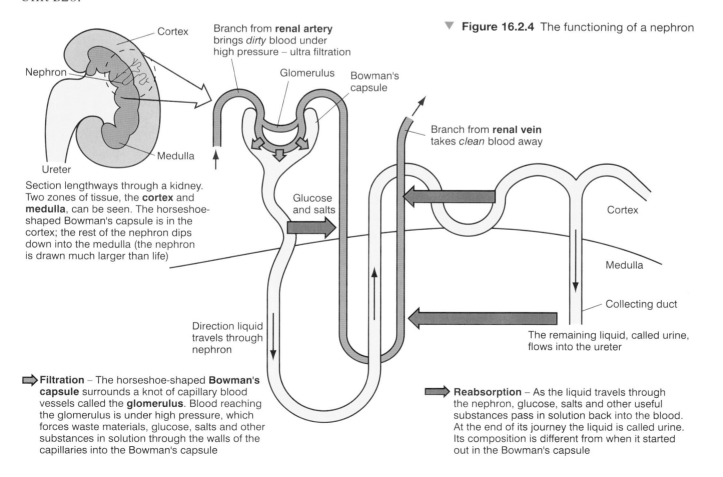

▼ **Figure 16.2.4** The functioning of a nephron

Section lengthways through a kidney. Two zones of tissue, the **cortex** and **medulla**, can be seen. The horseshoe-shaped Bowman's capsule is in the cortex; the rest of the nephron dips down into the medulla (the nephron is drawn much larger than life)

Branch from **renal artery** brings *dirty* blood under high pressure – ultra filtration

Branch from **renal vein** takes *clean* blood away

Glucose and salts

Direction liquid travels through nephron

The remaining liquid, called urine, flows into the ureter

Filtration – The horseshoe-shaped **Bowman's capsule** surrounds a knot of capillary blood vessels called the **glomerulus**. Blood reaching the glomerulus is under high pressure, which forces waste materials, glucose, salts and other substances in solution through the walls of the capillaries into the Bowman's capsule

Reabsorption – As the liquid travels through the nephron, glucose, salts and other useful substances pass in solution back into the blood. At the end of its journey the liquid is called urine. Its composition is different from when it started out in the Bowman's capsule

In Unit B7 you learnt about osmosis. You should remember that when there is an imbalance in the concentration of dissolved substances, the water tends to move from the region of lower concentration of dissolved substances to the region of higher concentration of dissolved substances to reach a balance.

Osmoregulation is the process of maintaining the balance between water and salts in body fluids. This is very important for keeping the conditions in cells constant and balanced. It means that organisms have to find ways of balancing the amount of water and salts they take in with the amount of water and salts they excrete. In humans, this is one of the main jobs of the kidneys.

Controlling water gain and loss

Figure 16.3.1 shows you how the human body gains and loses water on a daily basis. The pie charts show you the proportions of water gained and lost by different means.

The amount of water you lose through urination is largely controlled by the kidneys. When you drink a lot of water (or other liquids) you produce more urine and you need to urinate more often. This is because the extra fluid dilutes your blood. If this extra fluid was not removed from the blood there would be an imbalance in your cells, so the kidneys remove more water from the blood during filtration. Your body excretes this in the form of very dilute urine.

The opposite happens when you do not drink enough fluids. Your blood becomes more concentrated, raising the levels of salts and other substances dissolved in it. Again, this would lead to an imbalance if it was not corrected, so the kidneys remove less water from the blood during filtration and you produce a smaller amount of very concentrated urine.

The graph in Figure 16.3.2 shows you how the kidneys maintain the balance of water and salts in the body. The graph shows the volume of urine and the concentration of salt in urine measured at given periods after drinking a large amount of water. Note that the excess water is removed from the body without the loss of valuable salts.

The role of ADH in osmoregulation

If you drink lots of liquid or you eat very salty food or you exercise on a hot day without drinking, your kidneys have to adjust their functions to make sure your fluid and salt levels remain balanced. So, how does the kidney know when it has to remove more water from the blood and when it has to remove less water from the blood?

The action of the kidney is controlled by a hormone called antidiuretic hormone or ADH. A diuretic is any substance that increases the rate of urine production. An antidiuretic has the opposite effect: it decreases the rate of urine production.

When your body is short of water your blood becomes more concentrated. This change in the blood is detected by special cells called osmoreceptors in the hypothalamus region of the brain. The osmoreceptors send a message to the posterior pituitary gland which releases stored ADH. The ADH makes the walls of the collecting ducts in the renal tubules more permeable so most of the water from the nephrons is reabsorbed into the blood. The result is that less urine is produced, but the urine is more concentrated (see Figure 16.3.3).

Objectives

By the end of this topic you will be able to:

- relate the structure of the kidney to its function in osmoregulation
- explain the role of the hormone ADH in osmoregulation.

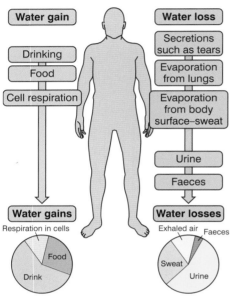

▲ **Figure 16.3.1** Daily water gain and loss by the human body needs to be balanced

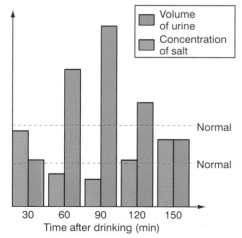

▲ **Figure 16.3.2** If you drink a large amount of liquid you will produce more urine, but it will be diluted so it will contain a lower concentration of salt than normal

If you drink lots of fluids, the blood becomes dilute. This change is also detected by the osmoreceptors in the brain and they stop the release of ADH. Without the ADH, the walls of the collecting ducts in the renal tubules remain impermeable and the kidneys do not reabsorb much water from the nephrons back into the blood. The result is that you produce large amounts of dilute urine. Figure 16.3.4 shows you how water excretion is controlled.

The process of releasing ADH relies on a system of negative feedback. You will learn more about negative feedback systems in Unit B20 when you deal with homeostasis in more detail.

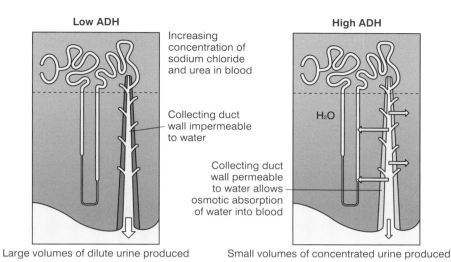

▲ **Figure 16.3.3** ADH controls how much water is reabsorbed from the collecting ducts

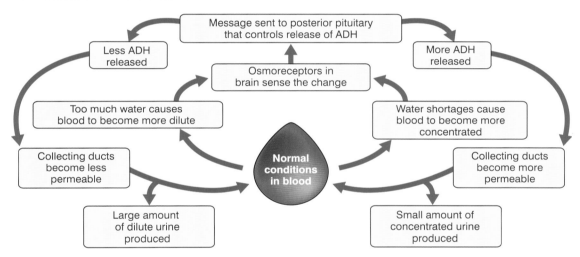

▲ **Figure 16.3.4** ADH plays an important role in osmoregulation

Questions

1 Match the functions listed in column A to the parts of the urinary system listed in column B.

	Column A	Column B
a	Takes urine from the kidney to the bladder	Sphincter
b	Prevents urine from leaking from the bladder	Renal artery
c	Removes urea from the blood	Renal vein
d	Carries urine out of the body	Nephron
e	Carries 'dirty' blood to the kidney	Kidney
f	Is the working unit of the kidney	Urethra
g	Carries blood away from the kidney	Ureter

2 Besides excretion, list two other functions of the kidneys in mammals.

3 What is 'osmoregulation'? Why is it important in living organisms?

4 A student plays volleyball on the beach on a hot day. She sweats a lot and she swims to cool down, but she does not drink much.
   a What will happen to this student's blood? Why?
   b How will her body react to this change?
   c What role will her kidneys play in maintaining her water balance? Explain fully.

5 Why do you produce lots of light coloured urine if you drink a lot of water?

The skeleton supports the body and protects the internal organs. The muscular system allows the body to move. These two systems work together – muscles move bone and bone supports muscle. In this unit you will look at the skeleton and its functions, learn how bones are built and how they are joined. You will also look at how the muscular system is structured to enable us to move.

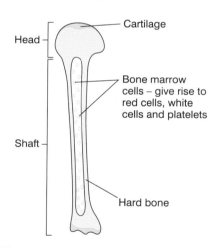

▲ **Figure 17.1.1** The basic structure of a long bone – the femur

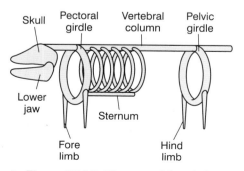

▲ **Figure 17.1.2** Diagram of the skeleton, showing division into axial and appendicular parts

B17.1   The skeleton

You might think, from looking at the bones in a museum, that a skeleton is dry and rigid, but this is not so. Bones are living tissue. They store minerals, like calcium and phosphorus, which the body needs to grow. The marrow in the bones is the site where red blood cells and some white blood cells are produced.

The bones that make up the skeleton are strong enough to support weight and light enough to enable you to move. There are 206 bones in the skeleton, of various shapes and sizes. The bone in Figure 17.1.1 is the femur, which is the main bone.

The skeleton is divided up into two main parts:

- The central bones of the skull, ribs, vertebral column and sternum form the central axis. This is called the axial skeleton.
- The bones of the arms and legs, along with the scapula, clavicle, and pelvis, make up the appendicular skeleton.

In humans, the axial skeleton is upright, or vertical, and in animals it is horizontal (see Figure 17.1.2).

The human skeleton is made of bones and cartilage. Cartilage is a softer tissue than bone that acts as a shock absorber and it is found at the ends of the bone, where two bones meet to form a joint. It allows the bones to move smoothly over one another. Tendons are tough fibres that join the muscles to the bones and ligaments join one bone to another. Ligaments are elastic fibres, which allow the joint to move.

Because the human skeleton is found inside the body, it is called an endoskeleton. All vertebrates have endoskeletons. Insects, on the other hand, have a skeleton on the outside of their bodies, called an exoskeleton. You will learn more about this in topic B17.5.

The functions of the skeleton

The skeleton has four main functions:

- It provides protection for the soft, internal organs. The skull protects the brain, the ribs protect the lungs and heart and the vertebrae protect the spinal cord. The pelvis protects the reproductive organs.

- It provides **support** for the body, giving it shape and form. Without the skeleton, the body would collapse.
- It enables **movement**. The skeleton and the muscles work together to perform this function.
- It produces **blood cells**. Red blood cells, and certain white blood cells, are made inside bones.

Key fact

The fossil remains of vertebrates are usually parts of skeletons. Bone is very hard and therefore preserves well.

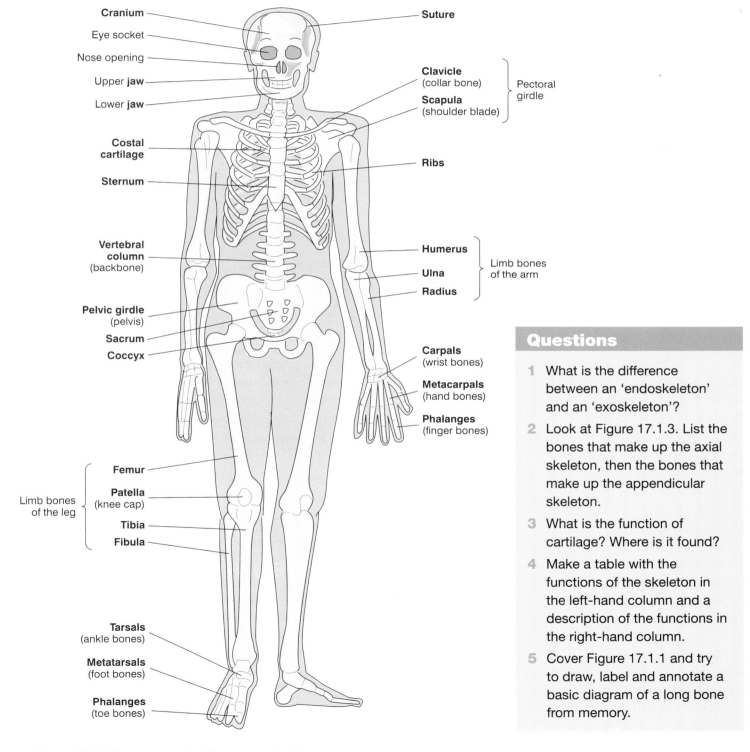

▲ **Figure 17.1.3** The main parts of the human skeleton

Questions

1 What is the difference between an 'endoskeleton' and an 'exoskeleton'?

2 Look at Figure 17.1.3. List the bones that make up the axial skeleton, then the bones that make up the appendicular skeleton.

3 What is the function of cartilage? Where is it found?

4 Make a table with the functions of the skeleton in the left-hand column and a description of the functions in the right-hand column.

5 Cover Figure 17.1.1 and try to draw, label and annotate a basic diagram of a long bone from memory.

By the end of this topic you will be able to:

- draw, label and annotate a diagram of a long bone
- distinguish and identify the differences between kinds of vertebrae
- state the functions of the spine in humans

B17.2 Bone structure

Bone is a type of connective tissue that is very strong and very light. It is made up of specialised cells and protein fibres, woven together into a matrix, and is composed of water, mineral salts and carbohydrates. Bone tissue is not completely rigid. It continually breaks down and rebuilds both during the growing process and when it is renewing itself after an injury.

Inside a bone

On the outside is a thin, dense layer of hard bone. It is hard because 70% of it is made up of calcium salts. Underneath this is a layer of spongy bone, made of criss-crossing fibres, which has canals in it, containing blood vessels. The centre of the bone is filled with bone marrow. Yellow marrow contains mainly fat and red marrow is where the red blood cells are made. Some white blood cells and platelets are also made in the bone marrow. The ends of the bone are covered with a layer of cartilage. (See Figure 17.2.1.)

The vertebral column

The axial skeleton consists of the skull, vertebral column and the ribs. These bones protect the vital organs and tissues and form a strong support for the body. The skull and the vertebral column form a protective sheath around the brain and the spinal cord.

- The **skull** consists of plates of bone fused together to form the cranium, which encloses and protects the brain. A hinged jaw allows powerful muscles to move the lower jaw against the upper jaw.
- The spine or **vertebral column** supports the skull and the limb girdles and ribs are attached to it. The vertebral column is a strong and flexible support that keeps the body and head upright and allows the body to bend and twist.
- The **ribs** form a curved, bony cage around the heart and lungs. At the front they are attached by cartilage to the sternum. At the back they form joints with the thoracic vertebrae.

Vertebrae

Each section of the spine, or vertebral column, is adapted to its function. The **cervical vertebrae** support the head and neck, the **thoracic vertebrae** anchor the ribs and the **lumbar vertebrae** support the strong weight-bearing regions towards the bottom of the spine and provide a stable centre of gravity during movement. You can see the structure of each type of vertebra in Figure 17.2.2.

Between each of the 33 vertebrae are spongy discs of tough cartilage that squash down under pressure to absorb shocks. If you look at Figure 17.2.3 you will notice that the join between the vertebrae is formed by the round-ended process of one bone fitting into a matching process of the bone above. Other processes form anchor points for muscles. The neural cavity in each vertebra creates space for the spinal cord to pass through it.

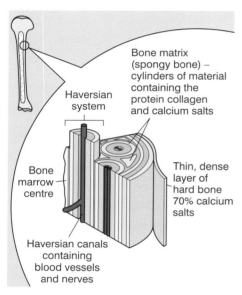

Bone matrix (spongy bone) – cylinders of material containing the protein collagen and calcium salts

Haversian system

Bone marrow centre

Thin, dense layer of hard bone 70% calcium salts

Haversian canals containing blood vessels and nerves

▲ **Figure 17.2.1** Section through the upper end of a femur

(!) Key fact

The joints in the spine work together to enable you to arch backward, twist round or curve forward.

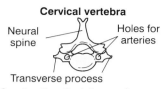

Cervical vertebra

Neural spine

Holes for arteries

Transverse process

Small, with articulating surfaces to allow for movement of the head. Two small holes for asteries on each side.

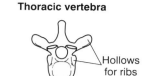

Thoracic vertebra

Hollows for ribs

Long neural spine for attachment of upper back muscles. Long transverse processes to join onto ribs.

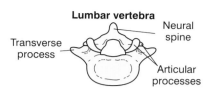

Lumbar vertebra

Neural spine

Transverse process

Articular processes

Large and strong. Neural spine and transverse process for attachment of lower back muscles.

▲ **Figure 17.2.2** Different vertebrae

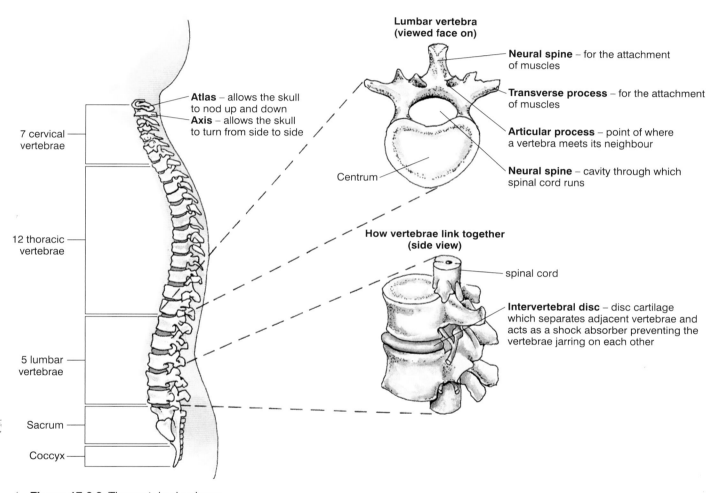

Lumbar vertebra (viewed face on)

Neural spine – for the attachment of muscles

Transverse process – for the attachment of muscles

Articular process – point of where a vertebra meets its neighbour

Neural spine – cavity through which spinal cord runs

Centrum

Atlas – allows the skull to nod up and down

Axis – allows the skull to turn from side to side

7 cervical vertebrae

12 thoracic vertebrae

5 lumbar vertebrae

Sacrum

Coccyx

How vertebrae link together (side view)

spinal cord

Intervertebral disc – disc cartilage which separates adjacent vertebrae and acts as a shock absorber preventing the vertebrae jarring on each other

▲ **Figure 17.2.3** The vertebral column

 Practical activity

Drawing bones

Your teacher may use this activity to assess: Drawing.

Your teacher will give you a long bone that has been cut in half down the middle. Draw and label the bone. Give your drawing a title, and make sure that you use these labels: hard bone, spongy bone, canals, marrow, cartilage, head, shaft.

▲ **Figure 17.3.1** Athletes use their muscles to move, so do we

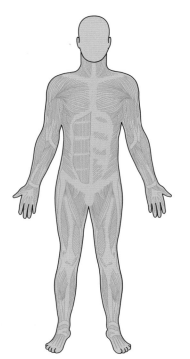

▲ **Figure 17.3.3** A view of the muscular system from the front. The back of the body is also covered in muscles.

B17.3 Muscles and movement

Look at the athletes in Figure 17.3.1. How are humans able to move so smoothly and quickly? In humans, movement relies on the interaction of our rigid skeleton with our muscles.

How do muscles help us to move?

Without muscles we would not be able to move. It is muscles that allow our hearts to beat, our blood to flow and our lungs to function.

Muscles are made of contractile tissue and they are controlled by the nervous system. There are three types of muscles (see Figure 17.3.2):

- Cardiac muscle that is only found in the heart is an extremely strong muscle which allows the heart to beat continuously without getting tired.
- Smooth muscle that is found in the intestinal tract, in the walls of arteries and in the lungs.
- Skeletal muscle that is attached to the bones. It is this muscle that allows us to move.

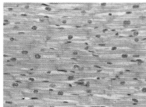
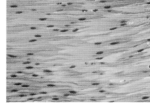
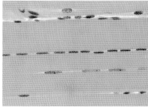

a Cardiac (heart) muscle　　**b** Smooth muscle　　**c** Skeletal muscle

▲ **Figure 17.3.2** The three types of muscle viewed under a microscope

Muscle cells consist of thousands of strands or fibres. These are supplied with nerves and blood vessels. When a stimulus reaches the muscle along a nerve, the muscle responds by shortening its fibres or contracting.

The relationship between muscles and bones

The entire human skeleton is covered with over 600 skeletal muscles. You can see part of the muscular system in Figure 17.3.3.

Muscles are attached to bone by strips of tough, fairly inelastic tissue called tendons. Tendons are made of collagen, a protein which resists pulling forces and allows muscles to contract.

Antagonistic pairs of muscles

The muscles in the arm are arranged in pairs which stretch across the joints at the shoulder and the elbow (see Figure 17.3.4). Muscles can pull bone in one direction but they cannot push, so two muscles are needed to move one joint. One muscle in a pair has the opposite effect to its partner. Hold your arm out and bend your elbow. You are able to do this because the biceps muscle contracts (gets shorter) and the triceps muscle relaxes (gets longer). These two muscles are called antagonistic muscles because they act in opposite ways to allow the same function (see Figure 17.3.5).

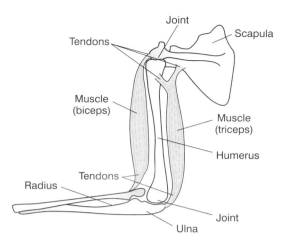

▲ **Figure 17.3.4** The arrangement of muscles in the human arm. Note that the bones of the skeleton are surrounded by muscles which are attached to the outer surface by tough tendons.

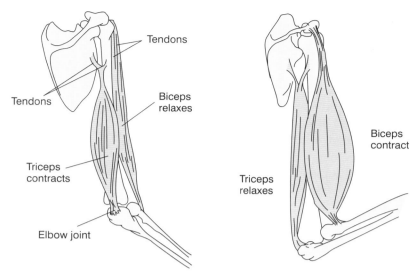

▲ **Figure 17.3.5** The action of antagonist muscles in the movement of the arm

Muscles which cause joints to bend when they contract are called flexor muscles. Muscles that cause limbs to straighten out when they contract are called extensor muscles. In the upper arm, the biceps is the flexor and the triceps is the extensor.

In order for the muscles to work well, the bones in the limbs need to be able to move freely. This happens at the joints. You will learn more about the joints in the human body in topic B17.4.

! Key fact

If you don't use your muscles regularly, they become weak. Muscles which are not used at all eventually shrink and atrophy. Besides disuse, muscles can atrophy if you are bed-ridden or ill. Some of the illnesses which can cause muscle atrophy are poliomyelitis (polio), diabetes, muscular dystrophy, Lou Gehrig's disease and Guillain–Barre syndrome, as well as rheumatism and arthritis. Even slight muscle atrophy usually results in a loss of mobility or strength.

Questions

1 Explain the meanings of the terms:
   a antagonistic pair
   b flexor
   c extensor.

2 Explain what causes muscles to contract.

3 Why is it important for muscles to be elastic and flexible but for tendons to be inelastic?

4 Now examine Figure 17.3.5 and answer these questions.
   a Which muscle contracts when the arm is raised?
   b Which muscle contracts when the arm is straightened?
   c Why are the biceps and triceps called an 'antagonistic pair' of muscles?
   d How are the arm muscles attached to the arm bones?

5 Look at Figure 17.3.6. Imagine the person is lifting her arm away from her side.
   a Which muscle is contracting?
   b Which muscle is relaxing?
   c How will the antagonistic relationship between these two muscles change when the person drops her arm?

6 What happens to muscles if they are not used? Why?

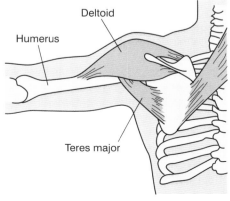

▲ **Figure 17.3.6** Muscles work together

Objectives

By the end of this topic you will be able to:

- describe the types of joint action at moveable joints
- identify different types of joint and their functions
- discuss various problems related to joints and muscles.

B17.4 Joints

Bones are joined in different ways. The function of most joints is to allow the bones to move in different ways.

There are three main types of joints in the human skeleton, each with a different function:

- immovable joints (also called sutures), where the bones are fixed together so that they do not move
- partially moveable joints (gliding joints and pivots), where bones are able to move over each other to allow some movement
- moveable joints (also called synovial joints), which allow free movement of bones.

You already know that the vertebrae in the spine are joined by intervertebral discs of cartilage, which help to make the backbone supple. Cartilage is a smooth, elastic tissue that helps to absorb shock. Cartilage is also present at the ends of bones in synovial joints, where it reduces friction and wear on the bones.

(!) Key fact

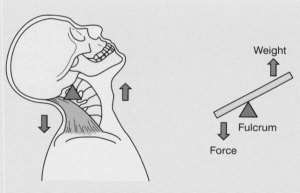

▲ **Figure 17.4.1** The head tilts back – a first-class lever

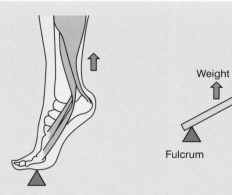

▲ **Figure 17.4.2** Standing on tiptoes – a second-class lever

A first-class lever works like a seesaw, with the fulcrum lying between the force and the weight. If you tilt your head back, the lever at the base of the skull pivots on the fulcrum of the neck joint and the neck muscles pull the head back.

In a second-class lever, the weight lies between the force and the fulcrum. When you rise up on your toes, the calf muscles are the force that lifts your body weight, the heels and foot form the lever and the joints in the toes provide the fulcrum.

▶ **Figure 17.4.3** Bending your arm – a third-class lever

In a third-class lever, which is the most common type found in the body, the force is applied to the lever between the weight and the fulcrum. A typical example is flexing the elbow joint, by contracting the biceps in order to lift the forearm. Can you think of any other examples of this kind of lever in the body?

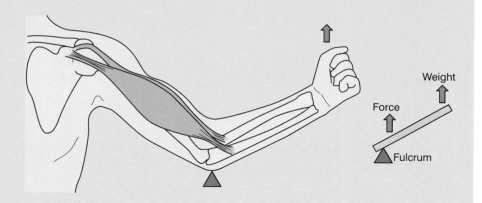

Joints are stabilised by ligaments. A ligament is a tough but flexible band of tissue that holds two or more bones together. Ligaments prevent excess movement of bones at joints and prevent the joints from dislocating. Exercise can stretch the ligaments at joints to make the joint more supple.

The ligaments joining the bones form a capsule containing synovial fluid. The synovial fluid functions to reduce friction at the joint and prevent cartilage from being worn away.

Action at moveable joints

Moveable (synovial) joints are found where two bones need to move freely. Examples are the joints in the elbow, shoulder, knee and hip. These joints are called synovial joints because they are surrounded by synovial fluid, which acts as a lubricant that enables the bones to slide smoothly against each other. The joint is enclosed in a capsule containing the synovial membrane, which secretes the synovial fluid.

Limbs work together as a series of levers. The joint serves as the fulcrum and the effort is produced by the muscle. There are three types of levers in the body. If you need to refresh your memory about levers, look at the 'Key fact' box on p176.

Figure 17.4.4 shows the hip joint, where the head of the femur fits into the socket of the pelvis. This is called a ball-and-socket joint. The head of the femur swivels in the socket of the pelvis, allowing movement in all directions. The shoulder is also a ball-and-socket joint – you can move your arm forward, back and round in a circle.

The elbows and knees, on the other hand, are hinge joints – you can move your arm or your leg in one plane only, like the hinge on a door. A pivot joint at the top of the vertebral column allows your head to move up and down and from side to side.

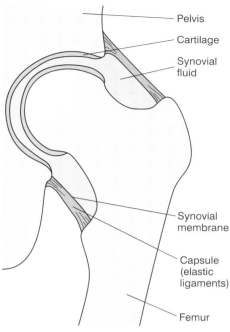

▲ **Figure 17.4.4** The structure of the hip joint

> ## ! Key fact
>
> At the base of the thumbs you find saddle joints. These allow movement back and forth, and from side to side. These are the only saddle joints in the body. Humans and primates are the only mammals with these opposable thumbs.

Questions

1 Look at these three diagrams. Give each a label, and say where you might find examples of them in the body.

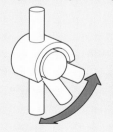  

▲ **Figure 17.4.5**

2 What job does each of the following structures do?

  a Tendons

  b Ligaments

  c Synovial fluid

  d Intervertebral discs

3 Make a labelled diagram of a hinge joint, and then write down:

  a the name of the joint

  b where it is found in the body

  c a short description of how it is moved by muscles.

4 Given the functions of our joints, write down three problems a person might experience if their joints were damaged (by arthritis for example) and unable to function normally.

5 Carry out some research of your own to find out about the medical problems that people may experience with both muscles and joints.

Objectives

By the end of this topic you will be able to:

- identify how different animals move
- tabulate the different forms of locomotion
- discuss the importance of locomotion in animals.

Key fact

Plants do not need to move from place to place in the same way as animals do. However, plants need to move to grow and be able to respond to conditions in their environment (light and water). Some plants also move in order to disperse their seeds. You will learn more about plant movements and responses in Unit B18.

B17.5 Locomotion in animals

Locomotion is the ability of an organism to move around in its environment. In terms of survival, locomotion is an essential ability for all animals for the following reasons:

- **Nutrition** – most animals need to move from place to place to find food. Herbivores move around in search of good grazing, carnivores need to move around so that they can hunt and catch other animals.
- **Reproduction** – animals move from place to place in search of a suitable mate and the young offspring of animals may move away from their parents as they grow older to avoid competition and to increase species diversity.
- **Safety** – animals need to be able to escape from predators and also to avoid dangers such as floods, fires and humans.
- **Environmental conditions** – animals need to adapt to changing conditions and this means that if it is too hot, cold, dry or wet they need to move to find conditions that are more suitable. In addition, animals (even microorganisms) tend to move away from their own waste products.

In this unit you will look at some of the ways in which animals are adapted to move in different ways. You will then draw up a table comparing skeletons, muscles and movements in different animals, including human beings.

The bodies of all living creatures are adapted to suit the medium in which they live. Birds need to move efficiently through the air, earthworms through the soil, and fish through water. Each animal's skeletal and muscular structure needs to support it as it moves.

How do birds fly?

Birds are adapted to move smoothly through the air. Their bodies are streamlined, their bones are light and their powerful wings are designed to move air aside with maximum efficiency (see Figure 17.5.1).

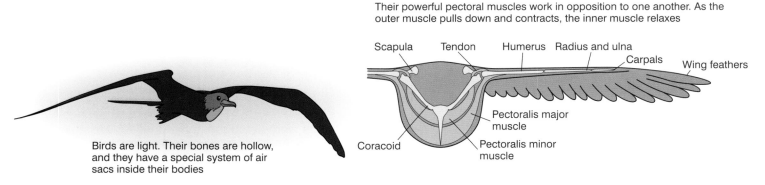

▲ **Figure 17.5.1** Transverse section through the thorax of a bird

Birds have other features that help them to fly. They are covered in feathers, which overlap and give them a light, streamlined covering. They angle the tips of their wings to turn and their tail acts as a stabiliser as well as a brake. The tail fans out when the bird lands.

When the bird glides, the wing acts as an aerofoil. Air flows faster over the top, with less pressure than underneath. This gives the bird lift. The designers of aeroplanes use the same system. Figure 17.5.2 shows this in more detail.

Exam tip

In an examination you might be asked to describe how a bird is able to fly. Remember the bones of a bird are hollow, making them very light.

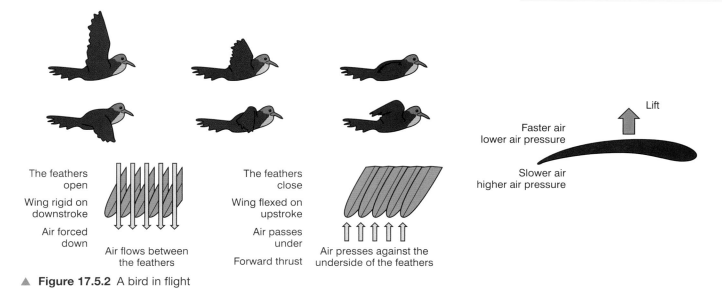

▲ **Figure 17.5.2** A bird in flight

How do insects move?

Insects have a completely different skeleton to vertebrates. Instead of an internal skeleton, insects are supported by a tough exoskeleton made of chitin.

Insects that move by flying have muscles in the thorax (the part of the body between the head and abdomen). When these muscles contract, the wings go up and down. Insects that move by hopping have jointed legs. Figure 17.5.3 shows the peg-and-socket joint in a grasshopper's leg. Can you see how the antagonistic muscles work in an insect's leg?

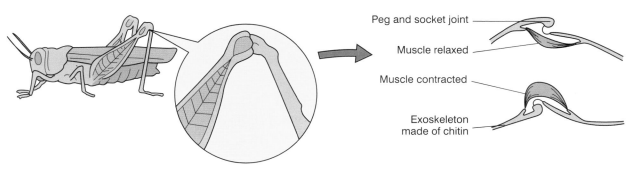

▲ **Figure 17.5.3** A grasshopper

How do earthworms crawl?

Earthworms have hydrostatic skeletons – a strong muscular wall which contains the fluid inside them. The fluid presses outward and gives the body its shape.

If you look at Figure 17.5.4, you will see that earthworms have a long, cylindrical shape, which is adapted for squeezing through burrows in the soil. The mucus on the skin helps them to slide forward. Hard bristles, called chaetae, on their underside, help them to grip the sides of their burrow.

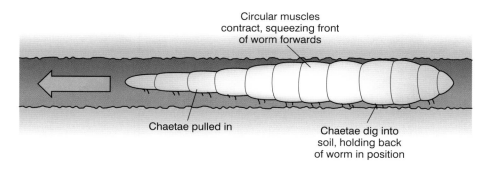

Circular muscles contract, squeezing front of worm forwards

Chaetae pulled in

Chaetae dig into soil, holding back of worm in position

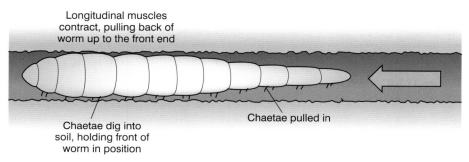

Longitudinal muscles contract, pulling back of worm up to the front end

Chaetae dig into soil, holding front of worm in position

Chaetae pulled in

▲ **Figure 17.5.4** How an earthworm moves

Earthworms also move with the help of a set of antagonistic muscles. Circular muscles contract, to make the earthworm long and thin, and longitudinal muscles contract to make the earthworm short and fat. In this way it moves forward.

How do aquatic organisms move?

Look at Figures 17.5.5 and 17.5.6. Which one is an amoeba, and which is a hydra? Both are simple organisms that live in water. Read the descriptions, and then decide for yourselves which is which.

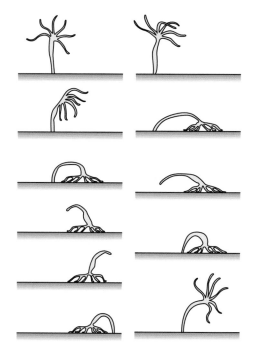

▲ **Figure 17.5.5**

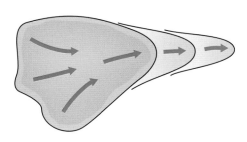

▲ **Figure 17.5.6**

Description 1

An amoeba moves when the runny protoplasm flows towards one end of the cell. The bulge that forms is called a pseudopod, or 'false foot'. The amoeba oozes from place to place.

Description 2

A hydra moves by somersaulting or looping. It is attached to stone or weeds by a foot. When it needs to feed, the muscular tails contract and whip the tentacles overhead. The body stretches out, then closes up, and the tentacles catch the prey.

How do fish swim?

Fish swim by pushing their bodies and fins against the water. Their streamlined shape helps to reduce resistance.

There are blocks of powerful muscles on either side of the ventral vertebral column. These muscles contract and relax in antagonistic pairs and propel the fish forwards (see Figure 17.5.7).

Exam tip

In an examination you may be asked to compare how different organisms move. Remember to describe each type of movement properly, include drawings if possible.

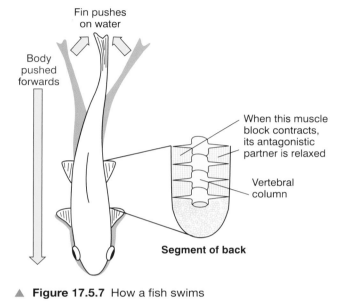

▲ **Figure 17.5.7** How a fish swims

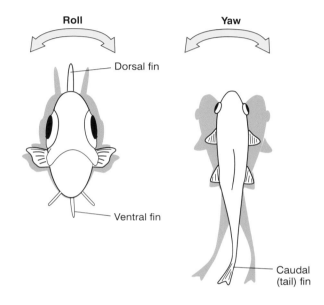

A swim bladder helps to control buoyancy and the tail and fins stabilise the fish in the water in an upright position (see Figure 17.5.8).

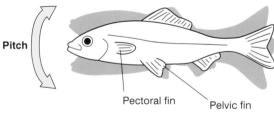

▶ **Figure 17.5.8** How tail and fins stabilise a fish when swimming

Questions

1 Explain what the terms dorsal, ventral and caudal mean using everyday words.
2 How do fish manage to stay upright in water?
3 Read through this topic again, then copy and complete this table:

Animal	Type of skeleton	Examples of antagonistic muscles	Description of how it moves
Human being			
Bird			
Insect			
Earthworm			
Amoeba			
Hydra			
Fish			

Plants and animals have to react to conditions in their environment in order to function effectively and to survive. Many of these reactions are triggered by changes or signals received from the environment. In this unit you will look at how plants and simple animals respond to these signals.

B18.1 Plant responses to stimuli

A stimulus is any change in the internal or external environment of an organism that causes some sort of change in the body or behaviour of the organism. The stimulus does not provide the energy for the change. The change in the body or behaviour of the organism is called a response. The ability to respond to stimuli means that organisms can change their activities according to the conditions around them and this helps them to survive.

Most plants are rooted and they do not move around from place to place like animals do. Plants do not have sense organs, like eyes and ears, or a nervous system connected to a brain. However, plants do detect and respond to stimuli in the environment. Some of the stimuli to which plants respond are light, gravity, water, touch and temperature. Figure 18.1.1 shows you some of the ways in which plants respond to various stimuli.

Some plants respond to light intensity by opening flowers during the day and closing them at night

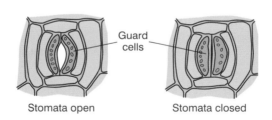

Guard cells

Stomata open   Stomata closed

Stomata on the leaves open and close in response to light intensity, water availability and strong winds

The leaves of plants like the *Mimosa pudica* respond to touch or strong winds by collapsing

The Venus fly trap plant closes its 'jaws' in response to insects touching it

Light

The stems of plants respond to light by growing towards it

The roots of plants respond to gravity by growing downwards

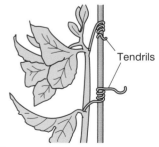

Tendrils

Some climbing plants respond to repeated contact with objects by twining around them

▲ **Figure 18.1.1** Plants respond to a variety of stimuli

Plant growth movements

Plants can respond to stimuli by growing towards or away from the stimulus. These growth movements are called tropisms. Tropisms are positive if the plant grows towards the stimulus and negative if the plant grows away from the stimulus.

Tropisms are named according to the stimulus that causes the movement. So, tropisms stimulated by light are called phototropisms, those stimulated by gravity are called geotropisms and those stimulated by water are called hydrotropisms. Figure 18.1.2 shows how these can be both negative and positive.

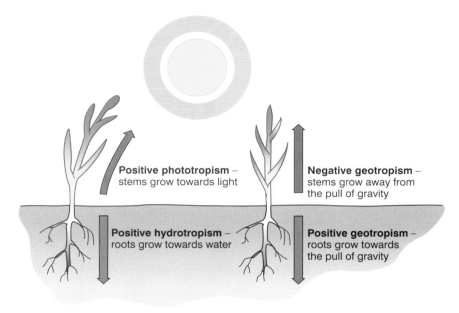

Positive phototropism – stems grow towards light

Negative geotropism – stems grow away from the pull of gravity

Positive hydrotropism – roots grow towards water

Positive geotropism – roots grow towards the pull of gravity

▲ **Figure 18.1.2** Different tropisms

Phototropism

Phototropism is the growth response of plants to the stimulus of light. Stems and shoots of plants are positively phototropic. If they are grown with light on one side only (unilateral light) they will grow and bend towards the light. Roots do not usually respond to light, but some, like rice and maize, are negatively phototropic and they grow away from the direction of light.

Geotropism

Geotropism is the growth response of plants to gravity. This causes the roots of germinating seeds to grow downwards because they are positively geotropic. It makes the shoots grow upwards because they are negatively geotropic.

Although plant roots are positively geotropic, they are more strongly positively hydrotropic. So, if the water is below the roots, they will grow downwards, but if the water supply is to the side or above the roots, they will respond to the water by growing sideways or upwards.

The response reactions to various stimuli are very important for the survival of plants. If roots did not grow down, they would not be able to anchor the plant and if they did not respond to water they would die. If shoots did not grow up or towards light, they would not be able to photosynthesise.

Questions

1 Name four environmental stimuli to which plants respond.
2 How is a plant likely to respond to the following stimuli:
   a light from the left-hand side only
   b water in the upper layers of the soil?
3 Does it matter which way up a seed or bulb is planted? Explain why.
4 Explain how roots and shoots of plants respond differently to gravity.
5 Why is it important that plants respond to stimuli such as light and gravity?

Investigating plant responses to stimuli

You are going to carry out some controlled experiments with small seedlings to see how they respond to light and gravity. You will need to have patience in order to observe the changes in plants because they take place over days, not immediately.

 Practical activity

How do plants respond to light from one side?

Your teacher may use this activity to assess: ORR; A&I.

To find the direction of growth if light is present on one side of the plant.

Materials

- Two Petri dishes lined with moist cotton wool
- Tomato seeds
- A dark box with a slit cut in one end

Method

1 Place a layer of damp cotton wool in each Petri dish and sprinkle some seeds on them.

2 Allow the seeds to germinate by leaving them in a warm place for two or three days. Do not allow the cotton wool to dry out.

3 Once the seeds have germinated, place one of the Petri dishes of seedlings inside the box. Place the slit of the box so that it receives sunlight.

4 Place the other Petri dish in a light sunny place. This will be your control. You will need to turn it a few times each day so that the seedlings get light from all sides.

5 Leave both dishes in position for a week. Check each day that the cotton wool has not dried out and add water as needed.

Observations

Sketch the seedlings in each Petri dish at the end of the week.

What conclusions can you draw from your experiment?

What does this mean for plants growing in natural environments?

 Practical activity

How does gravity affect plant roots?

Your teacher may use this activity to assess: ORR; A&I.

To find out whether gravity affects the direction of root growth in plants.

Materials

- Four glass jars with damp soil in them
- Four small seedlings with roots and shoots

Method

1 Plant one seedling at the side of each jar as shown in Figure 18.1.3.

2 Place the four jars in a shaded place for a week.

Observations

What happens to each seedling?

What does this show you about plant roots and their response to gravity?

What does this show you about plant shoots and their response to gravity?

Questions

1 Why did you have to place the seedlings in a shaded place?

2 Why is it important for plant shoots to grow above ground?

3 Why is it important for plant roots to grow below ground?

A   B   C   D

Seedlings grown in moist soil

▲ **Figure 18.1.3**

Practical activity

How adult plants respond to gravity

A student decided to set up an experiment to show that the shoots of plants are negatively geotropic. Figure 18.1.4 shows what she did.

Questions

1 Formulate a hypothesis for this experiment.

2 Why did the student place the plant on its side?

3 Why do you think she didn't place it upside down?

4 What did she find out from this experiment?

Force of gravity

▲ **Figure 18.1.4**

 Practical activity

Investigating whether plant roots respond more strongly to water than gravity

Roots are positively geotropic. They normally grow down into soil in response to gravity. What happens when there is more water at the side of the plant than below the plant?

Method

Set up the apparatus as shown in Figure 18.1.5.

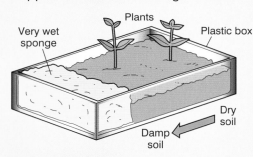

Plants

Very wet sponge

Plastic box

Dry soil

Damp soil

▲ **Figure 18.1.5**

Leave the plants to grow for a week. Do not water the soil, but replenish the water in the sponge each day.

Questions

1 Predict what will happen to the roots of the plants in this experiment.

2 How could you check what happens to the roots?

3 What does this experiment show?

4 What does this experiment suggest for plants that grow in the following places?
   a Next to rivers.
   b Near drains and other household water sources.
   c On the sea shore.

Questions

1 Explain how plants respond to unilateral light.

2 Explain how gravity affects the growth of both roots and shoots of plants.

3 Your grandmother complains that the houseplants she grows on the bookshelf at the back of her sitting room, opposite the window, are all falling over and growing at an angle.
   a Explain to her why this is happening.
   b Suggest what she could do to make the plants grow more upright.

4 Why do trees in tropical forests tend to be tall and thin?

B18.2 Invertebrate responses to stimuli

A taxis or taxic response is a movement of a cell or an invertebrate in response to an external stimulus. Taxes can be positive or negative, but organisms can also move in any direction in response to the stimulus. Examples of taxic responses are bacteria that move towards oxygen (positive aerotaxis) or insects that move away from insect repellent (negative chemotaxis). The term 'taxic response' is only used to describe responses of cells (that are able to move) and simple invertebrate animals.

Responses to light, temperature and moisture

You have probably already observed taxic behaviour in invertebrates. For example, you may have seen that earthworms, fly larvae, woodlice and cockroaches move away from light. We can say they are negatively phototaxic. Moths and fruit flies on the other hand move towards light. We can say they are positively phototaxic.

Invertebrates tend to move towards conditions they like, such as warm, moist places or cool, dry and dark places. They also tend to be more active and to move around more rapidly when they are in a place they do not like. For example, woodlice in a warm, dry and light environment will move around rapidly because the conditions are not ideal for them. Woodlice in cool, dark and moist conditions will tend to settle down and move more slowly.

Using a choice chamber

A choice chamber is a simple piece of apparatus that can be used to test the responses of small invertebrates to different conditions. The idea is that you set up different areas, each with different conditions and then release some animals into the choice chamber. By allowing the animals to move freely between the areas, you are able to observe which conditions they choose or prefer. Figure 18.2.1 shows the basic structure of a choice chamber.

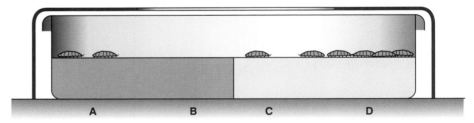

▲ **Figure 18.2.1** The basic structure of a choice chamber

In the choice chamber in the diagram, four separate areas have been set up, each with different conditions. These are:

Area A – dark and dry [anhydrous calcium chloride (drying agent) in area below gauze, black cover].

Area B – light and dry [anhydrous calcium chloride (drying agent) in area below gauze, no cover].

Area C – light and moist (water in area below gauze, no cover).

Area D – dark and moist (water in area below gauze, black cover).

The surface of each area is covered by fine mesh gauze to support the animals and to prevent any invertebrates that are placed in the choice chamber from being harmed by the drying agent or drowning in the water. The lid is transparent so that you can see where the animals settle. Animals can be introduced to the choice chamber through a hole in the centre of each area. If you use this method you will place the same number of animals in each area. You can also lift the lid and place all the animals together in one particular area to see how they respond.

Once in the choice chamber, the animals are free to move about. By counting the number of animals in each area at given intervals, you can see which conditions they move towards and which they prefer. So, for example, if you placed earthworms or woodlice in the choice chamber in Figure 18.2.1, they would probably show a taxic response to both moisture and light and move towards the dark, moist area.

You can build a choice chamber in the laboratory using plastic Petri dishes or lids. You need four dishes (or lids) and a sheet of perforated zinc or netting (made from stockings or net fabric) to use as a floor. Figure 18.2.2 shows you how to do this.

Practical activity

Investigating invertebrate responses

Your teacher may use this activity to assess: ORR; M&M; Planning and Design (P&D).

Design and carry out an investigation in which you use a choice chamber to investigate the response of small invertebrates to light, moisture and heat.

Record your findings.

Write a report on your investigation using the following headings:

- Title
- Hypothesis
- Aim
- Apparatus
- Method
- Observations
- Results recorded
- Interpretation of results
- Conclusion

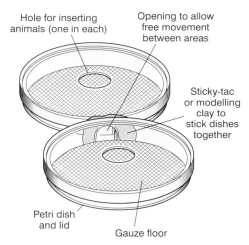

▲ **Figure 18.2.2** How to make a choice chamber

Labels:
Hole for inserting animals (one in each)
Opening to allow free movement between areas
Sticky-tac or modelling clay to stick dishes together
Petri dish and lid
Gauze floor

Animals respond to changes in their environment in order to use less energy and keep their conditions as close to optimum as possible. Taxic responses allow invertebrates to avoid danger and to avoid situations which are too hot, cold, dry or wet. As suitable conditions are normally necessary for reproduction, the main benefit of responding adequately to stimuli is the survival of the species.

Questions

1 What is a taxic response?

2 How do responses to light, moisture and heat affect the survival of insects, such as woodlice, in their natural environment?

All the organs and systems in animals and humans need to work together as a whole. We say that they are coordinated. The nervous system is important because it allows information to be carried throughout the body to bring about coordination.

B19.1 Senses and the nervous system

You learnt in Unit B18 that plants and simple invertebrate animals need to be able to respond to the things that are happening in their environment. For example, plants grow towards light and insects move towards conditions that are suited to them, such as dark and damp soil.

More complex animals, including humans, have to detect information from the external and internal environment in order to survive and function effectively. For example, we may detect the smell of smoke and remove ourselves from danger in the event of a fire, we may get hungry when we smell delicious food cooking, or find a cool place to sit down and rest when we get too hot.

It is not enough to just detect information. We also have to interpret the information and react in the appropriate way. This is one of the functions of our nervous system.

Receptors and effectors

You already know that any information that makes a plant or animal respond is called a stimulus. There are many different stimuli in the environment and we use our sense organs: the eyes, ears, tongue, nose and skin, to detect these stimuli.

Sense organs

The sense organs of animals and humans contain many special cells, called **receptors**, which detect these stimuli and send information about conditions to the control centres in the body. For example, your eyes contain light receptors. Information from these receptors in the eyes passes along nerve fibres to your brain. (You will learn about the eye in more detail in topic B19.5.) Your nose detects smells and sends information about the smell to the brain. Your tongue, skin and ears also have receptors, as shown in Figure 19.1.1.

Table 19.1.1 shows you the main sense organs, the stimuli to which they respond and the type of response or sensation that is experienced.

Receptors change external and internal stimuli into signals that the body can respond to. The signals are called **nerve impulses**. Nerve cells, called **neurones,** conduct nerve impulses to the other parts of the body.

Responses to stimuli are caused by **effectors**. These may be muscles or glands. When nerve cells send impulses to muscles, they respond by contracting or relaxing. When nerve cells send nerve impulses to glands, they respond by

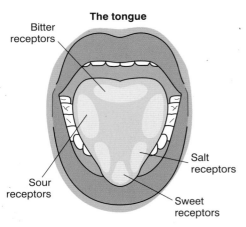

The tongue

Bitter receptors

Sour receptors

Salt receptors

Sweet receptors

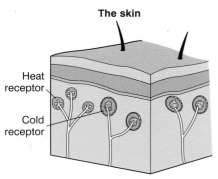

The skin

Heat receptor

Cold receptor

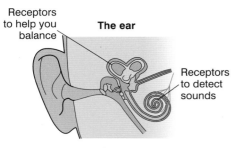

The ear

Receptors to help you balance

Receptors to detect sounds

▲ **Figure 19.1.1** Sense organs and receptors

secreting substances. For example, the salivary glands will produce saliva when you see or taste food. The stimulus–response pathway always happens in the same sequence:

stimulus → receptor → control centre → effector → response

The receptors in the sense organs are an important part of the nervous system.

▼ **Table 19.1.1** Main sense organs, stimuli and responses

Sense organs	Stimuli to which they respond	Response
Eyes	Light	Sight
Ears	Sound, position of body or movement	Hearing, balance
Tongue	Chemical (tastes)	Taste
Nose	Chemical (smells)	Smell
Skin	Warmth, cold, touch	Warmth, coldness, pressure, pain, pleasure

The nervous system

Figure 19.1.2 shows the main parts of the human nervous system. The nervous system is the main coordinating system in the body. The human nervous system can be divided into two parts:

- the **peripheral nervous system**, which consists of the nerves that join all parts of the body to the central nervous system
- the **central nervous system**, which consists of the brain and the spinal cord (nerve cord).

The receptors in sense organs are linked to the peripheral nervous system. Their role is to detect stimuli and pass impulses to the various control centres in the body. The brain interprets impulses and sends nerve impulses through the spinal cord, through the nerves to the effectors so that they can respond to the stimuli. This process is called coordination.

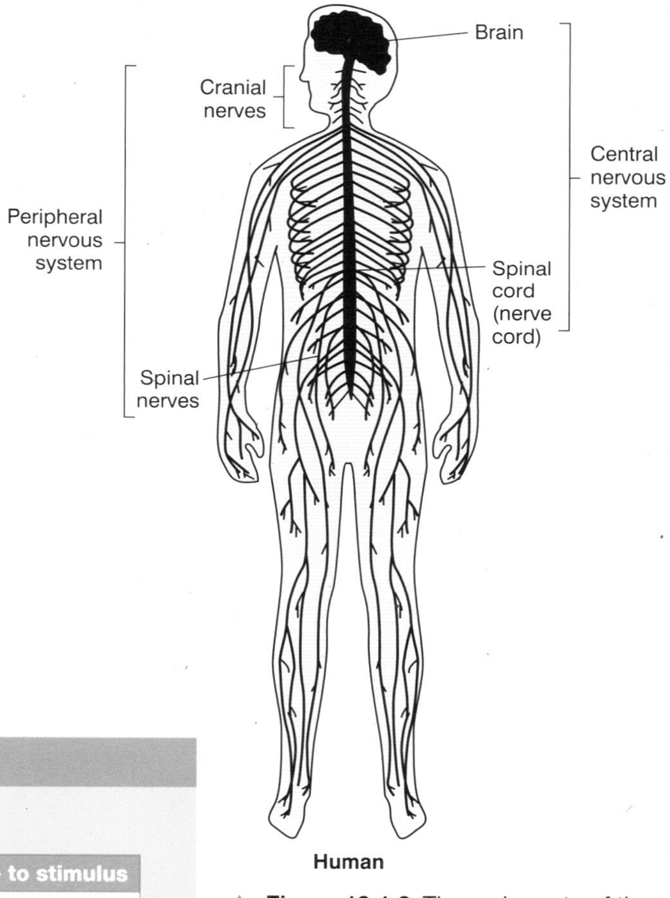

Human

▲ **Figure 19.1.2** The main parts of the human nervous system

Questions

1 Copy and complete this table:

Stimulus	Where receptors are located	Response to stimulus
Light		
		Hearing
	Skin	
Chemical		

2 What is the main job of the nervous system? Why is this important?

Explain what is meant by the each of the following terms and give an example to support each explanation.

a Stimulus   c Control centre   e Response
b Receptor   d Effector

Objectives

By the end of this topic you will be able to:

- state the roles of sensory neurones and motor neurones in the nervous system
- distinguish between cranial reflexes and spinal reflexes
- use flow diagrams to show how impulses travel in a reflex
- investigate reflexes and responses.

B19.2 Neurones, nerves and reflexes

If you look at nerves with the naked eye, they look like fine, silver threads. However, if you examine them with a microscope you can see that they actually consist of bundles of specialised nerve cells called neurones. Figure 19.2.1 shows you the structure of a nerve.

Neurones link receptors (sensory cells) with effectors. They effectively conduct impulses from one part of the body to another.

Sensory neurones and motor neurones

The nerves of the peripheral nervous system are made up of two types of neurones: sensory neurones and motor neurones.

Sensory neurones transmit impulses from receptors in the sense organs to the spinal cord and brain. Motor neurones transmit impulses from the spinal cord to the various effectors (muscles and glands) of the body (see Figure 19.2.2). Figure 19.2.3 shows the structure of these two types of neurones.

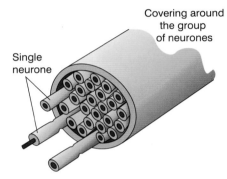

▲ **Figure 19.2.2** The typical path between receptors, the central nervous system and effectors

Table 19.2.1 compares the structures found in sensory and motor neurones.

▼ **Table 19.2.1** The structures in sensory and motor neurones

Structure and function	Sensory neurone	Motor neurone
Cell body – contains nucleus, cytoplasm and cell organelles	Near end of neurone close to where it enters the spinal cord	At start of neurone inside the spinal chord
Dendrites – thin, branched extensions of the cell body which carry impulses to the cell body	Found at ends of neurone	Extensions of the cell body
Axon – long, thin fibre that carries impulses away from the cell body	Short	Very long (up to 1 m in length)

Transmitting impulses

Figure 19.2.4 shows a human motor neurone causing a muscle to contract.

Neurones (nerve cells) are quite long because they have to extend from one part of the body to another. The main part of each neurone is a long, thin fibre, called an axon, that carries the nerve impulses. The axons are often covered by a thin layer of myelin. Myelin is a fatty substance that is believed to insulate nerve fibres. The myelin sheath helps to speed up the transmission of nerve impulses.

It takes more than one neurone to link a receptor to an effector. However, adjacent neurones do not touch each other. They are separated by a small gap called a synapse. The synapses are found between the terminal branch of an axon of one neurone and the dendrite of another. Neurones transmit impulses from one to another across the synapses.

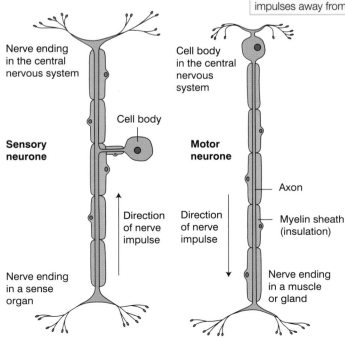

▲ **Figure 19.2.3** A sensory neurone and a motor neurone

▲ **Figure 19.2.1** A nerve

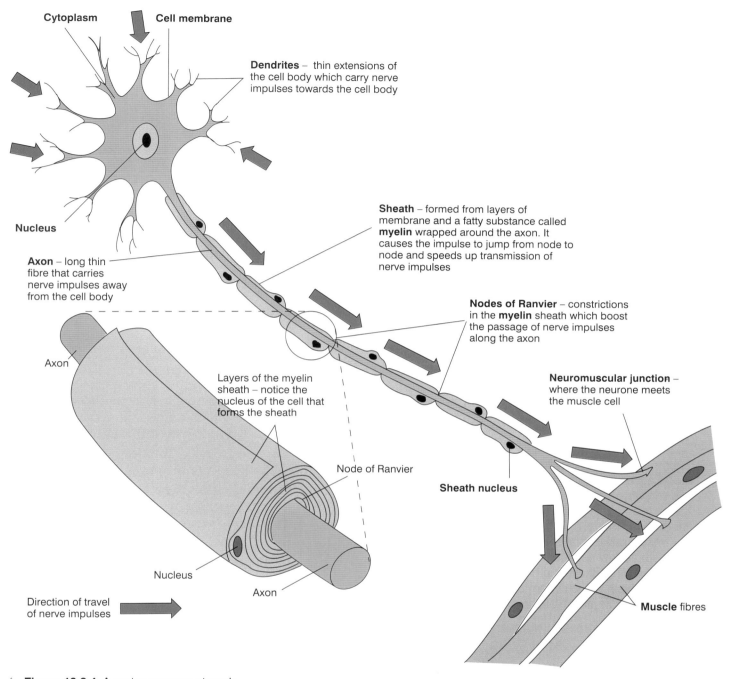

▲ **Figure 19.2.4** A motor neurone at work

When nerve impulses arrive at the end of the axon they stimulate the production of a special chemical substance called a neurotransmitter. The neurotransmitter diffuses across the synapse to the dendrites of the adjacent neurone. The neurotransmitter stimulates the dendrites to causes a new nerve impulse to start in the next neurone.

Nerve impulses always travel in one direction from the axon of one neurone to the dendrite on another. Neurotransmitters are released from only one side of a synapse to ensure that impulses can only be transmitted from that side.

The bundles of nerve fibres that make up the peripheral nervous system provide a very effective communication system for impulses in the body.

Key fact

Drugs can affect how easy or difficult it is for neurotransmitters to cross a synapse. Tranquilisers block receptor molecules and make transmission difficult, so your responses are slower. Stimulants make conduction easier, so responses are speeded up.

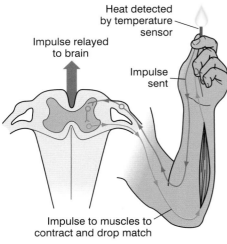

▲ **Figure 19.2.5** The reflex arc that makes you drop a match when it burns your fingers

Cranial and spinal nerves

Nerves that are directly connected to the brain are called cranial nerves. There are 12 pairs of cranial nerves in humans. They supply the sense organs and muscles of the head, neck and internal organs. The optic nerve, which links the eye and the brain, is an example of a cranial nerve.

Nerves that are connected to the spinal cord are called spinal nerves. Humans have 31 pairs of spinal nerves, which leave the spinal cord between each vertebra. Each spinal nerve contains both motor and sensory neurones, so they are called mixed nerves.

Reflex responses

If you touch a hot surface you automatically pull your hand away. Similarly, if you get dust in your eye, you automatically blink. In these examples you respond to a stimulus without even thinking and your response is involuntary – you have no control over the response. We call these automatic responses reflex responses. The nerves involved in a reflex response form a reflex arc. You can see the reflex arc that results from putting your finger close to a flame in Figure 19.2.5.

Different types of neurone form a reflex arc. A synapse separates each type of neurone from the next neurone in the arc.

- Sensory neurones transmit nerve impulses from sensory receptors to the central nervous system. When you touch a hot object a pain-receptor cell in your skin detects the stimulus (heat) which triggers off nerve impulses. These are transmitted to the spinal cord by the sensory neurones.

- Relay neurones in the spinal cord receive nerve impulses from the sensory neurons and pass them to the motor neurones.

- Motor neurones receive nerve impulses from the relay neurones and transmit them to the effector. In the example of Figure 19.2.5, the effector is your arm muscles, which contract, and you drop the match.

Reflex actions often happen before the brain has had time to process the information. However, when the brain catches up with the events, it takes over and brings about the next set of voluntary responses. These responses could be a shout of pain, the decision to run your finger under cold water to stop it burning, or the decision to stamp on the burning match you dropped to prevent a fire.

Spinal and cranial reflexes

Some reflexes are controlled by the spinal cord, so they are called spinal reflexes. Examples of spinal reflexes are: pulling your finger away from a sharp pain, removing your hand from a hot surface and jerking your knee when your leg is tapped with a hard object (see Figure 19.2.6).

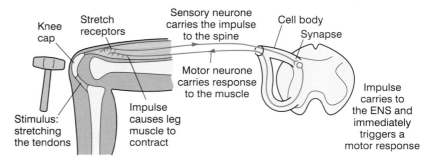

▶ **Figure 19.2.6** The pathway followed by the impulse shows the reflex arc

Other reflexes are controlled by the brain, so they are called cranial reflexes. Examples of cranial reflexes are blinking when you get something in your eye, coughing if food enters your windpipe and contraction or dilation of the pupils in your eye in response to bright light.

Both spinal and cranial reflexes follow the same pathways or reflex arc. This can be represented using a simple flow diagram like this one:

stimulus → receptor → control centre → effector → response

sand in your eye → eyeball → brain → eyelid muscles → rapid blinking

Now you are going to investigate different types of reflex response.

 Practical activity

Testing your reflexes

Work with a partner to test some of your reflexes.

Carry out the following tests and record what happens in each case.

1 Sit on a chair with your legs crossed in a relaxed way, as shown in Figure 19.2.7. Your partner will tap the tendon just below your knee with a ruler.

2 Look straight ahead. Your partner will suddenly wave a hand in front of your eyes.

3 Kneel on a chair and let your feet hang loose. Your partner will tap the back of your foot just above your heel.

4 Close your eyes. Open them and let your partner note the size of your pupil (the small black opening). Now have your partner shine a torch into your eyes and observe the pupil again.

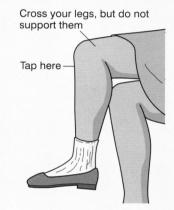

Cross your legs, but do not support them

Tap here

▲ **Figure 19.2.7**

Questions

1 What is the difference between voluntary responses and involuntary responses?

2 What is the advantage of having automatic reflexes?

3 Sandra Joy was walking in a shallow rock pool near the beach when a crab pinched her toe. She kicked it off automatically as shown in Figure 19.2.8.
   a What type of response did she have?
   b Draw a flow diagram to show the pathway followed by the impulses in this reflex reaction.
   c Explain why it is important that the impulses in a reflex arc are not transmitted via the conscious brain.
   d Sandra Joy kicked the crab off before she even realised it had pinched her. What do you think her response was likely to be once her brain caught up with the reflex action? Why?

4 Newborn babies have a number of special reflexes that disappear as they grow. Find out about the gripping and sucking reflexes shown in human and primate babies. Explain why these are important reflexes in a newborn.

▲ **Figure 19.2.8**

B19.3 The brain

The brain is the most highly developed part of the central nervous system. The brain controls both actions and feelings. The brain consists of millions of interconnected neurones, which receive and send thousands of impulses each day. The neurones in the brain are called multipolar neurones because each one has many dendrites which can form synapses with incoming axons. Scientists estimate that there are up to 6 million cell bodies in every 1 cm³ of brain matter and that each neurone is connected to as many as 80 000 others.

The functions of the major parts of the brain

Figure 19.3.1 shows a section through a human head. If you look at the diagram you can see that the brain is divided into three regions: the forebrain, midbrain and hindbrain. In humans, the forebrain forms the cerebrum (pronounced *se-ree-brum*) which is so large it almost covers the rest of the brain.

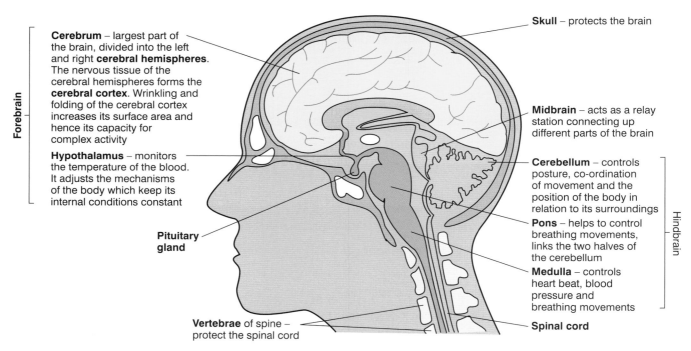

▲ **Figure 19.3.1** The parts of the brain and their functions

The cerebrum receives impulses from all the sense organs. Separate areas in the cerebral cortex of the cerebrum receive impulses from different senses and interpret them. The cerebrum sends out impulses that control or coordinate conscious, voluntary, muscular movements, such as walking, reaching for objects or bending.

The cerebrum is also important for thought, speech and memory.

Figure 19.3.2 shows the functions of different parts of the cerebral cortex in the cerebrum.

The cerebellum (pronounced *se-reh-bell-um*) controls the coordination of all our movements and makes it possible for us to move smoothly and gracefully. It is the cerebellum that allows us to bend down and pick up items

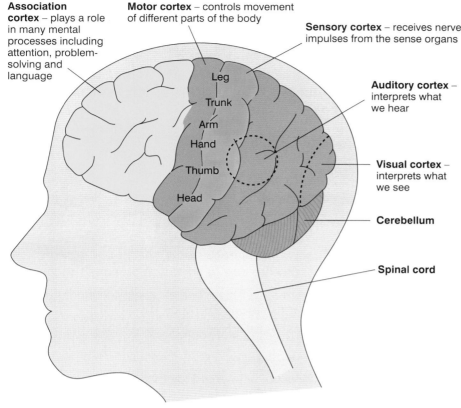

Association cortex – plays a role in many mental processes including attention, problem-solving and language

Motor cortex – controls movement of different parts of the body

Sensory cortex – receives nerve impulses from the sense organs

Auditory cortex – interprets what we hear

Visual cortex – interprets what we see

Cerebellum

Spinal cord

Leg
Trunk
Arm
Hand
Thumb
Head

▲ **Figure 19.3.2** The cerebrum coordinates and controls many voluntary actions

without falling over and makes it possible for us to dance by coordinating all our limbs. The cerebellum also influences posture and balance by sending impulses to muscles.

The medulla joins the brain to the spinal cord. The medulla controls many unconscious body functions, such as breathing, heart rate and peristalsis. The medulla also contains the reflex centres for vomiting, coughing, sneezing, hiccupping and swallowing. The medulla functions below the level of consciousness to maintain body functions without any input from the cerebrum.

The flow diagram in Figure 19.3.3 shows you how the brain (as part of the central nervous system) is linked to the peripheral nervous system in humans.

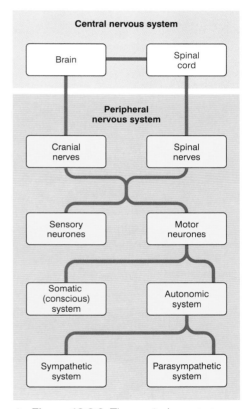

▲ **Figure 19.3.3** The central nervous system is linked to the peripheral nervous system

The autonomic nervous system

You have no conscious control over your internal organs. You can decide to move your hands or feet up or down, but you cannot decide to make your liver stop working or your heart stop beating. The continued coordination and functioning of your internal organs is involuntary and unconscious. These actions are controlled by a part of the peripheral nervous system called the autonomic nervous system, which controls your heart rate and breathing rate.

The autonomic nervous system consists of motor neurones which link to the smooth muscles of internal organs, such as the heart.

The autonomic nervous system is divided into two systems:

- The sympathetic system speeds up your heart beat and breathing rate. It is dominant when you are in danger or under stress and it effectively causes the fight or flight response.
- The parasympathetic system slows up your heart beat and breathing rate. It is dominant when you are relaxed and at rest and it controls normal body functions.

Questions

1 Match each biological term in column A with its function in column B.

Column A	Column B
Cerebellum	Transmits nerve impulses from the central nervous system to a muscle
Medulla	Transmits nerve impulses from a sense receptor to the central nervous system
Synapse	Maintains coordination and functioning of internal organs
Cerebrum	Controls learning and memory
Sensory neurone	Controls pulse, breathing, blood pressure and other involuntary actions
Motor neurone	Controls balance
Autonomic nervous system	Links a sensory neurone with a motor neurone or relay neurone

B19.4 Drugs

A drug is any chemical substance that affects the functioning of the body. Medicines, such as antibiotics and painkillers, are drugs that are used to prevent and treat disease. Other drugs such as solvents, illegal substances like heroin and marijuana, alcohol and the nicotine and other chemicals in cigarettes may harm the body.

The effects of drugs

Drugs taken as medicines under doctor's orders can be of great benefit as they help ill people fight disease and control pain. However, the amount taken and when it is taken is very important or it may cause harm. For example, if drugs that affect the nervous system are taken under the wrong circumstances, people can become addicted to them. When you are addicted to a drug, you want more and more of the drug and you don't care about the harm is does to your body. When drugs are used improperly, we talk about drug abuse.

Besides harming the body, drug addiction has social and economic effects. Addiction is expensive because it is illegal to obtain most drugs without a doctor's prescription. Addicts therefore can only buy the drugs they need from drug dealers who make a lot of money (which is illegal, so it is not taxed and there is no community benefit). The life of the addict is one of ill-health and declining self-respect, with little regard for family or community values. Unless the addiction is broken, the life of the addict is normally short. When drugs are injected, there is a further danger of spreading infectious diseases such as hepatitis A and viruses such as HIV which causes AIDS.

Table 19.4.1 shows the main types of drug, their effects and examples of each type.

▼ **Table 19.4.1** Different types of drugs and their effects

Type of drug	Effects	Examples
Depressants	Slow down the actions of the nervous system	Barbiturates, heroin, morphine, tranquilisers and alcohol
Stimulants	Speed up the actions of the nervous system, highly addictive	Amphetamines, cocaine (and crack cocaine), ecstasy, caffeine and the nicotine in tobacco
Hallucinogens	Affect the nervous system and produce feelings of false reality	Cannabis (marijuana), LSD and solvents such as glue or lighter fuel

Some drug addictions arise from the use of prescription drugs, such as sleeping tablets, diet pills and painkillers. Chronic abuse is the result of high consumption over a long time. Abuse of painkillers, such as aspirin or other headache tablets, can lead to kidney damage, raised blood pressure, anaemia and digestive problems. If the abuse continues, kidney failure is likely and the person may die without treatment.

Drug abuse among young people

The Organisation of American States carried out research into drug and alcohol use among Form 2, 4 and 6 students (a sample of 38 534 students) in 12 Caribbean states. In 2010, they published the findings in a report with the title Comparative Analysis of Student Drug Use in Caribbean Countries. Table 19.4.2 summarises some of the data from that report.

If you examine the table, you see that alcohol is the substance that is most abused. This is problematic because alcohol is addictive and people quickly become dependent on it. Drinking large amounts of alcohol over long periods of time can lead to stomach ulcers, heart disease, brain damage and cirrhosis of the liver.

 Link

For more detail relating to the age and gender of drug users in your own country, and an analysis of the problems linked to drug and alcohol use, you can access the entire report online at www.cicad.oas.org/Main/pubs/StudentDrugUse-Caribbean2011.pdf.

▼ **Table 19.4.2** Students who have ever used tobacco, alcohol and other substances (figures are percentages)

Country	Alcohol	Cigarettes	Marijuana	Tranquilisers	Stimulants	Inhalants	Cocaine	Crack cocaine	Ecstasy
Antigua and Barbuda	71.10	17.33	23.94	2.77	2.44	12.10	1.80	1.75	1.28
Barbados	75.60	21.46	18.97	3.00	3.35	18.00	2.01	2.02	1.93
Dominica	80.18	30.69	29.54	5.22	4.22	7.78	0.69	0.86	0.56
Grenada	80.77	34.53	25.43	5.58	2.72	9.42	1.50	1.40	1.13
Guyana	61.02	17.66	12.12	6.10	6.99	21.46	4.12	4.30	3.86
Haiti	47.72	9.20	2.20	24.72	20.27	3.23	2.69	2.65	2.95
Jamaica	65.83	24.61	21.56	4.44	5.42	25.52	3.12	1.63	2.79
St Kitts and Nevis	64.77	11.82	24.14	2.80	3.05	12.48	2.27	2.47	2.12
St Lucia	86.20	27.84	26.51	6.85	6.12	9.39	1.48	0.99	1.54
St Vincent and the Grenadines	65.34	21.01	20.13	3.25	3.15	5.26	0.53	0.32	0.54
Suriname	61.15	33.06	5.53	9.10	4.12	7.32	0.70	0.66	1.45
Trinidad and Tobago	82.02	28.86	12.09	2.61	3.27	24.81	0.91	0.77	0.90

Exam tip

In an examination you might be asked to describe the effects of alcohol or marijuana abuse. Remember to include a definition of drug abuse before you describe the effects of the drug.

Table 19.4.3 shows the effects and dangers of alcohol abuse and dependence.

▼ **Table 19.4.3** The effects and dangers of alcohol abuse

Effects of alcohol abuse	Dangers of alcohol abuse
In small amounts can be relaxing and create a sense of wellbeing	Slow reactions make it dangerous to drive or handle heavy equipment
	Impaired judgement can lead to criminal activity and irresponsible sexual behaviour
Alcohol is a depressant. With greater amounts people lose muscle control and lack coordination, reaction times are slowed and judgement becomes impaired.	Longer term drinking leads to alcoholism and related family and social problems and possible loss of employment
	Heavy drinking damages the liver and can cause brain damage and ulcers
Mood swings and violence are common when people are drunk	Drinking during pregnancy can harm the foetus and alcohol can pass through the placenta. There is an increased risk of miscarriage, premature birth and underdevelopment of the foetus.

Giving up the use of alcohol or other drugs is not easy. People who are trying to give up need lots of help and support, especially in the first few weeks when they may experience serious withdrawal symptoms as their body reacts to no longer having the addictive substance.

Questions

1 What is a 'drug'?

2 Give two examples of legal drugs. For each one, describe its benefits and the possible consequences if it is abused.

3 How does using an illegal drug such as cocaine affect:
   a the body
   b families and communities?

4 Alcohol is the most commonly abused drug in the Caribbean. Alcohol is a depressant that is addictive.
   a What is meant by the terms 'depressant' and 'addictive'?
   b List three physiological effects of long-term alcohol consumption.
   c List two social and economic effects of alcoholism.
   d The law states that you cannot drive if you have consumed more than a set number of units of alcohol (the legal limit differs across Caribbean countries – find out the limit in your country). Why do you think laws like this are necessary?

5 Alcoholism is a major problem in many parts of the world. Find out what can be done to prevent and treat alcoholism. Present your ideas to the class.

6 Do you think there is a serious youth drug problem in your country. Justify your answer with reference to the data in Table 19.4.2.

B19.5 The human eye

In topic B19.1 you were introduced to the five sense organs and the types of stimuli that they can detect. In this topic you are going to learn more about the eye. The eye is a sense organ that allows us to focus on objects and see shapes and colours. To understand how the eye works, we need to understand its structure.

The structure of the eye

Figure 19.5.1 shows you a section through a human eye. The labelled parts of the eye are listed in Table 19.5.1 with their functions.

Objectives

By the end of this topic you will be able to:

● relate the structure of the human eye to its functions
● draw and label diagrams showing sections through an eye
● examine the dissected eye of a mammal
● explain, with the use of diagrams, some common sight defects
● explain how sight defects can be corrected.

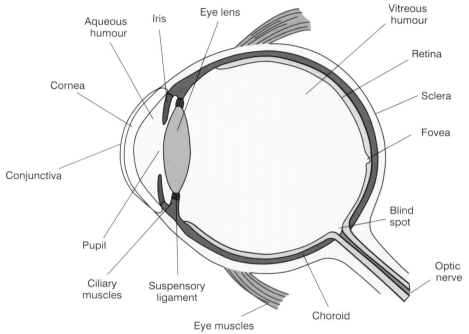

▲ **Figure 19.5.1** The structure of the human eye

▼ **Table 19.5.1** The functions of parts of the eye

Part of the eye	Function
Aqueous humour	Transparent watery liquid that supports the front of the eye and maintains the shape of the cornea
Blind spot	Region where the retina is not sensitive to light (no receptor cells present)
Choroid	Black layer of blood vessels that carry food and oxygen to the eye and remove waste products. Black colour prevents reflection of light inside the eye.
Ciliary muscles	Muscles which contract and relax to change the thickness of the eye lens
Conjunctiva	Thin transparent membrane that protects the surface of the eye from dust and other particles
Cornea	Helps to focus light onto the retina
Eye muscles	Move the eye in its socket
Fovea	Region of the retina where the retinal cells are densest. Light is normally focused here and it is where colours are detected.
Iris	Coloured ring of muscle that controls the amount of light entering the eye
Lens	Focuses light onto the retina by refracting it
Optic nerve	Carries nerve impulses from the retina to the brain
Pupil	Hole in the centre of the iris though which light enters the eye
Retina	Light-sensitive layer around the inside of the eye
Sclera	Tough white layer that surrounds and protects the eyeball
Suspensory ligament	Attaches the ciliary muscle to the eye lens
Vitreous humour	Transparent jelly-like substance that supports the back of the eye and maintains the shape of the eyeball

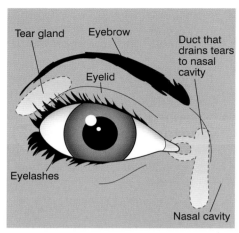

▲ **Figure 19.5.2** The main structures that keep the eye clean

Protecting and cleaning the eyes

Figure 19.5.2 shows the structures that protect and clean the eye.

Your eyelids and eyelashes help to keep dust and sweat from entering the eye. You have probably noticed that you blink automatically when something passes close to your eye. This is an involuntary reaction to protect the eye.

The surface of the eye is kept moist by fluid produced in the tear glands. This fluid contains lysosome which kills germs. When you blink, the eyelid moves across the eye and spreads this fluid. Excess fluid drains away through the tear ducts into the nasal cavity.

How we see

In order to see, light enters our eyes through a transparent, curved surface called the cornea. Light passes through a convex (converging) lens which focuses the light to form an image on the receptor cells in the retina. The image formed on the retina is upside-down. The retina sends impulses to the brain through the optic nerve. Our brain then interprets the image and we 'see' it the right way up.

Focusing

When we look at objects close up or far away, the lens in the eye changes shape to keep the object in focus. The adjustment of the lens shape to focus light coming from different distances is called accommodation. The ciliary muscles alter the thickness of the eye lens. These muscles run round the eye lens and are attached to the lens by suspensory ligaments. The tension in the suspensory ligaments, and therefore the shape of the eye lens, is altered by the contraction and relaxation of the ciliary muscles.

When the muscle fibres contract, the suspensory ligaments are loosened and the eye lens becomes fatter. When the muscles relax, the suspensory ligaments tighten, pulling the eye lens and making it thinner. You can see the differences in the eye lens when you look at close objects and objects far away in Figure 19.5.3.

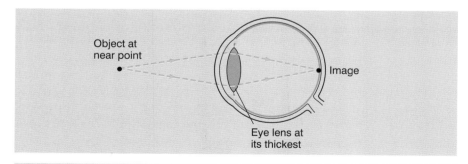

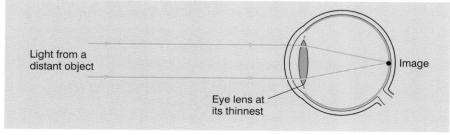

▲ **Figure 19.5.3** The eye lens accommodates for light coming from different distances

The light which enters the eye hits light-sensory cells in the retina. The light causes a chemical reaction in these cells which in turn triggers nerve impulses. The impulses are transmitted along the optical nerve to the brain. The brain interprets the impulses and corrects the image so that we see it the right way up.

light → sensory cells in the retina → sensory neurons in optic nerve → brain

In humans, two eyes are positioned so that each one gives a slightly different view of the surroundings. This means that humans have binocular vision. Each eye makes an image or picture of what you are looking at. Information about both images is sent to the brain. The brain combines the images from each eye and we see things in three-dimensions. You can see how this works by closing your right eye and looking at something. Now, without moving your head, open your right eye and close the left. Repeat this a few times. The thing you are looking at seems to change position. When you look with both eyes, you see the object at the correct size and distance.

The sensory cells in the eye are very sensitive to light. Light enters the eye by passing through the pupil. The muscles in the iris control the pupil and open and close to control the amount of light entering the eye.

In very bright light, the iris muscles work to make the pupil constrict (get smaller) to limit the amount of light entering the eye. In dim light, the muscles of the iris allow the pupil to dilate (open wider) so that more light can enter the eye.

The action of the pupil is an example of a reflex action.

Certain drugs can affect how the pupil in the eye reacts to light. Drugs like heroin make the pupil constrict and become unreactive. Drugs like cocaine and amphetamines make the pupil dilate and become slow to react or unreactive to light. Marijuana, alcohol and depressants do not make the pupil change size, but they do make it slow to react or unreactive to light.

Seeing shape and colour

When you look at an object, an image (picture) of the object is formed on the retina. The retina consists of many light-sensitive cells which send nerve impulses to the brain as soon as light falls on them. The brain recognises the pattern of the signals from the cells covered by the image and so it recognises the shape of the object.

The retina consists of two types of cells – rods and cones (see Figure 19.5.4). Rods occur mostly near the edges of the retina. They are not sensitive to colour and only respond to the brightness of light. Cones are packed most densely at the middle of the retina. This area is called the fovea. Each cone is sensitive to red or blue or green light. For example, when red light falls on the retina, it activates the red-sensitive cones, so you see red. Other colours activate more than one type of cone. Yellow light, for example, activates the red- and the green-sensitive cones so they send messages to the brain. When the brain received signals from adjacent red- and green-sensitive cones, it knows that yellow light is on that part of the retina.

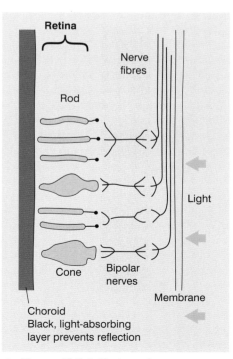

▲ **Figure 19.5.4** Rods and cones

Questions

1 Trace or draw the diagram of the eye shown in Figure 19.5.1. Try to label the parts correctly without looking at your textbook.

2 Think back to practical activity 'Testing your reflexes' on p193, where you investigated pupil size when you dealt with reflexes. Redraw Figure 19.5.5 to show what happens to the pupil in bright light. Apply what you have learnt about the function of the eye to write labels for your drawing.

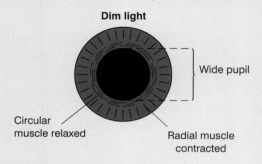

Dim light

Wide pupil

Circular muscle relaxed

Radial muscle contracted

▲ **Figure 19.5.5**

3 When you go from daylight into a darkened room you cannot see properly at first. Why is this?

4 Why do you think nocturnal animals (those that are active at night) tend to have large pupils and lots of rods in their retinas?

Sight defects

Human eyes do not always work perfectly and many people cannot see properly. We say they have sight defects. Many sight defects can be corrected by spectacles (glasses) that contain lenses.

Correcting sight defects with lenses

There are three common sight defects that can be corrected with lenses. These are:

- short-sightedness (myopia)
- long-sightedness (hypermetropia)
- lack of accommodation (presbyopia).

Short-sightedness

If you are short-sighted you can see objects clearly that are close to you, but you cannot see objects clearly that are far away. So, a short-sighted person can read a book easily but he or she would find it difficult to read writing on the chalkboard.

Short-sightedness happens when the whole eyeball is too long, or when the lens is thickened. Refraction of the light through the lens causes the light from distant objects to come into focus in front of the retina (rather than on it) and the images seem blurry.

Diverging (concave) lenses are used to correct short-sightedness. Concave lenses work because they diverge the rays of light from objects far away, so that they appear to come from a point close to the eye. The image then falls directly onto the retina.

Figure 19.5.6 shows what happens when you are short-sighted and how a concave lens can correct the problem.

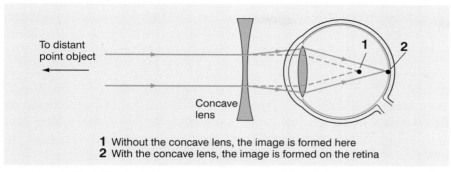

1 Without the concave lens, the image is formed here
2 With the concave lens, the image is formed on the retina

▲ **Figure 19.5.6** Short-sightedness is a common vision defect that is corrected easily using concave lenses

Long-sightedness

If you are long-sighted you can see objects that are far away clearly, but objects that are close up seem blurred because you cannot focus on them. So, a long-sighted person would be able to read the writing on the chalkboard clearly, but would struggle to read the words on the page in front of them.

Long-sightedness happens when the eyeball is too short or the lens is a bit thin. The rays of light from close objects are refracted and they cannot focus before they reach the retina.

Converging (convex) lenses are used to correct long-sightedness. The convex lens makes the light from close objects appear to have come from a point further away. The eye can then focus the rays so that they fall directly onto the retina.

Figure 19.5.7 shows you what happens when you are long-sighted and how a convex lens can correct the problem.

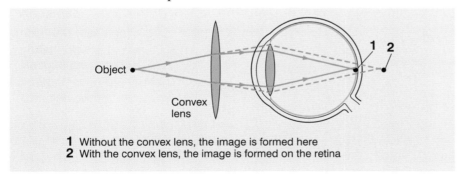

1 Without the convex lens, the image is formed here
2 With the convex lens, the image is formed on the retina

▲ **Figure 19.5.7** Long-sightedness is a common vision defect that is corrected easily using convex lenses

Lack of accommodation

As we get older, the lenses in our eyes usually get a bit stiffer and are not able to change their shape as easily to accommodate objects at different distances. You might have noticed that older people hold newspapers or menus at arm's length to read them properly.

Converging (convex) lenses are normally used to correct for lack of accommodation.

If you are short-sighted and you suffer from lack of accommodation you need different kinds of lenses. Opticians have developed bi-focal lenses so that people don't need two pairs of glasses. A bifocal lens is a diverging lens at the top and a converging lens at the bottom. If you wear bifocals, you look through the top of the glasses when you are looking at objects far away. You look down through the bottom of the lens to read or see things that are close up.

Contact lenses

Contact lenses are small lenses that are worn directly on the eyeball in front of the cornea. Contact lenses can be convex or concave, depending on the person's vision defect. People who wear contact lenses find they have more natural vision than with glasses. There are two reasons for this:

- there is no distortion of vision caused by looking through different parts of a lens, so objects look normal and they appear the right size
- the lenses move with the eyes, so the person is always looking through them and he or she gets a wider, clearer field of vision.

 Practical activity

Examining a mammalian eye

You will need the eye of a mammal and equipment for dissection.

Examine the outside structure of the eye.

Sketch the eyeball and attached muscles. Label these using your knowledge of the human eye.

Slice through the eye, starting at the centre of the cornea. Sketch the internal structure and label the parts of the eye.

 Practical activity

Investigating your vision

1 Find your blind spot using Figure 19.5.8.
  - Position the black spot in front of your left eye. Cover your right eye.
  - Move the page closer to your face and keep staring at the spot.

The X disappears when its image falls on the blind spot of your left eye.

Compare the distance at which this happens for different students.

2 Hold your hands in front of your face with the tips of your index fingers touching. Stare past your hands at a distant object and move your hands towards your face. What happens?

Why is this?

▲ **Figure 19.5.8** Blind spot test

Questions

1 What causes short-sightedness? How can it be rectified?

2 What causes long-sightedness? How can it be rectified?

3 Why do older people often need bifocal lenses?

For cells to work efficiently, the composition of the tissue fluid that surrounds them should be kept fairly constant. In this unit you will learn about homeostasis and the feedback mechanisms that help the body maintain a constant internal environment.

B20.1 Homeostasis and negative feedback

The world in which an organism lives is its external environment. The cells that make up an organism exist inside the organism, in an internal environment. The internal environment of an animal is the tissue fluid that surrounds and maintains the cells of the body. This internal environment needs to be maintained and kept constant so that the cells can function efficiently. Different mechanisms help to regulate the body and to keep the internal environment as constant as possible.

Homeostasis

Cells are very sensitive to changes in the environment. Cells work best when the temperature, pH and fluid levels are kept within narrow limits and when levels of waste products are kept at a low level. The process of keeping conditions constant is called **homeostasis**.

Homeostasis is controlled by the nervous system The human brain contains a number of centres that regulate factors such as osmoregulation, blood pressure and the level of glucose in the blood.

Negative feedback

In Unit B16 you learnt that any change in blood composition as a result of water gain or loss is detected by receptors in the brain. These receptors cause the body to respond to correct the change and then return the situation to normal. As soon as conditions return to normal, the receptor is no longer stimulated. This process of feedback and response is called **negative feedback** because it results in a response that is opposite to the present conditions. Figure 20.1.1 shows you a typical negative feedback loop. In humans, negative feedback plays an important role in the following processes:

- ensuring balanced levels of oxygen and carbon dioxide in the blood
- keeping the heart rate constant
- maintaining normal blood pressure
- regulating the release of hormones
- controlling the level of glucose in the blood
- osmoregulation (water balance)
- regulating pH
- controlling body temperature.

You will learn more about controlling body temperature in topic B20.2.

Objectives

By the end of this topic you will be able to:

- define homeostasis and state why it is important
- explain how negative feedback systems work in the body.

(!) Key fact

A good example of negative feedback is the thermostat in an oven. When you heat the oven to a set temperature, say 200 °C, the thermostat detects that the correct temperature has been reached and it switches off the oven. If the temperature drops below 200 °C, the thermostat again detects the change and switches the oven back on. This feedback loop will continue as long as necessary to maintain a constant temperature in the internal environment of the oven.

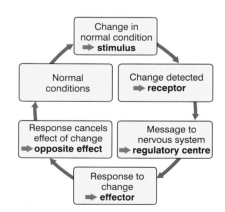

▲ **Figure 20.1.1** Negative feedback allows the body to cancel out the effect of a change in conditions

Hormones play a role in homeostasis

The hormone system plays an important role in regulating body systems and homeostasis. For example, in Unit B16 you learnt that the hormone ADH plays a role in osmoregulation. This is a good example of homeostasis. Figure 20.1.2 shows how ADH and negative feedback are part of the process of osmoregulation.

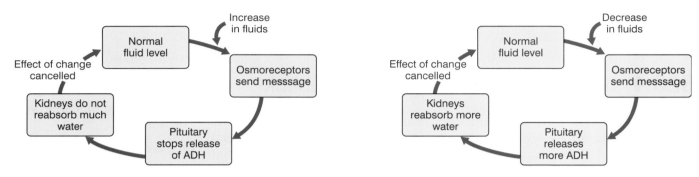

▲ **Figure 20.1.2** Osmoregulation relies on negative feedback and the hormone ADH

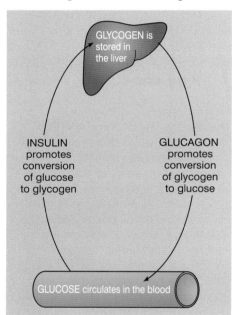

▲ **Figure 20.1.3** Homeostasis is important for control of blood sugar levels

When you experience emotional stress in the form of excitement, pain or irritation, your blood pressure rises. Any increase in blood pressure is detected by receptors in your aortic and carotid sinuses. These receptors send a message to the regulatory centre in your brain, which in turn causes the walls of your arteries to relax. Once the artery walls relax, your blood pressure drops again.

The hormones insulin and glucagon also rely on negative feedback to make sure that the level of glucose in the blood remains constant. When the glucose level is high the hormone insulin is released to normalise the levels. When the glucose level is low the hormone glucagon is released to normalise the levels. These two hormones work together to maintain a blood sugar level that is constant at more or less 90 mg per 100 cm^3 of blood. Figure 20.1.3 shows you how this works.

Homeostasis ensures that blood and tissue components and values stay within a normal, and usually narrow, range. All of the organ systems in the body play a role in homeostasis. The liver is especially important for keeping blood sugar level constant and the kidneys are very important for osmoregulation and the maintenance of pH in tissue fluids.

Questions

1 What is homeostasis? Why is it important in living organisms?

2 What is a negative feedback system? Give an example of a biological negative feedback mechanism in humans.

3 Read the information in the box on the left about blood pressure. Use it to draw a flow diagram showing how negative feedback restores the body to its original state (homeostasis).

4 In positive feedback systems, a change leads to responses that increase the change even further. For example, when you cut yourself, your body releases chemicals to activate blood platelets. Once they are activated, the platelets release chemicals that activate more platelets, causing a massive increase in blood platelets and the formation of a blood clot.
   a Explain why positive feedback is rare in biological systems.
   b Why is a positive feedback mechanism not useful for homeostasis?

B20.2 Temperature regulation

You know that enzymes control many of the chemical reactions that take place in your cells. You also know that most enzymes work best at temperatures of around 37 °C. In lower temperatures enzymes work slowly, or not at all, and once temperatures rise above 40 °C most enzymes are destroyed. This is one of the main reasons why we need to maintain a constant temperature of about 37 °C inside our bodies.

If you touch something very cold, the temperature of your fingers will decrease. If you lie in the sun, the temperature of your skin will increase. These temperature changes are surface changes. They do not affect your metabolic processes. The temperature at the centre of your body is called your core temperature and it is this temperature that needs to be maintained at a constant level.

Controlling body temperature

Humans (and other mammals and birds) gain most of their body heat from their own metabolic processes. This heat is carried throughout the body in the blood and it helps to keep our body temperature constant. However humans also lose heat, mainly through evaporation of water from body surfaces, when we exhale or when we sweat. So, how does the body manage to balance heat gains and losses to maintain a constant core temperature of 37 °C?

The skin and temperature control

Human skin is the largest single organ in the body. It is also the organ that plays the biggest role in regulating our body temperature. Figure 20.2.1 shows you the structure of the skin.

Objectives

By the end of this topic you will be able to:

- use temperature control as an example of homeostasis
- describe the function of the skin in temperature control and protection in humans.

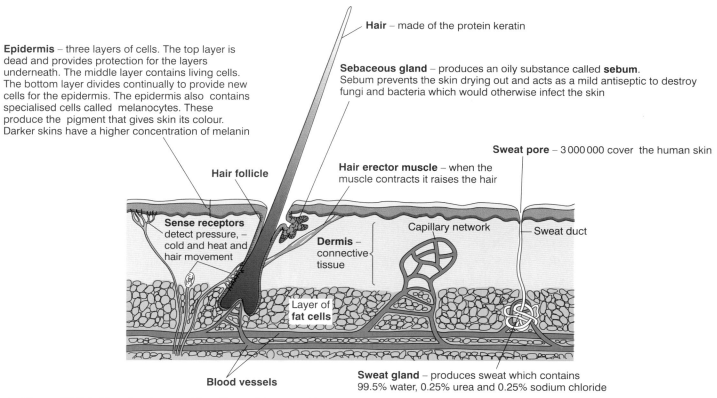

Epidermis – three layers of cells. The top layer is dead and provides protection for the layers underneath. The middle layer contains living cells. The bottom layer divides continually to provide new cells for the epidermis. The epidermis also contains specialised cells called melanocytes. These produce the pigment that gives skin its colour. Darker skins have a higher concentration of melanin

Hair – made of the protein keratin

Sebaceous gland – produces an oily substance called **sebum**. Sebum prevents the skin drying out and acts as a mild antiseptic to destroy fungi and bacteria which would otherwise infect the skin

Sweat pore – 3 000 000 cover the human skin

Hair follicle

Hair erector muscle – when the muscle contracts it raises the hair

Sense receptors detect pressure, cold and heat and hair movement

Dermis – connective tissue

Capillary network

Sweat duct

Layer of fat cells

Blood vessels

Sweat gland – produces sweat which contains 99.5% water, 0.25% urea and 0.25% sodium chloride

▲ **Figure 20.2.1** The structure and functions of human skin

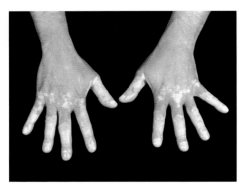

▲ **Figure 20.2.2** Melanin protects the skin from certain cancers and prevents premature ageing. Skin-lightening creams act by blocking melanin production, leaving the person vulnerable to skin cancer and longer-term organ damage. Regular use of these products damages the skin and actually causes more pigmentation and a rough, blotchy appearance.

The skin works together with receptors in the hypothalamus to control temperature. Any changes to the external temperature are sensed by the skin. Changes in the temperature of the blood are sensed by the hypothalamus. When body temperature drops below the normal 37 °C, the hypothalamus is activated. This sends a message (via the nerves) to the blood vessels in the skin and they constrict (close up) to prevent heat loss. At the same time, the hairs on the skin stand up so that they can act as insulation by trapping a layer of warm air next to the skin. This is why you get goose-bumps when you get cold.

If the body temperature falls further, messages are sent to the skeletal muscles and they start to contract and relax very quickly, causing you to shiver. Shivering generates heat and your body temperature rises as a result.

When your body temperature rises above normal, the hypothalamus sends messages to the blood vessels to make them dilate. This allows more blood to flow close to the surface of the skin and more heat is lost to the environment. The hypothalamus also activates the sweat glands, so you sweat more. The evaporation of sweat also helps to lower your body temperature.

Table 20.2.1 summarises the homeostatic functions of the skin.

▼ **Table 20.2.1** Homeostatic functions of the skin in humans (and other mammals)

Mechanisms to encourage heat loss	Mechanisms to conserve heat
Increased blood flow through capillaries close to skin to increase heat loss from skin surface	Decreased blood flow through capillaries close to the skin surface to reduce heat loss from skin surface
Amount of sweat produced by sweat glands increased, heat lost as sweat evaporates	Less sweat produced, so heat loss by evaporation is reduced
Hair lies flat against body to reduce insulating layer	Hair stands up to trap air and provide an insulating layer next to the skin
Metabolic rate drops (we become less active) so that less heat is produced in the body	Metabolic rate rises producing extra heat, shivering may occur in muscles to generate more body heat

Besides its role in regulating temperature, the skin also functions as a physical barrier between our internal and external environments. Skin prevents damage to underlying tissue, protects the body from harmful ultraviolet (UV) rays and prevents harmful microorganisms from entering the body.

Questions

1 Why is it important for humans to maintain a core body temperature of 37 °C?

2 Look at the simplified diagram of the skin in Figure 20.2.3.
   a Name the parts labelled A to D.
   b What do parts B and D do when you get hot?
   c How does this help you to maintain a constant core temperature?
   d What do parts B and D do when you get cold?
   e How does the skin know how to react to the cold?

3 Why do you shiver when you get very cold?

4 In very hot or very cold conditions you can make it easier for your body to maintain a constant 37 °C temperature.
   a List three things you can do in hot weather to help your body remain cool.
   b List three things you can do in cold conditions to help your body remain warm.
   c Why do health care workers recommend that you drink more liquids when it is very hot?

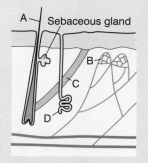

▲ **Figure 20.2.3**

B21 Growth and development

All living organisms grow and develop. These processes are controlled by growth substances in plants and by hormones in humans. Both growth and development can be observed and measured using different scientific methods.

B21.1 What are growth and development?

Growth is a permanent increase in size caused by an increase in the number and size of cells. For example, plants grow taller, the size of their leaves increases and the thickness of their stems and length of their roots increase. Animals may get taller and heavier and the size of their organs or limbs may increase.

Development is the process by which organisms become more complex as they grow. This is due to cell differentiation. For example, plants develop from simple seeds, to shoots, to leafy plants and then they flower and produce fruit. Humans develop from embryos to foetuses to newborn babies. They then develop further in stages, such as during puberty when sexual characteristics become more pronounced in both males and females.

Stages of growth and development

Figure 21.1.1 shows you how growth and development (in both plant and animal cells) happen in three stages.

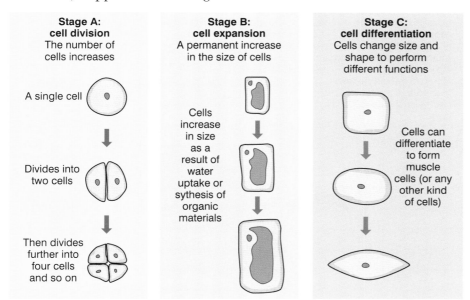

▲ **Figure 21.1.1** Cellular changes are involved in growth and development

Growth and development in plants

Most plants grow from seeds. The seed contains the embryo of the plant. In suitable conditions, the seed will germinate and roots and shoots will develop from it. The roots and shoots grow in length, with the roots extending

Objectives

By the end of this topic you will be able to:

- define the terms 'growth' and 'development'
- give examples of growth and development in plants and arthropods
- read and interpret graphs showing growth curves for plants and insects.

Key fact

In countries like the UK, wood grows seasonally. The growth cycle is repeated each year to form cylinders of wood which can be seen in the cross-section as annual growth rings, such as those below:

downwards and sideways and the shoot growing upwards to form the stem of the plant. This type of growth is called primary growth.

Some plants, especially woody shrubs and trees, also grow widthways, with the stems (or trunks) and roots getting thicker. This is called secondary growth.

Figure 21.1.2 shows you the main stages in the growth of a woody shrub. The graph in Figure 21.1.3 shows you the growth curve for a woody perennial. You can see that growth continues throughout the life of the plant.

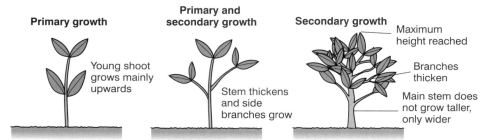

▲ **Figure 21.1.2** Woody plants show primary and secondary growth

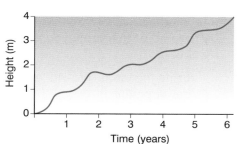

▲ **Figure 21.1.3** A growth curve for a woody perennial (a mango tree)

Annual plants have a limited growth cycle. In these plants, growth does not continue for the life of the plant. The plants grow to maturity and then they decrease in size and mass before they die. Figure 21.1.4 shows you a growth curve for a bean plant as it grows from a seed to a mature plant.

You will examine plant growth and development in more detail in Unit B22 when you deal with reproduction in plants.

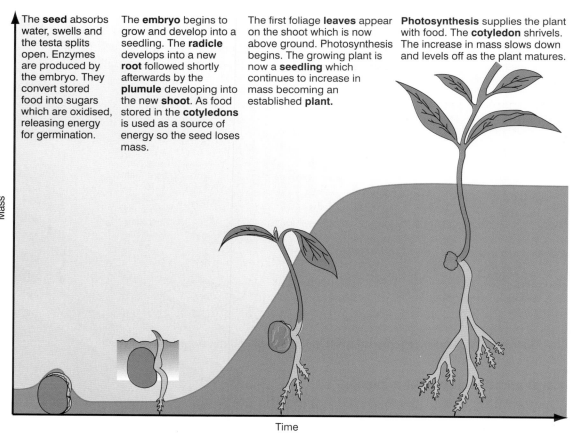

▲ **Figure 21.1.4** The growth curve for a broad bean

Questions

1 Write brief notes to explain how a young plant grows and develops into a mature tree.

2 Study the growth curve of a broad bean in Figure 21.1.4 on p210 and answer the following questions:

   a What does 'germination' mean?

   b Why does the mass of the seed initially increase as germination begins?

   c After this initial increase in mass, why does the germinating plant then lose mass?

   d What happens to the plant to make it gain mass after the decrease in mass after germination?

   e What happens to the mass of the plant as it reaches the end of its lifespan? Why?

   f Compare this curve with the curve for a woody plant shown in Figure 21.1.3 on p210. How are the curves different?

Growth and development in arthropods

The growth curve for arthropods, such as crustaceans and insects, is not smooth like the curves shown in Figures 21.1.3 and 21.1.4. Instead, the growth curve is stepped, as shown in Figure 21.1.5.

Arthropods grow like this because the hard exoskeleton that surrounds the body cannot stretch. An increase in length occurs only when the old exoskeleton is removed in the process of moulting or ecdysis and replaced by a new one. The body tissue expands while the new exoskeleton is still soft and able to stretch.

Insects change a lot as they moult and grow into adults. These changes are an example of metamorphosis. In insects like locusts, the metamorphosis is gradual. Young locusts (called hoppers) look similar to adult locusts except that their wings and sex organs are not developed. With each of the five moults that they go through, the hoppers get bigger (as shown in Figure 21.1.5). At the last moult they become adults with fully developed wings and sex organs. This type of gradual change is called an incomplete metamorphosis. The young of insects that show incomplete metamorphosis are called nymphs.

Metamorphosis is more dramatic in insects like butterflies, wasps, moths and flies. The young are called larvae and they do not look at all like the adult. The larvae moult and grow but then they turn into pupae. The final changes into the adult occur inside the pupa. When the changes are complete, the adult emerges from the pupa, dries off and flies away. This complete change in appearance from young to adult is called a complete metamorphosis.

Two examples of the stages in complete metamorphosis are shown in Figure 21.1.6.

Insect development is controlled by hormones which activate and deactivate genes at different stages in the life of the insect. The hormone ecdysone

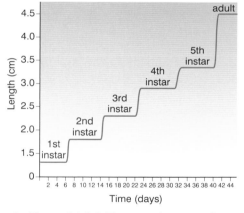

▲ **Figure 21.1.5** The growth curve of a locust. Each stage between moults is called an 'instar'.

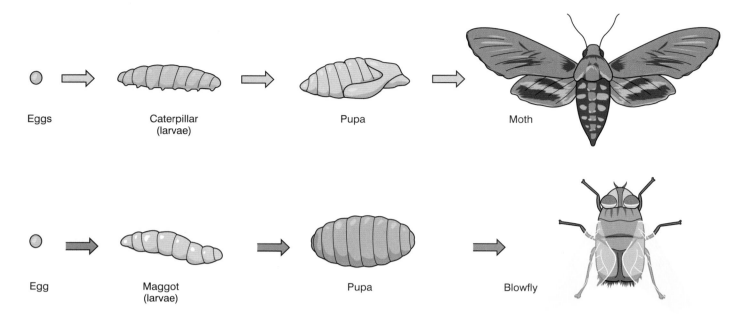

▲ **Figure 21.1.6** Moths and flies both undergo complete metamorphosis as they grow and develop

makes the young insect grow and moult its exoskeleton. The hormone does this by switching on the genes that control these processes at the right time in the development.

Methods of measuring growth

There are several ways of measuring the growth of plants and animals. You can measure increases in length or height; body volume; mass of the organism or parts of the organism; area of different parts of the organism, for example, leaf area and the number of leaves produced by a plant.

Human and large animal growth is normally measured using height and/or body mass. However this is not an ideal method as there are many variations from person to person. Also, organs and body parts grow at different rates at different times and body mass increases more rapidly during some stages of growth than others.

Questions

1 State three ways in which growth in arthropods is different to growth in plants.

2 Why is the growth curve of an insect, such as a cockroach, not a smooth curve?

3 Study the graph of a locust's growth in Figure 21.1.5 and answer these questions:

   a How many moults does this insect undergo before it is fully grown?

   b When does the insect increase in body volume?

   c Why does the insect's body volume remain constant during each instar?

   d Give four examples of other animals whose growth curves would show a similar pattern.

B21.2 Measuring growth

How do you know whether a plant or animal has grown? In real life, you probably just look at it and decide that it is bigger. Scientists, however, need more accurate measurements, so they use a range of different methods to measure growth.

Wet and dry mass

The **wet mass** of an organism is its mass including the water it contains. Wet mass varies from day to day because plants may take up more water at certain times and animals may drink more or less depending on their environmental conditions. This water does not become part of the biomass of the organism, so it is not an indicator of growth.

Because wet mass varies, dry mass is often used as a measure of growth. The **dry mass** is the mass of the organism without any water. To measure dry mass, you have to dry out the organism in an oven to remove the water. Obviously this kills the organism, so it is not a suitable method for use in natural environments as it can impact on the trophic levels of an ecosystem.

In laboratory or test conditions, dry mass measurements are taken to monitor and work out patterns of plant growth. To do this, hundreds of seedlings of the same variety and genetic makeup are planted in similar conditions. As they grow, samples (10 or more plants) are taken and dried at various stages to work out patterns of growth from seed to mature plant stage.

Table 21.2.1 summarises the methods you can use to measure growth.

▼ **Table 21.2.1** Different methods of measuring growth.

Measurement	Advantages	Disadvantages	Used to measure
Length or height	Easy to measure Does not harm organism Can be used in laboratory or natural environment Can be applied to different parts of the organism (e.g. legs, wings)	Gives information about one aspect of growth only, may be misleading if mass decreases with height or length Difficult with very tall plants or trees	Plant growth Length of animal bodies Humans
Wet mass	Easy to measure Does not harm organism Can be repeated over time on the same organism Can be used in laboratory or natural environment	Readings may be inconsistent due to changes in water content Impractical in the field for very large animals Plants need to be uprooted to take measurements and this can disturb their growth patterns	Most animals Small plants (can be used with pot plants if the pot and soil is measured before planting and subtracted from the mass each time you measure)
Dry mass	Gives most accurate measurement of true growth	Kills the organism, so cannot be repeated over time Requires special equipment Requires large sample for accuracy	Plants in controlled conditions Small animals (invertebrates and insects)
Number of leaves	Good indicator of plant growth Easy to measure or calculate	Measures one dimension of growth only	Small plants
Area or volume of body parts, including leaves	Good indicator of plant growth Can give specialised data about animal parts, including organ size and growth rates	Not always easy to calculate accurately with irregular shapes May require removal of parts	Area: leaves and flowers Volume: specific organs, for example, volume of human brain Body volume of arthropods Volume of biomass in large trees
Number of organisms	Useful to show population growth	Can be difficult to calculate	Fungi such as yeasts and moulds

213

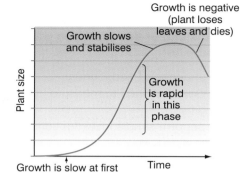

▲ **Figure 21.2.1** How to interpret a growth curve

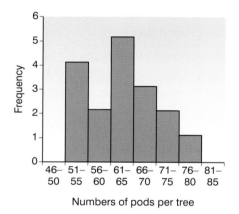

▲ **Figure 21.2.2** Histogram showing number of pods per cocoa tree

Interpreting and drawing growth curves and histograms

The graphs that you looked at in topic B21.1 are called growth curves. Growth curves are generally described as S-shaped (sigmoid) curves. An S-shaped growth curve normally shows four different stages, as described in Figure 21.2.1.

A histogram is a type of bar graph which shows the value of each group of data as the area of a bar. In a histogram, the bars always touch each other and their width is related to the period (class interval) shown on the horizontal axis. Figure 21.2.2 is a histogram. It shows the number of pods found on different cocoa trees in a small plantation. The bars are the same width because the class interval is equal (five pods). The frequency is shown on the vertical axis.

Questions

1 Select the methods that you would use if you were to measure growth in each of these and explain why you selected each method.

a Reef fish   c Palm trees   e A human baby

b House plants   d Your pet dog

2 The table below gives you the average dry mass in grams of samples of plants grown from seed and measured every two days for 38 days.

Time in days	0	2	4	6	8	10	12	14	16	18
Dry mass (g)	3.0	1.0	3.0	3.5	4.0	4.5	6.0	9.0	14.0	15.0
Day	20	22	24	26	28	30	32	34	36	38
Dry mass (g)	20.0	28.0	37.0	45.0	46.0	46.2	46.5	46.2	45.0	42.0

a Why is the mass measured as dry mass?

b Plot a growth curve for these plants.

c Label the four stages of growth on your graph.

d Do you think these are annual or perennial plants? Why?

e Why does the dry mass decrease after day 34? What causes this?

3 The lengths of one species of insect in a population are measured and averaged daily for the first five instars. These are the data collected:

Days	1–9	10–16	17–22	23–32	33–46
Length (mm)	4	7	11	15	22

a Why are the class intervals in days not all the same?

b Plot a histogram to show the growth of these insects over time.

c Describe the shape of the curve formed by the tops of the bars. Why is the graph this shape for this species?

Investigating growth and development

Now that you know how to measure and record growth, you are going to carry out some simple investigations that demonstrate growth in living organisms. You will use your observations and conclusions to make deductions about the ways in which different organisms grow.

Practical activity

Growth in plant roots

Your teacher may use this activity to assess: ORR; M&M.

Materials

- Three bean seedlings with roots 1–2 cm long. (You can germinate your own beans for this activity.)
- Thread and Indian (waterproof) ink
- Cork and a pin
- A glass jar with some water
- A sheet of glass

Method

1 Dip the thread in the ink and use it to make ink lines 2 mm apart along the length of the root on each seedling.

2 Pin each seedling to a piece of cork. Make sure the root is pointing downwards.

3 Place the corks with the seedlings in the jar with a little water in the bottom to keep them moist.

4 Cover the jar with the glass sheet.

Questions

1 Examine the marks on the roots after three days. What do you notice?

2 What does this tell you about where most growth occurs in plant roots?

3 Explain why you get more accurate results by using more than one seedling in this experiment.

 Practical activity

Growth in a pot plant

For this activity you will need a young plant in a pot. You can grow your own plants from seed, but this will take longer than working with an established, young plant.

1 Measure the height of your plant from the soil to the top of the plant every day (if possible) for three weeks.

   a Use a table like this one to record your measurements:

Day					
Height (cm)					

   b Plot a growth curve of your results.

   c At what stage of growth is this plant? How can you tell this from the graph?

2 Count the number of leaves on your plant every three days for the three-week period.

   a Record the data in a table.

   b Draw a line graph of your results.

   c What does the graph show?

3 Choose four different-sized leaves on the plant. Mark them with a spot of correction fluid so that you know which ones you have chosen.

   a Use graph paper to measure the area of the leaves every three days for the three-week period. Figure 21.2.3 shows you how to do this. Remember each small square on the graph paper represents 1 mm^2.

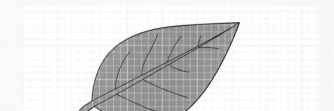

The outline of a leaf is drawn, then the area is calculated

▲ **Figure 21.2.3**

   b Decide on an appropriate format and graph your results.

4 Write a paragraph describing what you have learnt about plant growth from this investigation.

5 List three other measurements

Practical activity

Investigating growth in invertebrates

To do this investigation you will need to collect some caterpillars (all the same kind), worms or slugs. Place the animals in a glass tank lined with damp soil and provide caterpillars and slugs with lots of fresh leaves to keep them alive during your investigation. You will return them to their natural environment after the investigation is complete.

1 Use a ruler to measure the body length and a balance to measure the wet mass of each animal every three days for a three-week period.

2 Calculate the average length and average wet mass. You can do this by adding up each set of measurements and dividing the total by the number of animals in the tank.

3 Use a table like the one below to record the average lengths and wet masses and the average increase in length and in wet mass.

4 At the end of the three-week period, plot growth curves of average length and wet mass on the same set of axes.

5 Write a few sentences interpreting the graph.

Look at the figures which show you the average increase in length and in wet mass. What can you deduce from these figures?

Day	Average length (mm)	Average increase in length (mm)	Average wet mass (g)	Average increase in wet mass (g)

Practical activity

Observing animal growth

1 Design an investigation that would allow you to observe growth in a chick, puppy, kitten or other young animal in your environment.

2 Consider how you would observe, measure and record changes in length or height, body mass and increase in size of particular body parts, for example, size of beak, length of ears, area of feet, number and size of teeth.

3 Decide how you would present the results of your investigation.

4 Discuss with your teacher whether or not to carry out your investigation.

Living things have a limited lifespan, after which they die. However, species continue to exist because individual organisms reproduce during their lifespan to produce offspring. Reproduction may be sexual or asexual.

B22.1 Sexual and asexual reproduction

Reproduction means producing offspring. Sexual reproduction requires two parents (one male and one female) while asexual reproduction can take place with only one parent.

Sexual reproduction

Most flowering plants reproduce by means of sexual reproduction (although many can also reproduce asexually as well). In sexual reproduction, the plant produces special sex cells, or gametes, in the reproductive organs. Both male and female gametes are produced in the parent plants. Male and female gametes, normally from two different plants, combine in the process of fertilisation to form a cell known as a zygote. It is the zygote that develops into a new plant. The new plant will be similar to its parents, but it will not be identical because it contains characteristics from both parent plants. We say that offspring from sexual reproduction show variation (differences or changes). You will study sexual reproduction in flowering plants in more detail in topic B22.2.

Asexual reproduction

Some plants can reproduce asexually. Asexual reproduction involves only one parent plant which does not produce gametes, so no fertilisation takes place. When the parent plant produces new offspring asexually from buds, it is called vegetative propagation.

Figure 22.1.1 shows some of the ways in which plants reproduce asexually.

Humans can propagate new plants using asexual methods. For example, you can take cuttings from plants and use these to grow new plants or you can graft parts of plants on to the rootstock of others. Plants can also be cloned bio-genetically from tissue culture. Cloning is covered in more detail in Section C.

The offspring produced by asexual reproduction are identical to their parent so they do not show variation. We say this type of reproduction is conservative because it conserves the characteristics of the parent.

Comparing sexual and asexual reproduction

The advantages and disadvantages to plant species of using each method of reproduction are summarised in Table 22.1.1.

a–c Rhizomes, tubers, corms and bulbs are all types of underground stem that can function as reproductive organs by budding and producing new individuals.
a – Ginger, a rhizome
b – Potato, a tuber
c – Onion, a bulb

d In plants like the spider plant, the above ground stem produces shoots called runners or stolons, which form new plants.

e Cell division along the margins of some leaves can lead to the development of new plantlets that fall off and form new plants. The *Bryophyllum* species (Kalanchoe or 'leaf of life') does this, as do several cacti.

f Some plants use their roots for vegetative propagation. The tree in the photograph has sent up new stems from its roots. New trees will grow from these shoots.

▲ **Figure 22.1.1** Different methods of asexual reproduction in plants

▼ **Table 22.1.1** Comparison of advantages and disadvantages of sexual and asexual reproduction

	Asexual reproduction	Sexual reproduction
Advantages	Reproduction can take place quickly. Requires only one parent plant. No gametes are necessary. All good characteristics of the parent are passed on to offspring. If a plant is successful in its environment, the offspring are likely to be successful there too.	Offspring show variation so they can adapt to changing conditions, ensuring survival. Variation allows plants to develop resistance to pests and diseases. Seeds can be dispersed, so new plants develop away from parents, reducing competition.
Disadvantages	No variation means that adaptation to changing conditions is unlikely. All plants are likely to be affected if they are attacked by pests or diseases. Offspring may not be dispersed, so they compete with parent plant for water, light and nutrients.	Reproduction can be slow as it takes time for a plant to grow from seed to maturity. Two parents are needed (but some plants can self-pollinate).

Questions

1 Define sexual and asexual reproduction.

2 Name four different methods plants can use to reproduce asexually.

3 What is variation? How is the degree of variation found in offspring linked to reproduction?

4 What are the advantages of asexual reproduction in a constant environment?

5 What are the advantages of sexual reproduction in a changing environment?

B22.2 Sexual reproduction in flowering plants

Flowers are the reproductive organs of angiosperms. The flower contains both male and female reproductive organs in the form of stamens (male) and carpels (female). The stamens produce male gametes in the form of pollen and the carpels produce female gametes in the form of ovules (egg cells). When a pollen grain fuses with an ovule, it fertilises it and a zygote is formed.

Before you can understand in detail how reproduction takes place, it is important to know the parts of the flower and their functions.

Flowers

Flowers are actually shoots which are specialised for reproduction. There are many different types of flower but they are all made up of similar parts. Figure 22.2.1 shows a cross-section through a flower with the parts labelled. Table 22.2.1 gives the function of each part.

Objectives

By the end of this topic you will be able to:

- name and draw the parts of a flower and their functions
- describe how flowers are pollinated by wind and insects
- compare the structures of insect-pollinated and wind-pollinated flowers
- draw, label and annotate local examples of insect- and wind-pollinated flowers
- understand the processes that take place in pollination, growth of the pollen tube and fertilisation in flowering plants.

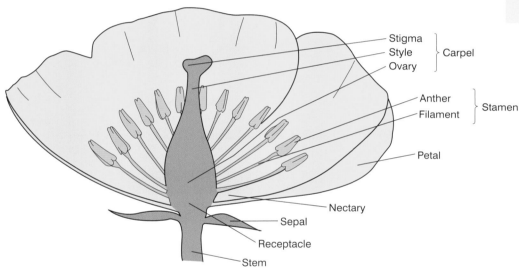

▲ **Figure 22.2.1** The parts of a flower

▼ **Table 22.2.1** Flower parts and their functions

Part	Function
Sepal	Protects the flower while it is in bud
Petal	Has colour, scent and a nectary at its base to attract insects. Acts as a landing area for insects.
Stem (also called stalk or petiole)	Supports the flower
Receptacle	Swollen top of the stem to which the flower parts are attached
Nectary	Produces sugary liquid called nectar
Stamen (consists of anther and filament)	Male reproductive organ
Anther	Contains pollen sacs filled with millions of pollen grains. Each pollen grain contains and protects the male gametes.
Filament	Supports the anther and allows it to move
Carpel (consists of stigma, style and ovary)	Female reproductive organ, contains the ovules
Stigma	Has a sticky, sugary coating to attract insects and trap pollen
Style	Joins the stigma to the ovary. Pollen tubes grow through it.
Ovary	Contains the ovules. Develops into the fruit after the ovules are fertilised.
Ovule	Contains the female gametes. Develops into seed when fertilised.

Although all flowers are made up of similar parts, the parts of different types of flower may be arranged in different ways. Some flowers have parts that are joined, or fused together, for example, carpels may fuse to form a single carpel containing a number of ovules, rather than many single carpels containing one ovule each. Some flowers do not have sepals or petals because they do not need them to attract insects. Two different arrangements of flower parts are shown in Figure 22.2.2.

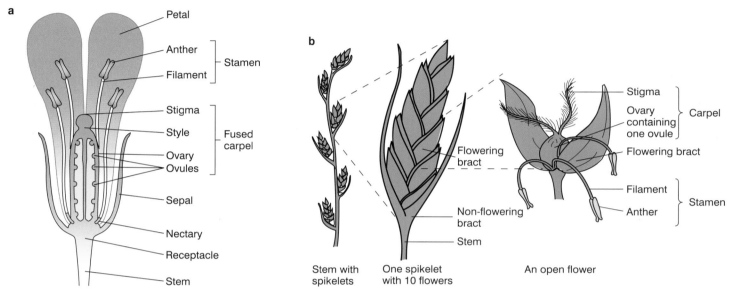

▲ **Figure 22.2.2** The flower in **a** has a fused carpel. The grass flowers in **b** have no sepals or petals.

Questions

1 Figure 22.2.3 shows different flowers, cut in half so that you can see their parts.

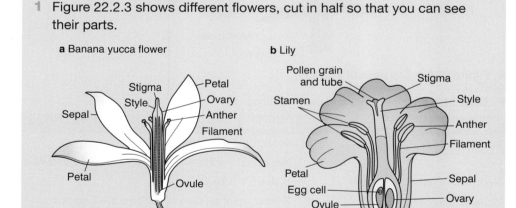

▲ **Figure 22.2.3** Sections through different types of flower

a Try to locate and name the different parts of each flower in the figure.
b Collect two different types of flowers from your local environment. Use a lens to examine the flowers in detail.
c Bisect (cut into two parts) the flowers as shown in Figure 22.2.3. Sketch what you see and label the parts.

Safety

When bisecting the flowers take care with sharp instruments.

Pollination

Pollen grains are made inside the anthers. When the pollen is ripe, the anthers split open to release the pollen (see Figure 22.2.4).

The pollen grains must pass from the anther to the stigma (part of the carpel) before the male gamete inside each grain can fertilise the female gamete in the ovule (see Figure 22.2.5). The transfer of pollen from male to female reproductive organs is called pollination.

Flowers are mostly pollinated by insects and birds (such as humming birds) and wind. Flowers that are pollinated by insects (or birds) are structurally different to flowers that are pollinated by wind.

Wind pollination

Wind-pollinated flowers, such as the one shown in Figure 22.2.6, are adapted to make sure that the pollen is scattered widely. Some have long slender anthers which hang clear of the sepals and petals because these parts could stop pollen from being blown away. The flowers of many grasses do not have sepals and petals at all. Some plants, such as the syringa tree, produce clouds of pollen that is blown away before the leaves are open, so that the leaves of the plant do not get in the way of pollination.

Insect pollination

Insects carry pollen from the anthers of one flower to the stigma of another flower. Insect-pollinated flowers are therefore adapted to attract the insects which pollinate them. Flowers are often large, brightly coloured and sweetly scented. They also produce sweet liquid called nectar. Insects are attracted by the colour and scent of the flowers and they visit them to feed on pollen and nectar. As insects feed at the flower, their bodies become covered in pollen which they carry to the next flower the insect visits. Figure 22.2.7 shows you how flowers are pollinated by bees.

The differences between wind-pollinated and insect-pollinated flowers are summarised in Table 22.2.2.

Self-pollination and cross-pollination

Self-pollination happens when pollen from the anthers of one flower lands on the stigma of the same flower, or another flower on the same plant. Many plants are adapted to prevent self-pollination and to encourage pollination with other

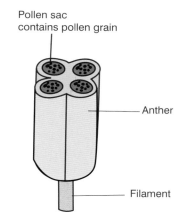

▲ **Figure 22.2.4** When pollen is ripe, the anthers split open to release the grains

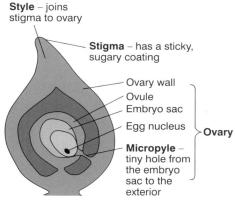

▲ **Figure 22.2.5** The ovule is part of the carpel, which contains the female gametes

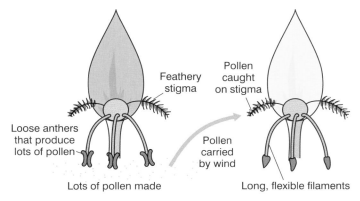

▲ **Figure 22.2.6** A wind-pollinated flower

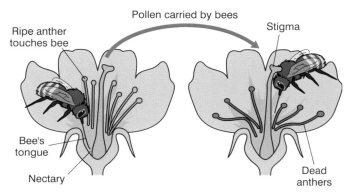

▲ **Figure 22.2.7** Insect-pollinated flowers are adapted to attract insects and transfer pollen

a Self-pollination. Pollen is transferred from the anthers to the stigma(s) of the same flower or the anthers of one flower to the stigma(s) of another flower on the same plant

b Cross-pollination. Pollen is transferred from the anthers of a flower on one plant to the stigma(s) of a flower on a different plant. Cross-pollination increases **genetic variation**

▲ **Figure 22.2.8** Self-pollination and cross-pollination

plants of the same species. When pollen from the anthers of one flower lands on the stigma of a flower on another plant of the same species, cross-pollination occurs. Cross-pollination produces offspring that show greater variation because the gametes come from two different parents (see Figure 22.2.8).

▼ **Table 22.2.2** Comparison of structures in wind-pollinated and insect-pollinated flowers

Part of flower	Wind-pollinated	Insect-pollinated
Petals	Often absent, if present small, green or dull colour, no scent, no nectar	Often large, brightly coloured and scented, most have nectaries
Anthers	Hang loosely on long, thin filaments so that they move easily in the wind	Positioned so that insects are likely to brush against them
Stigma	Long, branching and feathery to make a large catching area for wind-blown pollen grains	Positioned so that insects are likely to brush against them, sticky and flat or lobe-shaped
Pollen	Large amounts produced. Small, light grains with smooth surfaces which are carried easily by wind.	Small amounts produced. Large grains with rough or sticky surfaces which catch on insects' bodies.

Some plants, such as the garden pea, are self-pollinating. Pollination takes places before the flowers have opened to make sure this happens. Other plants will self-pollinate if cross-pollination does not occur. Some plants make sure that self-pollination does not happen by having male and female organs on separate flowers. A good example of this is the casuarina tree shown in Figure 22.2.9, which has male and female flowers on different trees.

▲ **Figure 22.2.9** Casuarina trees prevent self-pollination by having male and female organs on different trees

Questions

1 How is the position of each of the following parts of a plant related to its function?
   a Stigma
   b Anther
   c Petal

2 Examine the flowers shown in Figure 22.2.10. Which are likely to be pollinated by insects or birds and which are likely to be pollinated by the wind?

3 What is the advantage to plants of:
   a self-pollination
   b cross-pollination?

Figure 22.2.10 ▶

Fertilisation

The process of pollination is completed when the pollen grains land on the stigma. However, the male gametes inside each pollen grain still have to travel to reach the egg cell in the ovule of the plant. To do this, the pollen grains have to grow.

The sticky coating on the surface of the stigma helps pollen grains to stick to it. If conditions are right, the pollen grains begin to grow pollen tubes, as shown in Figure 22.2.11.

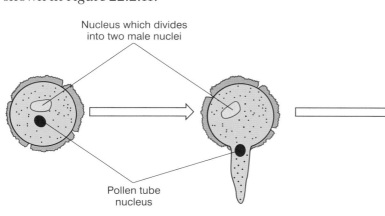

▲ **Figure 22.2.11** The growth of a pollen tube

The pollen tube grows down through the style towards the ovary where it penetrates the ovary wall and enters an ovule through the micropyle. The tube nucleus dies and the two male nuclei pass down the pollen tube and into the embryo sac. There one nucleus fuses with the egg nucleus to form the fertilised zygote. This fusion of male and female nuclei is called fertilisation. You can see this in Figure 22.2.12.

Although more than one pollen grain may grow a pollen tube, it is the male nucleus of the first pollen tube to reach the egg nucleus which fertilises it. In an ovary which has more than one ovule, each egg nucleus is fertilised by a different male nucleus.

The zygote (fertilised egg) divides and develops into the embryo which will become the new plant. The other male nucleus from the pollen tube fuses with two more nuclei in the embryo sac, developing into a special tissue called the endosperm. The endosperm forms a food store for the embryo to use as it grows.

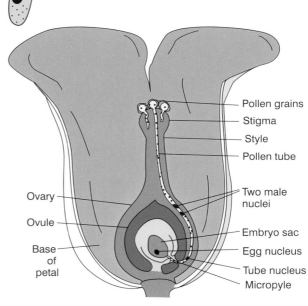

▲ **Figure 22.2.12** The male nucleus from the pollen fertilises the female egg nucleus

 Practical activity

Investigating wind-pollinated and insect-pollinated flowers

Your teacher may use this activity to assess: A&I; ORR.

1 Collect at least six different types of flower from the local environment.

2 Examine each flower carefully – use a hand lens if you need to. Record all the features in a table.
   a Decide whether each flower is wind-pollinated or insect-pollinated and explain how you can tell.

b Which of the features listed in Table 22.2.2 on p222 does the flower have?

c Are there any other structures or features of the flower that play a role in pollination? If so, what are they?

223

Practical activity

Observing methods of pollination

Observe flowers being pollinated by insects or birds in the environment.
For each one, make notes about:

a What type of insect or bird pollinates it.

b What the insect or bird does to assist pollination.

c How the flowers are adapted to being pollinated by these insects or birds.

 Practical activity

Growing pollen tubes

Your teacher may use this activity to assess: ORR; M&M.

Materials

- A 10% sucrose solution and some plain water
- Two cavity slides with cover slips
- Ripe pollen grains from a hibiscus or other flower

Method

1 Place a drop of sucrose solution on one slide and label it Slide A.

2 Shake some pollen grains onto the solution.

3 Place a cover slip on the slide.

4 Repeat this procedure for Slide B using plain water instead of sucrose solution. This will be your control.

5 Place both slides in a warm, not too bright place for 30 minutes.

6 After 30 minutes examine both slides under a microscope and then every 10 minutes for the rest of the period. Sketch what you see on both slides each time you examine them.

Questions

1 What is the difference between the pollen on the two slides? What can you conclude from this?

2 What does your experiment suggest about the stigmas in a flower? How could you test this suggestion?

Questions

1 Define the terms 'pollination' and 'fertilisation'.

2 Choose one wind-pollinated and one insect-pollinated flower that you have studied. Explain how each flower is adapted for pollination.

3 Can fertilisation take place before pollination? Explain why or why not.

4 Copy the diagram in Figure 22.2.13 and write the correct names of the parts labelled **a** to **f**.

5 Explain what happens when the pollen tube reaches the ovule.

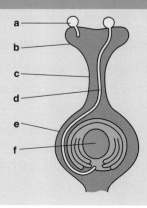

Figure 22.2.13 ▶

B22.3 Seeds and fruits

A characteristic of flowering plants is that they produce seeds. The seeds can survive without the parent plant and under ideal conditions they will germinate to form new plants.

Seeds

A seed is a fertilised ovule. Inside the seed is an embryo plant and its store of food which develops after fertilisation. The seed is covered by a tough outer skin called the testa.

When the embryo is almost fully developed, the tissues around it lose water, leaving the seed hard and dry. This seed can remain like this for a long time, until conditions are right for it to germinate (grow).

Food may be stored in a thick, fleshy, wing-like structure called the cotyledon. Figure 22.3.1 shows the seed of a broad bean. Note that the bean seed has two cotyledons, so bean plants are dicotyledonous. The diagram also shows which parts of the embryo will grow into the different parts of a new plant.

Grasses, such as rice and maize, produce seeds which store food in only one cotyledon. They are called monocotyledonous plants.

Fruits

After fertilisation the ovary of most plants develops into the fruit. The wall of the ovary is then called the pericarp. As the fruit develops the pericarp becomes either dry and hard, as in ochro, peas and balata, or juicy and fleshy as in succulent fruits such as tomatoes, mangoes, plums, limes and paw-paws. Figure 22.3.2 shows the parts of the flowers that develop into fruit in plum trees and almond trees.

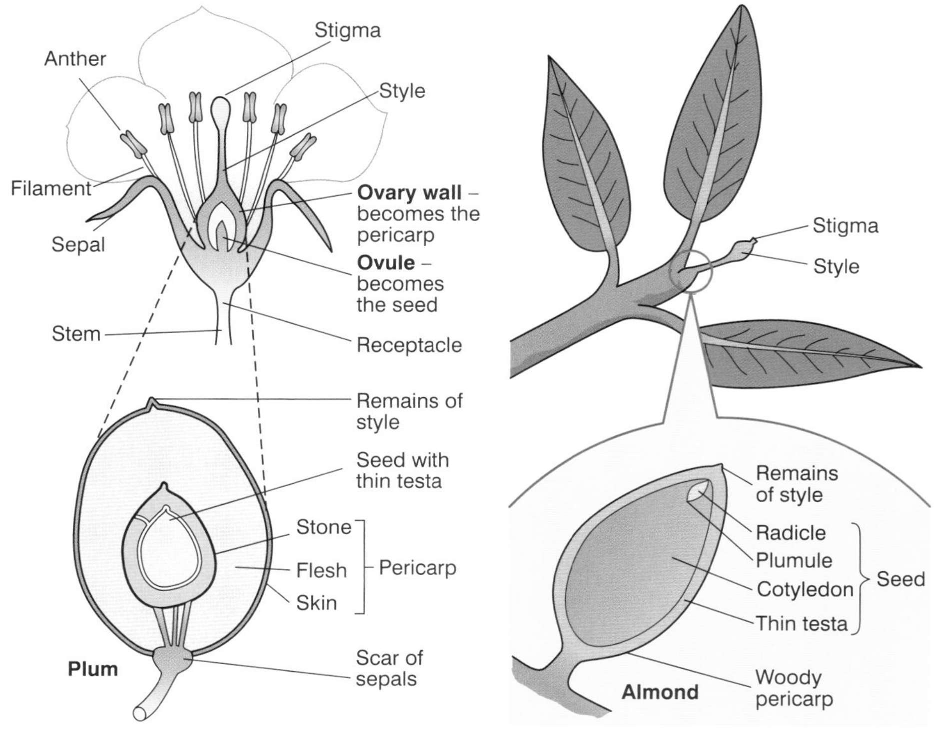

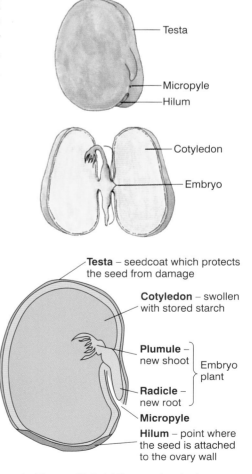

Testa – seedcoat which protects the seed from damage

Cotyledon – swollen with stored starch

Plumule – new shoot ⎤
                              ⎬ Embryo plant
Radicle – new root ⎦

Micropyle

Hilum – point where the seed is attached to the ovary wall

▲ **Figure 22.3.1** The seeds of a bean, a typical dicotyledonous plant

▲ **Figure 22.3.2** The parts of the flower that develop into parts of the fruit

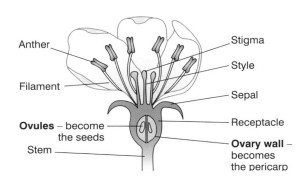

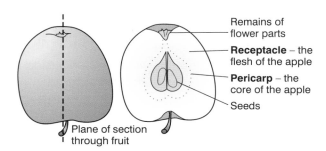

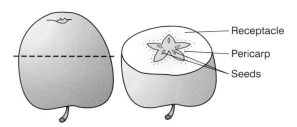

▲ **Figure 22.3.3** The apple is an example of a false fruit

The fruit contains the seed or seeds. The number of seeds in a fruit depends on how many ovules there were in the ovary to begin with, and how many were fertilised.

In some plants, parts of the flower other than the ovary develop into the fruit. These are called false fruits. In many false fruits, it is the receptacle that grows to form the fruit. Apples, pineapples, breadfruits and figs are examples of false fruits. Figure 22.3.3 shows you the parts of the flower that form the false fruit in an apple.

Germination

The stages of growth from the embryo inside the seed to the time when the seedling no longer depends on stored food is called germination. To germinate successfully, most seeds need:

- Warmth – the correct temperature allows for enzyme action. If the temperature is too low, germination is prevented.
- Water – when the seed absorbs water, it swells and the testa bursts open so that the embryo plant can begin to grow. Water is also essential to make the food stores soluble so that they can feed the embryo. Water allows enzymes to be activated. The enzyme amylase breaks down starch to maltose, while protease breaks down proteins to amino acids.
- Oxygen – the seedling needs more oxygen than when it was an embryo inside the seed. The oxygen is used during aerobic cellular respiration which releases the energy the plant needs for cell division and the process of growth.

During germination, the seed respires and digested food from cotyledons is translocated (moved) to the growing points to produce a small root and a shoot known as the radicle and the plumule. The radicle grows downwards to form the root system of the plant. The plumule grows upwards, above the soil, to form the stem and leaves of the new plant. As soon as the new plant forms its own leaves, it begins to photosynthesise and produce its own food. At this stage, it no longer needs the food stored in the cotyledons and they wither away.

Different kinds of germination

In the broad bean plant, the cotyledons stay below the ground during germination. This is called hypogeal germination. Other seeds which show hypogeal germination are the oil palm and grasses such as maize and rice.

In some seeds, the cotyledons are lifted out of the soil with the growing shoot, so they are visible above ground. This is called epigeal germination and it is found in plants like the sunflower, castor oil, kidney bean, black-eyed pea and flamboyant.

Both types of germination are shown in Figure 22.3.4a and b. After germinating, the young plant continues to grow and mature independently until it is ready to produce flowers and reproduce, continuing the life cycle of the species.

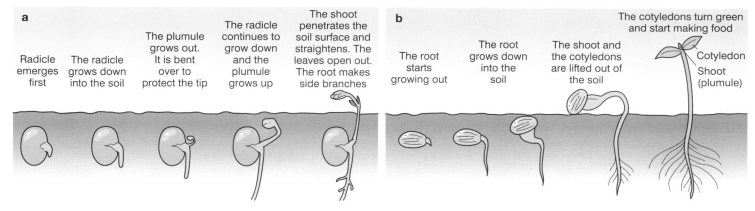

a

Radicle emerges first

The radicle grows down into the soil

The plumule grows out. It is bent over to protect the tip

The radicle continues to grow down and the plumule grows up

The shoot penetrates the soil surface and straightens. The leaves open out. The root makes side branches

b

The root starts growing out

The root grows down into the soil

The shoot and the cotyledons are lifted out of the soil

The cotyledons turn green and start making food

Cotyledon

Shoot (plumule)

▲ **Figure 22.3.4 a** Hypogeal germination and **b** epigeal germination

B22.4 Seed dispersal

Dispersal means spreading out over a wide area. Seed dispersal gives plants a better chance of survival by reducing overcrowding and competition between parent plants and offspring. It also allows plants to spread to and colonise new habitats. Flowering plants produce seeds and fruits that are dispersed by wind, water or animals. In many plants, the seeds and fruits have specialised structures which help with dispersal.

Dispersal of fruits and seeds

When a fruit is ripe, it breaks away from the parent plant and the seeds are dispersed. The pericarps of different fruits have developed and adapted in different ways for different methods of dispersal. Figure 22.4.1 shows seed development in different plants.

Objectives

By the end of this topic you will be able to:

- describe the structure of different fruits to show how they are adapted for seed dispersal
- draw examples of local fruits and seeds to show how they are adapted for seed dispersal
- carry out food tests on seeds before and after germination.

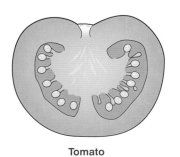
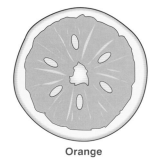
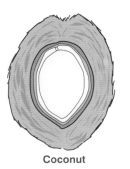

Tomato   Orange   Coconut

▲ **Figure 22.4.1** The internal structure of different fruits

The main methods of dispersal are by **wind** and by **animals**. Figure 22.4.2 shows you some fruits and seeds that are dispersed by wind and by animals. Read the labels carefully to see how each fruit or seed is adapted for dispersal.

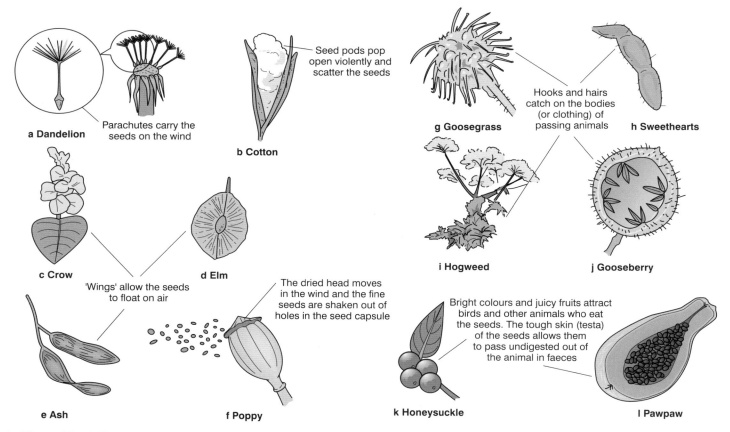

a Dandelion

Parachutes carry the seeds on the wind

b Cotton

Seed pods pop open violently and scatter the seeds

g Goosegrass

Hooks and hairs catch on the bodies (or clothing) of passing animals

h Sweethearts

c Crow

d Elm

'Wings' allow the seeds to float on air

e Ash

f Poppy

The dried head moves in the wind and the fine seeds are shaken out of holes in the seed capsule

i Hogweed

j Gooseberry

Bright colours and juicy fruits attract birds and other animals who eat the seeds. The tough skin (testa) of the seeds allows them to pass undigested out of the animal in faeces

k Honeysuckle

l Pawpaw

▲ **Figure 22.4.2** Fruits and seeds can be dispersed by wind or by animals

In some plants, dispersal of fruits and seeds is mechanical. In other words, the plant disperses its own seeds. The fruit wall of these plants dries and splits open. As this happens, the seeds are thrown out. Examples of seeds that disperse in this way are shown in Figure 22.4.3. A few fruits are dispersed by water currents, for example, the coconut and the water lily (see Figure 22.4.3).

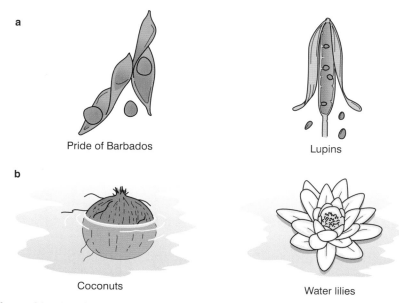

a

Pride of Barbados

Lupins

b

Coconuts

Water lilies

▲ **Figure 22.4.3 a** Seeds dispersed mechanically; **b** seeds dispersed by water currents

Practical activity

Investigating food stores in seeds

Design and carry out an investigation that uses food tests to find out what food substances are found in the cotyledons of a bean or sunflower seed before and after germination.

Questions

1   What is the difference between a seed and a fruit?

2   Seeds are normally covered by a hard coating. What is this layer called and what is its function?

3   Collect five different types of seed from local plants.
   a   Draw and label the external structure of each seed.
   b   Cut the seeds open and draw and label the inside structure of the seed.
   c   Write a few sentences describing how the structure of the seed is related to both the flower and the fruit of the plant.

4   Look at the five fruits shown in Figure 22.4.4. For each one, explain how you think the fruit is dispersed.

Safety

Take care with sharp instruments when cutting the seeds open.

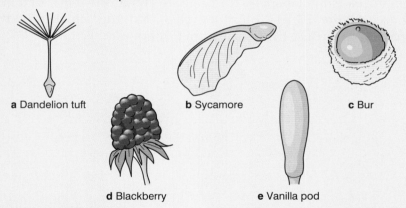

a Dandelion tuft   b Sycamore   c Bur

d Blackberry   e Vanilla pod

▲ **Figure 22.4.4**

5   Collect at least five examples of local fruits and seeds. Sketch the fruits and label your diagrams to show how each fruit or seed is adapted for dispersal.

6   Give two reasons why dispersal of seeds is important in plants.

Among animals, there are two methods of reproduction: asexual reproduction, which involves only one parent and sexual reproduction which involves two parents, gametes and fertilisation. In humans and other mammals, reproduction is sexual, so it produces offspring which show variation.

Objectives

By the end of this topic you will be able to:

- describe the structure and functions of the reproductive systems in humans
- label and annotate diagrams of the male and female reproductive systems.

B23.1 The reproductive system

The biological function of the human reproductive system is to produce children. The male and female reproductive system and organs are different because they have different functions, so we will deal with them separately before looking at how cells from the male and the female parent combine to create children.

The male reproductive system

The male reproductive system produces male gametes or sperm cells. Spermatozoa (singular spermatozoon) are about one-tenth of a millimetre long (see Figure 23.1.1) and they pass into the female's body during intercourse to fertilise the female gamete, or ovum.

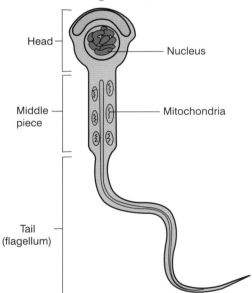

▲ **Figure 23.1.1** A sperm cell

The visible parts of the reproductive system are called the genitalia. A man's genitalia consist of the penis and the testes. The testes are contained in a bag-like scrotum which hangs down between the legs. This position protects the testes from injury. It also keeps their temperature about 3 °C lower than normal body temperature. This is important because spermatozoa only develop properly inside the testes in these slightly cooler conditions. The male reproductive system is illustrated in front view and side view in Figure 23.1.2. The function of each part is described in Table 23.1.1.

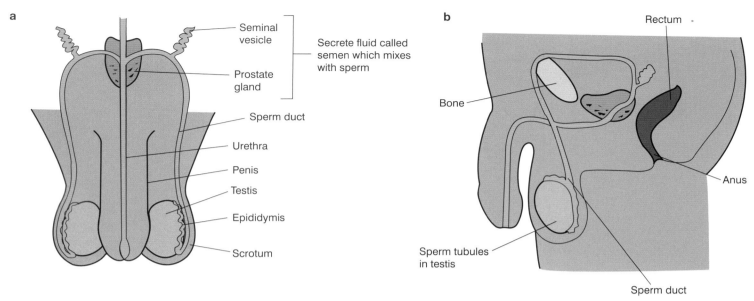

▲ **Figure 23.1.2** The male reproductive system: **a** front view and **b** side view

▼ **Table 23.1.1** The parts of the male reproductive system and their functions

Part	Function
Seminal vesicle	Opens into the sperm duct and produces seminal fluid which combines with spermatozoa to form semen. The secretions stimulate the sperm to swim.
Prostate gland	Opens into the urethra and produces an alkaline fluid which neutralises any urine in the urethra and stimulates sperm to swim
Sperm duct	Muscular tube which links the testis to the urethra to allow the passage of semen containing spermatozoa
Urethra	Conducts both semen and urine
Penis	Becomes erect for transmission of semen during intercourse
Epididymus	Spermatozoa mature here and some spermatozoa are stored here
Testis	Produce spermatozoa and sex hormones
Scrotum	Contains testes and holds them outside the body to regulate temperature for spermatozoa production

The female reproductive system

The female gamete is the ovum (plural: ova), illustrated in Figure 23.1.3. The female reproductive system produces ova. The ovaries usually each produce an ovum on alternate months from the beginning of puberty to the menopause. Ovum production is controlled by hormones during the menstrual cycle. You will learn about this in more detail in topic B23.2.

The female reproductive system is inside her body. The genitalia cover and protect the opening to the reproductive system.

Figure 23.1.4 shows you the parts of the female reproductive system in front view and side view. Table 23.1.2 describes the function of each part.

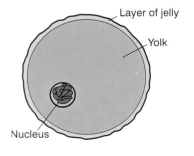

▲ **Figure 23.1.3** An ovum

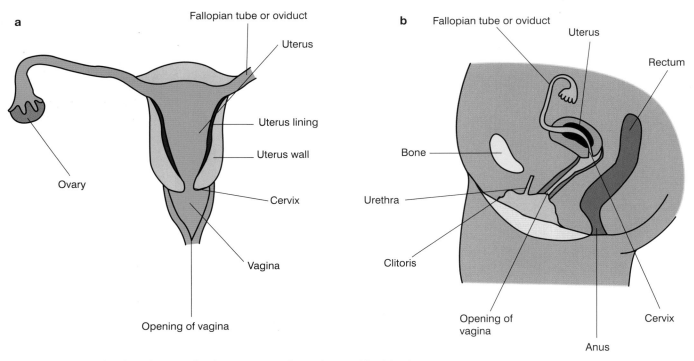

▲ **Figure 23.1.4** The female reproductive system: **a** front view and **b** side view

▼ **Table 23.1.2** The parts of the female reproductive system and their functions

Part	Function
Oviduct (Fallopian tube)	Carries the ova to the uterus, site of fertilisation
Ovary	Produces ova and sex hormones
Uterus (womb)	Cavity with thick muscular walls where the embryo and foetus develop, lining is where fertilised ovum is implanted
Cervix	Ring of muscle which forms neck of uterus, opens into vagina, produces watery mucus to help sperm swim to the uterus
Vagina	Receives male penis during intercourse, sperm deposited here
Urethra	Carries urine from the bladder, no role in reproduction

Questions

1 Which part of the male reproductive system is responsible for:
   a making sperm
   b carrying sperm and urine at different times
   c adding fluids to sperm to make semen
   d carrying sperm from the testis to the penis?

2 What is the main function of the following parts of the female reproductive system?
   a The ovary
   b The oviduct
   c The uterus
   d The cervix

3 What is the difference in function of the urethra in males and females?

B23.2 The menstrual cycle

When females reach puberty they begin to experience a menstrual cycle (they start to have periods). This is a cycle in which changes take place in the uterus and ovaries over approximately a 28-day period. The menstrual cycle is controlled by a number of hormones.

Objectives

By the end of this topic you will be able to:

- describe the menstrual cycle
- explain the role of hormones oestrogen and progesterone and the effect of pregnancy on the menstrual cycle.

Ovulation and the menstrual cycle

The human female usually ovulates to produce one mature ovum each month from the beginning of puberty (from age 11 to 14 years) to the start of the menopause (around age 45). This monthly cycle is called the menstrual cycle (from the Latin word *mensis* meaning month).

At the beginning of the menstrual cycle (days 1 to 5) there is a low level of female sex hormones in the body. This causes the lining of the uterus to break down. As this happens, blood vessels rupture and a flow of blood and cells passes out of the vagina. This is called menstruation.

From days 6 to 13, the lining of the uterus thickens again under the influence of oestrogen and a new ovum starts to develop in the ovary. The ovum grows inside a ball of fluid called a follicle. As the follicle grows, it moves towards the edge of the ovary, closer to the oviduct. Ovulation takes place around day 14 of the cycle, when the ovum is mature. At this stage, the follicle bursts open to release the ovum into the oviduct. The empty follicle forms a structure known as a corpus luteum.

The ovum travels down the oviduct towards the uterus. The oviduct is full of fluid and lined with small hairs (cilia) that vibrate and create currents which move the ovum along the tube.

After ovulation the lining of the uterus thickens and becomes richly supplied with blood in preparation for receiving a fertilised ovum. If the ovum is fertilised (by a spermatozoon) then the fertilised ovum will become implanted in the thick lining of the uterus. When this happens, we say the woman has become pregnant.

If the ovum is not fertilised, no pregnancy occurs. The unfertilised ovum dies within 24 hours. The corpus luteum breaks down in the ovary and the lining of the uterus breaks down. These pass out of the vagina during the next menstruation. Then the whole cycle starts again (see Figure 23.2.1).

Hormones and the menstrual cycle

The ovulation and the menstrual cycle are controlled by two important hormones released by the pituitary gland: follicle-stimulating hormone (FSH) and luteinising hormone (LH). These hormones are carried to the ovaries in the bloodstream.

The cycle is started by the release of FSH from the pituitary. This hormone causes one of the follicles in the ovary to mature and produce an ovum (ova). The ovum developing in the follicle signals the ovary to produce oestrogen.

Oestrogen stimulates cell division in the lining of the uterus. The uterus thickens and its blood supply increases. Rising levels of oestrogen feedback negatively, reducing the production of FSH from the pituitary.

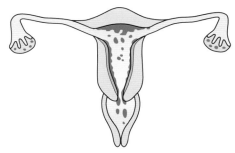

During menstruation, the uterine lining (endometrium) breaks down and blood and cells flow out of the vagina

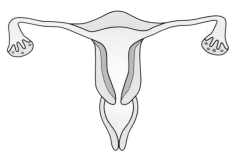

From day 6 to 13 the uterus lining thickens in readiness for implantation of a fertilised ovum

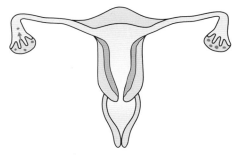

During ovulation, an ovum is released into the oviduct, where it is moved along by fluid and small hairs. The empty follicle remains in the ovary as a corpus luteum

▲ **Figure 23.2.1** The three main stages in the menstrual cycle

As oestrogen levels drop, LH is released from the pituitary. This triggers ovulation by signalling the follicle to burst and release the ovum. The corpus luteum (remains of the follicle) then produces progesterone which stimulates the uterus lining to thicken even more.

If no pregnancy occurs, the corpus luteum breaks down and production of progesterone drops. This stimulates the walls of the uterus to break down again.

If implantation occurs, the developing embryo produces progesterone and oestrogen. These hormones stop the pituitary from producing FSH and they maintain the thickness of the uterus lining. This is why there is no ovulation and no menstruation during pregnancy. You will learn more about this in topic B23.3.

Figure 23.2.2 shows you how hormones control the menstrual cycle. Figure 23.2.3 shows you the feedback loops involved in the process.

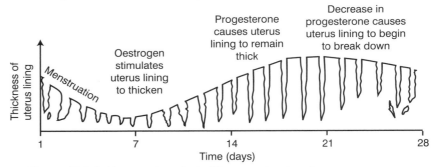

▲ **Figure 23.2.2** Hormonal control of the menstrual cycle

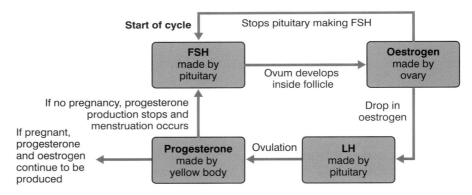

▲ **Figure 23.2.3** Feedback is important in regulating and controlling hormone release

Questions

1 What is the menstrual cycle?

2 Why does the uterus lining thicken during the menstrual cycle?

3 What happens to the uterus lining if no pregnancy occurs?

4 How do the following hormones affect the menstrual cycle:
   a FSH
   b LH
   c Oestrogen
   d Progesterone?

5 Explain how pregnancy affects the menstrual cycle.

B23.3 From fertilisation to birth

A woman cannot become pregnant unless the ovum in her oviduct is fertilised by a spermatozoon cell. During sexual intercourse the man ejaculates and releases semen into the vagina of the woman. The spermatozoon cells in the semen move from the vagina through the uterus into the oviduct. The spermatozoa reach the top of the oviduct about 40 minutes after ejaculation and they swarm around the ovum if one is present.

Figure 23.3.1 shows you how spermatozoa travel to reach the ovum.

Objectives

By the end of this topic you will be able to:

● outline how gametes are brought together for fertilisation

● describe how a human embryo is implanted and how it develops

● briefly explain the functions of the amnion, placenta and umbilical cord.

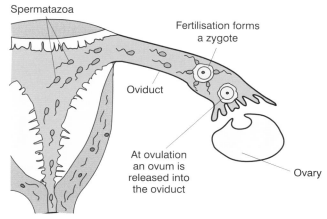

▲ **Figure 23.3.1** Spermatozoa have to travel a long way to reach the ovum in the oviduct

Fertilisation and development of the embryo

Although thousands of spermatozoa may reach an ovum, only one enters it. The tail of the successful spermatozoon is left outside as the head of the spermatozoon travels through the cytoplasm of the ovum to the nucleus. Fertilisation occurs when the spermatozoon nucleus fuses with the ovum nucleus to form a zygote (see Figure 23.3.2). Fertilisation is also called conception and the woman has become pregnant.

Figure 23.3.3 shows you what happens after fertilisation has taken place.

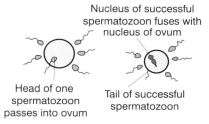

▲ **Figure 23.3.2** Fertilisation of the ovum forms a zygote

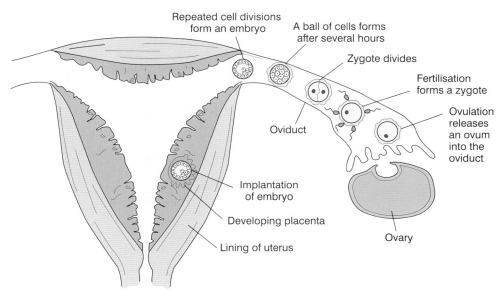

▲ **Figure 23.3.3** The stages from ovulation to implantation

The zygote travels down the oviduct. As it travels, the cells divide and a ball of cells forms. The journey may take up to seven days. By the time the ball of cells reaches the uterus it has formed an embryo. Remember that at this stage of the menstrual cycle, the wall of the uterus has a thick lining. The embryo sinks into this thick lining in a process known as implantation.

As the embryo develops it is surrounded by a membrane called the amnion. This fills with amniotic fluid, which protects the growing embryo. Finger-like extensions called villi project from the embryo into the uterus lining. The surfaces firmly bind together forming a region called the placenta. In the next few weeks, the embryo develops into a foetus which is attached to the placenta by the umbilical cord. An artery and a vein run though the umbilical cord and connect the foetus's blood system to the placenta. Figure 23.3.4 shows that the foetus's blood system is not directly connected to the blood system of the mother. The exchange of oxygen, food and wastes between mother and foetus depends on diffusion across the thin wall of the placenta.

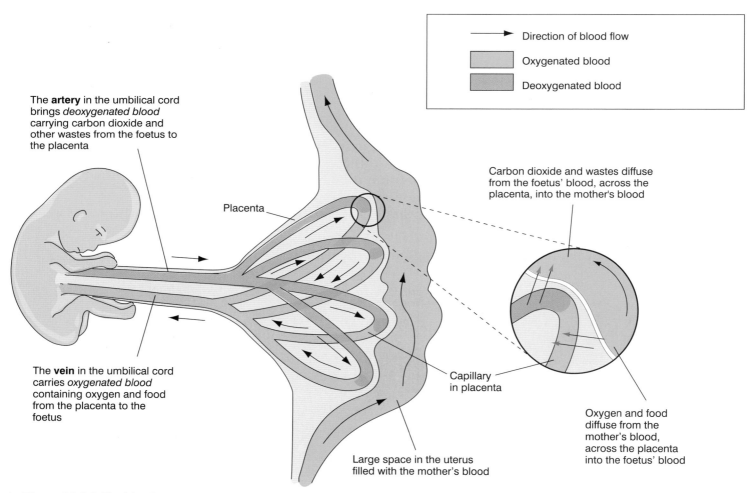

Direction of blood flow

Oxygenated blood

Deoxygenated blood

The **artery** in the umbilical cord brings *deoxygenated blood* carrying carbon dioxide and other wastes from the foetus to the placenta

Carbon dioxide and wastes diffuse from the foetus' blood, across the placenta, into the mother's blood

Placenta

The **vein** in the umbilical cord carries *oxygenated blood* containing oxygen and food from the placenta to the foetus

Capillary in placenta

Oxygen and food diffuse from the mother's blood, across the placenta into the foetus' blood

Large space in the uterus filled with the mother's blood

▲ **Figure 23.3.4** The blood systems of the mother and foetus exchange material by diffusion across the placenta

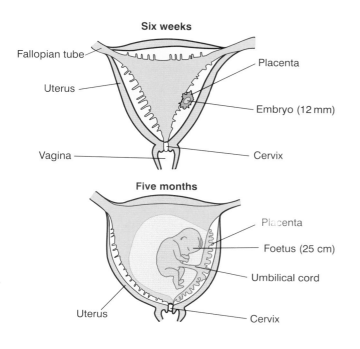

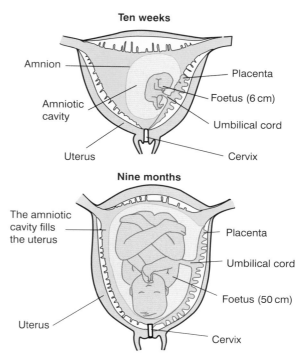

▲ **Figure 23.3.5** Growth and development of the foetus in the uterus

Figure 23.3.5 shows the growth and development of the foetus from the early stages of pregnancy to just before the baby is due to be born.

When the baby is ready to be born, the mother goes into labour. This is triggered by the hormone oxytocin. During labour the muscles of the uterus contract, causing the amnion surrounding the baby to break and the amniotic fluid to escape. The muscles of the uterus then contract very strongly and push the baby out. The cervix opens (dilates) and baby then moves, normally head first, out through the vagina.

Once the baby is born, it starts to breathe air. The umbilical cord is tied or clamped and cut to separate the baby from the placenta. The placenta and remaining umbilical cord come away from the uterus wall and they are pushed out through the vagina as the afterbirth.

When the baby is born, progesterone levels fall, FSH and LH are released once again and the menstrual cycle starts again.

 **Key fact**

The time taken for the foetus to develop from conception into a baby is called the gestation period. This lasts approximately 40 weeks (9 months) in humans.

 **Key fact**

Your navel or belly button is the stump of the umbilical cord that used to attach you to your mother.

Questions

1 Draw a simple flow diagram to show the sequence of events from fertilisation to birth in humans.

2 Figure 23.3.6 shows a foetus developing in the uterus. Copy and complete the table by naming the parts labelled **a** to **d**, stating the function of each part.

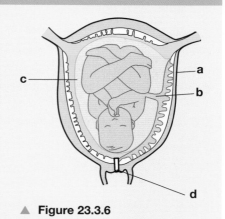

Part	Name	Function
a		
b		
c		
d		

3 Why should the mother not smoke or take harmful drugs during pregnancy?

▲ **Figure 23.3.6**

Objectives

By the end of this topic you will be able to:

- identify different methods of birth control
- discuss the advantages and disadvantages of different methods of birth control.

B23.4 Birth control

If a couple want to have sexual intercourse but do not want to have children, they must use some form of contraception to prevent pregnancy. Using methods of contraception allows people to choose when they want to have children and the number of children they have. This choice is called birth control or family planning.

In order to prevent pregnancy, contraception has to either stop the spermatozoa from reaching the ovum, or stop ova from being produced, or stop the fertilised ovum from developing in the uterus.

There are four main methods of contraception:

- natural methods
- chemical methods
- mechanical methods
- surgical methods.

Today, people may also use one method of contraception, condoms, to prevent transmission of sexually transmitted infections (STIs) including HIV and AIDS.

Different methods of contraception are described in Table 23.4.1 and their advantages and disadvantages are listed

▼ **Table 23.4.1** Methods of contraception and their advantages and disadvantages

Method	Example	Procedure/mechanism	Comments
Natural	Abstinence	Refrain from sexual intercourse	No spermatozoa in vagina, 100% safe, no transmission of STIs
	Coitus interruptus (withdrawal)	Male withdraws penis before ejaculation, preventing spermatozoa from being deposited in vagina	Only 80–90% effective, requires self-control and some semen is released before orgasm
	Rhythm method	Time of ovulation is predicted and intercourse is avoided around this time	Time of ovulation can vary, so not always reliable (about 80%), sexual activity is restricted for some time each month
Chemical	Contraceptive pills	A hormone pill is taken every day by the woman to prevent ovulation	Must be taken every day, some side effects, especially in smokers, reliable, almost 100% effective
	Depo-Provera injection	Woman gets four injections of progesterone-like substance each year to stop release of FSH and LH	Must be given by a doctor or health professional, some women report side-effects and weight gain, almost 100% effective
	Skin implants	Tube of progestin inserted under skin, releases hormones directly into blood to prevent ovulation	Effective for up to five years, no known risks
	Spermatozooni-cides	Cream or foam inserted into vagina before intercourse to kill spermatozoa	Needs an applicator, can be messy, not very effective used alone, only about 70% effective on its own
Mechanical	Condoms: male and female	Forms barrier between penis and vagina and prevents transfer of spermatozoa	Can be used by men and women, effective in stopping spread of most STIs, no side-effects
	Cervical cap or diaphragm	Latex cap inserted in vagina to cover cervix	Women must be taught how to insert it correctly and it must be the correct fit, must remain in place for at least six hours after intercourse, best used with a spermatozoonicide, if used correctly, around 90% effective
	Intra-uterine device (IUD)	Fitted inside the uterus to prevent implantation	Reliable, but must be fitted by a health professional, best used by women who have had a child, some women get an infection from IUD
Surgical	Sterilisation	Involves cutting and tying off sperm ducts in men and oviducts in women to prevent spermatozoa from reaching the ovum	Usually permanent (irreversible), can be used by men and women, almost 100% effective

Methods of contraception vary in their reliability. Sterilisation and the contraceptive pill are almost 100% effective, but some people may choose not to use these methods for religious or moral reasons. Many women also find they suffer from side-effects when they use hormonal contraception, so they prefer other methods.

The diagrams in Figure 23.4.1 show you how some of these different methods of contraception are used.

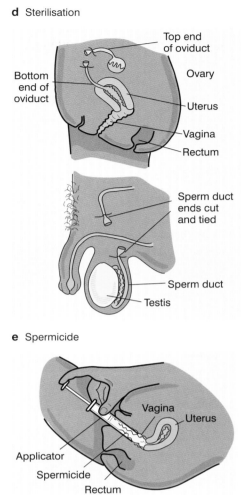

d Sterilisation

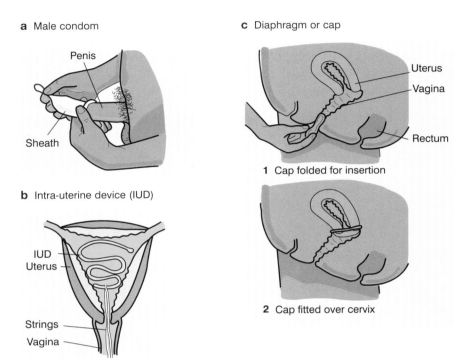

a Male condom

c Diaphragm or cap

1 Cap folded for insertion

2 Cap fitted over cervix

b Intra-uterine device (IUD)

e Spermicide

▲ **Figure 23.4.1** Different methods of contraception

Questions

1 Copy this table and complete it by putting ticks in the correct columns.

Method of contraception	Used by women	Used by men	Used by men and women	Protects from STIs	Reliable and effective
The pill					
Sterilisation					
Rhythm method					
Abstinence					
Condoms					
Diaphragm					
IUD					
Injections					
Withdrawal					
None					

2 Which forms of contraception are the most and least popular in your country? Why?

3 Why do you think the pill and injection are the most widely used form of contraception in many countries?

4 Worldwide, the use of condoms has increased in the past 10 years. Why do you think more and more people are choosing to use this method of contraception?

Objectives

By the end of this topic you will be able to:

● discuss the transmission and control of HIV and AIDS and gonorrhoea.

B23.5 Sexually transmitted infections

Sexually transmitted infections (STIs) may be passed from person to person by sexual activity. Gonorrhoea and syphilis are examples of sexually transmitted infections caused by bacteria. Acquired Immune Deficiency Syndrome (AIDS) and herpes are examples of sexually transmitted infections caused by viruses.

Gonorrhoea is caused by the bacterium *Neisseria gonorrhoea*. The bacterium can live for only a short time outside the body and is very quickly killed by heat, lack of water and antiseptics. The bacterium that causes syphilis can be killed in similar ways. It is difficult to contract gonorrhoea other than by unprotected sexual contact. Table 23.5.1 summarises the effects and implications of this disease in men and women.

▼ **Table 23.5.1** Some effects of gonorrhoea in men and women

Gonorrhoea	
Men	**Women**
Becomes painful to pass urine, yellow discharge from the penis	Many women show no symptoms at all, but there may be pain in passing urine and a yellow discharge from the vagina
Symptoms disappear	Symptoms disappear
In the long-term, sperm ducts become blocked resulting in sterility, can also lead to bladder problems	Oviducts become blocked resulting in sterility. Babies affected in the uterus may be born blind

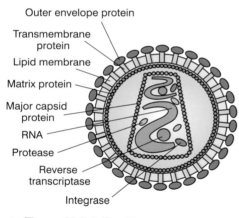

Outer envelope protein
Transmembrane protein
Lipid membrane
Matrix protein
Major capsid protein
RNA
Protease
Reverse transcriptase
Integrase

▲ **Figure 23.5.1** The Human Immunodeficiency Virus (HIV)

People who have contracted syphilis or gonorrhoea can be treated with antibiotic drugs like penicillin and streptomycin. These drugs cure the disease completely if treatment is started early enough.

AIDS

AIDS is caused by a virus called the Human Immunodeficiency Virus (HIV), which is shown in Figure 23.5.1.

HIV attacks the lymphocytes which play an important part in the body's defence against disease. This means that a person with HIV is far less protected against disease than normal. It is not normally the HIV itself which causes the suffering of AIDS patients, they usually die from another infection as a result of their loss of immunity.

Table 23.5.2 show you how HIV is transmitted and what can be done to control the spread of the virus. Unlike many other viral infections, controlling AIDS presents particular difficulties. There is a long time interval (from a few months to several years) between the virus entering the body and symptoms developing. During this period, the infected person is infectious and can pass the virus on to others without knowing it.

▼ **Table 23.5.2** Transmission and control of HIV

How HIV is transmitted	Methods of controlling the spread of HIV
Through unprotected sexual intercourse with an infected person (this is the most common method of transmission)	Abstain from sexual intercourse Always use a condom during sexual intercourse
Sharing needles, blades or other cutting instruments with an infected person (drug users may share needles and pass on the virus)	Never share needles, razors, blades, ear-piercing equipment without sterilising them properly (wiping them or washing them is not enough!)
Infected mothers can pass the virus to the foetus through the placenta and by breastfeeding	Pregnant women can take drugs which reduce the risk of infection in the foetus Feeding babies born to infected mothers with formula or milk from uninfected mothers
Transfusions of unsterilised and infected blood can pass on the virus, although the numbers infected in this way are low	Careful screening of blood used for transfusions
In hospitals the virus can spread if surgical instruments are not sterilised and through 'needle-stick' accidents	Proper sterilisation and strict measures for getting rid of medical waste (used needles, etc.) in hospitals

Although doctors and scientists are working on medications to kill HIV and vaccines to prevent transmission, there is presently no cure if you get infected. Current medications slow the progress of the disease and a healthy lifestyle allows infected people to manage the disease for years, but they are not cured and they are highly likely to develop AIDS in time and to die from the infections linked to AIDS.

Avoiding sexually transmitted infections (AIDS, syphilis, gonorrhoea) means avoiding sexual intercourse with an infected person. However, you cannot usually tell when someone is infected – there may be no symptoms at all. So, your safest option is to abstain from having sex until you are in a stable, monogamous relationship and you have both been tested for STIs. People who have a lot of sexual partners have a much higher risk of contracting a sexually transmitted infection.

> **! Key fact**
>
> Research into HIV and AIDS is on-going and health professionals are working hard to try and find a cure for AIDS. You can find out more about this work and access up-to-date country and regional statistics from the International HIV and AIDS charity, AVERT (www.avert.org).

Questions

1 Why is it easier to cure gonorrhoea than it is to cure herpes?

2 Study the figures in the table carefully:

Country	Living with HIV/AIDS		Deaths due to AIDS during most recent year (estimated)
	All people	Adult (15–49) rate (%)	
Bahamas	6500	2.8	<500
Barbados	1400	0.9	<100
Belize	4600	2.3	no data
Cuba	14 100	0.2	<200
Dominican Republic	44 000	0.7	1700
Guyana	6200	1.1	<500
Haiti	120 000	1.8	5800
Jamaica	30 000	1.8	1600
Suriname	3400	1.0	<500
Trinidad and Tobago	13 000	1.5	<1000

Source: http://www.avert.org (2013)

a Why are figures like these estimated and given with a degree of uncertainty?

b Infection rates in the Dominican Republic have dropped since the government introduced an awareness and education campaign. What behaviours do you think this campaign encouraged? Why?

c In Cuba, everyone who is infected with HIV is given free treatment. How do you think this affects the transmission and spread of the virus? Why?

A disease is any condition that disturbs the normal functioning of cells, tissues or organs and leads to poor health. In this unit you will learn about different types of disease, what causes them, how they are spread and how they can be treated or prevented.

B24.1 Different types of disease

Why is it important to understand types, causes, methods of transmission and methods of treating different diseases? Dr C. James Hospedales, Director of the Caribbean Epidemiology Centre (CAREC) gave these reasons in a report on the general health trends in the region: 'Economies of the Caribbean depend highly upon a healthy population and workforce. Societies depend on healthy individuals, families and communities for sustainability. The impact of compromised health is felt both in increased health service costs for treating avoidable illness and in the decline in productivity, loss of employability, etc.'

What is disease?

For most people, the word 'disease' means sickness or feeling unwell. However, biologically, a disease is any condition that impairs functioning of cells, tissues or organs.

Infectious diseases

Infectious or communicable diseases are diseases that can be passed from one person to another. They are caused by microscopic organisms called pathogens. A pathogen can be a bacterium, a virus, a fungus or a protozoan.

Table 24.1.1 shows you these groups of pathogens, how they affect the human body and gives examples of pathogenic diseases.

▼ **Table 24.1.1** Pathogens and their effects on the human body

Pathogen	Description	Effects on the human body	Diseases
Bacterium	Microscopic uni-cellular organisms that can reproduce by themselves by mitosis. Can live outside the body.	Some compete with body cells by killing them or by excreting toxins which damage the cells. Toxins can enter the blood and other body fluids. It is these toxins that make the person feel ill.	Tonsillitis, tuberculosis (TB), cholera, tetanus, typhoid fever, gonorrhoea.
Virus	Can only live and reproduce inside a living cell. Each virus contains a long thread of chemical information	Attaches to a living cell then injects the thread into the cell. The thread stimulates the invaded cell to produce new viruses. After a time, the cell will burst and release the new viruses into the blood. From there they will spread through the body and invade other cells. The person may fall ill or feel uncomfortable as the immune system tries to counteract the invading viruses.	Influenza (flu), dengue, HIV/AIDs, herpes, chicken pox, polio, measles
Fungus	Cannot make their own food, must find food in the environment in which they grow	Most fungi are decomposers, they feed on dead matter. Some feed on the skin and cause skin diseases. The fungi send out long thin threads into the skin and their feeding damages the living skin below the surface.	Ringworm (tinea), dandruff, thrush (Candida), athlete's foot (tinea)
Protozoan	Unicellular organisms found in different parts of the body	Relationship between protozoa and body is normally beneficial. Harmful protozoa are called parasites and a few can cause serious illness. These protozoa excrete toxic waste products and reproduce quickly.	Malaria, bilharzia, amoebic dysentery

Pathogens can infect humans, other animals and plants. The infected organism is called the host, because the pathogen lives on or inside it.

Non-infectious diseases

Not all diseases are infectious. Many non-infectious diseases develop because the body is not working properly. The way we treat our bodies affects the onset of non-infectious diseases. Many disorders can be avoided or at least delayed providing we live sensibly, paying attention to our health. There are three groups of non-infectious diseases: deficiency, hereditary and physiological diseases.

Table 24.1.2 gives you information about different non-infectious diseases.

▼ **Table 24.1.2** Non-infectious diseases and their effects on the body

Type of disease	Description	Examples
Deficiency	Poor diet may deprive the body of vitamins and other essential substances	Scurvy, rickets, kwashiorkor, anaemia (iron-deficiency)
Hereditary	Inherited defect that prevents an organ or tissue from working properly	Dwarfism, haemophilia, sickle cell anaemia, cystic fibrosis
Physiological		
Cancer	Cell division runs out of control and a cancerous growth (tumour) develops.	Lung cancer, leukaemia, skin cancer
Degenerative	Organs and tissues are damaged or worn out by 'wear and tear'.	Heart attacks, arthritis, hypertension
Metabolic	Defect that prevents an organ or tissue from working properly.	Diabetes (islets of Langerhans)
Psychological	Mental illness caused by imbalances in, or damage to the brain.	Depression, paranoia, schizophrenia

Questions

1 In column A there is a list of diseases. In column B there is a list of the pathogens that could cause them.

	Column A	Column B
i	Cholera	Fungus
ii	AIDS	Bacterium
iii	Dysentery	Protozoan
iv	TB	Virus
v	Dengue	
vi	Influenza	
vii	Tetanus	
viii	Athlete's foot	
ix	Malaria	
x	Polio	

   a List the numbers of the diseases i to x and next to each one, write the pathogen that can cause the disease.
   b Why are these diseases all called infectious or communicable diseases?

2 Explain the difference between a deficiency disease and a hereditary disease and give an example of each.

3 What are physiological diseases? How are they different from pathogenic diseases?

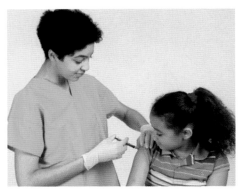

▲ **Figure 24.2.1** This child is being vaccinated against measles, mumps and rubella (German measles)

 Key fact

Treatment involves dealing with a disease once the person has contracted it. Control means acting to prevent the spread of diseases.

B24.2 Treatment and control of diseases

The treatment and control of disease is an important task for all Health Ministries.

Treating and controlling infectious diseases

The causes and spread of infectious diseases can be controlled by focusing on the interactions between the host (humans), the pathogen and the environment. Many of the diseases themselves can be treated with medicines and it is possible to be vaccinated or immunised against some diseases. The result is that the number of deaths from infectious diseases has generally declined in the Caribbean over the past 50 years, although the rise in the number of HIV infections since the 1980s has caused a slight increase in the numbers once again.

Infectious diseases can be controlled by measures which affect the host, the pathogen or the environment.

Measures that affect the host

Resistance to a disease is the ability to fight it off. Resistance to infectious diseases, such as polio, tuberculosis, diphtheria, whooping cough, tetanus, measles, mumps and German measles, can be increased by vaccination programmes. Resistance to diseases, such as colds and flu, can be increased by keeping fit and eating a balanced diet with adequate vitamins (especially vitamins A and C).

Early detection measures involve testing regularly people who are at risk of catching a disease to find out whether or not they are infected. Diseases such as TB and some sexually transmitted infections are easy to cure with medicines if they are detected early.

The most effective measure against infection is personal hygiene. Taking basic steps, such as washing your hands before preparing or eating food, can help to control the spread of pathogens.

Measures that affect the pathogen

Disease causing pathogens can be destroyed by using substances that kill them. These substances include antibiotics, disinfectants and antiseptics and sterilisation techniques, such as heating or boiling.

Viruses are the most difficult pathogens to kill because they live in the body of the host and most of them are not affected by antibiotics. Table 24.2.1 shows you some of the methods used to control viral diseases.

▼ **Table 24.2.1** Control of some viral diseases

Disease	Viral agent	Control
Flu	A number of DNA viruses	Vaccination with dead virus of the correct strain. As the virus changes regularly, new vaccines must be developed quickly to be effective
German measles	Rubella virus	Vaccination with living form of the virus
Rabies	RNA virus	Elimination of animal carriers, vaccination of pets and humans at risk
Foot-and-mouth disease	RNA virus	Slaughter of infected animals, vaccination
Tobacco mosaic	TMV (an RNA virus)	Destruction of infected plants

Many pathogens are controlled by disrupting their life cycle and preventing them from reaching their next host. Many of these measures involve changes to the environment.

Measures that affect the environment

Measures which create unfavourable conditions for pathogens to grow and reproduce can prevent the spread of disease. These measures include:

- improved standards of living, hygiene and the treatment of sewage
- eradication of insects, such as mosquitoes and houseflies
- provision of safe, clean drinking water
- food inspections, such as the inspection of meat at abattoirs
- better preparation and storage of food (pasteurisation and cold storage)
- laws which require notification of certain diseases, such as rabies and leprosy; this allows for quick treatment and quarantine (isolation of infected individuals)
- improved public health programmes, including vaccination programmes and education programmes.

Key fact

Surgical instruments and equipment that are used over and over again on different people are sterilised by boiling them under pressure in an autoclave to kill the pathogens. Boiling the water under pressure allows it to boil at a higher temperature (120 °C) which is more effective at killing the pathogens.

▲ **Figure 24.2.2** Spraying insecticides to kill mosquitoes and larvae

 Practical activity

Carry out a survey of infectious diseases

You are going to do a survey to find out about the treatment and control of infectious diseases in your community. Follow the steps outlined here.

1 Find out which four infectious human diseases are most common in your community. You can visit the local clinic or other health service to find this information.

2 Draw up a list of questions for your survey. These should help you to find out about the symptoms of the disease, how people became infected with the disease, what treatment they received and what efforts were made to control the spread of the disease.

3 Interview at least 10 willing members of your community who have been ill with at least one of the diseases you identified. Record their responses to your questions. Note that you should be sensitive to the people you are interviewing.

4 Use the information you have collected to compile a short report of the effects, spread, treatment and control of the diseases you investigated.

1 Give one reason for each of the following actions:

  a Doctors and dentists wear masks over their noses and mouths.

  b If you fall and cut yourself, you wash the wound and put antiseptic cream on it.

  c Many of the food items in stores are wrapped in cellophane.

  d Washing your hands after going to the toilet.

  e Animals brought into the country from overseas are put in isolation for a period of time.

2 Why are children with chicken pox or measles not allowed to attend school?

3 Imagine there is an outbreak of flu in your local area.

  a What can you do to avoid getting the flu?

  b What can you do to treat the flu if you do get it?

Treating and controlling non-infectious diseases

Chronic non-infectious diseases are the leading cause of death in the Caribbean, with heart disease, strokes, diabetes and cancer being among the top causes of death. It is often difficult to treat these diseases, although it is possible to prevent or delay them by making certain lifestyle changes. In this section you will focus on the role of diet and exercise in preventing heart disease, hypertension and diabetes.

The role of diet and exercise in disease prevention

Diet

The amount of sugar and fat you eat affects your risk of developing physiological diseases, such as heart disease, hypertension and diabetes. If people eat too much sugar and fat, they tend to gain weight. Overweight people have a higher risk of these diseases.

Too much of the wrong sort of fatty food increases the levels of cholesterol in the blood. Cholesterol is a fatty deposit which can block arteries and restrict the flow of blood through them. The more cholesterol there is in the blood, the greater the risk of a person having a heart attack (see Figure 24.2.3).

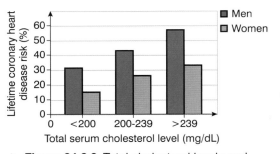

▲ **Figure 24.2.3** Total cholesterol levels and lifetime risk of coronary heart disease

Eating food containing a lot of saturated fat seems to raise the levels of cholesterol in the blood. However, polyunsaturated fats are good for us. It is recommended that for every gram of fat you eat, at least 0.45 g should be polyunsaturated. Figure 24.2.4 shows the proportion of saturated fats contained in different foods.

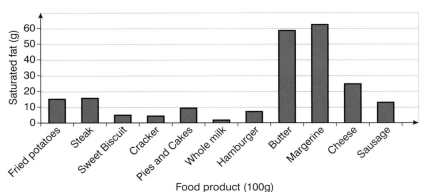

◀ **Figure 24.2.4** Grams of saturated fat (per 100g of food) for different foods

Too much salt in the diet can raise blood pressure. A person with higher than normal blood pressure is more likely to suffer from heart disease (see Figure 24.2.5).

Different studies show that changing your diet and exercising more can have an important effect on your blood pressure and your risk of suffering from heart disease. People who are a normal weight, who eat well and who exercise regularly have a much reduced risk of developing diabetes. People with diabetes find they can reduce their dependence on injected insulin if they control their diet, eat well and exercise regularly.

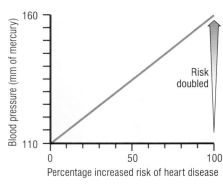

▲ **Figure 24.2.5** Blood pressure and the risk of heart disease

Exercise

Many studies strongly support the idea that regular exercise protects against heart disease. Some of the evidence from these studies is summarised in Figure 24.2.6.

Exercise and...

Blood pressure
• Blood pressure is lower in physically fit people
• Regular exercise can help control high blood pressure and reduce the risk of heart disease

Overweight
• Being overweight is often due to lack of exercise and is linked with high blood pressure
• Regular exercise increases fitness, reduces body fat, lowers blood pressure and reduces the risk of heart disease

Stress
• Stress increases blood pressure and the risk of heart disease as well as making people irritable and depressed
• Regular exercise reduces the risk of heart disease and gives an increased feeling of well being

Coronary arteries
• Regular exercise reduces the build-up of atheroma and makes coronary arteries wider reducing the risk of heart disease
• Exercise can promote the growth of new blood vessels after a heart attack

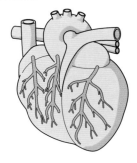

▲ **Figure 24.2.6** Exercise and heart disease

Living sensibly means getting regular exercise to maintain the fitness of your heart, but it also means avoiding other controllable risk factors which contribute to hypertension and heart disease such as smoking and stress. Figure 24.2.7 shows the number of deaths caused by leading risk factors in 2004. According to the World Health Organization, eight risk factors – alcohol use, tobacco use, high blood pressure, high body mass index, high cholesterol, high blood glucose, low fruit and vegetable intake, and physical inactivity – account for 61% of cardiovascular deaths.

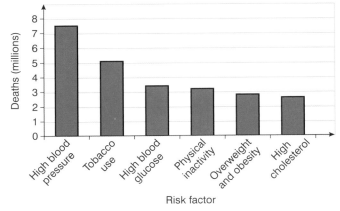

◀ **Figure 24.2.7** The number of deaths caused by leading risk factors in 2004

Exercise (combined with a healthy diet) can also reduce your risk of getting diabetes. A study by the Diabetes Prevention Program (DPP) indicated that the risk of getting diabetes is reduced by 58% when the following lifestyle changes occur:

- calorie and dietary fat reduction in the diet
- physical activity: total of 150 minutes a week
- weight loss: 7% body weight reduction as a result of diet and exercise.

The same study found these lifestyle changes were effective in treating and controlling Type 2 diabetes in people who already had the disease.

Practical activity

Testing your fitness

You can measure your physical fitness using a simple step test. The exercise can be done in pairs or in a group. Before you begin, make sure you know how to measure your pulse.

Materials

- A sturdy chair or box about 45 cm high
- A stopwatch

Method

1 Step up onto the chair and then down again for 5 minutes. You should do this about 30 times each minute.

2 Sit down and take (and record) your pulse for 30 seconds at the following intervals:
   - after resting for 1 minute
   - after resting for 2 minutes
   - after resting for 4 minutes.

3 Calculate your fitness points using the following formula:

$$\frac{\text{duration of exercise in seconds} \times 100}{2(\text{pulse after 1 min + after 2 min + after 4 min})} = \text{points}$$

4 Rate your fitness by finding your point score from the table:

If your results are not what you would like, then try exercising regularly for 15 minutes each day for a month. Then take the test again and see how you have improved.

Points scored	Fitness level
Less than 50	Poor
50–65	Below average
66–80	Average
81–90	Good
Above 90	Excellent

Questions

1 Briefly explain how a man with a family history of hypertension and heart disease can reduce his risk of having a heart attack.

2 A 25-year-old overweight woman with Type 2 diabetes would like to reduce her dependence on injected insulin. Write down three lifestyle changes she could make to achieve her aims.

B24.3 Transmission of disease

How are diseases transmitted?

Pathogens are found everywhere, on clothes, on skin, on money and on food. By touching these objects, the pathogens get onto your hands. If you touch your nose or mouth, or if you have open sores on your skin, the pathogens can enter your body. Pathogens can also enter your body in the water you drink or the food you eat.

Pathogens can also be exhaled by one person and then inhaled by others. This is why disease often spreads in places where people live or work close to each other.

Insects also carry pathogens. Insects, such as flies, may spread pathogens as they move from place to place to feed. Dysentery, typhoid fever and cholera can be spread by houseflies. We say the fly is a vector for pathogens that cause disease. Mosquitoes are vectors for the dengue virus, tiny worms that cause filariasis (swelling of the limbs) and the protozoa that cause malaria.

Vectors

A **vector** is an organism that carries pathogens and helps them to spread. The vector is not usually affected by the pathogen it carries. For example, the female *Anopheles* mosquitoes that carry the *Plasmodium* protozoa that cause malaria are not harmed by the protozoa. Similarly, flies are not harmed by the pathogens they transmit.

Understanding the life cycle of insect vectors can help health workers find ways to control the diseases that are spread by the vectors, by breaking the life cycle and preventing the spread of the disease. Figure 24.3.1 shows you the role of mosquitoes as vectors in the malaria life cycle.

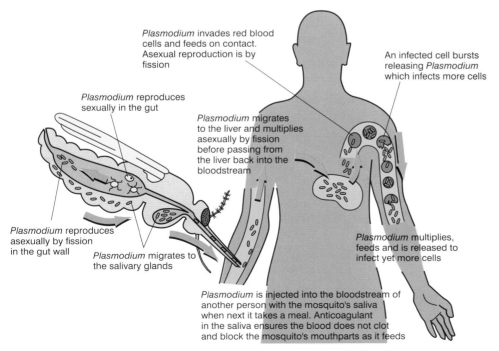

Plasmodium invades red blood cells and feeds on contact. Asexual reproduction is by fission

An infected cell bursts releasing *Plasmodium* which infects more cells

Plasmodium reproduces sexually in the gut

Plasmodium migrates to the liver and multiplies asexually by fission before passing from the liver back into the bloodstream

Plasmodium reproduces asexually by fission in the gut wall

Plasmodium migrates to the salivary glands

Plasmodium multiplies, feeds and is released to infect yet more cells

Plasmodium is injected into the bloodstream of another person with the mosquito's saliva when next it takes a meal. Anticoagulant in the saliva ensures the blood does not clot and block the mosquito's mouthparts as it feeds

▲ **Figure 24.3.1** The life cycle of the *Plasmodium* parasite, including the role of the mosquito as a vector for malaria

By the end of this topic you will be able to:

- explain the roles of vectors in the transmission of diseases
- identify stages in the life cycle of a mosquito as a vector of disease
- collect eggs and larvae of mosquitoes
- make observations and drawings of stages in the metamorphosis of the vector
- suggest methods of control at each life stage of the life history of the vector
- display and interpret information about diseases spread by mosquitoes in your country.

Treatment and prevention of malaria

Fighting malaria depends on destroying the mosquito vector, destroying the protozoa or preventing contact between the vector (the mosquito) and people. Control measures include:

- Draining marshes, ponds and ditches and emptying old tins, bottles and old car tyres if water collects in them, thus preventing the mosquito from laying eggs and preventing eggs which have been laid from hatching.
- Biological control in the form of fish which eat mosquito larvae.
- Insecticides sprayed onto the surface of water to kill mosquito larvae and pupae and sprayed into the air to kill adult mosquitoes.
- Drugs like quinine, mefloquinine and primaquine which prevent fission of *Plasmodium* in the liver or red blood cells of the host.
- Vaccines which are being developed to inhibit different stages in the protozoan life cycle.
- Sleeping under mosquito nets impregnated with insecticide to prevent the mosquito from biting the human host.
- Chemical repellents sprayed or rubbed onto the skin and clothes to stop mosquitoes from landing and biting.

Key fact

A vector, such as a mosquito, is the secondary (or intermediate) host in which pathogens reproduce. As a result the vector acts as a reservoir for the pathogens, constantly spreading them. Control of vector-borne diseases must include destroying the vector.

Safety

Avoid being bitten and infected by wearing insect repellent and protective clothing.

Practical activity

Collecting mosquito eggs and larvae

Your teacher may use this activity to assess: ORR; M&M.

You are going to identify places where mosquitoes can breed and collect eggs, larvae and pupae for inspection and observation.

Materials

- A glass jar
- A hand lens
- A notebook
- A tray
- A small net
- A pair of tweezers
- A pencil

Method

1 Explore an area near your school or home to find sites where mosquitoes are likely to breed.

2 Record the location of each site on a sketch map of the area. Annotate the sketch map to describe each breeding site.

3 Use the net to collect mosquito larvae and pupae. Place these in the glass jar and observe them. How do they move? Do they remain at the surface? Why?

4 Use a hand lens to examine a single larva and pupa. Sketch and label what you can see.

5 Return to the breeding site. Can you find eggs, larvae and pupae in the water at the same time?

6 Write a short report detailing practical methods of reducing the number of sites available to mosquitoes for breeding in your area.

As a class, you could play a role in the health of the community by carrying out the best and most practical suggestions from this activity.

Questions

1 What is a 'vector'?

2 What role do insect vectors play in the transmission of disease?

3 Mosquitoes are also vectors for dengue and yellow fever.
   a Find information about the incidence of dengue and yellow fever in your country.
   b Display the information graphically.
   c Write a few sentences interpreting the information you have collected.

B24.4 Plant and animal diseases

Plant diseases

Plant diseases are also caused by pathogens. However, the impact of pathogens on plants is different. Bacteria, for example, can cause serious diseases in humans and other animals, but they pose few problems for plants. Fungi, on the other hand, are a major source of plant disease. More than 1000 species of fungi cause plant disease with serious effects on crops and food production.

Figure 24.4.1 shows you some of the fungal diseases that are problematic in the Caribbean.

Objectives

By the end of this topic you will be able to:

- discuss the social and economic implications of disease in plants and animals
- display and interpret statistical data for local examples.

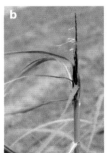

▲ **Figure 24.4.1** Some problematic and costly fungal diseases of plants: **a** potato blight, **b** sugar cane smut, **c** papaya ringspot, **d** pepper mottle virus and **e** banana wilt

Fungal and viral diseases in plants are spread easily and quickly as a result of planting infected plants and leaving infected left-over plant parts in the soil for the next year's planting. Spores are carried by wind or rain to other plants in the crop and viruses spread in the saliva of biting plant pests.

The following article on p252 from the *The San Pedro Sun* (Belize) tells of another problematic plant disease – lethal yellowing in coconuts.

Lethal yellowing is a fatal disease of coconut and other palms that has killed millions of palms in the Caribbean region since 1970. The disease has affected the coconut growing regions of Jamaica, Cuba, the Cayman Islands, Honduras, Belize and Trinidad.

Lethal yellowing is caused by a small virus-like organism called a phytoplasma, and is spread by small plant-sucking insects known as plant-hoppers. There is no effective cure for the disease, and the palm will die within 3 to 6 months after the appearance of the first symptom. The first visible sign that a coconut has been infected is the dropping of all of its fruit, irrespective of their size. Over the next two months or so, the new flowers produced by the palm wither and blacken. Then the leaves progressively yellow and hang, starting from the lower leaves and finishing with the top leaves. Once the top leaves have gone, the palm is dead and all which is left is something resembling a telephone pole.

The disease occurs in discrete areas known as 'foci'. These foci slowly grow larger, gradually taking in more palms. Once lethal yellowing becomes established in an area, most of the coconut palms will die within the next 3 years. The disease may also jump over several kilometres to establish new foci.

Even though there is no cure for lethal yellowing, the disease can be controlled. Short-term control can be effected by injecting the coconut palms with the antibiotic, oxytetracycline. This control method prevents the death of the palm in the short-term but is also quite expensive. A more long-term and cheaper solution to the problem is to plant resistant coconut varieties and palm species. It is recommended to use the two control methods in conjunction to keep the old coconut palms alive until the new resistant ones have grown up sufficiently.

Planting resistant coconut and other palm species are the only long-term solution to lethal yellowing.

Animal diseases

Animal diseases are often bacterial. For example, anthrax in farm animals, mastitis in cows and scours in piglets are all caused by bacteria. Animals can be vaccinated against these diseases and good sanitation measures can often prevent outbreaks and control the spread of disease.

Animal diseases such as avian flu, found in chickens, and bovine spongiform encephalopathy (BSE or mad cow disease) are called zoonotic diseases because they can spread to humans. When there is an outbreak of these diseases in a country, most of the animals are destroyed, with serious economic consequences for farmers and a drop in food production.

The effects of plant and animal diseases

According to the Food and Agriculture Organization of the United Nations (FAO) there are six serious economic and social effects of plant and animal disease. These are:

- **Decreased and lost production**: plants and animals die from diseases leading to lower yields, plants may produce less as a result of disease and animals may not reproduce as a result of illness.
- **Price and market effects**: when yields decline or crops and herds are lost, there is often an increase in the price of food, similarly, the price farmers are paid for poor or diseased crops is very low.

- **Trade**: many countries ban the importation of products from specific countries when a crop or animal disease breaks out, which can have serious effects on the economy of the country where the disease has broken out.

- **Food security and nutrition**: if food crops or animals are badly affected by disease, a country may not be able to produce enough food for its population.

- **Human health and the environment**: plant and animal diseases can impact on human health as a result of eating infected food or not having access to food and measures to control the disease can have environmental consequences, particularly if ecosystems are disturbed.

- **Financial costs**: measures taken by individuals, farming collectives and governments to control and eradicate pests and diseases cost money, these include the cost of inspections, monitoring, prevention and response.

Questions

1 Figure 24.4.2 shows the production figures of hot peppers in Jamaica over a five-year period.

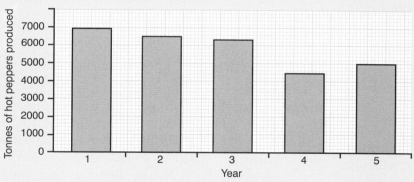

▲ **Figure 24.4.2** Hot pepper production in Jamaica

a Describe the general trend shown on the graph.

b Peppers are very susceptible to fungal and viral diseases. Explain how these are spread from plant to plant.

c At the start of year 4, there was an outbreak of pepper mottle virus. How did this impact on the production of peppers?

d What social and economic effects do you think this disease had for pepper farmers?

2 Name one plant or animal disease that has been found in your country, then answer the following questions about it:

a What causes the disease?

b How is it spread?

c How does it affect the plant or animal?

d How is it treated or controlled?

e What social and economic impact does the disease have?

Biology in the real world

Case study A

Diet and health

The topic of diet and healthy eating is a popular one and you will regularly find articles in the newspapers and magazines about healthy eating, balanced diets and new fads 'guaranteed' to help you lose weight. However, you will also find a lot of unsubstantiated facts as well as misleading and possibly dangerous information.

Read through the statements below. Have you read or heard people say these things? Which of these do you think are true?

- Salt in your diet causes high blood pressure.
- Carbohydrates are bad for you.
- Dairy products are fattening and unhealthy.
- Red meat is bad for you.
- Brown bread is better for you than white.
- Everyone needs a lot of protein.

Essentially all of these statements are myths, yet many people believe them. The reason they seem plausible is because there is an element of truth in each, but actually the statements are too generalised to be true for everyone. The information below will help you to dispel each of these misconceptions.

Salt and high blood pressure (hypertension)

As early as 1940, researchers at Duke University in North Carolina restricted the salt intake of patients with high blood pressure. A number of other studies showed that cutting down on salt helped to reduce hypertension. However, adults need some sodium in their diet to maintain the body's fluid balance. The problem is not salt per se, but rather the amount of salt we consume. The maximum recommended intake of salt is 6 g per day, but most people consume 9 g or more. People who eat lots of processed food such as packet or canned soups, sauces and processed meats take in much more salt than they need. Adding salt as you cook or at the table is not 'bad' for you. Generally this salt only forms a fraction of your salt intake.

Carbohydrates

You already know that carbohydrate-rich foods are an important source of energy. They can also provide a lot of fibre and nutrients. Many vegetables are rich in vitamins, including potatoes. However, carbohydrates have fallen out of favour because people think they are fattening. Media coverage and celebrity support of low-carb diets, such as the Atkins diet, have added to this myth.

The reality is that carbohydrates are not more likely to make us gain weight than any other food. Weight gain is caused by taking in more kilojoules than your body needs, and often these kilojoules are contained in the things we add to carbohydrates – butter and jam on bread, fats and oils to fry potatoes or sugar to make things taste better.

Dairy products

Curtin University of Technology in Perth, Australia, did a study which showed that dieters following low-calorie diets which included cheese, yoghurt and milk lost more weight than those on low-dairy diets. Those on the diet including dairy also had the least stomach fat, lower blood pressure and a significantly better chance of avoiding heart disease and diabetes.

Dairy products provide essential nutrients and they are good sources of protein, zinc and some B vitamins. Dairy products also provide calcium, which helps to build strong, healthy bones.

Red meat

In 2012 the World Cancer Research Fund recommended that people limit their intake of red meat to 500 g (cooked weight) a week to avoid colon cancer. The results of this study made people panic and think red meat was dangerous.

But 500 g of meat is roughly the equivalent of five or six medium portions of roast beef, lamb or pork. Red meat provides minerals and vitamins, particularly iron. Red meat is healthy provided your intake is moderate. Processed meat of all kinds, however, should be avoided.

Brown bread versus white

Wholemeal bread is made from flour containing all the goodness of wheat grains. The outer husk has not been removed, so the resulting brown bread is rich in fibre, protein and vitamins B1, B2, niacin, vitamin B6, folic acid and biotin. Brown bread, in contrast, is made from finely milled wheat, from which the bran has been extracted, and some darker coloured breads are simply coloured with caramel to make them look healthier – basically they are dyed white bread and subsequently are no better for you than white bread.

We all need lots of protein

You learnt that protein is essential for growth and development. The Centres for Disease Control (CDC) in the USA recommend that 10–35% of your daily kilojoule intake be protein. On average, this means girls aged 14–18 need 46 g, boys aged 14–18 need 52 g, adult women need 46 g and adult men need 56 g. However, in some countries average daily intake of protein can be over 80 g for men and over 60 g for women, which is more than that needed.

So why do we think we need so much? One of the main reasons is that some diets advocate speedy weight loss by cutting the carbohydrates and eating mainly proteins. High-protein intake can put a strain on the liver and the kidneys and other bodily systems.

Case study B

Organs for sale – moral and ethical issues

Spare parts – buying and selling human organs

It is against the law in most countries to buy or sell human organs. However, that does not stop desperate people from doing so. The organs which are most commonly traded are kidneys, parts of the liver, corneas and blood.

Moral and ethical issues

Buying and selling of human organs raises ethical and moral questions. Most health workers involved in organ transplantation believe that human organs should not be bought or sold under any circumstances. In 2008, a group of transplant specialists gathered and drew up a document known as the Declaration of Istanbul which declares 'human organ commercialization' to be unethical and illegal.

But there are other professionals who have a different viewpoint. They feel that legalising the trade in human organs would make the process safer. By legalising the trade, and then overseeing it, the people who pay the true price, those who are poor and are selling their organs, would at least get decent medical care afterwards. Currently, many of these people are left to their own devices and many of them become ill or die as a result of the original organ removal. The debate about legalising the trade in organs is taking place in many countries, including the United States and Great Britain. The country of Singapore is considering changing its laws to accommodate for the sale and purchase of organs.

Illegal kidney trade booms as new organ is 'sold every hour'

Denis Campbell and Nicola Davison in Shanghai

The illegal trade in kidneys has risen to such a level that an estimated 15,000–20,000 black market operations involving purchased human organs now take place annually, or more than one an hour, World Health Organisation (WHO) experts have revealed.

Evidence collected by a worldwide network of doctors shows that traffickers are defying laws intended to curtail their activities and are cashing in on rising international demand for replacement kidneys driven by the increase in diabetes and other diseases.

Patients, many of whom will go to China, India or Pakistan for surgery, can pay up to $200,000 (nearly £128,000) for a kidney to gangs who harvest organs from vulnerable, desperate people, sometimes for as little as $5,000.

The vast sums to be made by both traffickers and surgeons have been underlined by the arrest by Israeli police last week of 10 people, including a doctor, suspected of belonging to an international organ trafficking ring and of committing extortion, tax fraud and grievous bodily harm. Other illicit organ trafficking rings have been uncovered in India and Pakistan.

The Guardian contacted an organ broker in China who advertised his services under the slogan, "Donate a kidney, buy the new iPad!" He offered £2,500 for a kidney and said the operation could be performed within 10 days.

The resurgence of trafficking has prompted the WHO to suggest that humanity itself is being undermined by the vast profits involved and the division between poor people who undergo "amputation" for cash and the wealthy sick who sustain the body parts trade.

"The illegal trade worldwide was falling back in about 2006–07 – there was a decrease in 'transplant tourism'," said Luc Noel, a doctor and WHO official who runs a unit monitoring trends in legitimate and underground donations and transplants of human organs. But he added: "The trade may well be increasing again. There have been recent signs that that may well be the case. There is a growing need for transplants and big profits to be made. It's ever growing, it's a constant struggle. The stakes are so big, the profit that can be made so huge, that the temptation is out there."

Lack of law enforcement in some countries, and lack of laws in others, mean that those offering financial incentives to poor people to part with a kidney have it too easy, Noel said.

Kidneys make up 75% of the global illicit trade in organs, Noel estimates. Rising rates of diabetes, high blood pressure and heart problems are causing demand for kidneys to far outstrip supply.

Data from the WHO shows that of the 106,879 solid organs known to have been transplanted in 95 member states in 2010 (legally and illegally), about 73,179 (68.5%) were kidneys. But those 106,879 operations satisfied just 10% of the global need, the WHO said.

The organisation does not know how many cases involved the organ being obtained legitimately from a deceased donor or living donor such as a friend or relative of the recipient.

But Noel believes that one in 10 of those 106,879 organs was probably procured by black marketeers. If so, that would mean that organ gangs profited almost 11,000 times in 2010.

Proof of illegal trafficking is being collected by networks of doctors in various countries known as "custodian groups". The groups work to support the Declaration of Istanbul, the 2008 statement against global organ exploitation that was agreed by almost 100 nations.

Made up of hospital specialists who treat patients with end-stage kidney failure who survive on dialysis, and surgeons who operate on those lucky enough to get a new kidney, the groups monitor reports of black market activity in their own country or involving compatriots abroad.

A medical source with knowledge of the situation said: "While commercial transplantation is now forbidden by law in China, that's difficult to enforce; there's been a resurgence there in the last two or three years.

"Foreigners from the Middle East, Asia and sometimes Europe come and are paying $100,000 to $200,000 for a transplant. Often they are Chinese expats or patients of Chinese descent."

Some of China's army hospitals were believed to be carrying out the transplants, the source added.

The persistence of the trade is embarrassing for China. The health ministry in Beijing has outlawed it and has also promised to stop harvesting organs from executed prisoners by 2017, a practice that has brought international condemnation.

John Feehally, a professor of renal medicine at University Hospitals of Leicester NHS trust, said: "Since the Declaration of Istanbul the law on trafficking has been changed in the Philippines – which was one of the centres of transplant tourism – and the Chinese government realises that things have to change." Feehally is also president of the International Society of Nephrology, which represents 10,000 specialist kidney doctors worldwide. "Trafficking is still continuing – it's likely that it is increasing," he said. "We know of countries in Asia, and also in eastern Europe, which provide a market so that people who need a kidney can go there and buy one."

The key issue, Feehally said, was exploitation. "You are exploiting a donor if they are very poor and you are giving them a very small amount of money and no doctor is caring for them afterwards, which is what happens.

"The people who gain are the rich transplant patients who can afford to buy a kidney, the doctors and hospital administrators, and the middlemen, the traffickers. It's absolutely wrong, morally wrong."

Noel wants countries to defeat the traffickers by maximising the supply of organs from deceased and living donors, and encouraging healthy lifestyles to stop people getting conditions such as diabetes in the first place.

Extract from: http://www.theguardian.com

Case study C

Climate change and dengue fever

According to the World Health Organization (WHO) about 2.5 billion people (roughly 40% of the world's population) live in areas where there is a risk of dengue transmission. Dengue is endemic in the regions between 45°N and 35°S, this includes at least 100 countries in Asia, Africa, the Pacific and Caribbean. There are approximately 50 to 100 million cases per year with around 500 000 of these being the more severe dengue haemorrhagic fever (DHF). Dengue causes 22 000 deaths per year, mostly among children.

The map shows the dengue risk areas in Central America and the Caribbean.

Dengue haemorrhagic fever is relatively new to the region, with the first cases in the Caribbean only being confirmed in the early 1980s.

The table shows the number of dengue cases, severe dengue cases (DHF and dengue shock syndrome) and deaths from dengue reported to the Pan-American Health Organisation (PAHO) from 2010 to 2013 (data till August only).

Atlantic Ocean

Pacific Ocean

No Known dengue risk

Dengue risk area

Caribbean (including Hispanic Caribbean)	2010	2011	2012	2013
Dengue cases	132 646	27 437	40 328	32 375
Severe dengue	2229	194	424	282
Deaths	130	21	93	56

Recently, researchers concerned with climate change have undertaken studies to see whether climate change, particularly global warming, have an impact on the number of dengue vectors (*Aedes* mosquitoes) and subsequently the number of dengue cases and fatalities. The results have been fairly surprising.

This is what the Centers for Disease Control (CDC) have to say about the impact of climate on dengue.

Dengue viruses are transmitted by *Aedes* mosquitoes, which are highly sensitive to environmental conditions. Temperature, precipitation, and humidity are critical to mosquito survival, reproduction, and development and can influence mosquito presence and abundance. Additionally, higher temperatures reduce the time required for the virus to replicate and disseminate in the mosquito. This process, referred to as the 'extrinsic incubation period', must occur before the virus can reach the mosquitoes salivary glands and be transmitted to humans. If the mosquito becomes infectious faster because temperatures are warmer, it has a greater chance of infecting a human before it dies.

Although environmental factors are important they are not the only factors critical to dengue transmission. Virus must be present, there must be sufficient numbers of humans still susceptible, or non-immune, to the virus, and there must be contact between those susceptible humans and the mosquito vectors.

In countries where transmission does routinely occur, short-term changes in weather, particularly temperature, precipitation, and humidity, are often correlated with dengue incidence. These associations, however, do not describe the occurrence every few years of major epidemics in these areas, suggesting that long-term climate variability does not regulate long-term patterns in transmission. A more important regulator of epidemics might be the interplay of the four different dengue serotypes. The level of prior exposure of a human population to each of the dengue serotypes may be a more critical determinant of whether a large epidemic occurs than climatic cycles.

Globally, the reported incidence of dengue has been increasing. Although climate may play a role in changing dengue incidence and distribution, it is one of many factors; given its poor correlation with historical changes in incidence, its role may be minor. Other important factors potentially contributing to global changes in dengue incidence and distribution include population growth, urbanization, lack of sanitation, increased long-distance travel, ineffective mosquito control, and increased reporting capacity.

Extract from: http://www.cdc.gov/dengue/

Case study D

HIV and AIDS data for the Caribbean

The following case study has been drawn from the UNAIDS Report on the global AIDS epidemic (2012).

You can find more information, reports and fact sheets online (www.unaids.org).

The global epidemic at a glance

Globally, 34.0 million [31.4 million–35.9 million] people were living with HIV at the end of 2011. An estimated 0.8% of adults aged 15-49 years worldwide are living with HIV, although the burden of the epidemic continues to vary considerably between countries and regions.

Sub-Saharan Africa remains most severely affected, with nearly 1 in every 20 adults (4.9%) living with HIV and accounting for 69% of the people living with HIV worldwide. Although the regional prevalence of HIV infection is nearly 25 times higher in sub-Saharan Africa than in Asia, almost 5 million people are living with HIV in South, South-East and East Asia combined. After sub-Saharan Africa, the regions most heavily affected are the Caribbean and Eastern Europe and Central Asia, where 1.0% of adults were living with HIV in 2011.

However, there is some good news. Fewer new infections are reported as well as fewer deaths from AIDS-related causes and, there is generally greater awareness and access to treatments. You can see the trends for the Caribbean region (selected countries only) in the graphs and the table.

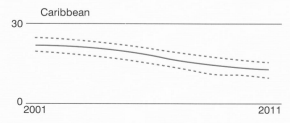

▲ Number of people newly infected with HIV (thousands)

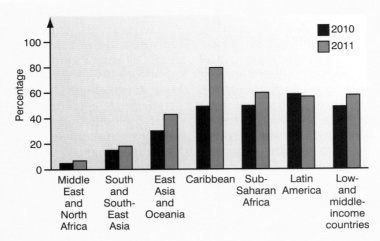

▲ Percentage of pregnant women living with HIV receiving effective antiretroviral regimens for preventing mother-to-child transmission, by region, 2010 and 2011

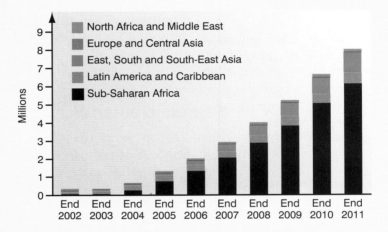

▲ Number of people receiving antiretroviral therapy in low- and middle-income countries, by region, 2002–2011

Country	Number of people living with HIV		Number of new infections		Young people (15–24) living with HIV (2011) (%)		Deaths from AIDS-related illness	
	2001	2011	2001	2011	Male	Female	2001	2011
Bahamas	6500	6500	<1000	<500	0.5	0.3	<1000	<500
Barbados	1200	1400	<200	<100	0.2	0.3	<100	<100
Cuba	3600	14000	No data	No data	<0.1	0.1	<500	<200
Dominican Republic	52000	44000	4900	1500	0.4	0.1	4000	1700
Haiti	130000	120000	12000	6400	1.1	0.4	12000	5800
Jamaica	36000	30000	2900	2000	0.6	0.9	3100	1600
Trinidad and Tobago	11000	13000	1200	<1000	1.0	0.6	<1000	<1000

▲ All reporting countries have a multi-sectoral strategy to respond to HIV

Extracts, figures and data from: http://www.unaids.org

Key concepts

B7 Cell biology

- The cell is the basic unit of life. Plant and animal cells are slightly different from each other, and plant cells contain structures not found in animal cells, but all cells have similar characteristics.

- The structures found in cells have specific functions that keep the cell alive and allow it to function properly.

- Some organisms consist of only one cell, we say they are uni-cellular. However, most cells cannot survive on their own, so they join together to function as multi-cellular organisms.

- In multi-cellular organisms, cells become specialised to perform specific functions. Cells group together to form tissues. Tissues combine to form organs. Organs work together to form organised systems.

- Substances, such as water and dissolved minerals, need to move in to and out of cells. The movement of dissolved substances through cells takes place by diffusion. The movement of water from areas of high concentration to areas of lower concentration takes place by osmosis.

- Osmosis is the way that plants take up the water they need to stay alive. Water moves from the soil through the cell membranes into the roots.

B8 Plant nutrition

- Plants make their own food by changing the energy they get from sunlight into sugar and oxygen in the process of photosynthesis.

- Most photosynthesis takes place in the leaves of plants because the leaves contain chlorophyll. The products of photosynthesis are transported from the leaves to other parts of the plants by the phloem tubes.

- The leaves of plants are specially adapted to allow for maximum photosynthesis. The colour, shape and size and position of the leaves all help in this regard. Internally, the cells in which photosynthesis takes place are tightly packed and close to the surface.

- In order for photosynthesis to take place plants need sunlight, chlorophyll and carbon dioxide. Oxygen and sugars are produced during photosynthesis.

- You can test parts of plants to show that they contain reducing sugars or starch. These tests are often used to prove that photosynthesis has taken place.

- Factors which prevent photosynthesis from taking place are called limiting factors. The amount of sunlight, the level of carbon dioxide, the temperature and how much water is available can all act as limiting factors to photosynthesis.

- Plants need minerals in order to grow well. Macro-nutrients, such as nitrogen, phosphorus and potassium, are needed in large amounts. Micro-nutrients, or trace elements, are needed in much smaller amounts. Plants will not grow well in soils which are mineral deficient. Minerals can be replaced by adding fertilisers to the soil.

B9 Life chemicals and nutrition

- Life processes require energy. Energy comes from the carbohydrates, proteins and lipids in the food we eat.

- Carbohydrates contain carbon, hydrogen and oxygen. Sugars, starch and cellulose are all carbohydrates.

- When organic molecules combine they may produce a water molecule in a condensation reaction. Molecules can recombine with water in hydrolysis reactions.

- Lipids are made up of glycerol and fatty acids. Fats and oils are lipids.

- Proteins contain carbon, hydrogen, oxygen, nitrogen and sometimes sulfur or phosphorus.

- You can carry out tests using different substances to find out which chemical nutrients are contained in foods.

- Enzymes are special groups of large proteins which control the rate at which chemical reactions take place in cells.

- Enzymes are catalysts. This means they help reactions to take place without being used up in the process.

- Enzymes work best at particular temperatures and specific pH values.

- A balanced diet contains carbohydrates, proteins, lipids, vitamins, mineral salts, fibre and water in the right amounts and proportions.

- Vitamins and minerals are organic substances which are important for controlling metabolism and for growth and repair in the body.

- The body is almost 70% water. Water is important in the body as it is the solvent in which chemical reactions take place, is it also the solvent in which waste matter is transported and passed out of the body. Water is an important component of blood and **lymph**.

- Fibre can be soluble or insoluble. It is important in the diet as it adds bulk to food and maintains peristalsis in the digestive system.

B10 Human digestion

- **Digestion** is the process of breaking down food. It takes place in the organs of the digestive system.

- Food enters the digestive system through the mouth (**ingestion**). It then moves through the digestive system where it is broken down by mechanical and chemical digestion before being passed out of the body in the process of **egestion**.

- In mechanical digestion, food is physically broken down into smaller pieces. In chemical digestion, food is chemically changed into smaller, water-soluble molecules. Enzymes play an important role in the reactions that break down food.

- The human digestive system consists of the mouth, the oesophagus, the stomach, the pancreas, the liver, the gall bladder, the small intestine and the large intestine.

- Some food is not digested. Some vitamins are small soluble molecules already and cellulose cannot be digested by humans. Food is moved through the intestines by the process of **peristalsis**.

- Teeth are important in digestion. Without teeth we cannot chew and break down solid food.

- Humans have four different types of teeth: incisors, canines, premolars and molars. These teeth are positioned in the mouth according to their function.

- **Absorption** is the movement of substances into the cells of an organism. Most absorption takes place in the ileum, where the villi increase the surface area to allow for maximum absorption.

- Once food is absorbed, it is transported to the liver for distribution to the various cells of the body. Once the food has been ingested, digested, absorbed and transported to the cells, it becomes part of the body. In other words it becomes **assimilated** and forms the raw material for metabolic processes and chemical reactions.

- The amount of energy you get from food is measured in kilojoules. The number of kilojoules that you need depends on your gender, age, how active you are and whether you live in a warm or cold place.

- A **balanced diet** contains the right amount of food from different groups in the right proportions.

- An unbalanced diet can lead to **malnutrition**, which can lead to health problems and nutritional diseases such as marasmus.

- Some people follow a **vegetarian** diet. This does not include meat.

B11 Respiration

- Food is converted to chemical energy by the process of **cellular respiration**. Respiration is not the same as breathing.

- **Aerobic respiration** is the breaking down of glucose in the presence of oxygen to release energy. Glucose and oxygen are the raw materials for aerobic respiration. Carbon dioxide and water are the products of aerobic respiration.

- During respiration, energy is released slowly in small amounts so that it does not kill cells. ADP in cells is converted to ATP. This is the chemical that carries energy to the parts of the body that need it.

- **Anaerobic respiration** is the breaking down of glucose without oxygen to release energy. It takes place in the cytoplasm of cells and does not involve the production of ATP.

- In plants, cellular respiration and photosynthesis form a cycle. The products of one process are the raw materials for the other.

B12 Gaseous exchange

- **Gaseous exchange** is the ability to exchange gases across a surface. In humans, breathing allows gaseous exchange to take place across the respiratory surfaces of the lungs.

- The human respiratory system consists of air passages, a pair of lungs and breathing muscles which move the chest and allow air to enter and exit.

- The surfaces of the air passages and lungs are covered by mucous membranes which trap bacteria, viruses and dust and also keep the air moist and warm so that dry air does not enter and harm the lungs.

- In the lungs, the alveoli enlarge the surface area for gaseous exchange between the air in the lungs and the blood in the capillaries of the body. The oxygen that passes into the blood dissolves or combines with haemoglobin to be transported to the tissues of the body. At the same time, carbon dioxide is passed from the blood into the lungs to be exhaled.

- Breathing depends on the muscles in the chest cavity. Breathing involves inhaling air, a short rest period and exhaling air.

- All gaseous exchange surfaces are thin, moist, large in surface area, well supplied with blood vessels and in contact with the atmosphere so that a sufficient supply of gases can move across the surfaces quickly and continuously.

- Fish and other organisms that live in water use oxygen that is dissolved in the water. The exchange of gases can take place across the surface of the body wall or through gills.

- People who smoke cigarettes expose their lungs to serious risk. Cigarettes contain many harmful chemicals and toxins. Smokers face the risk of lung damage, heart disease and various cancers.

B13 Transport and circulation

- Multicellular organisms do not have a large enough surface area to absorb what they need from the atmosphere. They need a transport system so that cellular needs can be met.

- In humans, the transport system is called the **circulatory system** and the medium of transport is the blood.

- Oxygen, carbon dioxide, digested foods, urea and other nitrogenous wastes, hormones and heat are transported in the blood.

- The circulatory system is made up of the heart and the blood vessels. The heart acts as a pump to keep the blood circulating through the body in the blood vessels. There are three types of blood vessel: arteries, veins and capillaries.

- Blood from the heart flows in the arteries. Blood that flows to the heart flows in the veins. Capillaries are tiny vessels that link arteries to veins and form dense networks in the organs and tissues so that materials can be exchanged.

- **Tissue fluid** is a liquid that leaks from the blood into the spaces between cells and allows for the exchange of materials between cells and the blood. The tissue fluid passes back into the circulatory system through the lymphatic system.

- Mammals have a double circulation. The heart is divided into two halves and the blood in these two halves does not mix. The route followed by the blood is:

  body ——→ heart ——→ lungs ——→ heart ——→ body.

- The heart is the pump that moves the blood through the arteries and veins. It is made of smooth cardiac muscle and it pumps continuously throughout your life.

- The heart works by contracting and relaxing. When the heart relaxes, it fills up with blood, when it contracts, it forces the blood through the body.

- The movement of the heart produces a two-tone sound (the heartbeat) that can be heard through a stethoscope.

- Blood has many different functions in mammals. It transports substances through the body, it protects the body from microbes, it regulates the body temperature and it clots if the skin is broken to prevent excess blood loss.

- Blood is composed of plasma (water and dissolved substances) and blood cells. There are three main types of blood cell: red blood cells, white blood cells and platelets.

- Red blood cells contain the protein haemoglobin which combines readily with oxygen. White blood cells are larger than red blood cells; their main function is to help the body fight invasion by harmful substances. Platelets are important for helping blood to clot.

- The human body's defence system against pathogens is called the **immune system**. The immune system includes the skin, parts of the respiratory and digestive systems and the blood.

- **Immunity** is the body's resistance to a specific disease. Substances which cause an immune response are called **antigens**. The immune response involves the blood and the production of antibodies.

- Natural immunity is obtained when your body recognises a pathogen and fights it off. Natural immunity gives resistance to diseases such as chicken pox and measles.

- **Immunisation** makes you immune to a disease by giving you a substance that provides artificial immunity. The substance is normally called a **vaccine**. Vaccines can provide either **active** or **passive immunity**.

B14 Transport and water relations in plants

- Plants are multi-cellular organisms, so they need a transport system. This consists of a network of tubes and specialised tissue called xylem and phloem. Xylem transports water and phloem transports food.

- Xylem tubes or vessels are made from dead cells thickened with woody material called lignin. The tubes are long, thin and well suited for transporting water.

- The movement of water through plants depends on transpiration (the evaporation of water from the leaves of the plant to the air). In the xylem, water forms an unbroken column. The water that is lost through transpiration has to be replaced by water taken in through the roots or the plant will die. This constant movement of water through the plant is called the transpiration stream.

- The water lost through the leaves creates a transpiration pull which draws water upwards to replace the water that is lost. At the same time, more water enters the xylem through the roots to replace the water drawn up the xylem.

- Transpiration normally takes place during the day but it is affected by various environmental factors, such as temperature, humidity, wind speed, light intensity and the water content of the soil.

- Plants take in mineral ions through their roots by active transport. Once in the roots, these mineral ions are transported to the rest of the plant in the xylem.

- Phloem transports food materials, mostly in the form of sugars, up and down the stem to all parts of the plants. The movement of sugars and other substances from one region to another through the sieve cells is called translocation.

- Plants also need to maintain a water balance and to conserve water and prevent water loss through transpiration.

- Plants are adapted to slow or reduce the rate of transpiration, to store water in times of shortage and to increase water uptake as much as possible.

B15 Food storage

- Humans and other animals are able to store energy in their bodies in the form of glycogen and fat.

- The main storage organ for glycogen is the liver, but it can also be stored in the muscles where it is rapidly converted into glucose by metabolic processes.

- Fat is an important storage compound for energy. Fat is stored in adipose tissue under the skin of humans and other animals.

- If your energy intake is greater than the amount of energy your body needs, the excess is stored as fat. Too much stored fat can lead to obesity and other health problems.

- Plants store food so that they have a supply of glucose for cellular respiration during periods when they are not photosynthesising, and so that they have the energy they need to produce new plants.

- Plants store food in the form of sugar and oil. Food can be stored in the roots, stems, leaves, fruit and seeds of plants.

B16 Excretion and osmoregulation

- Excretion is important because it allows the body to get rid of waste products, such as carbon dioxide, urea, bile pigments and oxygen formed by metabolic activity.

- The main excretory product in plants is oxygen which is the product of photosynthesis. Other organic waste products include acids, calcium ions and calcium oxalate.

- The main excretory products in animals are carbon dioxide, nitrogenous compounds and bile pigments.

- Different animals have different structures for excretion. These include Malphigian tubules and trachea in arthropods; gills, skin, liver and kidneys in fish and amphibians; and the skin, lungs, liver and kidneys in humans and other mammals.

- The main excretory organs in humans are the kidneys. The kidneys filter 'dirty' blood and produce urine which is passed out the body during urination.

- Besides excretion, the kidneys also play a role in osmoregulation, they maintain osmotic pressure in the body fluids and they regulate the pH of blood by controlling the acid–base balance in the blood.

- Osmoregulation is the process of maintaining the balance between water and salts in body fluids. The amount of water you gain and lose is largely controlled by the kidneys. The action of the kidneys is controlled by ADH. The process of releasing ADH relies on a system of negative feedback.

- Plants also need to maintain a water balance and to conserve water and prevent water loss through transpiration.

- Plants are adapted to slow or reduce the rate of transpiration, to store water in times of shortage and to increase water uptake as much as possible.

B17 Support, movement and locomotion

- The human skeleton consists of 206 bones and cartilage divided into the axial and the appendicular skeleton.

- The skeleton has four main functions: protection, support, movement and the production of blood cells.

- Bone is a type of light, strong, connective tissue. The outside layer is dense and hard because it is made up of calcium salts. Underneath this is a layer of spongy bone. The centre of the bone is filled with marrow. The ends of the bone are covered with a layer of cartilage.

- The axial skeleton consists of the skull, vertebral column and the ribs. In the vertebral column, there are different types of vertebra, adapted to suit their function.

- The cervical vertebrae support the head and neck, the thoracic vertebrae anchor the ribs and the lumbar vertebrae support the strong, weight-bearing regions towards the bottom of the spine.

- Muscles and bones work together to produce movement. When muscles contract they pull against bones so that they move at a joint. Muscles work in antagonistic pairs.

- Different types of muscle perform different functions in the body. Smooth muscle contracts and relaxes slowly and steadily, it is found in the walls of the intestine and the air passages. Skeletal muscles are striated and their action is voluntary. This type of muscle is found in the arms and legs. Cardiac muscle is striated, it never becomes tired and its action is involuntary.

- Limbs work together as a series of levers. The joint serves as a fulcrum and the effort is produced by the muscles. Bones are joined in different ways: synovial joints, ball-and-socket joints and hinge joints.

- Different animals move in different ways depending on the type of skeleton they have. Insects move using muscle pairs and joints, earthworms move using their hydrostatic skeletons and fish swim by pushing their bodies and fins against the water.

B18 Stimulus and response

- A stimulus produces a change in action or behaviour in an organism. The change or action is called a response.

- Plants respond to various stimuli, including light, temperature, water and contact. Their responses are called tropisms. Some plant tropisms include phototropism, geotropism and hydrotropism.

- Invertebrates respond to stimuli such as light, temperature and moisture by moving towards or away from the stimulus. These responses are called taxic responses.

B19 Coordination and response

- Organisms need to be able to respond to stimuli in their environment in order to survive.

- Humans have five senses which allow them to detect stimuli and respond to them. We use our sense organs the eyes, ears, tongue, nose and skin to detect stimuli. These organs are called receptors. The muscles and glands that allow the body to respond to the stimuli are called effectors.

- The nervous system is responsible for coordinating responses to stimuli. The human nervous system is divided into a peripheral and a central nervous system.

- The nervous system contains nerves and neurones. There are two types of neurones: sensory neurones and motor neurones.

- Sensory neurones transmit impulses from receptors to the spinal cord and brain. Motor neurones transmit impulses from the spinal cord to the various effectors.

- Nerve impulses travel along neurones and across synapses. Nerve impulses always travel in one direction from the axon of one neurone to the dendrite on another.

- Nerves which are directly connected to the brain are called cranial nerves. Nerves which are connected to the spinal cord are called spinal nerves.

- An autonomic response to a stimulus is called a reflex response. The nerves involved in a reflex response are called a reflex arc.

- The brain is the most developed part of the nervous system. The brain is divided into three regions: the forebrain, the midbrain and the hind-brain.

- The actions of your internal organs are controlled by the autonomic nervous system.

- Drugs are substances that affect the functioning of the body. Drugs given as medicines can help people to fight disease and control pain. However, some people take drugs they do not need and they may become addicted to these.

- Some drugs are illegal substances that people abuse because they become addicted to the substances. Depressants, stimulants and hallucinogens are all examples of drugs that are abused.

- Tobacco, alcohol and caffeine are also drugs. People can become addicted to these in the same way they become addicted to illegal drugs. Tobacco and alcohol can harm the body. Alcohol abuse can lead to social and economic problems as well.

- The human eye is a sense organ. The structure of the eye is related to its function. The eye has a lens that allows light into the eye. This light forms an image on the retina. Impulses from the retina are sent to the brain via the optic nerve. The lens also accommodates to make sure that objects are in focus.

- Sight defects include short-sightedness and long-sightedness. These defects can be corrected by spectacles or contact lenses containing concave or convex lenses.

B20 Homeostasis and control

- The process of keeping conditions inside cells constant is called homeostasis. This process relies on negative feedback.

- Negative feedback plays an important role in ensuring oxygen levels in the blood are constant, blood pressure is stable and body temperature is stable, etc.

- Hormones play an important role in homeostasis. For example, insulin and glucagon make sure the glucose levels in the blood are constant.

- In humans, the skin is the largest single organ and it plays an important role in temperature control. The skin works together with receptors in the hypothalamus to control temperature.

B21 Growth and development

- Growth is a permanent increase in size. Development is the way that organisms become more complex as they grow. Cellular changes are involved in growth and development.

- Most plants grow from seeds. The seed contains the embryo of the plant which develops into roots, stems and leaves. The growth of plants can be shown on a graph called a growth curve.

- Arthropods grow in stages because they have to moult and shed their hard exoskeleton at each stage of growth, the body can only expand when the new exoskeleton is soft enough to stretch. Growing in a series of moults is called an incomplete metamorphosis.

- In some insects, such as butterflies and wasps, the changes from stage to stage are more dramatic because they involve a complete change from larvae, to pupae to adult insect. This is called complete metamorphosis.

- Growth in plants and animals can be measured using wet and dry mass or other indicators like length, height, number of leaves, area or number of organisms.

- Growth statistics can be shown on curves and histograms

B22 Reproduction in plants

- Reproduction means producing offspring. Plants can reproduce asexually or sexually. Asexual reproduction involves only one parent and no gametes are involved. Sexual reproduction involves two parents and the production of gametes.

- Plants produced asexually show no variation from the parent plant. Plants produced by sexual reproduction show variation from the parent plants.

- Flowers are the reproductive organs in flowering plants. The flower contains both male and female organs. The parts of the flower are specialised for their function in reproduction.

- Pollen grains must pass from the anthers to the stigma so that the male gametes can fertilise the female gamete in the ovule. This process is called pollination.

- Flowers can be pollinated by birds, insects and wind. Flowers that are pollinated by wind are structurally different from flowers that are pollinated by birds and insects.

- Self-pollination happens when pollen from a flower fertilises the same flower or another flower on the same plant. Cross-pollination takes place when the pollen from one flower fertilises a flower on another plant.

- **Fertilisation** takes place when the pollen grains land on the stigma. Once fertilisation has taken place, the pollen grows a tube to reach the ovule. Once it reaches the ovule, the pollen nucleus fuses with the ovum nucleus to form a fertilised **zygote**.

- A **seed** is a fertilised zygote. After fertilisation the ovary of most plants develops into the fruit. The fruit contains the seed or seeds of the plant.

- To germinate, most seeds need warmth, water and oxygen. Germination below the ground is called **hypogeal germination**. Germination above the ground is called **epigeal germination**.

- Seeds are spread out or **dispersed** to give plants a better chance of survival. The main methods of dispersal are by wind and by animals. However some seeds are dispersed mechanically and some by water.

B23 Human reproduction

- Male and female human beings have different sexual organs which are adapted to their functions in reproduction.

- The male reproductive system consists of the penis and the testes. Their function is to produce **spermatozoa** and to transfer these to the female reproductive organs for fertilisation.

- The female reproductive system consists of the ovaries and uterus. Its function is to produce **ova** which can be fertilised to develop into an embryo and foetus that is carried inside the uterus until the mother gives birth.

- The **menstrual cycle** in females is the cycle in which a mature ovum is produced each month. The menstrual cycles is controlled by hormones: follicle stimulating hormone and luteinising hormone. **Ovulation** takes place around the fourteenth day of the cycle.

- During sexual intercourse, the female ovum can be fertilised by a male sperm cell. Fertilisation takes place when the male gamete fuses with the female gamete to form a zygote. After fertilisation, the zygote develops into an embryo which is **implanted** in the uterus wall.

- The **placenta** connects the embryo to the mother's blood system and oxygen. Food and waste products are passed between mother and foetus by diffusion across the placenta.

- The time taken for the foetus to develop into a baby is called the **gestation period**. At the end of the gestation period the mother gives birth and a human baby is born. After the birth, the placenta is expelled through the vagina.

- Humans are able to make decisions about whether or not to have children. There are various methods of birth control that can be used to prevent pregnancy. Each of these methods has advantages and disadvantages.

- **Sexually transmitted infections** (STIs) are passed from person to person by sexual activity. Some STIs are very serious, and there is no known cure for HIV/AIDS, so it is important to protect yourself from STIs by appropriate behaviour and preventative methods.

B24 Understanding disease

- A **disease** is any condition that impairs the functioning of cells, tissues and organs. There are four main groups of diseases: **pathogenic**, **deficiency**, **hereditary** and **physiological**.

- Pathogenic diseases such as TB, cholera and measles, are caused by pathogens (bacteria, viruses, fungi or protozoa). **Infectious** or **communicable** diseases can be passed from person to person.

- Non-infectious diseases cannot be passed from person to person. Deficiency diseases, hereditary diseases and physiological diseases are not infectious.

- Infectious diseases can be controlled by measures which affect the host, the **pathogen** or the environment.

- **Resistance** is the ability to fight off disease. Resistance can be improved by keeping your body healthy and by improving hygiene. Diet and exercise can also play a role in preventing disease, particularly non-infectious diseases.

- Diseases can also be transmitted by vectors. A **vector** is an organism, such as a mosquito, which carries the pathogen and helps it to spread.

Do you know these key terms?

- uni-cellular organisms (p74)
- multi-cellular (p74)
- tissue (p77)
- organ (p77)
- diffusion (p80)
- osmosis (p82)
- turgid (p83)
- turgor pressure (p83)
- plasmolysed (p84)
- osmoregulation (p84 and 168)
- photosynthesis (p86)
- limiting factors (p94)
- macro-nutrients (p95)
- micro-nutrients (p95)
- monosaccharides (p98)
- disaccharide (p98)
- condensation reaction (p98)
- hydrolysis (p98)
- polysaccharides (p99)
- saturated fats (p99)
- monounsaturated fats (p99)
- polyunsaturated fats (p99)
- enzymes (p101)
- digestion (p105)
- ingestion (p105)
- egestion (p105)
- peristalsis (p108)
- absorption (p111)
- deamination (p112)
- assimilated (p113)
- balanced diet (p113)
- malnutrition (p116)
- vegetarians (p117)
- cellular respiration (p118)
- aerobic respiration (p118)
- anaerobic respiration (p120)
- gaseous exchange (p125)
- circulatory system (p137)
- capillaries (p137)
- tissue fluid (p138)
- immune system (p145)
- immunity (p145)
- antigens (p145)
- antibodies (p146)
- immunisation (p146)
- vaccine (p146)
- active immunity (p147)
- passive immunity (p147)
- xylem (p149)
- phloem (p149)
- vascular system (p149)
- transpiration (p151)
- transpiration stream (p152)
- transpiration pull (p152)
- capillarity (p152)
- root pressure (p152)
- evapo-transpiration (p153)
- relative humidity (p153)
- active transport (p155)
- translocation (p156)
- hydrophytes (p158)
- halophytes (p158)
- mesophytes (p158)
- xerophytes (p158)
- metabolism (p164)
- excretion (p164)
- cartilage (p170)
- tendons (p170)
- ligaments (p170)
- endoskeleton (p170)
- exoskeleton (p170)
- cervical vertebrae (p172)
- thoracic vertebrae (p172)
- lumbar vertebrae (p172)
- intervertebral discs (p176)
- synovial (p177)
- fulcrum (p177)

- ball-and-socket joint (p177)
- hinge joints (p177)
- stimulus (p182)
- response (p182)
- tropisms (p183)
- phototropisms (p183)
- geotropisms (p183)
- hydrotropisms (p183)
- taxis, taxic response (p186)
- reflex arc (p192)
- spinal reflexes (p192)
- cranial reflexes (p193)
- cerebrum (p194)
- cerebellum (p194)
- medulla (p195)
- autonomic nervous system (p195)
- sympathetic system (p196)
- parasympathetic system (p196)
- accommodation (p200)
- rods (p201)
- cones (p201)
- short-sighted (p202)
- diverging (concave) lenses (p202)
- long-sighted (p203)
- converging (convex) lenses (p203)
- bifocal lens (p204)
- homeostasis (p205)
- negative feedback (p205)
- growth (p209)
- development (p209)
- seed (p209 and 225)
- moulting, ecdysis (p211)
- metamorphosis (p211)
- incomplete metamorphosis (p211)
- complete metamorphosis (p211)
- wet mass (p213)
- dry mass (p213)
- reproduction (p217)

- sexual reproduction (p217)
- asexual reproduction (p217)
- gametes (p217)
- stamens (p219)
- carpels (p219)
- pollen (p219)
- ovules (p219)
- zygote (p219)
- pollination (p221)
- wind-pollinated (p221)
- insect-pollinated (p221)
- self-pollination (p221)
- cross-pollination (p222)
- fertilisation (p223)
- endosperm (p223)
- cotyledon (p225)
- dicotyledonous (p225)
- monocotyledonous (p225)
- germination (p226)
- hypogeal germination (p226)
- epigeal germination (p226)
- dispersal (p227)
- sperm (p230)
- ovum (p230)
- menstrual cycle (p233)
- ovulation (p233)
- implantation (p236)
- sexually transmitted infections (STIs) (p240)
- disease (p242)
- infectious or communicable diseases (p242)
- pathogen (p242)
- deficiency diseases (p243)
- hereditary diseases (p243)
- physiological diseases (p243)
- resistance (p244)
- cholesterol (p246)
- vector (p249)

Practice exam-style questions

Working through these questions will help you to revise the content of this section and prepare you for your examination. The number of marks available for each question gives you an idea about how much detail to put in your answer.

1 The diagram shows a leaf cut lengthways:

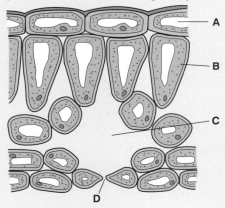

a) Label the parts A, B, C and D. [1KC]
b) Name and describe the stages involved in the process by which the food is made. [1KC, 4UK]
c) State THREE differences between plant and animal cells. [3KC]
d) Choose TWO of the cells show in the diagram, and for EACH:

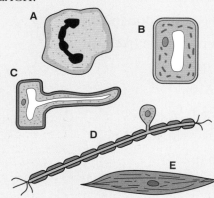

   i) name the cell chosen
   ii) describe how its structure allows it to perform its function efficiently. [2KC, 2UK]
e) With reference to the amoeba, explain why singled-celled organisms do not need cell specialisation. [2UK]

[Total 15 marks]

2 The following questions refer to the graph, showing the rate of reaction of enzymes A, B and C in a range of pH from 0 to 14.

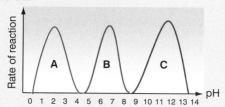

a) **i)** Where in the digestive system would enzyme A be secreted?
   ii) Which enzyme is enzyme A likely be?
   iii) Which enzyme is enzyme C likely be? [3KC]
b) A blue-black compound is formed when dilute iodine solution reacts with starch. This colour disappears if the starch is broken down. Three test tubes were set up as shown below:

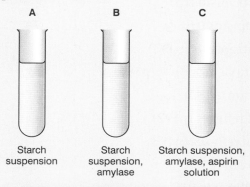

Add a few drops of iodine to each tube	Test tube A	Test tube B	Test tube C
Results after 15 minutes	Blue-black	Colourless	Pale blue

   i) What can you deduce about the action of amylase on the starch from test tubes A and B? [1UK]
   ii) How does the presence of aspirin, in test tube C, appear to affect the action of the amylase? [1KC]
   iii) Suggest TWO precautions that should have been taken to give the results greater validity. In EACH case explain the reason for the precaution. [2KC, 2UK]
c) Discuss THREE reasons why a person who is obese is equally at risk of health problems as an underfed person. [3UK]

[Total 12 marks]

3 a) What is the relationship between surface area : volume ratio and diffusion? [1KC]
b) Copy and complete the table below to briefly describe the mechanisms for increasing surface area in humans, fish and plants. [3UK]

Organism	Mechanisms for increasing surface area
Human	
Fish	
Plants	

c) The graph on p269 shows the percentage of children who say that they have smoked cigarettes (by age and gender).

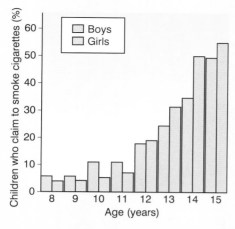

i) Draw ONE conclusion based on the graph. [1UK]

ii) One effect of smoking is the destruction of the lining of the alveoli and the formation of scar tissue. Describe how this affects gaseous exchange. [2UK]

d) i) Explain how carbon monoxide affects the way in which red blood cells function. [1UK]

ii) Explain the role of the blood in fighting off infection. [3UK]

e) What are parts A, B, C and D in the following diagram? [4KC]

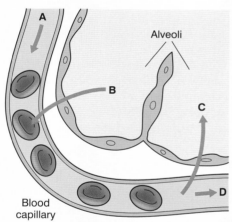

[Total 15 marks]

4 a) Explain the role of a named vector in the transmission of a named disease. [3KC]

b) Your friend has fallen ill and complains of high fever. He had taken some over-the-counter flu medication and by the time you visit he was well enough to be moving about. However, his symptoms begin returning every other day.

i) What disease could you tell him that these symptoms resemble? [1KC]

ii) What explanation could you give him about the cause of these symptoms? [3UK]

c) i) How does knowledge of the mosquito help us to reduce mosquito infestation in our environment? Include the habitat and mode of life of each stage. [5UK]

ii) The larvae of flies have been used to clean infected wounds.
Why would a wound like that be protected from flies? [3UK]

[Total 15 marks]

5 Two students each placed a stem of celery into separate beakers containing red coloured solution, and labelled them Student A and Student B. Student A forgot to place his celery outside in the sun as instructed. After one hour, when they each cut a cross-section at the top of the stem, student B saw red-stained tissue and student A saw none.

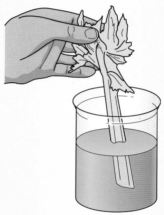

a) i) What tissue did student B observe? [1KC]

ii) Explain how water travels through the stem of the celery. [2UK]

b) Student A noticed the stain near the base of the stalk when a cross-section cut was made. Explain why student A did not observe a stain at the top of the stalk. [2UK]

c) Plants that live in dry, desert-like areas often have some leaves modified into spines and sunken stomata. State TWO ways in which these modifications help the plant to survive in deserts. [2KC]

d) i) Discuss the importance of food storage in living organisms using three examples. [3UK]

ii) Discuss the economic implications of a farmer planting his crops in soil that is nitrogen-deficient. [3UK]

iii) Explain how the structure of the phloem tubes facilitates the transport of food in plants. [2UK]

[Total 15 marks]

6 Study the table below and answer the questions that follow.

	Concentration (%)		
Substance	In liquid part of blood	In liquid that has been filtered in the kidneys	In liquid in the bladder
Protein	7.0	0	0
Salt	0.35	0.35	0.5
Glucose	0.1	0.1	0
Urea	0.03	0.03	2.0

a) **i)** Suggest ONE reason why urea levels are higher in the bladder than in the blood. [1UK]

ii) Name the parts of the kidney where the following occur:
- ultra-filtration
- reabsorption of water. [2KC]

iii) Discuss the causes and effects of diabetes. [3KC]

iv) High blood pressure (hypertension) and protein detected in the urine are two symptoms which may indicate that the kidney is malfunctioning. Explain fully. [3UK]

b) On a hot day, you may find yourself drinking more water. Explain the response caused by the hormone ADH. [4UK]

c) Explain the process by which tannins and calcium oxalate are excreted by plants. [2UK]

[Total 15 marks]

7 a) James lit a match but burnt his finger. Using a labelled diagram of a reflex arc, explain what happened. Include the words stimulus, response, reflex arc, motor neurones, and sensory neurones. [6UK]

b) Keith was reading a book under a shady plum tree and was distracted by a beautiful bird flying in the sky above him. Describe all the changes in his eyes from reading the book to looking on the bird. [4UK]

c) **i)** Copy and label the following parts on the lumbar vertebra:

- centrum
- neural spine. [2KC]

ii) What type of levers would be used in the following actions?
- Lifting a bag.
- Standing on your toes.
- Nodding your head. [3KC]

[Total 15 marks]

8 a) Describe the events which occur after the release of spermatozoa into the vagina of a human female until implantation of the embryo. [4UK]

b) The chart below shows how the thickness of the uterus lining and the levels of two hormones A and B, made in the ovaries, vary during the menstrual cycle. The first month is a normal menstrual cycle but fertilisation occurs during the second month.

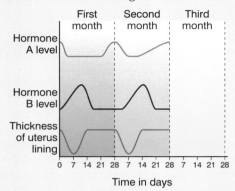

i) Which is the most likely time of ovulation in the first month?

ii) When in the second month is fertilisation likely to have occurred? [2 KC]

c) Copy and complete the chart above to show what happens, following fertilisation, to:
i) the uterus lining in the third month
ii) the levels of hormones A and B in the third month. [3 UK]

d) **i)** Suggest ONE method of contraception that is most effective in preventing transmission of HIV and other STIs. [1KC]

ii) Give ONE reason why some married couples are opposed to the use of contraceptives. [1KC]

iii) A couple has not been able to conceive. Suggest a possible reason for this. What advice would you give to overcome this problem? [1KC, 3UK]

[Total 15 marks]

9 A mother has decided to refuse immunisation for her child as she intends to breastfeed for a year.

a) In your explanation of the importance of immunisation, differentiate between natural and artificial immunisation. [4UK]

'Disease can cause loss of livestock and agricultural crops.'

b) Discuss the statement above by reference to **two** diseases [4UK]

c) **i)** State TWO immediate effects of alcohol abuse and TWO long-term effects. [4KC]

ii) Outline ONE way in which drug abusers may transmit a named disease without sexual contact. [3KC]

[Total 15 marks]

C25 Cell division

Cell division is the first step in the life of any organism. Cells divide to form new cells, which increases the number of cells that form the plant or animal. Cells can divide in two ways – the cells of the body divide by mitosis and the cells of the sex organs, which produce gametes, divide by meiosis.

C25.1 Mitosis

New cells are formed when old cells divide. The cells that divide are called parent cells and the new cells which form are called daughter cells. Two overlapping processes take place in cell division:

- the nucleus of the cell divides
- the cytoplasm divides.

However, before the cell can divide, the parts of the cell must be replicated (copied exactly) so that the daughter cells will have all the parts they need to continue with the process of life.

Chromosomes

The nucleus of a cell contains many thread-like chromosomes. These chromosomes control the activities in the cell and they carry the genes, made up of long strands of deoxyribonucleic acid (DNA, see p276) that determine the characteristics of an organism. Our genes are contained in our DNA (see Figure 25.1.1).

Each cell in the body has a specific number of chromosomes, arranged in homologous pairs. In humans, each cell of the body contains 23 pairs of chromosomes to give 46 chromosomes in all. Gametes (sperm, i.e. spermatozoa in males, and eggs, i.e. ova in females) have only 23 chromosomes. This is half the number of chromosomes in each body cell.

Each living organism has a specific number of chromosomes in each cell. Different species have different numbers of chromosomes. Humans have 23 pairs, cats have 19 pairs, chickens have 18 pairs, kangaroos have 6 pairs and fruit flies have only 4 pairs. When a new organism is formed, the chromosome number in each cell must remain the same. So, in humans, an embryo at the start of pregnancy must have 23 pairs of chromosomes. A sperm has 23 chromosomes and an egg has 23 chromosomes. When these gametes fuse during fertilisation, the new cell which is formed has 46 chromosomes, or 23 pairs, the normal number for a human.

Cell division by mitosis

You have seen that each new daughter cell formed by cell division must have the correct number of chromosomes. In the cells of the body, which have 46 chromosomes, cell division takes place by mitosis. You will look at how gametes divide by meiosis in topic C25.2.

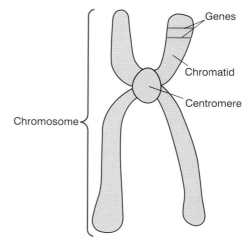

▲ **Figure 25.1.1** Structure of a chromosome

Mitosis divides the chromosomes of the parent cell into two identical groups. Cells that divide through mitosis to receive the full number of chromosomes from their parent cells and, in turn, pass these on to their daughter cells are described as having the diploid (or 2*n*) number of chromsomes.

Stages in mitosis

The diagram in Figure 25.1.2 shows you what happens during mitosis in a cell with four chromosomes.

The importance of mitosis

Because daughter cells each receive an identical full (diploid) set of chromosomes from the parent cell, daughter cells and the parent cell are genetically identical. This is why mitosis is the way in which living things repair damage to the body, grow and reproduce asexually. For example:

- parent cheek cells divide by mitosis into identical daughter cheek cells
- parent skin cells divide by mitosis into identical daughter skin cells
- parent root cells divide by mitosis into identical daughter root cells.

Mitosis replaces old body cells with new ones, with the result that the individual stays the same. This is why our appearance does not change from week to week, even though the surface cells of the skin have been replaced in the intervening period.

The role of mitosis in asexual reproduction

The cell division that takes place in asexual reproduction is as a result of mitosis. This means that the offspring produced during asexual reproduction are genetically identical to each other and also to the parent organism. Genetically identical individuals are called clones.

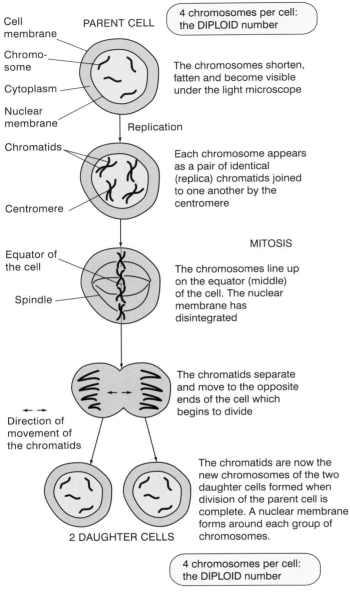

▲ **Figure 25.1.2** Cell division by mitosis

Remember that in asexual reproduction, only one parent organism is involved in producing the offspring. During mitosis, the parent's DNA is replicated (copied exactly) and these exact copies of the DNA are passed on to the daughter cells. We can represent this process as follows:

parent cells $\xrightarrow[\text{of DNA}]{\text{replication}}$ mitosis $\xrightarrow[\text{inherited}]{\substack{\text{exact copies} \\ \text{of parent DNA}}}$ daughter cells $\xrightarrow{\text{develop}}$ genetically identical offspring

In Unit B22, you dealt with different methods of asexual reproduction in plants. The ability to produce copies of the parent plant is important in agriculture, particularly in the production of crops such as sugar cane.

Sugar cane plants are generally produced by asexual reproduction using parts from the parent plant. The most common methods used in the Caribbean involve taking a piece of the stem from a parent plant (a sett) or a cutting from the parent plant. Cuttings must contain at least one node, as the primary roots of the new plant will grow from the node.

Laboratory cloning

For the past 30 or so years, scientists have been able to clone animals in laboratory conditions. To do this, they either use tissue from a donor animal or they split an early embryo into smaller groups of cells. These groups of cells are then allowed to develop into a new embryo. Cloned laboratory animals are often used in medical research. The fact that the animals are genetically identical provides a sort of 'control group' situation and allows researchers to be sure that their results are due to the experimental process rather than the genetic make-up of the animals.

Cloning by embryo splitting can also be used to increase numbers of endangered species. In this method, the split embryos are often implanted into surrogate mothers who then give birth to genetically identical offspring.

Cloning can also be used in human medicine although there may be ethical and moral issues involved in this. For example, human embryos can be produced outside the human body by extracting female ova and then artificially fertilising these (this is called in vitro fertilisation). The embryo produced by in vitro fertilisation can be split to produce a number of clones. Some of these clones are then subjected to genetic testing to make sure the resultant offspring will be disease-free. If the embryos are found to contain any genetically transmitted diseases they can be destroyed before implantation. If not, then one (or usually more) of the cloned embryos are implanted into the mother's uterus where they can develop into human babies.

> **! Key fact**
>
> Although most cells of the body can divide by mitosis, brain cells cannot. A human baby is born with approximately 30 000 brain cells and will not produce any more. Brain cells start to die as the body ages, which is why older people may find it difficult to remember things and why hearing and sight can be lost with old age.

Questions

1 What are chromosomes? Where are they found and what is their function?

2 Why do gametes contain half the number of chromosomes that other body cells have?

3 Where does mitosis take place?

4 Why does mitosis take place?

5 Uni-cellular organisms, such as amoeba, bacteria and viruses do not have male and female gametes. They only have one body cell. Explain how these organisms can reproduce quickly with reference to the diagram in Figure 25.1.3.

6 Explain what is meant by the term 'clone' and why the formation of clones is dependent on mitosis.

7 Why do you think some people are opposed to any form of human cloning?

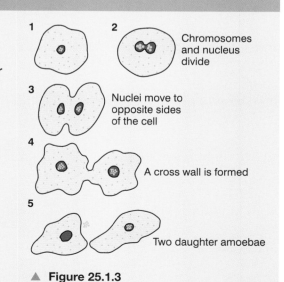

▲ **Figure 25.1.3**

C25.2 Meiosis

Objectives

By the end of this topic you will be able to:

- outline the process of meiosis
- use arrow diagrams to describe meiosis
- state the importance of halving the chromosome number in the formation of gametes
- understand the role of gametes in determining the sex of an individual.

Although most cells of the human body have 46 chromosomes in 23 pairs, the gametes are different. Each gamete has only 23 chromosomes. This means that an egg cell has 23 chromosomes and a sperm cell has 23 chromosomes. Only the cells in the reproductive organs divide to produce gametes. This type of cell division is called meiosis and it takes place in the ovaries and testes of humans and the anthers and ovaries of plants to produce the gametes (male and female gametes).

When a human egg cell and sperm cell fuse to form a zygote, their chromosomes combine to give the zygote 46 chromosomes in 23 pairs. Figure 25.2.1 shows you how this happens.

Once formed, the zygote continues to divide by mitosis to form more cells each with 23 pairs of chromosomes.

Cell division by meiosis

Meiosis halves the number of chromosomes in the parent cell. The half number of chromosomes in the daughter cells is described as haploid (or *n*). Figure 25.2.2 shows you the process of meiosis. Read the information next to the diagram carefully and notice that there are two cell divisions.

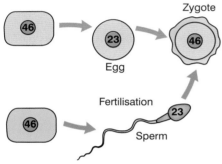

▲ **Figure 25.2.1** Gametes with 23 chromosomes each fuse to form a zygote with 46 chromosomes (23 pairs)

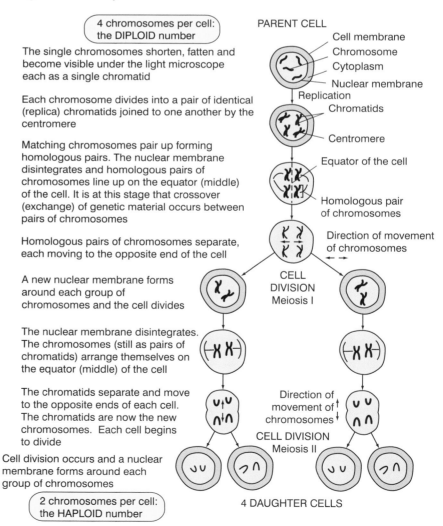

4 chromosomes per cell: the DIPLOID number

The single chromosomes shorten, fatten and become visible under the light microscope each as a single chromatid

Each chromosome divides into a pair of identical (replica) chromatids joined to one another by the centromere

Matching chromosomes pair up forming homologous pairs. The nuclear membrane disintegrates and homologous pairs of chromosomes line up on the equator (middle) of the cell. It is at this stage that crossover (exchange) of genetic material occurs between pairs of chromosomes

Homologous pairs of chromosomes separate, each moving to the opposite end of the cell

A new nuclear membrane forms around each group of chromosomes and the cell divides

The nuclear membrane disintegrates. The chromosomes (still as pairs of chromatids) arrange themselves on the equator (middle) of the cell

The chromatids separate and move to the opposite ends of each cell. The chromatids are now the new chromosomes. Each cell begins to divide

Cell division occurs and a nuclear membrane forms around each group of chromosomes

2 chromosomes per cell: the HAPLOID number

PARENT CELL
Cell membrane
Chromosome
Cytoplasm
Nuclear membrane
Replication
Chromatids
Centromere
Equator of the cell
Homologous pair of chromosomes
Direction of movement of chromosomes
CELL DIVISION Meiosis I
Direction of movement of chromosomes
CELL DIVISION Meiosis II
4 DAUGHTER CELLS

▲ **Figure 25.2.2** Cell division by meiosis

The importance of meiosis

Daughter cells (gametes) each receive a haploid set of chromosomes from the parent cell. During fertilisation, the chromosomes from both gametes combine. As a result, the zygote is diploid, but it inherits a new combination of genes from the parents. Each parent contributes 50% of the genes. The new individual that develops from the zygote inherits characteristics from both parents, not just from one parent as in asexual reproduction. You will study inherited characteristics in more detail in Unit C26.

Boy or girl?

The chromosomes determine what sex the new individual will be.

You know that a cell has 23 pairs of chromosomes. Of the 23 pairs, one pair consists of the sex chromosomes which determine whether a person is male or female. Sex chromosomes can be either X chromosomes or Y chromosomes. They get these names from their shape. Women have two X chromosomes and men have one X chromosome and one Y chromosome.

During meiosis, the sex chromosome pair (like all the other chromosome pairs) separates so that only one sex chromosome from the pair appears in each of the gametes. You can see how this happens in Figure 25.2.3.

The gametes fuse during fertilisation to form a zygote with two sex chromosomes. The combination of X and Y chromosomes in the zygote determines the sex of the baby. Two X chromosomes will cause the zygote to develop into a baby girl. One X and one Y chromosome will cause the zygote to develop into a baby boy. Because meiosis results in an equal number of X and Y sperm cells, the chances of a woman conceiving a boy or a girl are equal (see Figure 25.2.4).

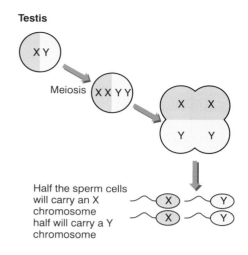

Testis

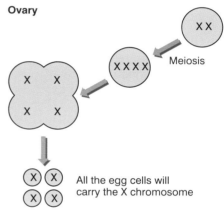

Ovary

▲ **Figure 25.2.3** Haploid gametes contain either an X or a Y chromosome

Questions

1 Match the statements in column B to the most suitable terms in column A.

	Column A	Column B
a	Testes	Produces diploid daughter cells
b	Mitosis	A process that allows growth and repair
c	Meiosis	Produces male gametes by meiosis
d	Ovary	Produces haploid daughter cells
e	Cell division	Produces female gametes by meiosis

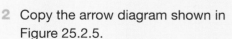

▲ **Figure 25.2.5**

2 Copy the arrow diagram shown in Figure 25.2.5.

   a Label and annotate the diagram to explain what is taking place.

   b Draw a similar arrow diagram to illustrate the process of mitosis.

3 Is it the gamete from the father or the mother which determines the sex of a baby? Explain why.

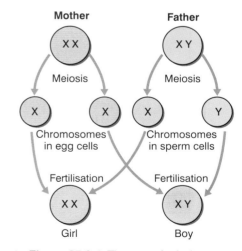

▲ **Figure 25.2.4** The sex of a baby depends on the combination of X and Y chromosomes in the zygote

All people are similar because they have some characteristics in common, for example, two eyes, a nose, a mouth, and so on. Yet, every human is unique because we inherit varied characteristics from our parents. In this unit you are going to learn more about variation and how we inherit characteristics.

C26.1 How characteristics are inherited

Each human being has around 100 000 characteristics and the combination of these makes each person unique. Table 26.1.1 shows you just five of these characteristics.

▼ **Table 26.1.1** Which of these characteristics do you have?

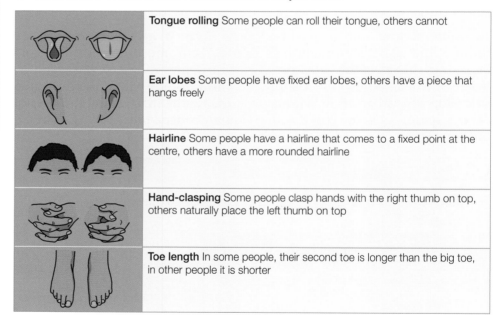

	Tongue rolling Some people can roll their tongue, others cannot
	Ear lobes Some people have fixed ear lobes, others have a piece that hangs freely
	Hairline Some people have a hairline that comes to a fixed point at the centre, others have a more rounded hairline
	Hand-clasping Some people clasp hands with the right thumb on top, others naturally place the left thumb on top
	Toe length In some people, their second toe is longer than the big toe, in other people it is shorter

The question biologists ask is, 'How are these characteristics transmitted from parents to their offspring?' The answer is contained in the study of genetics. All cells in the body that have a nucleus contain a complete genetic blueprint for human development. The genetic information is contained in the chromosomes inside the cell nucleus. Chromosomes are made up of a chemical called deoxyribonucleic acid (DNA). DNA contains genes and it is these genes that determine the characteristics of an organism.

The structure of DNA

A DNA molecule is made up of thousands of nucleotides. Each nucleotide consists of three molecules: a phosphate, a sugar and a base. If you look at Figure 26.1.1 you can see that the DNA is made of two strands of nucleotides. The sugars and the phosphates form the backbone of the DNA and the bases link the two strands together to give DNA its double helix shape.

There are four different bases in DNA: thymine (T), adenine (A), cytosine (C) and guanine (G). The pairs of bases are held together by hydrogen bonds, which help the DNA keep its shape. The bases always combine in the same way:

- adenine (A) pairs with thymine (T)
- cytosine (C) pairs with guanine (G).

You already know that the cells in the human body contain 46 chromosomes arranged in 23 pairs. (Remember females have 23 matching pairs, males have 22 matching and one unmatched XY chromosome.)

Chromosomes and inheritance

The 46 chromosomes in each cell contain approximately 100 000 genes. The genes contain the code that makes up each person. A gene is in effect a section of chromosomal DNA that gives the code for particular characteristics. A gene is always found in the same location on a given chromosome, but the genes themselves can take different forms. For example, one gene determines whether you are right- or left-handed. This gene has two different forms or alleles. The allele for right-handedness in humans is denoted by R while the gene for left-handedness is denoted by r.

Dominant and recessive genes

Each chromosome in a pair carries one allele for each particular characteristic (see Figure 26.1.2). In a pair of chromosomes you can either have two identical alleles (RR or rr) or you can have two different alleles (Rr or rR).

Usually one of the alleles is stronger. This allele is said to be dominant and it controls what happens when the characteristic is passed on. For example, R is dominant, so a right-handed person would have either the RR alleles or the Rr alleles. Only people with the rr combination of alleles will be left-handed. We say that the allele for left-handedness is recessive. In characteristics such as eye and hair colour, the darker colour genes are usually dominant over recessive, lighter colour genes. So the gene for black hair is dominant while the gene for blonde hair is recessive. The gene for brown eyes is dominant while the gene for blue eyes is recessive. Table 26.1.2 shows you some other examples of characteristics which are dominant or recessive.

▼ **Table 26.1.2** Some dominant and recessive features in humans

Dominant	Recessive
Dark hair	Light hair
Curly hair	Straight hair
Early grey hair	No early greying of hair
Brown eyes	Blue eyes
Freckles	No freckles
Lobed ears	Joined ear lobe
Tongue can roll	Non-tongue rolling
Normal skin colouring	Albinism

A geneticist, R.C. Punnett developed a system known as a Punnett square to show possible combinations of alleles. The alleles of the gametes of one parent are written along the top. The alleles of the gametes of the other parent are written down the side. The possible combinations of alleles are written in the blocks. The Punnett squares that follow show the possible results for different allele combinations for handedness:

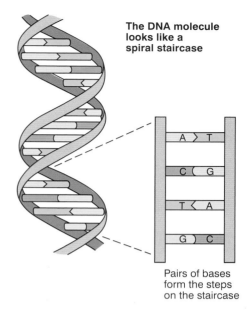
The DNA molecule looks like a spiral staircase

Pairs of bases form the steps on the staircase

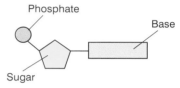
A single nucleotide

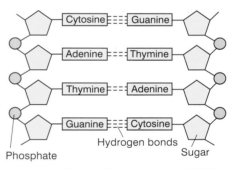
▲ **Figure 26.1.1** The structure of DNA

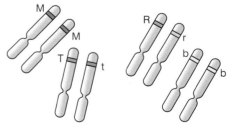
▲ **Figure 26.1.2** Each chromosome in a pair carries one allele for one particular characteristic

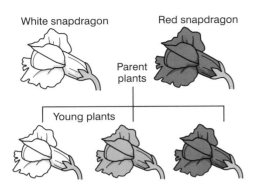

White snapdragon

Red snapdragon

Parent plants

Young plants

From this father and mother

... you can get all these different fruit flies (and more!)

▲ **Figure 26.1.3** Variation is the result of sexual reproduction and different combinations of genes

 **Key fact**

The Punnett square shows all possible offspring that can result from combinations of the alleles of the parents. However, you cannot assume that the offspring will appear in that order or in the exact ratio. It is simply an indication of what you can expect to see in the offspring.

Gametes	r	r
R	Rr	Rr
R	Rr	Rr

All offspring will be right-handed.

Gametes	R	r
R	RR	Rr
R	RR	Rr

All offspring will be right-handed.

Gametes	R	r
R	RR	Rr
r	Rr	rr

Three-quarters of offspring will be right-handed, one-quarter will be left-handed.

When you write down the kinds of alleles on a chromosome (for example RR), we refer to it as the genotype. The genotype describes the genetic make-up of all the genes of an individual. The physical appearance of each individual is known as the phenotype (for example right-handed). Our genotype is important in determining what phenotype is expressed, but it is not the only factor. For example, in the past, left-handed children were forced to develop and use their right hands at school, so many of them became right-handed as a result of social and environmental factors.

Genes and variation

When a species reproduces sexually, each offspring is made up of cells which contain chromosomes from both parents. This means they also have genes from both parents.

Parents may have different alleles of the same genes, so in the offspring, these alleles can be combined in many different ways. This is why offspring born to the same parents will be different from their parents and from each other. In other words, there is a great degree of variation produced by sexual reproduction, not only in humans, but in other animals and plants as well (see Figure 26.1.3).

When an individual carries two identical alleles (for example RR or rr), we say the individual is homozygous. When an individual carries two different alleles (for example Rr), we say the individual is heterozygous.

Questions

1 Define the terms 'chromosome', 'gene', 'allele', 'dominant' and 'recessive'.

2 Consider the alleles of two genes shown in the cells in Figure 26.1.2. Write down all the possible combinations that would be possible in the gametes if this cell divided by meiosis.

3 Francis is tall and her genotype is TT. Mathew is short, his genotype is tt. Tallness is dominant to shortness.
   a Use a Punnett square to show the possible combinations of alleles in offspring from these two parents.
   b What is the phenotype of their children likely to be? Why?

4 Consider the inherited characteristics shown in Table 26.1.1. Using your class as a sample, what characteristics would you say are dominant? Give reasons for your answers.

Genetic crosses

An Austrian monk called Gregor Mendel (1822–84) provided the basis for much of the knowledge we now have of inheritance and how characteristics are passed from generation to generation.

One of Mendel's important studies involved conducting breeding experiments with garden peas. Mendel chose the garden pea because it has easily observable characteristics including: seed shape, seed colour, seed coat colour, pod shape, pod colour, flower colour, plant height and position of flowers. The phenotypes of these are shown in Table 26.1.3.

▼ **Table 26.1.3** Characteristics that can be observed in pea plants

Round seeds		Wrinkled seeds	
Yellow seeds		Green seeds	
Coloured seed coat		White seed coat	
Smooth pod		Wrinkled pod	
Green pod		Yellow pod	
Purple flowers		White flowers	
Tall stem		Short stem	
Terminal flowers		Axial flowers	

Mendel worked with pure-breeding plants. These were plants that consistently produced the same results, for example, tall plants that produced only tall offspring generation after generation and purple-flowered plants that produced only purple-flowered offspring generation after generation.

Mendel was very systematic and he recorded his results carefully. He found that when he crossed pure-breeding purple plants with pure breeding white plants he got two different sets of results: all F_1 generation plants were purple, but when the F_1 generation was interbred both purple and white flowers were produced. These results are illustrated in Figure 26.1.4.

Note that the F_1 (first filial) generation is the name given to offspring produced by a parent generation. The F_2 (second filial) generation is the offspring of the first filial generation.

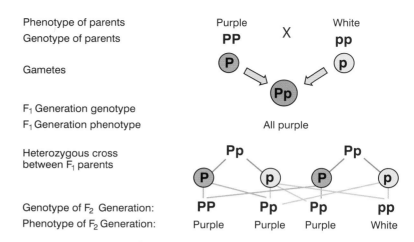

▲ **Figure 26.1.4** The results of one of Mendel's experiments shown as a genetic diagram

Mendel found that the characteristics in the left-hand column in Table 26.1.3 are dominant in peas.

The test cross or back cross

In Mendel's experiments, all the parents of the F_1 generation were homozygous while the offspring were heterozygous. You cannot tell whether an organism showing the dominant characteristic, such as a purple-flowered plant is homozygous or heterozygous by looking at it. To find out, you have to do a test cross, or back cross.

A test cross involves crossing the unknown purple parent organism with a homozygous, recessive parent. In our example, the homozygous recessive parent would be the white-flowered plant (which has to have the alleles pp to be white because purple is dominant and Pp would be purple). If the purple-flowered plant is homozygous (PP) then crossing it with the white-flowered plant would result in only purple-flowered offspring (Pp). If the purple-flowered plant is heterozygous (Pp), then crossing it with the white-flowered plant would result in 50% of the offspring being purple-flowered and the other 50% being white-flowered. This is illustrated in Figure 26.1.5.

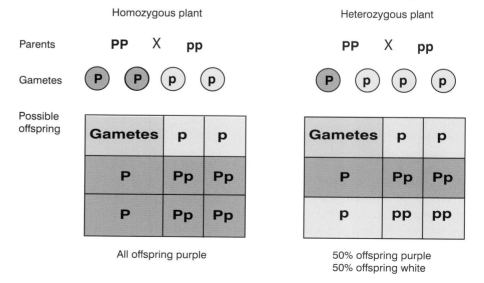

▲ **Figure 26.1.5** Two possible results from the test cross of purple- and white-flowered plants

Questions

1　Copy and complete the Punnett square to show the results of a cross between two round-seeded pea plants. (R represents the allele for roundness, r represents wrinkled.)

Gametes	R	r
R		
R		

   a　Describe the phenotypes of the F_1 generation.

   b　In what proportions are the different phenotypes expected to occur?

2　Use genetic diagrams to answer the following questions. In fruit flies, normal wing length (N) is dominant over short wing length (n). What proportion of the offspring are likely to have short wings in the following crosses?

   a　Short × short.

   b　Short × heterozygous normal.

   c　Heterozygous normal × heterozygous normal.

3　The table shows the results of breeding experiments with pea plants beginning with parents pure-breeding for tallness and shortness.

Cross	Original parent cross	F_1 plants from parental cross	F_2 plants from F_1 cross
Height	Tall × short	All tall	779 tall, 268 short

   a　Explain how you can tell from these results that tallness is dominant to shortness and that shortness is recessive.

   b　To the nearest whole number, what is the ratio of tall to short plants in the F_2 generation?

   c　All the F_1 plants are tall. Explain how the combination of their alleles is different from that of the parent tall plant.

   d　Draw a genetic diagram to show the F_2 results obtained from this cross.

   e　Explain how you could test whether a tall F_2 plant was homozygous or heterozygous.

4　In humans, long eyelashes (L) are dominant over short eyelashes (l). A woman whose father had short eyelashes has long eyelashes.

   a　What is her genotype?

   b　Predict the chance of her children having long eyelashes if she marries a man with short eyelashes. Explain your answer using diagrams if necessary.

5　Is it possible for two non-tongue rolling parents to have a child that can roll his or her tongue? Explain your answer.

Objectives

By the end of this topic you will be able to:

- understand what is meant by the terms 'incomplete dominance' and 'codominance'
- use genetic diagrams to explain the inheritance of blood groups in humans
- predict the results of crosses involving co-dominant alleles.

▲ **Figure 26.2.1** The pink flowers are a result of a cross between red-flowered and white-flowered parent plants

▲ **Figure 26.2.2** The F_1 generation has feathers that are a blend of their parents' colours

C26.2 Inheritance and partial dominance

The examples of crosses and inherited characteristics you studied in topic C26.1 dealt with alleles which were either dominant or recessive. For example, flowers were either purple or white, people were either right-handed or left-handed, and fruit flies either had wings of normal length or short wings. Not all crosses show a dominant or recessive pattern. For example, red and white flowers may cross to produce pink flowers, two grey mice may produce a black or white offspring and babies may be born with a blood group that is different to both their parents.

The characteristics which appear to be a blending of characteristics are a result of partial dominance. Partial dominance can take the form of incomplete dominance or codominance. You are now going to study examples of both of these kinds of dominance.

Incomplete dominance

Consider flowers such as the impatiens shown in the photograph in Figure 26.2.1. A red-flowering plant crossed with a white-flowering plant will produce an F_1 generation with all pink flowers. This happens because neither the red nor the white colour allele is completely dominant over the other.

When the pink plants are crossed with each other, the F_2 generation has plants with red, pink and white flowers. You can see how this happens in the Punnett squares below. We use the genotype RR for red flowers and WW for white flowers. We use capital letters for both to show that neither allele is dominant to the other. The genotype RW produces pink flowers.

F_1 cross

Gametes	W	W
R	RW	RW
R	RW	RW

F_2 cross

Gametes	R	W
R	RR	RW
W	RW	WW

This means that the F_2 generation contains red, pink and white flowers in the ratio 1:2:1. This suggests it is the phenotype and not the genotype that seems to blend in incomplete dominance.

Incomplete dominance is also found in animals. If you look at the domestic chickens in the photograph in Figure 26.2.2, you can see that when a black-feathered bird is crossed with a white-feathered bird the resulting offspring have greyish feathers. Again this is because the allele for black feathers is not completely dominant over the allele for white feathers. If you draw Punnett squares to show these crosses you can see that the F_2 generation will once again produce black, grey and white offspring in the ratio 1:2:1.

Codominance

The petunias in Figure 26.2.3 come from a cross of purple plants and white plants.

These plants are the heterozygous offspring (PW) of a cross between purple and white parent plants. They all have flowers with a mixture of both purple and white colouring. Both alleles (P and W) are expressed in the phenotype because they are not dominant to each other, so PW gives us an F_1 generation that has flowers with both purple and white colouring. Once again, when the F_1 generation crosses, they will produce purple, mixed purple and white, and white flowers in the ratio 1:2:1.

Human blood groups

Sometimes a characteristic is controlled by more than two alleles. Human blood groups, for example, are controlled by three alleles: A, B and O. An individual has two out of these three alleles.

The A and B alleles control production of the antigens which determine a person's blood group. The A and B alleles are codominant to each other but they are both dominant to the O allele. So, if the A and B alleles are both present, then the blood group will be AB. If neither the A nor B alleles are present, then the person's blood group will be O. The possible combinations of alleles in different blood groups is summarised in Table 26.2.1.

▼ **Table 26.2.1** Possible combinations of alleles in different blood groups

Genotype	Antigen on red blood cells	Blood group
AA or AO	A	A
BB or BO	B	B
AB	A and B	AB
OO	Neither A nor B	O

The genetic diagrams in Figure 26.2.4 show you the possible blood groups of children from parents with given blood groups. Note that it is possible for a child to have a blood group which is different from the blood groups of both parents.

Questions

1 Provide an example to illustrate what is meant by incomplete dominance.

2 How is codominance different from simple dominance?

3 In some plants, a cross between a dark purple-flowering plant and a white-flowering plant results in pale purple coloured offspring.

  a Is this an example of incomplete dominance or codominance? Explain why.

  b Draw a diagram to show the offspring and the proportions of each that you could expect if you crossed two pale purple-flowering plants.

4 Mrs Kelly has white cows and a black bull. When the cows mate with the bull, the resultant calves are all white with splotches of black.

  a Is this an example of incomplete dominance or codominance? Explain why.

  b What would you expect the genotype of the calves to be? Why?

  c The black and white cows are then mated with a black and white bull. Draw genetic diagrams to show the phenotypes possible in their offspring and state the proportions in which these phenotypes occur.

▲ **Figure 26.2.3** These offspring have the colours of both parents, but the colours do not blend

Example 1
Parents:
AA   **BO**

Gametes	A	A
B	AB	AB
O	AO	AO

Children: **AB or A**

Example 2
Parents:
AO   **BO**

Gametes	B	O
A	AB	AO
O	BO	OO

Children: **AB, A, B or O**

▲ **Figure 26.2.4** Possible blood groups from different sets of parents

By the end of this topic you will be able to:

- understand that some characteristics are sex-linked
- use genetic diagrams to explain the inheritance of albinism and sickle cell anaemia
- use pedigree charts to analyse the inheritance patterns of particular characteristics.

C26.3 Inherited conditions and diseases

Sex-linked conditions

You learnt in topic C26.1 that our sex (gender) at birth is determined by the 23rd pair of chromosomes inherited, one from each parent. The XX combination produces female offspring while the XY combination produces male offspring.

Some genes are carried on the sex chromosomes. We call these sex-linked characteristics because they are present on one of the chromosomes that determine the sex of the offspring. An example is the allele for colour-blindness, which is carried on the X chromosome only. The Y chromosome does not contain the allele. The allele for normal vision is dominant (C) and the allele for colour-blindness is recessive (c). This gives three possible genotypes for females and two for males (see Figure 26.3.1).

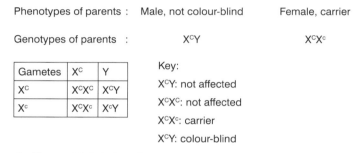

Phenotypes of parents :   Male, not colour-blind   Female, carrier

Genotypes of parents : X^CY X^CX^c

Gametes	X^C	Y
X^c	X^CX^c	X^CY
X^c	X^CX^c	X^cY

Key:
X^CY: not affected
X^CX^C: not affected
X^CX^c: carrier
X^CY: colour-blind

▲ **Figure 26.3.1** Possible genotypes for the sex-linked condition, colour-blindness

Key fact

We write these genotypes differently to show that they are sex-linked. We include the X and Y chromosomes and we write the dominant and recessive alleles above and to the right of them. So a heterozygous female will have the genotype X^CX^c.

Colour-blindness is more common in men than in women because the recessive gene carried on the X chromosome can show its effect when there is no matching dominant gene on the Y chromosome. Females who are heterozygous for colour-blindness will have normal vision because the presence of the dominant allele (C) cancels out the effect of the recessive allele (c). However, they will be carriers of the recessive allele and they can pass it on to their children. Whether the children are colour-blind or not will depend on whether or not the father is colour-blind.

Haemophilia is a genetic condition in which the blood does not clot properly after an injury, usually because the person with haemophilia fails to produce Factor 8, which causes blood to clot. The allele responsible for haemophilia is recessive and is located on the X chromosome. Therefore haemophilia is caused by a sex-linked recessive gene.

You can use genetic diagrams to show how sex-linked conditions are inherited. Figure 26.3.2 shows the offspring that could be born to a woman who is a carrier of haemophilia and a man who does not have the allele.

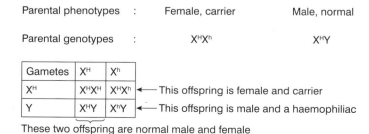

Parental phenotypes   :   Female, carrier   Male, normal

Parental genotypes   : X^HX^h X^HY

Gametes	X^H	X^h
X^H	X^HX^H	X^HX^h	←— This offspring is female and carrier
Y	X^HY	X^hY	←— This offspring is male and a haemophiliac

These two offspring are normal male and female

▲ **Figure 26.3.2** Inheritance of haemophilia, a sex-linked disease

Human genetic diseases and inherited conditions are caused either by abnormalities in the number of chromosomes or by mutations (random changes) in the genes themselves.

Albinism – an inherited condition

Albinism is an inherited condition. People with albinism (albinos) have very little or none of the melanin pigment that creates colour in their eyes, skin or hair. Most people with albinism have very pale sun-sensitive skin, their hair is very blonde or white and their eyes are usually very sensitive to sunlight.

The genes responsible for albinism are located on several different chromosomes, including the X chromosome. Albinism is determined by a recessive allele (a). So, for a person to have albinism, they have to inherit two recessive alleles (one from each parent). If the parents are homozygous (AA) and (aa), the offspring will not show any signs of albinism (see Figure 26.3.3).

Phenotypes of parents: Normal pigmentation   Albino pigmentation
Genotype of parents: AA   aa
Genotype of gametes: A A   a a
Genotypes of offspring

Gametes	A	A
a	Aa	Aa
a	Aa	Aa

Phenotypes of offspring: **all normal**

▲ **Figure 26.3.3** Possible outcome of a genetic cross between two homozygous parents, one of whom carries the recessive alleles for albinism

If both parents are heterozygous (Aa), they both carry the recessive allele, and they have a 1 in 4 chance of producing offspring with albinism. See Figure 26.3.4.

Phenotypes of parents: Normal pigmentation   Normal pigmentation
Genotype of parents: Aa   Aa
Genotype of gametes: A a   A a
Genotypes of offspring

Gametes	A	a
A	AA	Aa
a	Aa	aa

Phenotypes of offspring: **3 normal, 1 albino**

▲ **Figure 26.3.4** Possible outcome of a genetic cross between two heterozygous parents who each carry the recessive allele for albinism

Albinism occurs worldwide and affects people of all races. Males and females alike can have the condition.

Sickle cell anaemia – an inherited disease

Sickle cell anaemia is an inherited blood disease that causes red blood cells to develop an odd C-shape, like a sickle. You can see normal blood and blood from a person with sickle cell anaemia in Figure 26.3.5.

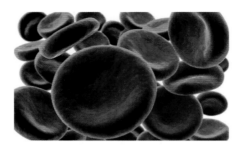

▲ **Figure 26.3.5** Normal red blood cells and sickle-shaped red blood cells

When a person has sickle cell anaemia the red blood cells contain abnormal haemoglobin, S, so they cannot carry oxygen as well as normal cells. The disease is caused by an abnormal allele which is not sex linked (it can be passed on by either parent). In order to develop sickle cell anaemia, a child must inherit the abnormal allele from both parents and be homozygous, Hb^S Hb^S (see Figure 26.3.6).

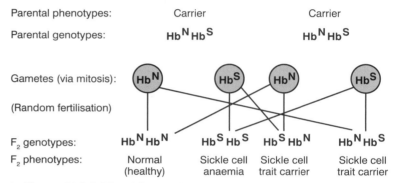

▲ **Figure 26.3.6** The children of heterozygous carriers of sickle cell anaemia have a one-in-four chance of being born with the disease

Many more people have sickle cell trait than have the disease. They inherit a normal allele from one parent and an abnormal one from the other. Interestingly, people who have the recessive allele show some immunity to malaria. This means the disease is more common in high malaria areas, as the heterozygous carriers do not get malaria, so they survive to adulthood and can pass on the allele.

When parents are deciding to have children, they may be concerned about passing on genetic disorders, particularly if there is a family history of an inherited disease. The possibility of passing on inherited conditions can be determined by a pedigree analysis.

Pedigrees

A pedigree is a method of charting the incidence of various conditions in families (related groups). A pedigree shows the patterns of inheritance of certain characteristics. When the pattern is repeated, or observed over many generations, a mode of inheritance can be worked out. The symbols used in a pedigree represent the individual males and females in families (normally as squares and circles) as well as showing which individuals show particular characteristics (often indicated by shading). Most pedigree charts are accompanied by a key which tells you what the symbols represent. Figure 26.3.7 is a pedigree which shows inheritance of night blindness (an inability to see well in low light).

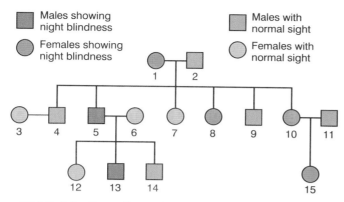

▲ **Figure 26.3.7** A family pedigree showing inheritance of night blindness

Genetic counsellors are specially trained to work with families to help them make informed choices about the risk of producing children with a genetic disorder.

Questions

1 In 2013 the world population was over 7 billion people. However, even with this huge number, there are approximately equal numbers of males and females. Explain, with the aid of a diagram, why this is the case.

2 Why are so few females born with red-green colour-blindness?

3 Describe briefly how albinism is inherited.

4 Explain how it is possible for two normally pigmented parents to have a child with albinism.

5 What is the advantage of being a heterozygous sickle cell anaemia carrier in a malaria area?

6 Explain, using diagrams as necessary, why both parents have to have the recessive allele for sickle cell anaemia in order for their children to have the disease.

7 Figure 26.3.8 shows a pedigree for a family in which some members have a rare genetic disorder.

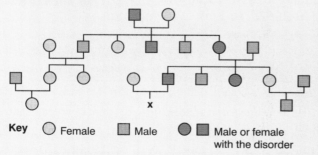

Key ◯ Female   ▢ Male   ● ▢ Male or female with the disorder

▲ **Figure 26.3.8**

a Is this condition caused by a recessive or a dominant allele? How can you tell?

b Is this condition sex-linked? Explain your answer.

c What is the chance that the individual marked x will be born with the disorder?

d How can a pedigree analysis help people who know they carry a genetic disorder to make decisions about having children?

Variation refers to the differences that exist between species. However, species also change in general over time. Humans today are far taller and larger than humans were in the past. Some animals which existed in the past, no longer exist today. In this unit you will learn more about the scientific reasons for variation and change.

C27.1 Variation

If you look closely at the organisms shown in Figure 27.1.1, you can see that the individuals in each photograph belong to the same species, however they also differ in certain characteristics. In other words, the individuals in each species show variation.

a Although people belong to the same species, each individual is unique

b These are all hibiscus plants, but they have different-sized leaves and different-coloured flowers

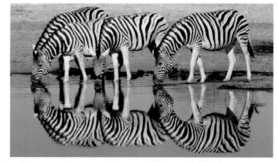

c Every zebra has a unique pattern on its coat. No two are ever identical

▲ **Figure 27.1.1** All individuals of a species have different characteristics as a result of genetic variation

Continuous and discontinuous variation

The variations shown by some characteristics are spread over a range of measurements. All intermediate (in-between) forms of the characteristic are possible between one extreme of the characteristic and the other. We say that the characteristic shows continuous variation. Height is an example of continuous variation. In a population where the heights range from 1.25–1.95 m, the individuals in the population can be any height in-between these two figures. When you graph the heights, you get a smooth, continuous curve (see Figure 27.1.2). Other examples of continuous variation are body mass, skin tone and intelligence in humans, and leaf size and height in plants.

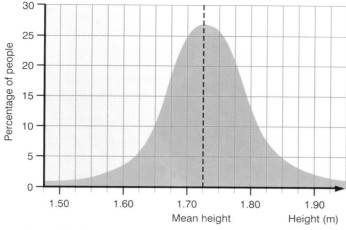

▲ **Figure 27.1.2** Continuous variation

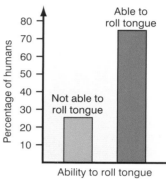

▲ **Figure 27.1.3** The ability to roll the tongue is an example of discontinuous variation

Other characteristics do not show a continuous trend in variation from one extreme to the other. They show categories of characteristics without any intermediate forms. For example, people can either roll their tongues or they cannot, there are no half-rollers. We say that this characteristic shows discontinuous variation (see Figure 27.1.3). Other examples of discontinuous variation include fixed or loose ear lobes and blood groups in humans, the presence or absence of horns in cattle, red or black eyes in fruit flies, plain green or variegated leaves in one species of plant.

 Practical activity

A survey of characteristics

In this activity you are going to use your class as a population to survey observable characteristics. Then you are going to select one characteristic to observe and record so that you can draw conclusions about the range of variation in that characteristic.

1 Observe at least 10 individuals in the class population. For each person you observe, write down one noticeable characteristic (be sensitive to each other). Once you have done this, complete the three columns by filling in the appropriate information.

2 Select one characteristic from the 10 you observed. Plan and carry out a survey of the entire population of the class to:

a record the incidence of the characteristic in the population – use a tally table or frequency table to record the data

b draw a graph to show the variation in the observed characteristic

c write a few sentences explaining what the graph suggests about the degree of variation in this particular case.

Characteristic	Inherited	Caused by environment	Continuous or discontinuous
1			
2			
3			
4			
5			
6			
7			
8			
9			
10			

 **Practical activity**

Investigating continuous variation in plants

In this activity you are going to measure the heights of one type of plant in different locations in your environment to find out how much variation there is.

1 Choose a plant that is common in your environment and that grows to a height that is measured easily.

2 Select five locations where the plant grows and measure the heights of five plants at each location. Record the results as a list.

3 Use the list of heights to draw up a frequency table. Your scale should run from the shortest height on your list to the highest and the class intervals should be equal.

4 Use your frequency table to draw a bar graph showing the variation in heights of the plants.

Questions

1 Calculate the range of heights found in the plants in your survey.

2 Describe the shape of the graph. What does this suggest about height variation in the observed species?

3 Give three other examples of continuous variation that could be observed in the plant species you selected for study.

4 Is it possible to find examples of discontinuous variation in the plant species you selected? If so, list these.

Sources of variation

Variation arises from genetic and environmental causes. Both these causes can affect the phenotype, but only variation arising from the genotype can be inherited.

The outward appearance of an organism (the phenotype) depends on a combination of inherited characteristics (the genotype) and characteristics due to the environment. For example, two genetically identical plants (clones) grown in different environmental conditions of light, water and soil will grow differently and so their appearance will be different – one plant may be bushy, green and healthy and bear lots of flowers while the other, genetically identical plant may be stunted, yellow and sickly because it does not have a suitable environment. Similarly, humans who grow up in different environments may show variations in height and mass as a result of nutrition and healthy or unhealthy teeth as a result of diet and other environmental factors.

The genetic and environmental causes of variation are summarised in Table 27.1.1.

▼ **Table 27.1.1** Genetic and environmental causes of variation

Genetic causes of variation	Environmental causes of variation
Meiosis – in meiosis, pairs of chromosomes exchange genes and split from each other producing gametes that are not identical	**Nutrients** – the food we eat and the minerals available to plants lead to variations
Sexual reproduction – the fusion of sperm and egg combines genetic material from each parent in new ways in the zygote	**Drugs** – for example, thalidomide was a drug given to pregnant women in the 1960s which caused serious deformities in some children born to many of these women
Mutations – these are random mistakes in the replication of DNA that make the new DNA slightly different to the original	**Temperature** – this affects the rate of enzyme-controlled reactions, for example, plants grown in warm conditions show faster rates of photosynthesis, so they develop faster and grow better than plants grown in cold conditions
	Physical training – when you use muscles you increase their size and power, for example, athletes develop strong muscles as they train for their sport

Variations that arise from genetic causes are inherited from parents by offspring. These offspring pass them on to their offspring, and so on, from generation to generation. Inherited variation is the raw material on which natural selection acts. You will study this in more detail in topic C27.2.

Variations that arise from environmental causes are not inherited because the sex cells are not affected. Instead the characteristics are said to be acquired. Children born to an athlete with strong muscles will not have strong muscles unless they also train physically. Variations as a result of acquired characteristics are not acted upon by natural selection and therefore they do not affect evolution.

Twins are often studied to help scientists understand which characteristics are inherited and which are determined by the environment. Identical twins have the same genetic material. If they are brought up together, they live under the same environmental conditions. Where the twins are separated (by adoption, for example) and brought up by different families, their environmental conditions are different, so variation between the twins will normally be a result of environmental causes. Table 27.1.2 shows you some of the differences observed in a study of identical twins. A small number indicates a small degree of variation between the identical twins in each study.

▼ **Table 27.1.2** Genetic and environmental variation between identical twins

Difference in	Identical twins reared together	Identical twins reared apart
Height	1.7	1.8
Body mass	4.1	9.9
Head length	2.9	2.2
Head width	2.6	2.9
IQ	3.1	6.0

The data in the table suggest that the environment is an important element in determining phenotype.

Genetic variation is important because it allows the species to adapt to changing environmental conditions and ensures their survival. You will examine these changes in more detail when you deal with natural selection in topic C27.2.

 Key fact

Ionising radiation, and some chemicals, increases the possibility of gene mutation. Emissions from radioactive substances are ionising radiations that cause mutations by directly damaging DNA, or by generating free radicals which cause the damage indirectly. Chemicals, such as the carcinogens in tobacco, may lead to mutations which inhibit cell division. A cancer develops when cell division runs out of control.

Questions

1 The patterns of fingerprints in humans can be divided into four main groups. These are shown in Figure 27.1.4. The bar graph shows the frequency of each type in a sample of 100 fingerprints.

   a What type of variation is this? Explain why.

   b Are fingerprints inherited or acquired characteristics?

   c Which fingerprint genotype do you think is dominant? Why?

   d Check the fingerprints of a sample of members from your class. Do you get the same pattern of distribution?

2 List the different sources of variation in living organisms.

3 Why does sexual reproduction produce much more genetic variation than asexual reproduction?

4 What is a 'mutation'? List two things that can cause mutations in genes.

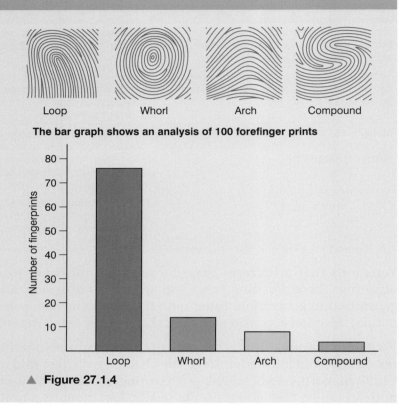

Loop   Whorl   Arch   Compound

The bar graph shows an analysis of 100 forefinger prints

▲ **Figure 27.1.4**

Objectives

By the end of this topic you will be able to:

- define natural selection
- explain how natural selection preserves useful characteristics
- describe one example of a single characteristic that can be changed by natural selection.

C27.2 Natural selection

Living species today are not exactly the same as they were millions of years ago. When a species changes over a long period of time, we say it has evolved. The process of changing slowly over time is called evolution.

Most scientists agree that species change and that new species develop over time. This is an aspect of the theory of evolution which suggests that all species have evolved from common ancestors by changing gradually.

The British naturalist, Charles Darwin was one of the first people to explain how species can evolve. After several exploratory trips aboard the research vessel *The Beagle*, Darwin tried to explain the variations he observed in different species.

Darwin understood that living organisms produce far more offspring than can normally be expected to survive. A tree, for example, may produce thousands of seeds each year. Hundreds of seedlings sprout from the seeds, but only one or two grow into mature trees. He also understood that the supply of food, amount of space and other resources in the environment are limited. Only those organisms with the structures and way of life that are well-suited (adapted) to make the best use of these limited resources survive long enough to reproduce. Less well-suited organisms produce fewer offspring or do not survive to reproduce at all. Therefore, variations which are favourable for survival accumulate from one generation to the next, while less favourable variations will die out (become extinct). Darwin called this process natural selection and suggested that this was the mechanism of evolution which allowed species to change over time. Figure 27.2.1 illustrates natural selection in action in mice.

The mouse has many offspring. Most are brown, but one is white

The hawk hunts the mice as a source of food. The white mouse is most visible as it lacks natural camouflage. The brown mice are well camouflaged, so they are more difficult for the hawk to spot

The hawk catches the white mouse. All the mice that survive to adulthood are brown. Brown colour is passed onto their offspring and, over time, the mice become better suited to their environment

▲ **Figure 27.2.1** Natural selection in mice

Natural selection explains why in a stable environment, a species becomes better suited to its environment and why most of the organisms are so similar.

 Practical activity

Modelling natural selection

Your teacher may use this activity to assess: ORR; A&I.

It is not practical to observe natural selection directly, as the changes to the species normally take several generations. The activity you are going to do here allows you to model natural selection in an experiment with a number of factors being controlled.

Aim
To model natural selection.

Materials
- About 60 toothpicks (half of them red, half of them green)
- An area of green grass

Method
1 Close your eyes and throw the toothpicks onto the grass.
2 Open your eyes. Collect as many toothpicks as you can in 15 seconds.
3 Count and record the number of each coloured toothpick that you pick up.
4 Repeat the experiment (using all the toothpicks) four times.
5 Calculate the average number of each colour of toothpick that you collected.

Questions
1 What colour toothpick was collected most often? Why?
2 What does this tell you about the 'survival rate' of red and green toothpicks?
3 Which factor of selection were you dealing with in this experiment?
4 What other factors would affect the survival of a population of red and green organisms?
5 If the toothpicks that survived the best bred and produced the same coloured offspring, how would this affect the population in the future?

Selection pressure

The offspring of asexual reproduction are genetically identical to each other and their parents. Mutation is the only source of genetic variation. Offspring from sexual reproduction inherit genetic material from both parents. They are genetically different from each other (except for identical twins) and from their parents.

Natural selection works on the genetic variation in populations of organisms by selecting the variations which enable individuals to adapt to a changing environment. In stable environments the selection pressure for organisms to adapt is low. Asexual reproduction therefore has advantages. One parent producing identical copies of itself can more easily exploit the environment than two parents reproducing sexually.

In rapidly changing environments, however, sexual reproduction is more favourable. Selection pressure is high and favours individuals that can change in response to changing circumstances. Only sexual reproduction is able to produce enormous amounts of genetic variation. Natural selection can then select the change which enables organisms to adapt to the new environment (see Figure 27.2.2).

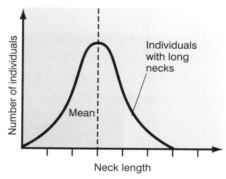

A long neck enables giraffes to browse on the leaves of trees. This is an advantage during the dry season when grass and other food plants are in short supply. More genes for long necks pass on to the next generation. The increase in mean neck length is a measure of change through evolution

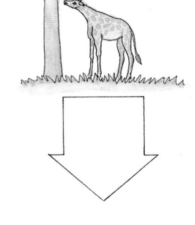

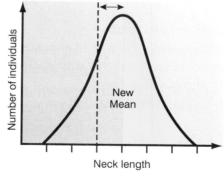

▲ **Figure 27.2.2** Passing on favourable characteristics

Natural selection in action

Natural selection has been observed in populations of pepper moths (*Biston betularia*) in England. Figure 27.2.3 shows two forms of the peppered moth. Separate moth populations are either predominately pale or predominately dark.

▲ **Figure 27.2.3** Different forms of the peppered moth

The speckled pale version (called the 'peppered variety') is found most often in the countryside where it merges into the light-coloured background of lichen-covered trees and rocks. In towns and cities, air pollution kills the lichens, leaving trees and other surfaces bare and sooty. The black moth (called the 'melanic variety') is the most common form in this environment, where it merges into the dark background.

Birds eat moths whose colour does not merge into the background because the moths are easier to see. The birds act as an agent of selection, which is to the advantage of the melanic variety in urban areas and the peppered variety in the countryside (see Figure 27.2.4.)

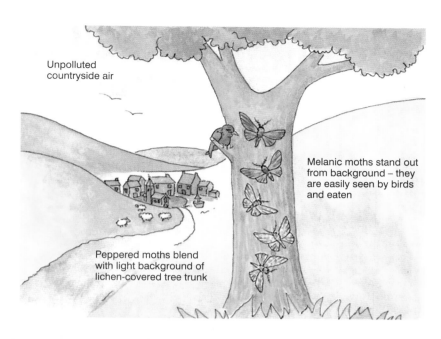

Unpolluted countryside air

Melanic moths stand out from background – they are easily seen by birds and eaten

Peppered moths blend with light background of lichen-covered tree trunk

Melanic moths blend with black background of soot-covered tree trunk

Peppered moths stand out from black background – they are easily seen by birds and eaten

▲ **Figure 27.2.4** Maintaining the balance between the peppered and melanic varieties of the moth *Biston betularia*

Resistance

When a new insecticide is used against an insect pest, a small amount is enough to kill most of the population. However, in subsequent sprayings, such small amounts are normally ineffective and stronger and stronger doses are needed. The few insects that survive the first spraying are naturally resistant and this resistance is passed on to their offspring. Over time, the population changes from being mainly susceptible to the insecticide to being mainly resistant (see Figure 27.2.5).

Resistance to antibiotics has evolved in bacteria in much the same way as resistance to insecticides has evolved in insects. Populations of bacteria always contain a few individuals with genes that make them resistant to an antibiotic. These individuals survive and reproduce. The new generation inherits the genes for resistance. Resistance develops rapidly in bacteria because they reproduce so quickly. The antibiotic acts as an agent of selection.

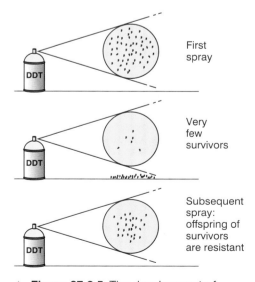

First spray

Very few survivors

Subsequent spray: offspring of survivors are resistant

▲ **Figure 27.2.5** The development of resistance to the insecticide DDT in mosquitoes

Key fact

Resistance in bacteria makes antibiotics less effective at treating diseases. People with TB, for example, who do not complete their treatment and who relapse and have to take more and more drugs, can develop a more serious form of TB known as 'drug-resistant TB'. This strain of the disease is normally deadly.

New species formation

Stable environments are rare. As environments change, so do the selection pressures which affect the survival of species. When populations adapt to new environmental conditions a new species may be formed. This is called speciation.

When organisms can no longer interbreed to produce healthy, fertile offspring, they are no longer members of the same species. Speciation can take place when some members of a species become isolated, usually because they are separated by mountains or bodies of water (on islands).

In his book *The Voyage of the Beagle*, Darwin made some observations about speciation in the finches he observed in the Galapagos Islands. Today many scientists believe that the 13 or more species of finches Darwin observed are descendents of finches found on mainland South America. The original finches would have migrated to the Galapagos Islands during a storm. Once there they adapted to the conditions in the environment and different conditions on different islands led to the natural selection of different features. Figure 27.2.6 shows you five of the Galapagos finches and the ways in which they are adapted to different sources of food.

The large ground finch has a large, strong, crushing beak

The large tree finch has a strong, sharp beak for grabbing and cutting

The warbler finch has a small pointed beak, for probing into cracks

The small ground finch, has a small but strong, crushing beak

The cactus finch, has a long, tough beak, for probing

▲ **Figure 27.2.6** Speciation in Galapagos finches

Questions

1 Explain what is meant by 'natural selection'. Describe the steps that take place in natural selection and give two examples of natural selection.

2 Figure 27.2.7 shows how the population of peppered moths found in Manchester, England in the 1800s changed.

   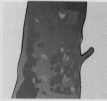  

Up to 1848 the creamy peppered moth was camouflaged on lichen-encrusted tree trunks

1848: the first black peppered moth was observed in the Manchester area

Industrial revolution: burning coal produced sulfur dioxide and soot

The smoke killed the lichen and caused tree trunks to appear darker

The creamy peppered moth was no longer camouflaged, but the black moth was well hidden on the dark tree trunks

By 1895, 95% of the peppered moth population in the Manchester area was black

▲ **Figure 27.2.7**

a Write a detailed explanation for these changes with reference to what you have learnt about natural selection.

b Today, Manchester (England) no longer has heavy smoke-creating industries and the city is much cleaner. How do you think this has affected the population of these moths?

3 The parrots of the Caribbean originally came from Central America. They all belong to the same genus *Amazona*, but different species are found on different islands. Make notes to explain how speciation may have occurred to produce the different species of parrots found on the Caribbean islands.

C27.3 Artificial selection

The fact that there is variation within a species, and that offspring resemble their parents more closely than they resemble other members of their species, has allowed humans to selectively breed plants and animals to suit specific purposes. For example, cows are bred to produce more milk, sheep are bred to produce more wool, plants have been bred to produce more or larger fruit and crops have been bred to produce more grain. Even domestic animals like cats and dogs have been selectively bred to produce the variety of breeds we know today. This process of selective breeding to bring out desired characteristics is called artificial selection.

Artificial selection differs from natural selection in that it produces new varieties in a relatively short time. Selection by nature takes much longer.

Artificial selection helps farmers

Artificial selection is used to improve the productivity of farm animals and crops.

For thousands of years, farmers have prized animals with a good pedigree. Dairy farmers want selected pedigreed cows from which to breed animals that produce lots of milk. Crops farmers need pure lines of cultivated plants. Characteristics, such as grain yield, fruit yield and disease resistance, are desirable qualities that can be maintained through artificial selection (selective breeding).

Figure 27.3.1 shows the variety of vegetables that have been produced through artificial selection from one species of plant, *Brassica oleracea* (a relative of the mustard plant). By choosing different characteristics, which make good eating, different vegetables have been developed to suit different tastes.

Objectives

By the end of this topic you will be able to:

- distinguish between natural and artificial selection
- give examples of selective breeding in animals and plants.

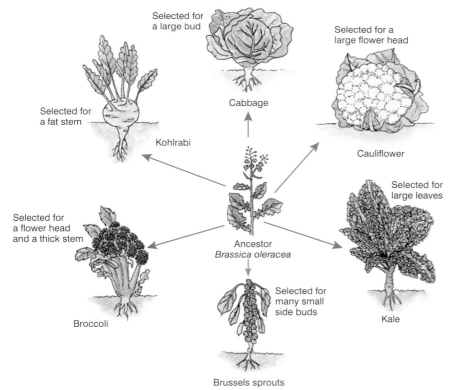

Selected for a large bud

Cabbage

Selected for a large flower head

Cauliflower

Selected for a fat stem

Kohlrabi

Selected for large leaves

Kale

Selected for a flower head and a thick stem

Broccoli

Ancestor *Brassica oleracea*

Selected for many small side buds

Brussels sprouts

▲ **Figure 27.3.1** A variety of vegetables artificially selected and bred from a single ancestral species

Rice

Wheat

Maize

Millet

▲ **Figure 27.3.2** Important cereal crops

Increasing yields of cereals

The grasses of the world provide the staple diet for most of the world's population. We know these as cereal crops. Humans have cultivated cereals since the earliest records of history. More people eat rice than any other food. Wheat, maize, oats, barley, rye and millet make up the bulk of the rest of the world's cereals (see Figure 27.3.2).

Today an enormous variety of cereals are available to farmers as a result of artificial selection over many generations. Planned hybridisation (crossing two different varieties) forms the basis of the development of new varieties. The aim of hybridisation is to concentrate as many desirable features as possible in a single variety. One variety of wheat, for example, may have food milling properties but poor resistance to fungal disease. Another may resist fungi but provide a low yield of grain. A third might not thrive in dry conditions but give a good baking flour when well irrigated. New varieties are constantly being developed by plant breeders to retain the favourable characteristics and eliminate the less favourable ones. In addition to the basic properties already mentioned, are others that vary according to the climate and soil in which the wheat is grown. The improvement in varieties as a result of selective breeding is largely responsible for the enormous increase in world wheat production since 1960.

Hybridisation and selection of varieties of rice has also boosted yields by 25%. It is a slower process than wheat breeding, but it is likely to produce crops that give higher yields in the future.

There is a disadvantage to selective breeding in that it greatly reduces variation in populations of animals and crops raised for food because the number of different alleles is reduced. Should conditions change, this reduced variation may make it impossible to selectively breed new populations that can survive the changed environmental conditions. Many plants and animals are now so selectively bred that they probably would not survive in nature.

Questions

1 Distinguish between artificial selection and natural selection. Give three examples of artificial selection.

2 Make a table listing the advantages and disadvantages of selective breeding for farmers.

3 Domestic dogs are selectively bred for characteristics such as size, strength, loyalty and a docile nature.
   a List four breeds of dogs and their characteristics.
   b Why do you think each of these dogs was bred?
   c Rate each breed on a scale of 1 to 10 to show how well you think they could survive in the wild (10 being an excellent chance of survival, 1 being very little chance of survival). Give a reason for your rating.

Biotechnologists use our understanding of genetics to develop useful products. New techniques, such as genetic engineering, help to fight diseases, make new products, improve food production and protect the environment. However there are social, ethical and ecological implications of using this technology to change the characteristics of organisms.

C28.1 Genetic engineering

The term biotechnology describes the way that we use plant cells, animal cells and microorganisms to produce substances that are useful to us. Although the word 'biotechnology' is modern, the processes of biotechnology have a long history. People have used fungi (mould) to make cheese and bacteria to make vinegar, for thousands of years. We have also used yeast to make bread, beer and wine. Ancient people even used lactic acid to preserve milk by turning it into yoghurt.

Today we have a far greater knowledge and modern technology. For example, in the 1950s and 1960s scientists unravelled the structure of DNA and showed how it synthesises proteins. Subsequent scientists have built on this knowledge so much that now they can change DNA inside a cell so that it synthesises different proteins. This process of changing the genetic structure of living cells in a laboratory is called genetic engineering.

The aim of genetic engineering is to remove a desirable gene from one organism and place it in another organism so its characteristics are expressed in the host organism. An organism which receives genes from another is called a transgenic organism.

To understand the principles of genetic engineering, we will study how scientists make use of genetically modified bacteria to produce herbicide-resistant crops and how they use different genetically modified bacteria to produce large amounts of human insulin.

Genetic engineering and food production

Scientists use genetic engineering to isolate desirable genes and insert them into crop plants. The bacterium *Agrobacterium tumefaciens* is an ideal cell for introducing desirable genes into host cells. Figure 28.1.1 shows the technique used.

Notice that the bacterial cell itself is genetically modified (GM) or transgenic. The plant is infected with modified *A. tumefaciens* and it produces a cancerous growth (tumour) called a 'crown gall'. Cells in the gall each contain the engineered gene. Plantlets can be cultured from the small pieces of tissue (explants) cut from the gall. The plantlets are genetically

Objectives

By the end of this topic you will be able to:

- state the purposes of genetic engineering
- outline the basic processes involved in genetic engineering using examples from food production and medical treatment.

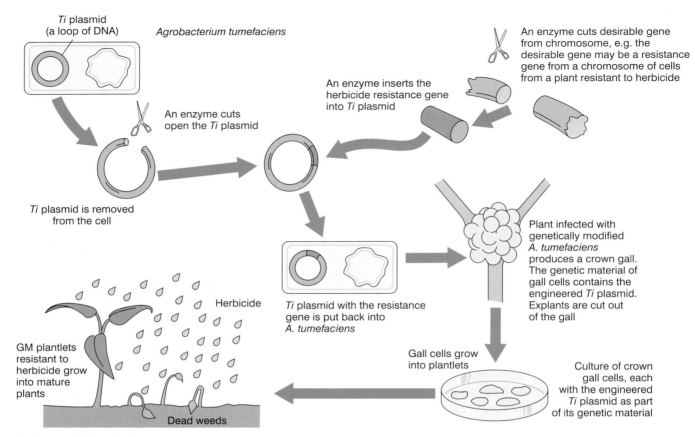

▲ **Figure 28.1.1** Engineering bacteria to produce herbicide-resistant plants

identical (clones). Each one carries the engineered gene and is therefore genetically modified. The GM plantlets are transferred to soil where they grow into a mature crop which has the desired characteristic, in this case resistance to herbicide.

Other examples of genetic engineering in food production include:

- Developing genes which are inserted into cells to increase nitrogen fixation in plants, which do not normally associate with nitrogen-fixing bacteria.

- Developing genes, which can be inserted into plants to make them resistant to insect pests.

- Developing hybrid plants (such as a cross between a potato and a tomato) or plants, which are disease-resistant.

- Improving animals by manipulating embryos. This includes: producing transgenic animals that can be used to produce useful proteins and medicines, transplanting embryos into surrogate mothers to conserve rare breeds and prevent extinctions, and embryo cloning to produce identical copies of animals with a desirable trait (such as milk production), although this latter example is not common practice yet.

- Helping to produce healthier farm animals, which produce higher yields. For example, the gene for bovine somatotropin (BST), which is a hormone that stimulates growth and increased milk production in cows, has been genetically engineered into bacteria. As a result, large amounts of the hormone are available for injection into cows to improve yields.

 **Key fact**

There are many examples of genetic engineering in food production – Bt corn, virus-resistant papaya, transgenic salmon and golden rice are all genetically engineered (modified). As scientists increase their skills and understanding in this field, more and more transgenic organisms are likely to be developed.

Genetic engineering and medicine

The human hormone insulin was the first substance made by genetic engineering to be given to humans. In 1980, volunteer diabetics successfully tried out genetically engineered insulin and by 1982 it was in general use. Before then, insulin was obtained from slaughtered cattle and pigs. It was expensive to produce and its supply was limited. The chemical structure of animal insulin is different from human insulin and some diabetics were allergic to the animal forms. Genetically engineered insulin is cheaper, available in large quantities and chemically the same as human insulin. Figure 28.1.2 shows how scientists use genetic engineering to produce insulin.

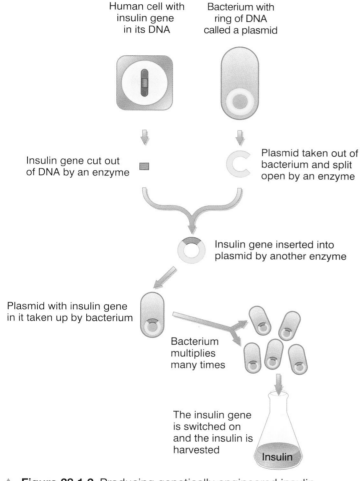

Human cell with insulin gene in its DNA

Bacterium with ring of DNA called a plasmid

Insulin gene cut out of DNA by an enzyme

Plasmid taken out of bacterium and split open by an enzyme

Insulin gene inserted into plasmid by another enzyme

Plasmid with insulin gene in it taken up by bacterium

Bacterium multiplies many times

The insulin gene is switched on and the insulin is harvested

Insulin

▲ **Figure 28.1.2** Producing genetically engineered insulin

Other genetically engineered hormones including human growth hormone and calcitonin (which controls the absorption of calcium into bones) are being produced by similar methods. Using human genes to produce hormones helps to prevent the harmful side effects of using products from animal tissues. It also reduces the use of animals for medical research.

Genetic engineering is also being used to produce antibodies that scientists hope will be useful in the fight against cancer, to mass-produce antibiotics from moulds (fungi), to produce substances known as interferons which are effective against viral diseases such as flu and genital herpes, and to develop safer vaccines against diseases like hepatitis B from viruses (see Figure 28.1.3).

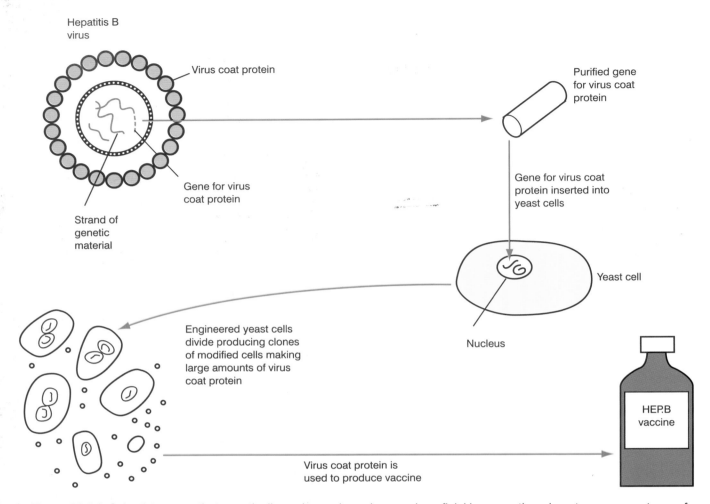

▲ **Figure 28.1.3** Scientists argue that genetically engineered vaccines are beneficial because they do not cause symptoms of the disease (like live vaccines can) since they do not contain the virus itself

A new development in genetic engineering is gene therapy. Gene therapy aims to control diseases caused by faulty genes, for example, sickle cell anaemia. Gene therapy for sickle cell anaemia would aim to add normal genes to the patient's genetic make-up so that he or she did not develop the disease.

Questions

1 What is 'genetic engineering'?

2 How does genetic engineering change organisms?

3 Give three examples to show how genetic engineering can be used in food production.

4 Describe how large amounts of insulin can be made from genetically engineered bacteria.

5 Vaccines protect millions of people worldwide from serious diseases. However, there are slight risks associated with their use. What are these risks? How is genetic engineering helping to reduce these risks?

C28.2 Changing genes – what are the issues?

Today humans are able to create genetically modified organisms for specific purposes. In the past, this was not possible and new organisms could only develop from artificial selection (selective breeding) or as a result of mutations. People tend to see genetically modified organisms as unnatural and there is some concern that creating transgenic plants and animals may carry some risks to human and animal health and the environment.

One concern that arises from genetic engineering is the use of large colonies of bacteria and viruses, which may escape into the environment. Scientists argue that the bacteria and other microorganisms used in genetic engineering are kept in sterile, contained environments and that there is no risk of contamination. Governments have also made strict laws to control the containment and use of microorganisms to prevent accidental release and spread of potentially harmful organisms.

However, many genetically engineered plants and animals are released into the general environment for use once they have been developed. Concerns also exist about whether or not this is environmentally harmful, because there is a danger of modified genes transferring to wild plants or animals.

There is no general agreement about whether or not genetic engineering is good or bad, and, like all technology, there are advantages and disadvantages to its use. These are summarised in Table 28.2.1.

Objectives

By the end of this topic you will be able to:

- discuss possible advantages and disadvantages of genetic engineering
- outline the social, ethical and ecological implications of genetic engineering.

▼ **Table 28.2.1** Advantages and disadvantages of genetic engineering

Genetic engineering	
Advantages	**Disadvantages**
Genetically modified (GM) bacteria can make large amounts of proteins that humans need in a pure form. Insulin is a good example of this.	Genetic engineering is new and largely unproven so the long-term effects are unknown. For example, insects may become pesticide resistant from eating plants that produce their own pesticide chemicals.
Engineered genes can help improve the growth rates of plants and animals, to improve food value of crops and reduce fat in animals. They are also used to produce plants which make their own pesticide chemicals.	People are concerned about possible health effects from eating GM plants and animals. They are also concerned that genes from these organisms might spread to natural species and contaminate the gene pool.
GM goods last longer in supermarkets and can be designed to grow in places that are too hot, too dry or too cold for normal production. This can help to reduce world hunger.	GM plant and animal technologies are often 'owned' by large companies. The crops are often not fertile (they do not produce seeds) so farmers in poor countries are at a disadvantage as they have to buy new seed each year.
A number of farm animals have been engineered to produce life-saving proteins in their blood or milk. For example, transgenic sheep produce the Factor 8 needed by haemophiliacs to make their blood clot.	Human genetic engineering may allow people who can afford it to manipulate the genes of unborn foetuses to produce clever, pretty or sporty children. This idea of producing designer babies raises serious moral and ethical issues.

Ethical and moral implications

Ethics and morals are the standards by which groups of people judge behaviour as acceptable or unacceptable. For example, people may feel it is unethical to interfere with natural God-given characteristics in human babies, but feel that it is ethical to carry out research on animals if it will cure diseases. Ethics are personal, and are based on personal knowledge and experience, so it is not possible to say which views are right and which views are wrong. The people in Figure 28.2.1 are expressing ethical and moral views about genetic engineering. Read what each person is saying and consider what your own views might be.

Our first child has a rare genetic defect. If we have another child I would be willing for doctors to change the genes in the embryo if they could to make sure I gave birth to a healthy child. I don't see any problems with this sort of technology.

I don't think it's right to interfere with nature. If scientists begin changing genes in the womb, there will soon be people who will want to design their children before they are born. Obviously only the rich will benefit from this technology.

Gene therapy allows us to change the genetic material in cells by adding healthy genes or switching off damaged genes. This can cure disease, but it doesn't stop the disease being passed on. If we were allowed to we would begin to cure genetic disease by changing genes in fertilised eggs or embryos. This would make sure that babies were born with healthy genes to pass on to future generations. In most countries, though, this type of gene therapy is banned for moral and ethical reasons.

I don't want to eat GM foods. I like to know what I am eating and I don't want modified bacteria in my food. I think we have enough natural fruits and vegetables and it's not good to mess with them. I think all food that is GM should be labelled so I can choose whether or not to eat it.

I am in favour of GM foods. If food lasts longer, the price should come down. Also, if plants make their own insecticide, then farmers won't have to spray them and the environment will be saved from insecticides.

I am worried about GM crops because they don't make seeds. I use seeds from my previous crop to grow my next crop because it is cheap and it works well. On the other hand, it might be useful to have a crop that can resist disease and grow well in poor soils. So, I am undecided.

▲ **Figure 28.2.1** People have different views about genetic engineering

Questions

Discuss these questions in groups.

1 Is genetic engineering a good idea in principle? Justify your answers.

2 In what circumstances is genetic engineering acceptable and in what circumstances is it unacceptable?

3 Is it right for large companies to patent gene technology and charge for its use? Why or why not?

4 Is it ethical to engineer animals so that they develop human diseases in order to research those diseases? Why or why not?

5 Are you happy to eat transgenic foods? Give a scientific reason for your opinion.

6 Consider a group of scientists who manage to engineer a rat sperm cell from stem cells. They implanted this in a female rat and produced offspring (although these were unhealthy and they soon died). Is it right for scientists to 'create' life in a laboratory? Justify your opinions.

Biology in the real world

Case study A

Biodiversity in the Caribbean

The Caribbean is regarded as a biodiversity hotspot with a very high number of species for the land area. The fact that many countries are island states also contributes to high levels of endemism, which is positive, but also a high extinction rate, which is negative – 54% of vertebrates (excluding fish) and 59% of plants are considered to be endemic to the region.

▲ Rainforests like this one in Trinidad are home to high numbers of endemic, but also threatened species

According to the United Nations Environmental Programme (UNEP), biodiversity in the region is under threat as a result of: unsustainable natural resource use, poorly managed tourism, mining, pollution, habitat destruction and change, natural phenomena such as hurricanes, as well as the introduction of alien species and the transformation of agricultural practises. Urbanisation and population pressure also contributes to biodiversity decline.

Table A shows the numbers of threatened and extinct species by country as well as the percentage of each country that is protected (data from 2003).

Table B shows the number of alien species in the Caribbean region by habitat type.

▼ Table B

Habitat	Number of alien species	Number of naturalised and/or invasive species
Terrestrial	479	390
Fresh water	55	10
Marine	18	16
Total	552	

Much more work and study needs to be done to ensure the ongoing protection of the region's biodiversity and natural resources. The International Union for Conservation of Nature (IUCN) does valuable research and monitoring to help nations develop clear and cohesive policies. You can find out more about their work at www.iucn.org.

▼ Table A

| Country | Animal species | | Plant species | | Protected areas | |
	Threatened	Extinct	Threatened	Extinct	Number	Percentage of country (including marine reserves)
Antigua and Barbuda	17	0	4	0	4	15.06
Bahamas	31	2	5	0	39	10.51
Barbados	15	1	2	0	3	0.57
Cuba	62	7	163	0	60	12.94
Dominica	19	1	11	0	7	27.19
Grenada	18	0	3	0	1	1.82
Guyana	35	0	23	0	3	2.26
Haiti	41	11	28	2	8	0.26
Jamaica	46	4	208	0	142	83.34
St Kitts and Nevis	16	0	2	0	1	0.06
St Lucia	23	1	6	0	37	10.06
St Vincent and the Grenadines	19	0	4	0	25	21.24
Trinidad and Tobago	22	0	1	0	18	5.99

Case study B

The evolution of antimicrobial resistance

Bacteria, fungi, viruses and some parasites can be killed by antimicrobial medicines (antibiotics, antifungals, antivirals and antimalarials). However, many of these microorganisms are developing resistance to such medicines (antimicrobial resistance or AMR). When microorganisms develop resistance to treatment, the treatment becomes ineffective and infections persist, get worse and become a threat to others. The evolution of resistance strains is a natural process that results from resistant traits being exchanged and passed on. The misuse of medicines as well as poor infection control can help accelerate the natural processes.

The WHO has made antimicrobial resistance a priority for the following reasons:

- AMR results in prolonged illness and a far higher risk of death.

- AMR reduces the effectiveness of treatments so patients remain infectious for longer, increasing the risk to others.

- AMR could result in some diseases becoming untreatable and uncontrollable and this would have serious implications for global health.

- Resistance increases the cost of health care as new treatments have to be developed and longer illness periods mean higher health costs.

- Without effective antimicrobials it is not possible to carry out organ transplants, treat cancers and perform major surgery as the risk of infection would be very high.

Multi-drug resistant TB

The bacteria that causes tuberculosis (TB) has developed resistance to TB medication. In 2011, 630 000 cases out of the 12 million cases in the world were estimated to be resistant to known TB medication, and those patients are therefore incurable. The map shows the percentage of new TB infections that are multi-drug resistant worldwide (data from 2012 WHO Report).

Antibiotic resistance

When bacteria develop resistance to antibiotics, even common illnesses can be deadly. For example, the only drug recommended by WHO for treating bloody diarrhoea in children is an antibiotic called ciprofloxacin because the shigella organisms that cause the diarrhoea have become resistant to all other previously effective antibiotics. However, increasing resistance to ciprofloxacin is now reducing the option for safe and effective treatment, particularly for children.

Resistance to antimalarial medicines

Chloroquine and sulfadoxine-pyrimethamine were previously effective in treating malaria. However, in most countries where malaria is endemic, the parasites have become resistant to these drugs. As a result, many people are infected for longer, and there is increased mortality from malaria.

Flu viruses

The virus that causes the flu in humans is constantly evolving and becoming resistant to antiviral drugs. This has serious health implications and WHO monitors outbreaks of flu worldwide to try and control and contain the spread of the virus.

The WHO takes AMR very seriously and is working to coordinate efforts and collect information so that AMR can be prevented.

Adapted from: World Health Organization (WHO) Fact Sheet 194 2012, updated May 2013

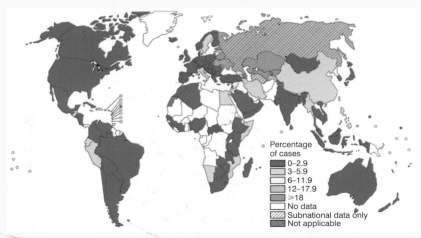

Percentage of cases
- 0–2.9
- 3–5.9
- 6–11.9
- 12–17.9
- ≥18
- No data
- Subnational data only
- Not applicable

◀ Percentage of new tuberculosis cases with multi-drug resistant tuberculosis (MDR-TB). (Source: *Global Tuberculosis Report, WHO 2012*.)

Key concepts

C25 Cell division

- The nucleus of a cell contains chromosomes. These are coiled threads of DNA and protein which carry genes. Humans have 46 chromosomes (23 pairs) in each cell except the gametes which contain only 23 chromosomes.

- Mitosis is a type of cell division in which the chromosomes of the parent cell divide into two identical groups before the cell divides so that each daughter cell gets the same number of chromosomes as the parent cell.

- Meiosis is a type of cell division that takes place in sex cells. In meiosis the daughter cells receive half the number of chromosomes of the parent cells.

- The chromosomes determine the sex of the child in humans. Two X chromosomes will produce a female child, an X and a Y combination will produce a male child.

C26 Continuity and inheritance

- Offspring inherit characteristics from their parents. In asexual reproduction, the offspring have exactly the same characteristics as the parent. In sexual reproduction, the gametes from both parents combine to produce unique characteristics which are not the same as either parent's.

- Inherited characteristics are determined by genes. Each gene has two different forms or alleles. The allele can be dominant or recessive. Dominant characteristics are seen in offspring more regularly than recessive characteristics.

- A genotype is a description of the alleles of a gene (for example Rr). A phenotype tells you about a characteristic, for example, right-handedness.

- Because parents may have different alleles of the same gene, these are combined in the offspring in different ways to produce variation.

- Studies of genetic crosses provide the basis for much of the knowledge we have of inheritance and how characteristics are passed on. A test cross is a method of working out whether an organism is heterozygous or homozygous.

- Characteristics which appear to be a blending of characteristics are a result of partial dominance. Partial dominance can take the form of incomplete dominance (grey feathers on offspring of black and white chickens) or codominance (blood groups in humans).

- Some characteristics are sex-linked. This means that they are carried on the 23rd pair of chromosomes. Examples of sex-linked conditions include colour-blindness and haemophilia.

- A pedigree is a chart which shows how conditions are inherited in members of a family. The symbols on the chart allow you to see which persons are male and female, and which persons carry the characteristic being investigated. Pedigrees are useful for determining whether or not a child is likely to carry a particular characteristic, such as sickle cell anaemia.

C27 Variation and change

- Characteristics, such as height, which range over a spread of measurements, show continuous variation. Characteristics which can be either one thing or another, such as left- or right-handedness, show discontinuous variation.

- Variation can arise from genetic and environmental causes. Both causes can affect the phenotype, but only variation arising from the genotype can be inherited.

- Genetic causes of variation include meiosis, sexual reproduction and mutations. Environmental causes of variation include nutrients, drugs, temperature and physical training.

- The process of slowly changing over time is called evolution. Scientists believe that species can evolve as a result of natural selection.

- In asexual reproduction the offspring are genetically identical to each other and their parents (clones). Genetic variation can only result from mutation. Offspring of sexual reproduction are genetically different from each other and from their parents.

- When populations adapt to environmental conditions, they may form new species. This is called speciation and it can be seen in finches of the Galapagos Islands and parrots found in different territories in the Caribbean.

- Artificial selection is the process of selectively breeding certain characteristics in a species. It is used in agriculture to produce new varieties of plants and animals that produce higher yields and which are resistant to diseases.

C28 Technology and genetics

- The process of changing the genetic structure of living cells is called genetic engineering.

- Genetic engineering allows scientists to take a gene from one organism and insert it into another organism. For example scientists can insert a desired gene into the bacterium *Agrobacterium tumefaciens* and infect plants with the bacterium, which causes the plants to grow tumours. The tumours are then used to produce new plants with the desired characteristics. It also allows scientists to insert genes into bacteria and to inject these into animals so that they can be used to produce medicines and other useful substances.

- Genetic engineering has possible advantages and disadvantages and there are social, ethical and ecological implications of genetic engineering.

Do you know these key terms?

- mitosis (p272)
- meiosis (p274)
- gene (p277)
- alleles (p277)
- dominant (p277)
- recessive (p277)
- genotype (p278)
- phenotype (p278)
- partial dominance (p282)
- incomplete dominance (p282)
- codominance (p282)
- pedigree (p286)
- variation (p288)
- continuous variation (p288)
- discontinuous variation (p289)
- evolution (p292)
- natural selection (p293)
- speciation (p296)
- artificial selection (p297)
- hybridisation (p298)
- genetic engineering (p299)
- transgenic organism (p299)
- genetically modified (GM) (p299)
- clones (p300)

Practice exam-style questions

Working through these questions will help you to revise the content of this section and prepare you for your examination.

The number of marks available for each question gives you an idea about how much detail to put in your answer.

1

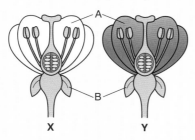

a) i) You were given plant X and plant Y. Describe how you would cross plant X and plant Y.   [2UK]

ii) Describe what happens after the ovule is fertilised.   [2KC]

iii) After crossing plant X and plant Y all of the offspring inherited the red flower colour. Explain this using a genetic diagram.   [3UK]

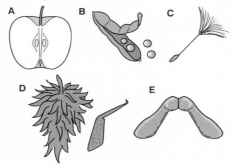

b) The above shows fruits and seeds. For any FOUR, describe how TWO features are adapted to the method of dispersal that the plant uses.   [8UK]

[Total 15 marks]

2 Huntington's disease is an inherited disease which causes mental deterioration. It is a non-sex-linked disease carried by the dominant allele H and the symptoms show up after age 30. The pedigree below shows inheritance in one family.

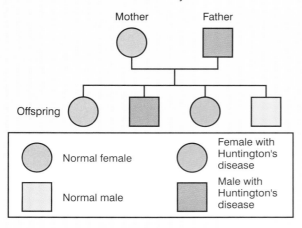

a) i) Use a genetic diagram to explain the inheritance of the Huntington's disease. (Use H for the dominant allele for Huntington's disease and h for the recessive allele.)   [4UK]

ii) Is it possible for a person with HH genotype to be unaware of the disease and pass it on to their children? Explain your answer.   [1KC, 3UK]

b) i) The agricultural sector has been able to use artificial selection to enhance the yield of crops. With reference to ONE named crop, outline how this can be done.   [1KC, 3UK]

ii) After the hurricane in Grenada, large-scale destruction of crops and agricultural lands occurred. Outline steps you would recommend for reversing the destruction and preventing future problems.   [3UK]

[Total 15 marks]

3 a) Copy the diagram. Indicate the sex of each parent and draw the chromosomes present in the gametes and the children.   [3UK]

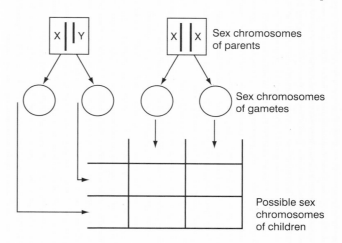

b) The diagram shows the chromosomes taken from an adult human.

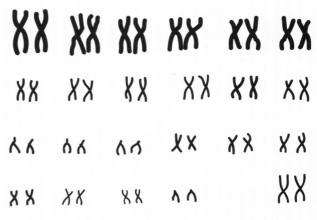

State whether the chromosomes come from a male or a female and give a reason for your answer.   [1KC, 1UK]

c) The diagram shows how Dolly the sheep was cloned.

i) Dolly is genetically identical to another sheep in the diagram. Which one? [1KC]

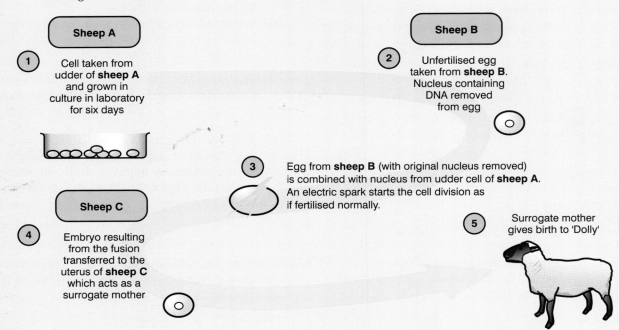

Sheep A

1 Cell taken from udder of **sheep A** and grown in culture in laboratory for six days

Sheep B

2 Unfertilised egg taken from **sheep B**. Nucleus containing DNA removed from egg

3 Egg from **sheep B** (with original nucleus removed) is combined with nucleus from udder cell of **sheep A**. An electric spark starts the cell division as if fertilised normally.

Sheep C

4 Embryo resulting from the fusion transferred to the uterus of **sheep C** which acts as a surrogate mother

5 Surrogate mother gives birth to 'Dolly'

ii) Explain why there was no variation in Dolly. [2UK]

iii) Suggest ONE advantage and ONE disadvantage in producing animal clones such as Dolly. [2UK]

d People are concerned that animal cloning may lead to human cloning.

i) What is your opinion? [1KC]

ii) Justify your answer. [4UK]

[Total 15 marks]

Index

Acknowledgements

The author and the publisher would also like to thank the following for permission to reproduce material:

Text permissions

P7, quote from Dr Perrie, a scientist from the Museum of New Zealand Te Papa Tongarewa; pp8-9, extract from http://www.sciencedaily.com, Pennsylvania State University; p40, 'Ecological footprint by region', © [2012] WWF (panda.org). Some rights reserved; pp40-42, various facts and figures from WWF, © [2012] WWF (panda.org). Some rights reserved; p47, Reproduced from 'The Living Planet Index, Ecological Footprint, Biocapacity and Water Footprint Through Time, 1961-2005', collected by WWF's 2008 Living Planet Report. Licenced by reproduction through the following Crown Copyright License: http://creativecommons.org/licenses/by-sa/3.0/deed.en; p56, 'Jamaican Bauxite Environmental Organization Wins Restoration of Alcan Tailings Pond', extract from http://www.miningwatch.ca, permission granted by MiningWatch; p57, 'Proposed project', extract from http://www.nrca.org, National Environment Planning Agency; p58, 'Carol reef are among the most diverse ecosystems, but they are also among the most threatened', adapted from National Oceanic and Atmospheric Administration (NOAA); p66 extracts from Statistical Institute of Jamaica (2009) *Environmental Statistics Jamaica 2007-12*, p43, and Forestry Department (n.d.) *Strategic Forest Management Plan 2009-13*, p3; pp66-67, 'Jamaica's response to manage its forests and watersheds', extract from http://www.nepa.gov.jm, National Environment and Planning Agency; p68, Boyan Slat, 'The Ocean Cleanup'; p68, 'The Truc stops here for old carrier bags', text: PRW Magazine, photo: Éléa Nouraud & the University of Brighton (3D Design course); p69, Scientific American; p95, 'Plants are good at maths', Telegraph Media Group 2013; pp133-134, table 12.3.2 and 12.3.3, www.cdc.gov; p197, table 19.4.2 reproduced with permission of the General Secretariat of the Organization of American States; p241, data: UNAIDS/ONUSIDA 2012, graphics www.avert.org; p242, quote from Dr C. James Hospedales, Director of the Caribbean Epidemiology Centre (CAREC); p246, figure 24.2.3 from 'Lifetime Risk of Coronary Heart Disease by Cholesterol Levels at Selected Ages' – Archives of Internal Medicine, September 2003; p246, data in figure 24.2.4 from Vera Lucia Chiara and Rosely Sichieri, 'Food consumption of adolescents. A simplified questionnaire for evaluating cardiovascular risk', *Arq. Bras. Cardiol*, 2001, vol. 77, n. 4, pp. 337-341; p247, figure 24.2.5 from *Framington Community Survey USA*; p247, figure 24.2.7, data reproduced with permission of the publisher, from Global Health Risks: Mortality and burden of disease attributable to selected major risks, World Health Organization, 2009 (http://www.who.int/healthinfo/global_burden_disease/GlobalHealthRisks_report_full.pdf, accessed 5th December 2013); p252, Lethal yellowing article, sourced from The San Pedro Sun Newspaper; pp252-253, Food and Agriculture Organization of the United Nations, 2001, [The State of Food and Agriculture 2001], updated 2013, http://www.fao.org/docrep/003/x9800e/x9800e16.htm. Reproduced with permission; p255, 'Illegal kidney trade booms as new organ is "sold every hour"' by Denis Campbell and Nicola Davison in Shanghai, Copyright Guardian News and Media Ltd 2012; p256, map of central and south America with data table from the Pan American Health Organization (PAHO); pp256-257, 'Climate change and dengue fever', Centres for Disease Control and Prevention (CDC), www.cdc.gov; pp257-258, 'HIV and AIDS data for the Caribbean', UNAIDS/ONUSIDA 2012; p305, table A sourced from United Nations Environment Programme (UNEP); p306, 'The evolution of antimicrobial resistance', adapted by Nelson Thornes Ltd with permission, from World Health Organisation (WHO), 'Antimicrobial Resistance', Face Sheet 194, 2012, updated May 2013.

Images

Corel/NT 10, 30c, 63; **Digital Vision/NT** 2, 288c; **JA/NT** 161t; **Ingram 500/NT** 218ct; **Alamy/JS Callahan/tropicalpix** 67, **/Aliki Image Library/Kathleen Watmough** 88l, **/Robert Harding/Louise Murray** 160, **/Medical-on-line** 208, **/H.Reinhard** 222(6), **/Phototake** 244l, **Brian Hoffman** 282c; **Peter Dean** 282b, idp garden collection 283; **/American Phytopathological Society**, used with kind permission 251c & e, **/Courtesy of D.L. Anderson** 251b; **/Corbis/Hal Beral** 30bl, **/Jeffrey L. Rotman** 30bc, **/Bill Gentile** 64tl; **Éléa Nouraud/ TRUC-Technic to Recycled Used Carrier Bags** 68; **/Eric Siegmund 288b; /Frank Lane Picture Library/ Norbert Wu** 8, **/Florian Kopp/ Imagebroker** 67, **/Alfred & Annaliese T/Imagebroker** 85, **/Ulrich Doering /Imagebroker** 252; **Getty Images/ Robert Nickelsberg** 64tr **/Getty Images Sport /Guang/** Staff 174, **Oxford Scientific Photos/G.I. Bernard** 182br; **iStockphotos** 14, 182b/209, 216 all, 222(3,4&5); **Mike van der Wolk/mike@springhigh.co.za** 15 both, 40, 51, 54 both, 61 both, 66, 85t, 130 both, 161b, 222tl&r, 222(1) &(2), 305, 298 all; **Neil Sealey** 13 both; **Rio Tinto Alcan** 57; **Science Photo Library/Georgette Douwma** 30br, **/Dr. Jeremy Burgess** 88r, **Sally Benusen** 97, **/Dr.David Furness, Keele University** 150, **/174c, /Astrid & Hanns-Frieder Michier** 174l **/Inerspace Imaging** 174r, **/J.C.Revy/ISM** 182c, **/Veronique Leplat** 218tl, **/Daniel Sambraus** 218c, **/Astrid & Hanns-Frieder Michler** 218cl, **/Jerome Wexler** 218tr, **/Duncan Smith** 218br, **/Debra Ferguson /AGStock USA** 245, **/Nigel Cattlin/Holt Studios** 251a, **/Geoff Kidd** 251d **/Francis Leroy, Biocosmos** 286 both, **Michael W. Tweedie** 294; **/Shawn Banton** 288a, 289;

Every effort has been made to trace the copyright holders but if any have been inadvertently overlooked the publisher will be pleased to make the necessary arrangements at the first opportunity.